Soviet and East European Studies

THE COMMISSARIAT OF ENLIGHTENMENT

Soviet and East European Studies

THE COMMISSARIAT OF ENLIGHTENMENT

The National Association for Soviet and East European Studies exists for the purpose of promoting study and research on the social sciences as they relate to the Soviet Union and the countries of Eastern Europe. The Monograph Series is intended to promote the publication of works presenting substantial and original research in the economics, politics, sociology and modern history of the USSR and Eastern Europe.

FIRST BOOKS IN THE SERIES

A. Boltho, *Foreign Trade Criteria in Socialist Economies*
Sheila Fitzpatrick, *The Commissariat of Enlightenment*
Donald Male, *Russian Peasant Organisation before Collectivisation*
P. Wiles, *The Prediction of Communist Economic Performance*

THE COMMISSARIAT OF ENLIGHTENMENT

SOVIET ORGANIZATION OF EDUCATION AND THE ARTS UNDER LUNACHARSKY OCTOBER 1917–1921

BY

SHEILA FITZPATRICK

CAMBRIDGE
AT THE UNIVERSITY PRESS
1970

Published by the Syndics of the Cambridge University Press
Bentley House, 200 Euston Road, London, N.W.1
American Branch: 32 East 57th Street, New York, N.Y.10022

Standard Book Number: 521 07919 5

Printed in Great Britain by Alden & Mowbray Ltd
at the Alden Press, Oxford

CONTENTS

PLATES

between pages 58 *and* 59

Acknowledgements for help in obtaining illustrations are due to I.A. Lunacharskaya, I.A. Sats, A.I. Deich, E.A. Dinershtein, K.S. Pavlova of the Lunacharsky Museum and staff of the State Museum of the Revolution

ACKNOWLEDGEMENTS

The basic material for this book was gathered in Oxford and London during the preparation of an Oxford D.Phil. thesis, and in Moscow, as an exchange student at Moscow State University. My thanks are due to the Association of Commonwealth Universities, which made it possible for me to study at Oxford in 1964–6 and 1967–8, and allowed me to suspend my scholarship to study in Moscow in 1966–7; St Antony's College, Oxford; the British Council, under whose auspices I studied in Moscow in 1966–7 and the spring of 1968; Lilia Pavlovna Demyanova, of the Foreign Department of Moscow State University, who assisted me in applications to the Soviet archive authorities; the Chief Archive Administration, Moscow, and the staff of the various archives I consulted; and my Moscow supervisor, A. I. Ovcharenko, of the philological faculty of Moscow State University.

My thesis and drafts of the present book were read by a number of people, for whose criticism and advice I am extremely grateful. I would like in particular to acknowledge the help of Mr Max Hayward, who supervised my Oxford thesis; Professor Leonard Schapiro who, as one of the examiners of the thesis, made detailed and penetrating criticisms; Mr E. H. Carr, to whom I, like all students of Soviet history, am greatly indebted, and who was kind enough to read and discuss my work; and Professor R. W. Davies, who provided a great deal of information on the economic aspect of the subject (including the material used in Appendix I) as well as making a number of general suggestions which I have tried to follow in revising the work for publication.

I wish to make special acknowledgement of the help I have received from Soviet scholars, and in particular from two relatives of A. V. Lunacharsky: his daughter Irina Lunacharskaya and his brother-in-law and former secretary I. A. Sats, who was until early 1970 on the editorial board of *Novyi mir*. Their time and knowledge, which was most generously given, cannot be valued too highly. With the greatest respect and affection, I therefore dedicate this book to Igor Aleksandrovich Sats.

S.F.

INTRODUCTION

I began the present work in Oxford as a study of Lunacharsky. It became, in the course of research in Moscow, a study of Narkompros, the commissariat in charge of education and the arts which Lunacharsky headed from 1917 to 1929. The decisive factor in this change was the archival material to which I had access in Moscow, which consisted largely of minutes and documents of the collegium of Narkompros and its departments. What most impressed me about the Narkompros archives, as compared to published materials of Narkompros and other Soviet institutions, was that they showed both the manner in which decisions were made in the commissariat and the gap which normally existed between a decision and its implementation. This is particularly true of the period 1918–19, when debates in the collegium of Narkompros were sometimes reported almost verbatim: from the beginning of the '20s protocols of meetings were entered more formally and professionally and have less to add to the material published in Narkompros' weekly bulletin. It would be difficult, I think, to read through the early Narkompros documents without catching the sense of excitement, of a world in flux but changing for the better, which was felt by the founding members of the commissariat. I hope something of this sense remains in my narrative.

The subject of this book is the establishment of a Soviet commissariat: its formulation of policy, internal workings, relations with other government departments and the Bolshevik Party, dealings with subordinate non-government institutions and the public. I have dealt only with the period 1917–21, ending with the introduction of the New Economic Policy when, for better or for worse, the institutional structure of the commissariat was stabilized and the scope and nature of its work for the next half-dozen years determined. I hope to deal with the later years of Lunacharsky's work in Narkompros (1921–9) in a separate volume.

This is institutional history; but as I came to write it through an interest in Lunacharsky, and as an historian and not as a political scientist, I have devoted considerable attention to the individuals creating the institution and working within it. Biographical data in this field is not easy to come by, and I have therefore included an appendix of biographical notes on the people who worked in Narkompros or influenced its early development. The information is by no means exhaustive, but I have done my best to check its accuracy.

Perhaps the narrative which follows will be more comprehensible to the reader if I introduce the main characters in advance. The most important of the *dramatis personae* are Lunacharsky, Krupskaya, Pokrovsky and Litkens within Narkompros, and Lenin outside it. Lunacharsky, the commissar, is a large, untidy man with pince-nez and a benevolent expression. During the winters of the Civil War he often wears an enormous fur-coat of the type worn by rich merchants under the old regime (a gift from Red Army men at the front), and can be seen striding through Moscow streets in animated conversation, arms waving, scarf flapping, coat unbuttoned and trailing behind him in the snow. He is an enthusiast but not a fanatic, tolerant—in the opinion of some of his colleagues—to a fault, with a past history of Party unorthodoxy; erudite, a lover of philosophy and the arts, a prolific playwright. Lunacharsky's deputy is the historian Pokrovsky: belligerent, sharp-tongued, radical in his political and intellectual views, intolerant to his former academic colleagues. Unlike Lunacharsky, who has little taste for political manœuvring at any level, Pokrovsky is a born academic politician. But neither he nor Lunacharsky plays an important role in internal Party politics, and neither is a member of the Central Committee of the Bolshevik Party.

Lenin's wife Krupskaya is, in Lunacharsky's phrase, 'the soul of Narkompros', and is deeply concerned in the formulation of its educational policy. She dislikes administrative work and has no pleasure in holding high office. She belongs to the honourable tradition of Russian revolutionary enlighteners. A number of the early members of Narkompros taught with her at the Smolenskaya evening adult-education classes in Petersburg in the 1890s: this experience remains her spiritual touchstone. She is by nature practical, self-contained, attached to old friends, suspicious of pretension and style.

Lenin, like Krupskaya, comes from the popular-educational as well as the revolutionary tradition of the Russian intelligentsia: his father was a radical inspector of schools under the tsar. Through Krupskaya, and through friendship with Lunacharsky, one of his neighbours in the Kremlin, Lenin is in particularly close contact with Narkompros. He attends virtually every educational conference during the period of his active participation in government (to 1922); and he is familiar with the minutiae of Narkompros affairs not only through Krupskaya, but directly through his presidency of the Party Central Committee's commission on the reorganization of Narkompros in 1921. He is in frequent telephone contact with Lunacharsky about educational matters, and in 1921 receives daily telephone reports from Litkens, who is in charge of the Narkompros reorganization.

Lenin, Krupskaya, Lunacharsky and Pokrovsky belong to the same generation and the same revolutionary tradition. Evgraf Litkens, who comes to Narkompros at the end of 1920, is of another generation and a new revolutionary tradition, born in the Civil War. The new revolutionary tradition carries its own style of dress: army boots and leather jackets *à la* Sverdlov (even Lunacharsky adopts the military-style 'French' jacket during the Civil War, though Lenin does not); and gives pride of place to the military virtues of discipline, organization and toughmindedness. Litkens perhaps models himself on Trotsky, who was sheltered by his father after the collapse of the Petersburg Soviet in 1905, when Litkens was still a schoolboy. He presents himself as a hard-headed practical revolutionary, making no concession to sentiment or intellectual self-doubt; he is nevertheless a graduate of the University of St Petersburg. Litkens comes from the front with a mandate from the Central Committee to turn Narkompros into an efficient administrative machine. He finds Narkompros deeply civilian and thus—as it seems to him—non-revolutionary in spirit. He is particularly offended by the retinue of self-centred, over-articulate, non-political poets, actors and musicians employed and supported by Narkompros and enjoying the protection of the commissar. He banishes the poets and—being an energetic and fairly efficient organizer—imposes a new rational organizational structure on the commissariat. But no sooner has he completed his work of rationalization than it is swept away in the wake of a general campaign to reduce costs and limit the number of government employees. Narkompros reverts to an irrational organizational state; the poets quietly return. Litkens is then murdered by Crimean bandits. The collegium of Narkompros, perhaps conscience-striken, resolves to publish a book of memorial essays; but this turns out to be one of many Narkompros resolutions never fulfilled.

These, then, are the characters of the story. The institution they created was incoherent, rambling, malfunctioning, over-staffed with middle-aged intellectuals and under-staffed with proletarian Communists. This condition was not peculiar to Narkompros, but common to all Soviet institutions during the Civil War. It extended even to Party bodies, usually considered to have been on a higher level of organization. The *agitprop* department of the Central Committee, for example, was no more and probably less operational at the end of 1920 than Glavpolitprosvet, the corresponding organ of Narkompros. Effective organization was achieved—partially and with great difficulty—only in the areas directly essential to national survival: the army, the Food Commissariat and the transport authority, Tsektran. Although it was frequently said that Narkompros was extraordinarily badly organized, and Narkompros as frequently claimed that it was extraordinarily badly treated, its condition appears to have been typical of commissariats not directly involved in the war effort: such complaints should not, in my opinion, be taken at face value.

The central organizational task facing Narkompros, as the Commissariat of Education, was the administration of the school system; and this was the area of its most conspicuous failure during the Civil War period. But Narkompros had a number of achievements to its credit. Universities, the Academy of Sciences, scientific research institutes and theatres were kept open with government subsidy, and without excessive interference from Narkompros in the face of considerable provocation. Public libraries, art collections and museums were preserved and opened to the public. Narkompros formulated basic principles of educational reform, and set up a large number of kindergartens and a network of experimental schools and children's colonies. It subsidized the arts on a fairly catholic basis which was in effect favourable to the development of experimental and avant-garde art, but at the same time discouraged the avant-garde from persecuting the conservatives. The leaders of Narkompros were exceptionally well-qualified for their work, democratic in their methods, appreciative of expert advice and co-operation.

What was the enlightenment Narkompros had to offer? Lunacharsky, if challenged, might have made three major claims. The first was in the sphere of educational theory, where Narkompros stood firmly on the side of the contemporary European and American progressive educational movement: for encouragement of the child's individuality and creativity, development of his social instincts, informal relations between pupils and teachers, activity methods of teaching, broadening of the school curriculum to include study of the surrounding environment, physical and aesthetic education and training in elementary labour and craft skills. These principles were more than once described by Lunacharsky as a cause of 'our legitimate pride before Europe'; and he told VTSIK that Narkompros' *Statement on the United Labour School* of 1918 would become 'an educational classic'.

The second claim was in the cultural and scientific sphere. An enlightened government, Lunacharsky believed, recognizes that creative work in science and the arts must be carried out with a minimum of outside interference and pressure. But it also recognizes that such work is to the ultimate advantage of the state, and so provides generous subsidies. In relation to the arts (and undoubtedly to the sciences, had the possibility of a Lysenko situation occurred to him), Lunacharsky held that the greatest possible misfortune was for the government to show special preference to any one group, thereby putting it in a position of artistic monopoly. He resisted the demands of Communist avant-garde artists like Mayakovsky and Meyerhold for special privileges, and did his best to protect the artistic traditionalists against their attacks. Believing that respect for scholarship was a mark of enlightenment, he supported the

Academy of Sciences in its demand for subsidized autonomy (although the Academy's secretary, Oldenburg, who put forward its claim, was a former member of the Cadet Central Committee and Lunacharsky's immediate predecessor as Minister of Public Education under the Provisional Government). He encouraged Communist artists and scholars, but not in persecution of their colleagues or bids for monopoly.

The third claim was on the principle of equality of educational opportunity. Narkompros held that the educational system should make it possible for a factory worker's child to become either a factory worker or an industrial manager or a member of the Academy of Sciences, without occupational choice being automatically restricted at an early age. This meant universal *general* education at both primary and secondary levels. It ruled out the possibility of early professional specialization in schools or trade apprenticeship for school-age children. Thus the United Labour School, according to the Narkompros programme, was 'polytechnical' but not 'professional': it taught a variety of labour skills without specializing in any one of them or providing a professional or trade qualification.

Narkompros' style and methods were often criticized for their lack of Bolshevik toughmindedness. Lunacharsky's commissariat—and Lunacharsky himself—were believed by many Bolsheviks to be too permissive, too liable to flights of fancy, too easily manipulated by the non-Party intelligentsia, not sufficiently vigilant in defence of Party orthodoxy. But Narkompros encountered relatively little serious objection on principle in the Civil War years. At this time, the official policy towards the arts was non-discriminatory. The natural tendency of a Communist government to give preference to Communist artists was counterbalanced by the instinctive dislike which most Communist politicians felt for the artistic avant-garde. Only Bukharin among Party leaders really sympathized—and then not for long—with the iconoclasm of the artistic left and its demand for monopoly privileges. The Central Committee (in its letter 'On the Proletkults' of December 1920) ruled against it. The most common objection to Narkompros' cultural activity was not on policy but on the extent of its patronage: it was said to be too generous and gullible a patron, and to spend too much money on the arts and too little on schools. Similarly, there was no basic disagreement with Narkompros' policy towards the scientific world. Indeed the initiative in granting autonomy to the Academy of Sciences belonged as much to Lenin—who believed that it was necessary to find a *modus vivendi* with specialists in all fields—as to Narkompros. Narkompros was criticized for its gentle handling of anti-Communist professors. But its respect for science and for some degree of scientific independence was not controversial.

The educational principles which Narkompros put forward in 1918 were received with indifferent approval by the Soviet government. VTSIK accepted the Narkompros *Statement on the United Labour School* without discussion, in view of its 'completely uncontroversial nature', as one delegate put it. However, the issue of professionalization of secondary education became controversial in 1920–1. The case for professionalization, argued by Otto Schmidt (head of Glavprofobr) and the trade unions, rested on the expected shortage of skilled labour during post-war reconstruction of Russian industry. The professional lobby was popular in the economic commissariats, the unions and local Party committees, which instinctively supported the more practical and utilitarian alternative offered. Part of the Central Committee supported professionalization. But Narkompros continued to oppose it, as a limitation on equality of educational opportunity; and it was defeated by the intervention of Lenin—using superior cunning from what was probably a position of weakness—in support of Narkompros.

The particular interest for the historian of Narkompros' first years lies in the struggle to translate ideas into practice, to find appropriate institutional forms in a revolutionary situation. In this respect, the early history of Narkompros presents a case-study in the problems of revolutionary government. But this is not all. Lunacharsky believed that Communism meant, above all, the enlightenment of the people. The October Revolution put him at the head of the Commissariat of Enlightenment: 'a true apostle and forerunner of enlightenment', as he was described in a greeting from revolutionary provincial teachers in 1918. The Civil War period was necessarily a time of limited practical achievement for Narkompros, but it was a time of great expectations. For Narkompros its new kindergartens were 'corners full of joy, full of the morning light portending future socialism; light grains of the future for which we struggle against the twilight, cruelly battle-coloured backdrop of our suffering land'. As Thomas Carlyle (contemplating the sky-blue coat which Robespierre had made for the Festival of the Supreme Being and wore on the day of his execution) wrote in his history of the French Revolution: 'O Reader, can thy hard heart hold out against that?'

ABBREVIATIONS

IN THE TEXT

agitprop	Agitation and propaganda. A department of the Central Committee of the Communist Party and of local Party committees.
Cheka likbez	Extraordinary commission for the liquidation of illiteracy under Glavpolitprosvet.
FON	Faculty of social sciences.
FOTO-KINO	Photography and cinema department of Narkompros.
Glavnauka	Chief administration for science and scientific institutions under Narkompros (from 1922).
Glavpolitprosvet	Chief administration for political education under Narkompros.
Glavpolitput	Chief political department (later administration) of Commissariat of Communications.
Glavprofobr	Chief administration for professional education (later 'for preparation of workers and higher educational institutions') under Narkompros.
Glavsotsvos	Chief administration for social training (=school education) under Narkompros.
Gosizdat	State publishing house (a department of Narkompros in 1918; from May 1919 an autonomous body within Narkompros).
GPU	Chief political administration (= security apparatus) of Commissariat of Internal Affairs, taking over functions of the Cheka in 1922. Later OGPU.
GUS	State Academic Council of Narkompros.
ispolkom	Executive committee (of local Soviet of workers' and peasants' deputies).
Istpart	Commission for collection and study of materials

	on the history of the October Revolution and RKP(b) under Central Committee.
IZO	Graphic arts department of Narkompros. (AK-IZO: graphic arts department of the Academic Centre of Narkompros, 1921).
KEPS	Commission for the study of the natural and productive resources of Russia under the Academy of Sciences, established 1915.
Komsomol	Union of Communist Youth.
KUBU	All-Russian commission for the improvement of the life of scholars under Sovnarkom, established 1919. Reorganized in 1921 as central commission for the improvement of the life of scholars (TSEKUBU).
LITO	Literary department of Narkompros.
MONO	Moscow education department (under Moscow Soviet and Narkompros).
MUZO	Music department of Narkompros.
Narkompros	People's Commissariat of Education (Enlightenment).
NEP	New economic policy.
NKVD	People's Commissariat of Internal Affairs.
NTO	Scientific–technical department of Vesenkha.
politprosvet	Political education. A sub-department of local education departments.
Proletkult	Proletarian cultural organization (used both for local organizations, and for the Central All-Russian Soviet of proletarian cultural organizations).
PUR	Political administration of the War Council of the Republic.
rabfak	Workers' faculty (of higher educational institution).
Rabis (Vserabis)	(All-Russian) Union of Art-workers.
Rabkrin	(People's Commissariat) of Workers' and Peasants' Inspection.
Rabpros	Union of Workers in Education and Socialist Culture (later, Union of Educational Workers).

RKP(b)	Russian Communist Party (Bolsheviks).
ROSTA	Russian Telegraph Agency (from 1919, a department of Narkompros, later under Glavpolitprosvet).
RSDRP	Russian Social-Democratic Workers' Party (parent Party of RKP(b)).
RSFSR	Russian Soviet Federative Socialist Republic.
sovkhoz	State farm.
Sovnarkom	Council of People's Commissars.
S-R	Member of Social-Revolutionary Party.
STO	Council of Labour and Defence.
TEO	Theatre department of Narkompros.
Tsektran	Central Committee of United Unions of Railway and Water-transport Workers, established 1920.
Tsentropechat	Central agency of VTSIK for the distribution of printed matter (1919–21).
Tsentroteatr	Central theatre committee of Narkompros, established 1919.
Vesenkha	Supreme Council of the National Economy. (Local economic councils referred to as *sovnarkhozy*.)
VTSIK	All-Russian Central Executive Committee (of the Congress of Soviets).
VTSSPS	All-Russian Central Council of Trade Unions.
VUS	All-Russian Teachers' Union (dissolved December, 1918).

IN THE NOTES

TSGAOR	*Tsentral'nyi gosudarstvennyi arkhiv oktyabr'skoi revolyutsii i sotsialisticheskogo stroitel'stva.*
TSGA RSFSR	*Tsentral'nyi gosudarstvennyi arkhiv RSFSR. Note:* in citation of archives, the name is followed by number of *fond/opis'/ edinitsa khraneniya.*

Krupskaya, *Ped. soch.*	N. K. Krupskaya, *Pedagogicheskie sochineniya v 10-i tomakh* (Moscow, 1957–62), plus vol. 11 (1963).
Lenin, *Pol. sob. soch.*	V. I. Lenin, *Polnoe sobranie sochinenii* (5th ed., 55 vols., Moscow, 1958–65).
Lunacharsky, *Sob. soch.*	A. V. Lunacharsky, *Sobranie sochinenii v 8-i tomakh* (Moscow, 1963–7).
Nar. pros.	*Narodnoe prosveshchenie* (weekly and monthly journals).
Sobr. uzak.	*Sobranie uzakonenii i rasporyazhenii rabochego i krest'yanskogo pravitel'stva* (Moscow).

LEF	Left Front in Art.
RAPP	Russian Association of Proletarian Writers.
TSIK	All-Union Executive Committee (of Congress of Soviets).
VOKS	All-Union Society for Cultural Links with Foreign Countries.

Dates before 14 February 1918 are given in the Old Style.

Russian proper names appear in the text in their most familiar English form: the soft sign ' is dropped, and the final –ii and –yi are rendered as –y (e.g. *Lunacharsky* rather than *Lunacharskii*; *Shulgin* rather than *Shul'gin*).

1

LUNACHARSKY

On 26 October 1917 the Bolshevik Central Committee announced the members of the new government to the Second Congress of Soviets in Petrograd. Lenin headed it as president of the Council of People's Commissars (Sovnarkom); Anatoly Vasilyevich Lunacharsky was People's Commissar of Education.

Nikolai Sukhanov noticed that as the names of the People's Commissars were read out only Lenin, Trotsky and Lunacharsky were loudly applauded. This, he thought, was because they were the names most familiar to non-Bolshevik delegates.[1] Sukhanov himself, although a friend of Lunacharsky, probably remained silent, for he had little faith in Lunacharsky's power to impose his undoubted goodwill on the Bolshevik Party. But Sukhanov was a Menshevik and, as he described himself, 'alien, indifferent and polemically-disposed'. Lunacharsky was a Bolshevik enthusiast, and for him this was a moment of historic victory of enlightenment over exploitation. 'These events are epoch-making!' he told Sukhanov. 'Our children's children will bow their heads before their grandeur!'[2]

Lunacharsky's office had, as he conceived it, a peculiar importance: he was at the head of the People's Commissariat of Enlightenment* in a revolutionary government whose historical mission was to achieve the enlightenment of the people. In this spirit he was greeted by provincial admirers as 'a true apostle and forerunner of enlightenment' and the representative of 'the spiritual dictatorship of the proletariat'. 'Hail to the sun, and may darkness vanish!' cabled the Novoladozhsky education congress to Lunacharsky in 1918.[3] It was an appropriate motto for Lunacharsky's commissariat.

Lunacharsky, 'poet of Revolution' and a lover of philosophy and the arts, described himself as 'an intellectual [*intelligent*] among

* The full title of the commissariat was Narodnyi Komissariat Prosveschcheniya (po Prosveschcheniyu), usually shortened to Narkompros. The word *prosveshchenie*—also used in the title of the former tsarist ministry—may be translated either as 'education' or 'enlightenment'.

Bolsheviks and a Bolshevik among intellectuals'. Although by no means the only Bolshevik lover of the arts, he made the most public profession of his love and—unlike other Bolsheviks—did not see this as incompatible with his role as a professional revolutionary. Within the Bolshevik group Lunacharsky was regarded as a political lightweight. 'An uncommonly gifted nature...' Lenin is reported to have said of him.[4] 'You know, I am fond of him, he is an excellent comrade! He has a sort of French brilliance. His lightmindedness is also French: it comes from his aesthetic inclinations.' In emigration Lunacharsky worked as a political and literary journalist, propagandist and orator. He took little part in Bolshevik organizational or conspiratorial activities.

Lunacharsky was born in Poltava in 1875, brought up in the family of a senior civil servant* and educated at the First Kiev gymnasium. In the fifth class he joined a Marxist revolutionary circle, and was warned on graduating from the gymnasium that this might prevent his admission to a Russian university. He persuaded his mother to send him to study with the philosopher Avenarius at the University of Zurich. In Switzerland, aged nineteen, he met Plekhanov, recommended his favourite philosophers—Avenarius, Herbert Spencer, Schopenhauer and Nietzsche—and found that Plekhanov had deep objections to all of them. Lunacharsky decided that Plekhanov neglected 'the emotional and ethical side of scientific-socialist ideology'.[5]

In 1898 Lunacharsky returned to Russia, joined a Social-Democratic group in Moscow organized by Lenin's sister Anna, and was quickly arrested. After a short period of imprisonment, he was exiled first to Kaluga and then to Vologda. In exile he found himself in congenial company, including the Marxists A. A. Bogdanov (Malinovsky), whose sister Lunacharsky married, and V. A. Bazarov, the S-R Boris Savinkov and Nikolai Berdyaev. Lunacharsky worked on philosophy with Bogdanov and Bazarov, debated against the

* Anatoly Vasilyevich Lunacharsky bore the surname and patronymic of his mother's first husband, a state councillor; but his natural father was Aleksandr Ivanovich Antonov, also a state councillor but of radical views, with whom the child and his mother lived in Nizhny Novgorod (now Gorky) until Antonov's death. (A. V. Lunacharsky, *Pochemu nel'zya verit' v boga?* (Moscow, 1965), p. 7, note. Quoted from unpublished autobiographical essay.)

idealist Berdyaev, and studied myth and the history of religion. It was a happy period of his life.

Shortly after his release from exile, Lunacharsky again went abroad and, for the first time, met Lenin. In 1904 both Lunacharsky and Bogdanov joined the Bolsheviks, who appealed to them as the most determined and professional of the Marxist revolutionaries. Lunacharsky later wrote:

> My whole outlook, and indeed my whole character, did not incline me for a moment towards half-hearted commitments, compromise and obscuring of the bright maximalist bases of fully revolutionary Marxism. Of course between me, on the one hand, and Lenin, on the other, there was great dissimilarity. He approached all these questions as a practical man [*praktik*] with an enormously clear grasp of tactics, a real political genius. I approached them as a philosopher and, I will say more definitely, as a poet of the revolution...[6]

To the philosopher–poet, the factional bitterness of emigré politics was surprising and distasteful. Lunacharsky conducted polemics with the Mensheviks 'with great ruthlessness', in his own words; but he did so as a matter of Party obligation and obtained satisfaction as an orator rather than as a natural partisan. Recalling these polemics during the Civil War, he wrote: 'I always received the arguments of opponents (as I do now) with every attention and objectivity. Because of this, I almost never hold any position with the absolute resolution which is the prerogative of a genuine fanatic.'[7] He had liked many of his political opponents, and reflected that 'among the more or less well-known Bolsheviks, there was perhaps not one who would have kept up human relations for as long as the Menshevik leaders did, and the ordinary members of their organizations as well'.[8]

Lunacharsky wrote of this period of his life that 'art and religion then occupied the centre of my attention, yet not as an aesthete but as a Marxist'.[9] It was in art and religion that he looked for the 'emotional and ethical' counterweight to Plekhanovite rationalism. He saw them as means of emotional expression and, in particular, expression of the individual need for communion with others. Religion, he wrote, carried the individual outside himself in search of fellowship: 'religion is a "bond" [*religiya*—"*svyaz*"]'.[10] He explained the social impulse in what he called 'biophysical' terms, but at the same time gave it ethical value. This was the basis of his ethical justification of Socialism.

The relationship of religion to Marxism was explored in the two volumes of Lunacharsky's *Religion and Socialism* published in 1908 and 1911. Lunacharsky argued that Engels and Plekhanov, in developing the rational and scientific aspects of Marxism, had overlooked the force of Marx's emotional and ethical commitment to Socialism. Marx, Lunacharsky suggested, was not only a social scientist but a moral philosopher—indeed a prophet in the great Jewish tradition of Christ and Spinoza—and Marxism, properly understood, was a synthesis of science and moral enthusiasm.

In this interpretation it was the Bolsheviks—'Marxist voluntarists', in Lunacharsky's phrase—who were the true followers of Marx. Plekhanovite Marxism was pure rationalism, which enabled the Mensheviks to analyse without influencing events. The Bolsheviks, like Marx himself, were rational but enthusiastic. They intended not only to interpret the world but to change it.

Lunacharsky knew that the Bolsheviks did not appreciate the implications of their own political position: they were voluntarists in politics, yet in philosophy they tried to squeeze themselves into an orthodox Plekhanovite Marxism which Lunacharsky thought was not really orthodox at all. Bolshevik propaganda, being purely materialist and scientific, could appeal to the proletariat but failed to gain the emotional sympathy of the intelligentsia or the peasantry. The Bolsheviks should propagate Marxism as an anthropocentric religion whose God was Man, raised to the height of his powers, and whose celebration was revolution—'the greatest and most decisive act in the process of "Godbuilding" [*bogostroitel'stvo*]'.[11] For 'religion is enthusiasm and "without enthusiasm it is not given to man to create anything great" '.[12]

The 'Godbuilding' thesis was illustrated by Maxim Gorky, then a close friend of Lunacharsky, in his novel *Confession* [*Ispoved'*], published in 1908. Gorky's hero, Matvei, is a Godseeker who meets many false prophets in his travels and, in the end, a true prophet, John. John speaks to him of God but directs him to a proletarian commune. Matvei begins to understand that the individual must seek God through union with other men. In the words of Lunacharsky's commentary:[13]

The God of whom the old man speaks is humanity, all of socialist humanity. This is the only divinity accessible to man; its God is not yet born, but is being built. But who is a Godbuilder? Above all, of course, the proletariat, in the historic moment we live in. John offers a general truth, not defining it exactly. In that general form it is more accessible to a man like Matvei. To him, a Godseeker, the high-sounding formula in which socialism is expressed here is the more comprehensible. Do you seek God? God is the humanity of the future...A marvellous formula. It is not in our terms, but in essence it is ours. It is the same music, our music, only they are playing it on new instruments.

Lenin thought otherwise. 'I too am a "seeker" in philosophy', he wrote; but what he sought was 'a stumbling block to people who under the guise of Marxism are offering something incredibly muddled, confused and reactionary'.[14] Lenin had not wished to make philosophy a party issue. But Bogdanov, the leading philosophical revisionist among the Bolsheviks, was at the same time a political rival to Lenin and opposed to him on the issue of Bolshevik participation in the Duma.* *Materialism and Empiriocriticism*, which Lenin wrote in 1908, was primarily directed against Bogdanov.

Bogdanov, like the empiriocritics Ernst Mach and Richard Avenarius (Lunacharsky's old teacher), was trained in the physical sciences; and empiriocriticism was essentially a scientists' philosophy, seeking to eliminate unnecessary concepts and establish a framework for the rational organization of empirical observations. Bogdanov's interest was in applying this framework to the social sciences, and developing an 'organizational science' of society and social consciousness. The empiriocritics regarded the existence of things outside our perception of them as unverifiable. The only non-metaphysical epistemology was one based on perception and cognition, not on matter: materialism itself was metaphysics.

* The question was how much use the Bolsheviks should make of legal institutions like the Duma, and how much they should continue to work (in post-1905 conditions) within the old underground revolutionary organizations. Bogdanov thought Lenin leant too far towards legal and parliamentary activity.

Lenin wrote in defence of materialism, which he saw as a political weapon not to be lightly abandoned for the convenience of scientists. He argued that the class struggle was reflected in the conflict of materialist and idealist philosophies, materialism being invariably supported by rational progressives and idealism by feudal-clerical reactionaries and fools. For the purposes of Lenin's argument, Lunacharsky's flirtation with religion (for which Bogdanov had little sympathy) pointed the inevitable path leading from empirio-criticism back to Bishop Berkeley.

In 1908, the year in which the philosophical controversy reached its height, Lunacharsky and Bogdanov were living on Capri at Gorky's invitation.[15] There, at the beginning of 1909, they began the organization of a 'Party school' which was to train 'permanent cadres of Party leaders from the working-class'.[16] The school was financed by private donations, notably from Gorky, his wife Maria Fedorovna Andreeva and Chaliapin.[17] Students were selected by local Social-Democratic committees, and smuggled out of Russia and through Europe to Capri. Leading members of all the Russian Social-Democratic groups in emigration were invited to lecture at the school. But neither Mensheviks nor Bolsheviks accepted the pretensions of the Party school to be 'inter-factional': it was regarded as a political manœuvre of the Bogdanovite group of dissident Bolsheviks 'to consolidate their position and get a powerful network of agents [*agentura*] in Russia'. This view, Lunacharsky commented in his memoirs, was 'not without foundation'.[18] Before the school opened in August its supporters had broken with the Bolsheviks and formed a separate group under the name *Vpered*. The Vperedists had no common platform, although many of them opposed Lenin's attitude to the Bolshevik representation in the Duma, and Bogdanov, Lunacharsky and Gorky were associated with philosophical revisionism.

The lecturers at the Capri school were all, in the event, Vperedists. Bogdanov lectured on economics and social thought, Lunacharsky on trade unionism, the history of the International and German Social-Democracy, Lyadov on the history of Russian Social-Democracy, Desnitsky on church and state in Russia, Volsky on the agrarian question and Pokrovsky on Russian history.[19] Gorky lectured on the history of Russian literature, and Lunacharsky conducted an excursion to the Naples museum, speaking so movingly on the Renaissance that all his listeners including Gorky were brought to tears.[20]

There were thirteen students. Lenin, determined to prevent the creation of any powerful Vperedist *agentura*, bombarded them with admonitory letters from Paris, and succeeded in alienating five students (one of whom turned out to be a police informer) from the Vperedist organizers of the school. The organizers themselves split under this pressure, Gorky and N. E. Vilonov—who had been largely responsible for bringing the students from Russia—inclining towards Lenin. The split was widened by personal animosities. Gorky's wife, Andreeva, had quarrelled with Anna Aleksandrovna Lunacharskaya and was on bad terms with Anna Aleksandrovna's brother, Bogdanov. The quarrel had caused the Lunacharskys to move, even before the opening of the Capri school, across the bay to Naples:[21] and although Gorky and Lunacharsky were perhaps unwilling participants in the original dispute, they remained estranged for almost a decade.

The Vperedists held a second Party school in Bologna in 1910–11. Again an attempt was made to put it on an inter-factional basis, and it was under the control of a commission of the Central Committee of the Russian Social-Democratic Workers' Party headed by the non-Vperedist Semashko. Gorky took no part in the Bologna school, and it was evidently financed by the profits of an expropriation carried out by a Bolshevik group in the Urals. This was greatly resented by the Bolsheviks. Lenin and Plekhanov were again invited to lecture and refused. Trotsky accepted, but the majority of the lecturers were Vperedists—Lunacharsky, Pokrovsky, Lyadov, Aleksinsky, Bogdanov and Volsky.[22]

After the Bologna school, the *Vpered* group began to disintegrate. Bogdanov returned to Russia in 1913, unreconciled with Lenin. Gorky and Lenin, their friendship reestablished, exchanged hostile comments on Lunacharsky's 'scientific mysticism'.[23] Lenin is reported at this period to have called Lunacharsky 'a real charlatan'.[24] Lunacharsky himself moved to Paris, and there established a 'circle of proletarian culture' whose members included the Vperedist

Fedor Ivanovich Kalinin (younger brother of the Bolshevik M. I. Kalinin) and the poet and theoretician of proletarian culture Aleksei Kapitonovich Gastev, who became director of the Moscow Central Institute of Labour (TSIT) in the '20s.[25]

On the outbreak of war, Lunacharsky took the internationalist position and cooperated with Trotsky and others in the publication of the internationalist journal *Nashe slovo* in France. In 1915 he moved to Switzerland where, he writes in his memoirs, 'I at once presented myself to Lenin and Zinoviev with a proposal of the fullest union' on the internationalist platform.[26] This marked Lunacharsky's reconciliation with Lenin, although he remained outside the Bolshevik group. Lunacharsky and his friend Lebedev-Polyansky revived the old *Vpered* journal, now published in Geneva and no longer anti-Bolshevik: the first issue announced that 'the idea of proletarian culture has now become the distinctive trait of Vperedism'.[27] The Vperedist idea of proletarian culture, as far as Lenin was concerned, hovered somewhere on the boundaries of philosophical heresy. Lunacharsky described the development of proletarian culture as a means of heightening the class awareness of the proletariat and promoting a spirit of militant enthusiasm for the achievement of class aims;[28] Bogdanov, whose influence on Lunacharsky was still strong, incorporated proletarian culture and the organization of proletarian consciousness within the framework of a general 'organizational science' (which Lenin distrusted), and believed that the sphere of proletarian cultural organization must be independent of the political sphere. This had overtones of Capri and Bologna—that is, of Bogdanov's attempts to establish a political and organizational centre independent of Bolshevik control. But in Bogdanov's absence Lenin saw no political threat in *Vpered's* proletarian culture, and probably dismissed it as political dilettantism.

In May 1917, Lunacharsky returned to Russia with a large group of political emigrés, mainly Menshevik, on the second 'sealed train' through Germany. In Petrograd he joined Gorky's Social-Democratic internationalist (but non-Bolshevik) paper *Novaya zhizn'* and, until July, headed the cultural-educational section of the Petrograd City Duma. He was arrested during the July Days. While in prison, he was readmitted to the Bolshevik Party and, after his release, stood as a Bolshevik candidate and was elected deputy to the mayor of Petrograd.[29] In September he became president of the newly formed cultural-educational commission of the Petrograd Party Committee.[30] He was one of the most popular Bolshevik orators, speaking almost daily at factories, barracks and mass meetings in the *Cirque Moderne*. 'My normal audience now is 4,000 people', he wrote to his wife.[31]

For Lunacharsky, who was inclined to see even prosaic things in a romantic light, the experience of revolutionary Petrograd was overwhelming. Life there, he wrote to his wife at the end of May, was 'colossal in everything, tragic and significant'.[32] The events of October raised him to an even higher pitch of emotional excitement. He had the characteristic, unusual in politicians, of wanting to share his own happiness with everyone; and in this spirit of universal goodwill he urged Sukhanov to join the Bolsheviks—'What a Foreign Minister he would make!'[33] His charity extended even to the dead: 'one could weep tears of blood', he wrote,[34] that the composer Scriabin had not lived to celebrate the revolution.*

Lebedev-Polyansky reported that after the February Revolution Lunacharsky predicted the downfall of the Provisional Government and its replacement by a government under Lenin, with Trotsky as Minister of Foreign Affairs and himself Minister of Education.[35] When the Bolsheviks took power, Lunacharsky's appointment to the Commissariat of Education was, according to Lebedev-Polyansky, uncontroversial: 'Everyone considered his candidature the most appropriate. It did not provoke arguments or hesitations.'[36]

Clearly Lunacharsky's record did not commend him as a reliable Party man. This was also the case with Trotsky, Rakovsky and Chicherin. It could be argued that the Bolsheviks had so low a regard for educational and cultural affairs that the Commissariat of Education was to be had for the asking (although the same could hardly be said of the Commissariats of War and Foreign Affairs, and the Ukraine). But it will be seen in later chapters that Lenin, at

* This attitude to Scriabin, in whose music Lunacharsky heard a prophecy of social upheaval, was not as eccentric as it might now seem to anyone familiar with his 'Divine' (*bozhestvennaya*) symphony and the *Poème d'ecstase*. Even the dour Plekhanov, who knew Scriabin, found an idealist and mystical reflection of a revolutionary epoch in his music.

least, had a very high regard for education, and was to give Lunacharsky's commissariat considerable personal support on almost all educational (though not artistic) issues. The more probable explanation is that Lunacharsky was appointed to the Commissariat of Education—as Semashko to the Commissariat of Health and Chicherin to Foreign Affairs—because he was recognized as the Party's leading specialist in the field. It is true, nevertheless, that neither in October nor subsequently was Lunacharsky admitted to the inner counsels of the Party; and the ambiguity of his status as a Party specialist but not a Party leader was reflected in the later reputation of his commissariat. The Bolsheviks, like Lunacharsky, were supporters of enlightenment, but without his all-embracing charity: they did not forgive his twelve-year apostasy from the Party or his temperamental preference for the company of poets rather than politicians.

Lenin's attitude to Lunacharsky in the post-*Vpered* period is probably accurately conveyed by Viktor Shulgin, a rather disapproving subordinate of Lunacharsky at Narkompros:

> At the sharpest moment of the struggle with Proletkultism* [1920], when Lunacharsky had not carried out Lenin's instruction, I said to Vladimir Ilyich reproachfully: 'And you are still fond of him.' Lenin then replied—and the reply was so unexpected that I wrote it down then and there—'And I advise you also to be fond of him. He is drawn towards the future with his whole being. That is why there is such joy and laughter in him. And he is ready to give that joy and laughter to everyone. Of course in this case he has been foolish; he should not get himself mixed up in Bogdanov's net. But we will pull him out of it.'[37]

* See below, pp. 177–80.

2

THE ESTABLISHMENT OF NARKOMPROS

The jurisdiction of Lunacharsky's commissariat covered the former Ministry of Public Education, the State Education Committee created by the Provisional Government, and the former Palace Ministry, which controlled the imperial theatres, the Academy of Arts and the royal palaces.

The former Minister of Education, S. F. Oldenburg (who replaced the first Provisional Government appointee, Manuilov, in July[1]) appears to have retired gracefully from his post in October and returned to his position as permanent secretary of the Academy of Sciences unmolested. One of his deputies, the S-R Salazkin, was less fortunate, and was briefly imprisoned in the Petropavlovskaya fortress. Lunacharsky's first and characteristic action as commissar was to secure his release.[2]

Lunacharsky's first task was to assemble workers for the new commissariat. Lenin, meeting him by chance in the corridors of Smolny, suggested that he seek the cooperation of Nadezhda Krupskaya (Lenin's wife) and the historian and former Vperedist M. N. Pokrovsky, who was then in Moscow.[3] Otherwise Lunacharsky was left to his own devices, and the first workers he recruited to Narkompros were his colleagues on the cultural-educational sections of the Petrograd Duma and Party Committee: Krupskaya, Vera and Ludmila Menzhinskaya, V. M. Pozner, Dora Lazurkina and D. I. Leshchenko. He also enrolled the former Vperedists F. I. Kalinin and Lebedev-Polyansky (who had returned to the Bolshevik Party in July with Lunacharsky, and had worked with him in the cultural-educational commission of the Petrograd Party Committee), together with Vera Bonch-Bruevich and I. B. Rogalsky. These were the members of the collegium which, according to Lunacharsky's recollection, was approved by Sovnarkom soon after his appointment to Narkompros.[4]

Having appointed a collegium, the next step should have been to take possession of the old Ministry of Public Education on Chernyshev bridge. But Lunacharsky hesitated, observing that other commissars attempting to occupy their respective ministries were meeting severe rebuffs. Trotsky and Uritsky went to the Ministry of Foreign Affairs on 27 October, and were locked out by its officials while the former deputy minister escaped through a back door with the Secret Treaties.[5] Shlyapnikov went to the Ministry of Labour a day later: none of the officials would tell him which was the minister's office.[6] Lunacharsky's appointee to the former Palace Ministry —Yuri Flakserman, then aged twenty-two—had the humiliating experience of being admitted but ignored by the ministry's officials when he came to announce their subordination to Soviet power:

> All the officials of that great organization were still at their posts. There was sabotage of all the ministries, banks and other institutions, and most of their officials and employees did not turn up to work. But in the Palace Ministry there was complete order; everyone came punctually to work and scribbled away as if nothing had happened.[7]

A non-Bolshevik paper reported with enjoyment that the Bolshevik commissars to the War Ministry

> went to the Petropavlovskaya fortress and appealed in great distress to General Manikovsky to join the administration of the War Ministry, in view of the fact that they did not know how to cope with supply, which had become completely disorganized. They stated that they would accept any conditions...[8]

On 8 November, Lunacharsky told VTSIK* that 'he could give no comforting news' about the position in the Ministry of Public Education. Its officials were on strike, as were the State Education Committee and the Teachers' Union (VUS). Lunacharsky had no illusions that agreement could be quickly reached because, he said, 'it has been observed that an empty-headed clerk will soon come to us, but all the intellectual [*ideinye*] workers stubbornly insist on their opinion that we have usurped power'. He added that 'it will be much easier to build everything afresh than to take account of old and decayed institutions'.[9]

* All-Russian Central Executive Committee of the Congress of Soviets, a body carrying out functions in many ways parallel to those of Sovnarkom. Lunacharsky was an elected member of VTSIK.

So for the time being the former officials of the ministry remained in possession of it, refusing any contact with the Bolsheviks, while Lunacharsky and his collegium worked from an office in the Winter Palace and the old office of the cultural–educational commission of the Petrograd Duma.

It is probable that Lunacharsky was an advocate of coalition with other Socialist parties. Trotsky quotes him as telling the Petrograd Bolshevik Committee on 1 November that

> Here we have been 8 days in power, but we do not know whether the people know of our decree on peace...Who is responsible? Technical staff, who are bourgeois or petty-bourgeois. They are sabotaging us... We ourselves can cope with nothing...Of course we can take the terrorist path, but why? What for?...I consider that in the face of all these difficulties, agreement is desirable. No proofs of yours about the Mensheviks will convince the masses. I know very well that to work as we are now is impossible.[10]

A number of members of the Bolshevik 'right'—Kamenev, Zinoviev, Rykov, Nogin, Milyutin, Teodorovich—resigned their posts over the coalition issue on 4 November. Lunacharsky was not among them. But his actions at this time, as so often, are not explicable in normal political terms. He resigned from the government on 2 November, hearing the false report of the destruction of St Basil's Cathedral during the fighting in Moscow. On 4 November, when the supporters of coalition resigned, Lunacharsky learnt that St Basil's had not been destroyed and withdrew his resignation. On Trotsky's evidence, a move to expel Lunacharsky from the Party as a supporter of coalition had been initiated by Lenin on 1 November, but defeated.[11]

Lunacharsky's resignation over the supposed destruction of St Basil's caused a good deal of ill-natured mirth in the Party at the time, and was even unexpectedly recalled by Khrushchev almost fifty years later.[12] But he was not alone in being deceived by false rumours. Telephone communication with Moscow had broken down on 31 October; and on 2 November, *Novaya zhizn'* reported 'horrifying news' from Moscow:

> In the Kremlin...cannons roar, shells fly, innocent blood flows...If

even one of the great historical monuments falls to the hands of vandals, blinded by malice, there will be no forgiveness for them, either from us or from those who come after...

On the same day, Lunacharsky is reported to have burst into tears at a meeting of Sovnarkom and rushed from the room crying 'I cannot stand it! I cannot bear the monstrous destruction of beauty and tradition!'[13]

Lunacharsky's resignation from the government was dated 2 November and published the next day in *Novaya zhizn'* and the Social-Revolutionary paper *Delo naroda*.

I have just heard, from eye-witnesses, what happened in Moscow.

St. Basil's and the Uspensky Cathedral are being destroyed. The Kremlin, where the most important artistic treasures of Petrograd and Moscow are collected, is being bombarded.

There are thousands of victims.

What will happen next? What more can happen?

I cannot bear it. My cup is full. I am powerless to stop this awfulness.

It is impossible to work under the pressure of thoughts which are driving me mad.

That is why I am resigning from Sovnarkom.

I understand the full gravity of this decision. But I can no more. (Signed) A. Lunacharsky.

The resignation was withdrawn on the day of its publication; and the next day (4 November) *Novaya zhizn'* published a statement from Lunacharsky explaining his resignation and its withdrawal and calling on the Russian people to treasure its cultural heritage. 'It is impossible to remain at a post where you are powerless', Lunacharsky wrote. 'But my comrades, the People's Commissars, considered resignation impermissible. I remain at my post, until your will may find a worthier representative...' Ironically, in the same number of *Novaya zhizn'* a reader applauded Lunacharsky's action in resigning:

You were not alone in your feelings, your suffering. With you were all those who see in socialism the bearer of a renewed mankind, purified of seeking bloody solutions to its problems. Your voice did not go out in vain...

Trotsky, explaining the incident to the Petrograd Soviet on 3 November, disposed of it briefly with the comment 'that Lunacharsky is not a militant politician; and news of the events in Moscow upset him so much that he said it was impossible to work. But then he withdrew his resignation.'[14]

The occupation of the Ministry of Education took place a fortnight later, on 18 November.[15] Lunacharsky's friend and colleague Leshchenko had found an intermediary, the left S-R Bakrylov, who reported that the officials of the ministry would leave the moment Lunacharsky appeared, but that the technical staff was prepared to remain. 'The prospect of being left with my comrades of the collegium, surrounded by a rather large number of messengers, stokers and doormen, was not attractive', Lunacharsky recalled.[16] Nevertheless, the expedition set off in several cars—but without military escort which, Lunacharsky wrote, 'I flatly refused.' There was no resistance at the ministry. A group of about fifty technical staff were waiting at the entrance 'and welcomed the People's Commissar and his colleagues with a loud "hurrah"'. Speeches were made. A representative of the technical staff expressed their feelings of solidarity with the proletariat and their eagerness to serve the workers' government.

> During our humble celebration, a young man with a thick beard came unexpectedly into the room, not taking off his coat...This young man turned out to have been sent by the absconding officials to inform me and my colleagues that they were very angry with us and that they considered us to be the destroyers of the glorious February Revolution, and to say how grieved they were that the administration of education was now ruined. All the time he was talking, Bakrylov kept wanting to arrest him...[17]

Narkompros issued an appeal to former officials of the ministry to appear there at 12 noon on 27 November for the transfer of business and the return of office keys.[18] Nobody came. On 28 November it was noticed that the departing officials had taken with them 93,000 roubles belonging to the teachers' pension fund. Countess Sofia Vladimirovna Panina, deputy to the Minister of Education from August 1917 and well known for her work in the field of popular education over many years, was arrested and brought before the Revolutionary Tribunal on 10 December. The money had in fact been removed from the ministry on Panina's instructions just before Lunacharsky's occupation of the building. Panina, who was defended before the tribunal by Yakov Yakovlevich Gurevich, one of the leaders of the Petrograd Teachers' Union, admitted responsibility but denied guilt, stating that she would return the money only to a legitimate authority—the Constituent Assembly.[19] *Novaya zhizn'*, in a front-page report of the trial on 13 December, warmly supported her stand.

The Revolutionary Tribunal—perhaps because of her past services to popular education, perhaps unwilling to make a political martyr—did not deal harshly with her. Their verdict was

> to leave citizeness S. V. Panina in prison until the return of the people's money, taken by her, to the treasury of the Commissariat of Public Education [*sic*].
>
> The Revolutionary Tribunal considers citizeness S. V. Panina guilty of opposition to the people's government but, taking into account the past of the accused, limits itself to consigning citizeness Panina to public contempt [*obshchestvennoe poritsanie*].[20]

Panina was prepared to remain in prison until her release by the Constituent Assembly and—true to her past—began organizing cultural activities for her fellow prisoners. But her friends were less optimistic of the future, and a subscription was raised among the Petrograd intelligentsia to buy her out. Professor Grevs brought 92,802 roubles 72 kopeks to Narkompros[21] and on 19 December Panina was freed.

This was not the last of Narkompros' problems with former officials of the ministry. Some of the senior officials 'created an organization, and entered into correspondence with various institutions in the name of the "Ministry of Public Education"'; and this organization continued for some months to conduct examinations, award diplomas and issue instructions to provincial officials.[22] The tsarist portraits in the ministerial building, including a more than life-size Alexander I in the minister's study, were still on the walls when Narkompros moved to Moscow in March 1918.[23]

Narkompros' jurisdiction was somewhat diminished in December 1917, when the left S-Rs joined the government and were given eight major offices, including a 'Commissariat of Property of the Republic' based on the old Palace Ministry. Karelin was appointed commissar. But the change took place on paper rather than in fact. Control of state theatres and museums remained formally under Narkompros;[24] and Flakserman, whom Lunacharsky had appointed to the Palace Ministry, remained as Karelin's deputy. According to Flakserman's account, Karelin took little interest in the commissariat, and soon resigned from the government over the Brest peace.[25] After his resignation Narkompros agitated for the return of the Commissariat of Property of the Republic, which Sovnarkom granted in August 1918.[26] It was subsequently reorganized as the Museum Department of Narkompros under Natalya Ivanovna Trotskaya.

A further consequence of the S-Rs' joining of the government was the appointment of the left S-R G. D. Zaks as assistant to the Commissar of Education. The left S-Rs in Narkompros, Lebedev-Polyansky recalled, were jealous of their rights and 'insisted that comrade Zaks should be present at the Commissar's receptions "to know what he was saying" '.[27] But Zaks—who was not only assistant to Lunacharsky, but deputy head of Vecheka—remained in Narkompros only for a short time: he was one of the leaders of the left S-R revolt in June 1918 and, although he survived the affair and even joined the Bolshevik Party in November, did not return to educational work.

In March 1918, Narkompros was evacuated with the rest of the government to Moscow. Lunacharsky, however, remained in Petrograd, combining the functions of Commissar of Education of the Republic, Commissar of Education of the Northern *Oblast'* and deputy head of the Council of Commissars of the Union of Communes of the Northern *Oblast'* under Zinoviev.[28] A number of departments of Narkompros remained in Petrograd with Lunacharsky, including the arts department (IZO), part of the theatre department and the teachers' pension fund.[29]

'Not one of the People's Commissars was placed in such a disadvantageous position as I', Lunacharsky wrote, 'because in my administrative and political work I had to tear myself in two . . .'[30]

The Central Committee of the Party wanted him to spend three weeks of each month in Moscow and one week in Petrograd, but finally allowed him to spend two weeks in each.[31] In fact Lunacharsky spent only ten weeks in Moscow between April and December 1918.[32] 'I am now so bound to this great and tragic Petrograd', Lunacharsky had written to his wife before the October Revolution, 'that I will not be able to tear myself away from it for long.' So it turned out; and he moved permanently to Moscow only at the beginning of 1919, 'on Sverdlov's insistence'.[33]

Narkompros began work in Moscow on 28 March—headed in Lunacharsky's absence by Krupskaya, and later Pokrovsky[34]—in the building of a former lycée at Ostozhenka 53. For the time being the effective governing body of the commissariat was not the collegium (which continued to have a formal existence) but the larger State Education Commission, established by Sovnarkom decree on 9 November 1917.[35] Except for Lunacharsky and the Menzhinskayas, most of the original Petrograd members of Narkompros moved to Moscow, heading departments of the commissariat and attending the meetings of the State Education Commission. The Petrograd group was joined by a group of Moscow Bolsheviks: M. N. Pokrovsky, who became deputy commissar in May; P. N. Lepeshinsky, a companion of Lenin's Geneva exile; P. K. Shternberg, professor of astronomy at Moscow University and one of the organizers of the Bolshevik rising in Moscow; Olga Kameneva, wife of L. B. Kamenev and sister of Trotsky, who became head of the theatre department in Moscow and thereafter a thorn in Lunacharsky's flesh; and L. G. Shapiro, a former Bundist and Menshevik who joined the Bolsheviks in 1918. Of the left S-Rs in Narkompros, those who most frequently attended the State Education Commission's meetings in Moscow were Sofia Azanchevskaya, an incompetent and querulous member of the Narkompros finance department; Dora Elkina, a staunch defender of S-R prerogatives with the face of a revolutionary heroine *à la* Turgenev; and A. Baryshnikov. Elkina and Baryshnikov continued to work in Narkompros throughout the '20s.

Among less regular attenders at the meetings of the State Education Commission were the Bolsheviks E. A. Preobrazhensky and

D. B. Ryazanov, the artist D. P. Shterenberg (who was a left Bundist), the composer A. S. Lourie and the Social-Democratic internationalist K. N. Levin, a former contributor to Gorky's Petrograd paper *Novaya zhizn'*.[36]

The serious business of constructing a functioning commissariat began only after the move to Moscow. But it was conducted informally, so that for some years Narkompros was not in a position to say exactly how many people it employed, and could only with difficulty compile a list of its departments. Lunacharsky, who could never believe that Narkompros could be the worse for gaining a man of goodwill, or the wife of a comrade, or the destitute granddaughter of a distinguished writer, had the habit of recruiting staff on a personal basis and directing them with letters of introduction to the head of a Narkompros department. But Narkompros continued to suffer from a chronic shortage both of qualified workers and of reliable Party members. It had difficulty in finding substitutes for the experienced officials who had fled the Petrograd ministry on Lunacharsky's approach (and, as far as can be seen from the Narkompros archives, did not return). Members of the radical and literary intelligentsia at first boycotted the commissariat, as an organ of Soviet power; and later joined it in increasing numbers, so that the arts departments proliferated beyond any functional rationality and to the detriment of Narkompros' reputation among other government and Party organizations.

Party members were notoriously unwilling to work in Narkompros, and those that did so were, with very few exceptions, female. Narkompros became—like the *zhenskii otdel** of the Central Committee and, in later years, Ryazanov's Marx–Engels Institute—a place of employment for wives and sisters of Bolshevik politicians: its members included the wives of Lenin, Trotsky, Zinoviev, Kamenev, Dzerzhinsky, Krzhizhanovsky and Bonch-Bruevich, Lenin's sister Anna Elizarova and the two sisters of Menzhinsky.

Most of the leading workers in Narkompros were recently returned from many years in emigration, where their occupation had commonly been literary and political journalism. Among the revolutionary wives, many had some experience of teaching in

* Department for work among women.

Russia, usually extramural; but almost nobody, male or female, had any administrative or organizational experience outside the sphere of emigré revolutionary politics.

This lack of experience was most keenly felt in dealing with financial problems. There was no accountant among the original members of Narkompros, and I. B. Rogalsky, who had no special qualifications for the task, was put in charge of Narkompros finances. 'I remember', Lunacharsky wrote,

that Rogalsky's face always bore a mark of the deepest astonishment when he brought us money from the bank. It still seemed to him that the Revolution and the organization of the new power were a sort of magical play, and that in a magical play it is impossible to receive real money.[37]

Immediately after Narkompros moved to Moscow, it faced the problem of drawing up budgetary estimates for presentation to Sovnarkom. The estimates were drawn up, according to Lunacharsky, on the basis of the 1917 budget, adding 30%. Pozner, however, claimed that 'the estimate was composed not according to 1917 but 1918. He [Pozner] saw Kerensky's estimate for the first half of 1918 and used it.'[38] In the absence of Rogalsky, Lebedev-Polyansky—then head of the literary-publishing department of Narkompros—was sent as Narkompros representative to the meetings on the budget.

There was some kind of meeting for consideration of the estimate. Nobody knew what the institution was or who the people were. We looked at them—neat, clean-shaven, in their starched collars. We whispered to each other: 'They look like old *chinovniki*. Why should we listen to them?' ...They tried to talk of concrete possibilities, norms and statistical inaccuracies, but in vain. We argued passionately, not conceding a single rouble...as if our estimate was really properly considered and well-founded...

Then the estimate had to be defended in a special commission of Sovnarkom...It was evening. Shlyapnikov was in the chair. There was endless noise and shouting...

'You want children's toys. Well, we can't run to toys now,' announced comrade Shlyapnikov.

'How can extramural work go on without them?' retorted comrade Lazurkina in defence.

'And publishing, that has to be halved as well.'

More noise. The Narkompros representatives hotly announced: 'We will leave the meeting if you mean to cut our estimates like this, not accepting any of our conclusions.' And so it went on over every clause...

In two hours the estimate was approved. Tired but satisfied of victory—although irritated with comrade Shlyapnikov—we went home.

Of course comrade Shlyapnikov, like us, was not prepared for such work. He knew only one thing: to reduce to a half, a third, a quarter. That is what he did.[39]

Sovnarkom approved the first Narkompros budget, at the sum of 511,285,100 roubles, on 5 April, 1918[40]—and this in spite of arithmetical mistakes in the estimates amounting to 3 million roubles, and almost total disregard of conventional presentation.[41] But seven weeks later Lunacharsky reported that

the financial position is bad...We are besieged with questions about money, but there are no allocations...We must find out what the Treasury wants from us, so that we can distribute the budget we have been given...A large part of the arts department was left completely without a budget...The finance department avoids spending the money it has, and has a lot left over. Gosizdat* has its own funds, but all the other departments are complaining of the absence of funds...[42]

Rogalsky and his deputy in the finance department, Azanchevskaya, went to Petrograd to negotiate with the Treasury but found the officials uncooperative. 'The Treasury is sabotaging us, exploiting the ignorance of many of us', Azanchevskaya reported plaintively to the State Education Commission on their return.[43] The Treasury was believed to hold a balance of 40 million roubles from the old ministry, but 'what part of this sum will be made available to Narkompros was still not clear'.[44] Treasury officials promised Rogalsky and Azanchevskaya to give 'telegraphic instructions to the provinces about the opening of credits with the Treasury', but it was discovered that the telegrams had not been sent because of the Treasury's unwillingness to pay the bill.[45]

The 'magical play' attitude to money which Lunacharsky noted in Rolgalsky was not his alone. Lunacharsky himself—who pro-

* The state publishing department of Narkompros.

tested against use of the word 'estimate' as bureaucratic—seems to have assumed in 1918 that Narkompros would be financed on demand. The Narkompros journal pointed out at the end of the year with satisfaction (though without allowing for inflation of the rouble) that educational spending in 1918 was almost double the 1917 figure, and applauded Narkompros' initiative in finding new categories like publishing and the arts to spend money on, since 'nothing which enriches mankind, adorns life, gives it new joy and new meaning, can be forgotten by a government which has set itself the aim of struggle for a new life, free from slavery and want'.[46]

Pokrovsky, speaking on the Narkompros estimates for the second half of 1918, saw the budget as primarily an exercise in propaganda: 'it is the most enormous budget for education which Russia has ever had', he said; and added that although the estimates had been criticized by short-sighted financial officials he was confident that, because of their 'agitational significance', they would be accepted by the 'more political people in Sovnarkom'. Pozner supported this view, suggesting that the budget should be widely publicized not only in Russia but abroad, because of its 'instructive significance [*prosvetitel'noe znachenie*]' for international public opinion. Pokrovsky admitted that there might be difficulty in spending so much money within the budgetary period, but thought that

> this fact is absolutely harmless. The money will be spent, if not in December then in January; if not in January then in March. If it is three months later, that is a matter of absolute indifference to the public and cannot have any importance.[47]

At the end of 1918, when the 1919 estimates were in preparation, departmental estimates were called for incorporation in the general Narkompros estimate. The protocols of the collegium for November[48] record forty-two separate meetings of departments, subdepartments, committees, sub-sections and commissions—from each of which estimates were submitted directly to the central collegium of Narkompros, since the constituent parts of the commissariat operated in chaotic independence of any general organizational structure. The bodies submitting budgetary estimates to the collegium were:*

- the secretariat
- department of the united labour school
- department of higher schools
- extramural department
- scientific-programming sub-department of the department of school reform
- department of conferences
- scientific department
- sub-department of adult schools
- statistical department for research into the conditions of universal primary education
- student social security committee
- sub-department of social education
- historical subsection
- bureau for the organization of school excursions of the sub-department of visual aids
- sub-section of new languages [Esperanto and others]
- financial collegium
- budgetary commission
- Proletkult
- pre-school department
- commission on the Shelaputinsky Institute
- sanitary education commission
- scientific commission on tuberculosis
- teacher training department
- chemical section
- music department
- department of school administration
- building department
- department of reform of professional education
- sub-section on defective children
- section of People's Houses [*narodnykh domov*]
- editorial commission
- orgburo for meetings on educational statistics
- commission on the transfer of educational institutions from the Commissariat of Communications to Narkompros
- lecturing sub-department
- cinema committee
- supply department
- committee on literacy
- sub-department on adolescents
- department of museums and preservation of historical and artistic monuments
- photographic and phototechnical committee [FOTO-KINO]
- chief archive administration
- theatre department
- library department.

Even this list does not exhaust the infinite variety of Narkompros institutions, since a number of departments then in existence—visual aids, school reform, state theatres, IZO—apparently failed to submit budgetary estimates to the collegium.

* Listed in order of consideration by the collegium in November 1918.

'The inflation of commissariats', Krupskaya wrote,

> is a continual, observable process... Very often there is no distinction between business entrusted to the commissar, the collegium and the departments. This is usually worked out on the spot. The functions of various sub-departments are not always clearly delineated. Lists of staff exist, but in the majority of cases these lists are very approximate...[49]

Certainly Narkompros was not the only commissariat meriting this description, although it seems to have carried organizational anarchy to a fairly extreme point. Its methods of appointment were haphazard, and it was not until January 1919 that the central collegium issued a firm instruction that 'all departmental collegiums must be endorsed by the collegium of Narkompros, and all unendorsed members of [departmental] collegiums must be submitted for endorsement within a week'.[50] The indiscipline of its staff was said to have provoked 'reproaches from the responsible workers of other Soviet institutions'; and in September 1918 the Narkompros secretariat complained 'that Narkompros employees are quite often late for work or absent; that they stroll round the corridors needlessly; and that they refuse on some excuse or other to perform the work delegated to them', adding the warning that 'idlers and saboteurs cannot be tolerated in the service of the Workers' and Peasants' Government'.[51]

In May 1919 Narkompros had a staff of 3,062—almost ten times the number employed in the central administration of the old ministry in October 1917[52]—which it was instructed to reduce to 2,265 by the Council of Worker–Peasant Defence. In preparing a scheme for the reduction of staff, Narkompros found that its biggest single departments were supply and museums, each with 345 employees. The combined strength of its music, cinema, theatre and arts departments was almost 600. The education departments, on the other hand, were comparatively understaffed, with 283 workers in the schools departments, 64 in professional-technical education, 40 in higher education and 30 in teacher training.[53] The total numbers employed in Narkompros seems subsequently to have dropped sharply as a result of famine and mobilization, but the disproportion between the educational and cultural departments remained.

Early in 1920, the collegium approved a plan rationalizing the internal organization of the commissariat.[54] Thereafter Narkompros was divided into five sectors: organizational, extramural (including adult education, Proletkult and the news agency ROSTA), scientific (including higher education) and artistic sectors, and the sector of 'social training' [*sotsial'nogo vospitaniya*], dealing with primary and secondary schools. Outside the sectors were the secretariat, the chief archive administration, the department for the education of national minorities and the State Publishing House (Gosizdat).

This structure was retained until the organizational reform of Narkompros at the beginning of 1921.

3

SCHOOL EDUCATION

THE NEW EDUCATIONAL SYSTEM

Lunacharsky's first declaration as Commissar of Education was published on 29 October, 1917. It anticipated a very modest role for the central commissariat, and announced that the Soviet education system was to rest on popular initiative. 'The labouring masses', Lunacharsky wrote, 'thirst after education':

> The government cannot give it to them, nor the intelligentsia, nor any force outside themselves. Schools, books, theatres, museums and so on can only be aids. The people themselves, consciously or unconsciously, must evolve their own culture...The State Education Commission is certainly not a central power directing educational institutions. On the contrary, all school affairs must be handed over to the organs of local self-government. The independent action of...workers', soldiers' and peasants' cultural-educational organizations must achieve full autonomy, both in relation to the central government and to the municipal centres...[1]

The problem, then, was to find a way of organizing popular initiative. The State Education Commission decided that this was to be done by 'educational soviets', elected by the population at *volost'*, *uezd*, *guberniya* and *oblast'* levels, and entrusted with the administration of education within their areas. The educational soviets were to be controlled 'in political respects' by the local Soviets of Deputies. Otherwise they would be responsible 'only to their own organs in the order of hierarchy': *volost'* to *uezd*, *uezd* to *guberniya*, *guberniya* and city to *oblast'*, *oblast'* to Narkompros.[2] Narkompros was thus in the position of an appointed government body topping a pyramid of elected soviets, but denying itself the right to act as a 'central directing power'.

Narkompros was so quick to abdicate central power and to repudiate a centralized system of educational administration that its announcement came before any decision had been made on the general administrative structure of the Soviet Republic. When the

Commissariat of Internal affairs (NKVD) completed its general administrative plan shortly afterwards, it was found—not surprisingly—to be at odds with the Narkompros plan.

NKVD's plan, published early in March, proposed to establish departments of each People's Commissariat at *uezd*, *guberniya* and *oblast'* levels. Members of the departments would not be elected, but appointed by the executive committees of the local Soviet of Deputies. Each department would be jointly subordinate to the local Soviet and its central commissariat.[3]

The Narkompros project had been approved by the cultural-educational section of the Third Congress of Soviets in January, but not sanctioned by the congress as a whole pending the completion of the NKVD plan. Narkompros was not prepared to abandon its elected soviets in favour of NKVD's appointed departments, and on 10 March published its project in *Pravda* with the introductory remark that

> in view of the fact that this project is the logical culmination of all that has been done up to this time by the State Commission on the reform of education, the Commissariat of Education considers itself bound to call attention to the necessity of the most immediate realization of the project.

The project, although strictly speaking superseded by the general NKVD plan and clearly incompatible with it, was by the fact of its publication 'looked on in a number of places as having the force of law'.[4]

It proved impossible for Narkompros to ignore NKVD's instruction completely, although Lebedev-Polyansky hopefully suggested to the State Education Commission that 'the instructions of NKVD cannot have any significance' for Narkompros, which should keep to its original plan.[5] Early in April it became clear that Narkompros would be forced to adopt what Lunacharsky called 'the bureaucratic procedure' of establishing local education departments. But the idea of educational soviets was not abandoned. It was decided that they should coexist with the education departments, having advisory functions to the departments—but, Lunacharsky added enigmatically, 'they may also perform executive functions'.[6] Evidently he still hoped that the educational soviets would drive the bureaucratic departments from the field. Only Krupskaya was concerned at the practical confusion this might cause. She pointed out that some cooperation with NKVD was desirable, if only because without it 'the [administrative] areas established by Narkompros may not correspond with the areas established by NKVD'.[7] Nobody else thought that this mattered.

Krupskaya was, nevertheless, the most ardent of all members of Narkompros in defence of the principle of the educational soviet. Its opponents, she thought,

> still cannot throw off the old view of the mass as an object of the intelligentsia's care, like a small and unreasonable child...We were not afraid to organize a revolution. Let us not be afraid of the people, let us not be afraid that they will elect the wrong sort of representatives, bring in the priests. We want the people to direct the country and be their own masters...We are always thinking in old terms, that if we do not spare ourselves and work day and night in the people's cause, that is enough. But it is nothing. Our job is to help the people *in fact* to take their fate into their own hands.[8]

She insisted that the administration of education should begin not at the *uezd* level (according to the NKVD instruction) but at the *volost'*, and therefore in closer contact with the people. In 1919, when NKVD tried to disband the *volost'* education departments established by Narkompros, Krupskaya protested and the attempt was abandoned.[9]

In June 1918 Narkompros issued a 'Statement on the organization of education in the Russian Republic' which established the educational soviet as a 'controlling advisory' body [*kontrol'no-soveshchatel'nyi*] under the education department. The soviet was to consist of elected representatives of all organizations represented in the Soviet of Deputies, in the same proportion, together with elected representatives of teachers, pupils and 'informed persons'. Its function was 'to listen to the reports of the education department ...and consider the plan of work in education proposed by the department'. The department itself was to be appointed by the executive committee of the local Soviet of Deputies (as in the NKVD instruction) and financed by the central commissariat. It was to hold the executive power in local educational administration, and its lowest unit (in spite of the NKVD instruction) was to be the *volost'* department.[10]

Narkompros' concern for local initiative and autonomy did not exclude a central educational policy, although it did leave some uncertainty on the means by which it could be implemented. Principles of educational policy were hotly argued in the State Education Commission during the spring and summer of 1918. There were two schools of thought on educational policy within Narkompros, the one centred in Petrograd and the other in Moscow. Both were progressive—in the sense of advocating activity methods of teaching, pupil-participation, informal relations between pupils and teachers and non-scholastic curriculum—and Marxist,[11] basing the educational system on the polytechnical school.

The Petrograders, led by Lunacharsky and Ludmila Menzhinskaya, were the more firmly based on what might be called the 'orthodox progressive' position of contemporary European and American educationalists. They believed in anti-authoritarian, non-scholastic education which would encourage full development of the child's individuality, using the methods of Dewey's 'activity school'. Their understanding of 'polytechnical' education was that it should acquaint the child with a number of basic technical skills, to be practised in a well-equipped school workshop, without beginning specialized trade training until late adolescence. A selective bibliography on 'the labour school' published by the Petrograd branch of Narkompros in 1918 included August Lay (*Die Tatschüle*), John Dewey, Kerschensteiner (the *Arbeiterschüle*), Ferrière, Montessori and the contemporary Russian educationalist K. N. Ventsel. Simultaneously the Petrograd branch of the anti-Bolshevik teachers' union VUS—no friend of Narkompros—published an almost identical bibliography on the same subject (with the addition of works by Tolstoy,* the Tolstoyan S. T. Shatsky, Kropotkin and Ushinsky).[12]

* There may have been a political, or at least a tactical, motive in Petrograd Narkompros' omission of Tolstoy and Kropotkin, but Narkompros was by no means entirely hostile to their educational ideas. Krupskaya was a friend of Tolstoyan I. I. Gorbunov-

The Muscovites, led by V. M. Pozner and P. N. Lepeshinsky, put their main emphasis on the school-commune [*shkola-kommuna*], which was to form the child's total environment, functioning for seven days in the week throughout twelve months of the year. They found the Petrograd interpretation of polytechnicalism too academic, and proposed that labour skills should be taught not in a school workshop but 'by life itself'—that is, through the practical experience of organizing and maintaining the school-commune. Like the later famous Ukrainian educationalist Anton Makarenko, the Muscovites were communalists above all, hostile to the family and only secondarily interested in leaving the child to development according to his individual bent. They accused the Petrograders of Tolstoyanism in their concern for freedom of individual development, and were in turn accused by the Petrograders of Tolstoyanism in glorifying physical labour for its own sake. The shadow of Tolstoy and the Tolstoyan tradition hung over both groups, acknowledged by neither.

Both Moscow and Petrograd groups drew up statements of educational policy, which were debated by the State Education Commission in August, at the First All-Russian Congress of Education in August–September, and again in the State Education Commission in September. The debates generated such passion that they overshot the beginning of the school year, which had to be postponed for a month until 1 October.[13]

The documents under discussion were the 'Declaration on the United Labour School' presented by Lunacharsky, and the 'Statement on the United Labour School' presented by Pozner. In jockeying for position, Pozner and the Muscovites had the support of a majority of the First All-Russian Congress on Education and the Moscow education department (MONO), and the advantage of fighting on home ground. The Petrograd group were at a disadvantage in being frequently absent from Moscow, where the debates took place, but scored a tactical success when it was agreed (on

Posadov, and published articles in his journal *Svobodnoe vospitanie* before the revolution. Shatsky's experimental school continued under Narkompros patronage, which was also extended to a Tolstoyan school at Yasnaya Polyana run by Tolstoy's daughter. Krupskaya recommended the publication of Kropotkin's work on education.

Pokrovsky's suggestion) that Lunacharsky's 'Declaration' should be considered 'as a literary document, not subject to alteration'.[14]

Pozner's 'Statement', not being a literary document but a set of precise propositions, was given for revision to a joint Moscow–Petrograd commission appointed by the State Education Commission. The main stumbling block to agreement proved to be school holidays, which Moscow wished to abolish altogether. This question was referred back to the State Education Commission where, to the great indignation of the Muscovites, Petrograd won by 6 votes to 5. MONO's representatives, who were present at the meeting without voting rights, lodged a formal protest claiming that their programme in its entirety was already successfully practised throughout Moscow (a claim which should undoubtedly be taken rhetorically and not literally). To this Lunacharsky tolerantly replied that 'Moscow could try working 12 months in the year and Petrograd 9, and we could draw conclusions from the results'.[15] Nevertheless, it was decided that the opinions of absent members of the commission should be sought. When this was done, Petrograd had a clear majority of 19 votes to 10—although its supporters included at least four persons not directly concerned with education: the constructivist artist Tatlin, the musician Lourie, the poet Bryusov and the politician Enukidze.[16]

The Petrograd Declaration and the amended Moscow statement were jointly presented by Pokrovsky to VTSIK on 30 September, 1918—one day before the delayed beginning of the school year. VTSIK was not struck by any incompatibility between the two documents, and indeed decided to accept them without discussion in view of their 'completely uncontroversial nature'.[17] They were published in *Izvestiya* on 16 October.

The 'Declaration' was a long, erudite and—in Pokrovsky's word—literary document, unmistakably on the side of the angels of progressive educational thought but not readily comprehensible to anyone unacquainted with educational theory. 'Our declaration will be held as an educational classic', Lunacharsky told VTSIK in 1920.[18]

It defined the 'united school' [*edinaya shkola*] as 'the whole system of normal school from kindergarten to university...a single, unbroken staircase...All children must enter the same type of school and begin their education alike, and all have the right to go up the ladder to its highest rungs.' This combined Binet's concept of *l'école unique*—a single primary school for children of all classes—with a repudiation of the tsarist educational system, under which graduation from one level did not necessarily qualify the student to enter the next, higher level of education.

The labour [*trudovoi*] principle meant, first, 'an active, mobile and creative acquaintance with the world', and second, 'the direct wish to acquaint pupils with what will be most necessary to them in life...with agricultural and industrial labour in all its variety'. Thus the labour school was both the 'activity school'* (after Dewey) and the polytechnical school (after Marx, and Kerschensteiner's *Arbeiterschüle*).

The 'Declaration' recommended that junior classes of the United Labour School [*edinaya trudovaya shkola*] be taught 'an encyclopedia of culture, centred on labour processes'. In the higher classes, this was developed into 'a course of sociology on the basis of the evolution of labour'. Labour processes should be taught in the school workshop, on the school farm and 'partly in factories etc.' Balancing uneasily between Moscow and Petrograd, the Declaration stated that 'labour must be real productive labour' although 'it never loses its pedagogical character'.

The sociological encyclopedia of culture supplemented, but did not displace, conventional school subjects—Russian (or native) language, mathematics, geography, history, biology, physics, chemistry and modern languages. These were to be taught as far as possible by activity methods: 'walking, making collections, drawing, photography, modelling and...observing and looking after animals'. Aesthetic education, including 'mass rhythmic gymnastics' (after Dalcroze), was recommended for 'the systematic development of the organs of perception'.

The school was to be self-administered by teachers and pupils, and the children were free to organize all kinds of societies. Schools and teachers were promised a minimum of outside supervision and

* The alternative Russian version of 'activity school'—*shkola deistviya*—was rarely used in Narkompros.

control: 'The central commissariat lays down some conditions whose fulfilment is considered absolutely obligatory, but at the same time envisages a wide field for independent initiative.'

The 'Statement on the United Labour School',[19] published together with the 'Declaration', was more specific but no less ambitious in its aims. It provided for free, compulsory, coeducational and secular education for all children from eight to seventeen years of age. The school would function seven days a week, with one and a half days devoted to clubs and excursions, and nine months of the year, with an additional month of open-air instruction in the summer. The school was to provide free hot breakfasts. Homework, punishment and examinations were abolished. Schools were to be self-administered through a school soviet consisting of teachers, representatives of the working population of the district, and senior pupils, together with one representative of the local education department. Teachers were to be subject to election.

The labour principle as described in the 'Statement' was a compromise between the Moscow and Petrograd positions, but—unlike the labour principle of the 'Declaration'—it leant towards Moscow:

> Productive labour must serve as the basis of school life, not as a means of paying for the maintenance of the child, and not only as a method of teaching, but as socially-necessary productive labour...The school is a school-commune, closely and organically linked through the labour process with its environment.

Instruction throughout the school was to have a 'polytechnical character'.

The possibility of schools arising on private initiative was not excluded either by the 'Declaration' or the 'Statement', though it was not positively encouraged as it would have been in the programmes of most Russian radical educationalists. According to the 'Declaration', 'a wide field will...be left for private initiative'—a phrase to which Potemkin of MONO had objected in earlier debates because 'it will arouse vain hopes among private proprietors'.[20] The 'Statement' was to be 'circulated among all schools arising from private initiative', and such schools 'may be given state support if the local education department recognizes [their] value'. But since, as Lunacharsky wrote in the Comintern journal,[21] 'abolition of all payment for the right to learn has made the private school in Russia impossible', the school which the 'Statement' had in mind must have been of purely altruistic or experimental motive, like Tolstoy's Yasnaya Polyana school, or Shatsky's pre-revolutionary 'Settlement'.

TEACHERS

The immediate problem before Narkompros was to find the teachers for its United Labour Schools. Of the small proportion of Russia's teachers capable of fully understanding the 'Declaration on the United Labour School', almost all were hostile to the Bolshevik government. Lunacharsky had hoped that the teacher's élite—the intellectuals of the capitals who dominated VUS* and the State Education Committee set up by the Provisional Government—would cooperate with Narkompros out of sympathy with its educational policies. But within a week of the October Revolution, the Petrograd branch of VUS had resolved 'not to perform the instructions of the self-styled power'.[22]

'Alas', Lunacharsky wrote,

> qualified personnel did not come our way. I made a special appeal...to the State Education Committee...I thought that at least some of those radical and liberal educationalists might agree to work with us. But that did not happen. At a personal meeting, the president of that Committee† (now a humble but respected worker in Narkompros) refused to shake hands with me as an enemy of the motherland...[23]

The State Education Committee, like VUS, passed a resolution calling on its members to take no part in educational work under the Soviet government, and to enter into no relations with it; and on 20 November 1917, VTSIK decreed that the committee be dissolved.[24]

* All-Russian Teachers' Union.

† V. I. Charnolusky, in fact deputy president of the committee. After the appearance of Lunacharsky's article in 1927, Charnolusky published an apology for his rudeness in 1917 (see *Narodnoe prosveshchenie* (1927), no. 10).

The Moscow branch of VUS, with an enrolment of 4,000 members, almost unanimously joined the strike of Moscow municipal workers and remained on strike until 11 March, 1918.[25] It was alleged that the teachers were supported during the strike by the merchant banking family of Ryabushinsky. In Petrograd, the teachers' strike lasted until 6 January, 1918.[26]

Narkompros was outraged by this response from the teachers. Lunacharsky wrote:[27]

> We are obliged to dismiss *for ever* from school activity these honourable gentlemen who, in spite of our appeal, prefer to continue in the role of political matadors rather than the role of teachers.
>
> I do not know with what quantity of repentant tears the individual teacher may, in the eyes of the people, wash away the black letters which he himself has painted on his forehead: *'In December 1917, in the hour of the people's terrible struggle against the exploiters, I refused to teach the children and received money for this from the exploiters' funds.'*

A minority of teachers dissociated itself from the strikes. In November, the Petrograd VUS expelled P. V. Dashkevich and Vera and Ludmila Menzhinskaya for working with the Bolsheviks. Fifty-nine others, including V. M. Pozner and Evgeny Poletaev (head of the department of middle schools of the Petrograd Narkompros in 1918) left the union in protest against its policy.[28]

Narkompros threatened to dismiss teachers taking part in the strike, but it was in no position to do so, for it had no replacements for them. Lunacharsky expressed the belief that better educationalists would come from the people, but this offered no immediate solution. In February it was announced that all teachers must submit their names to the local educational soviet or, in its absence, to the local Soviet of Deputies, for confirmation in their position by election.[29]

The teachers interpreted this as a punitive response to the strike. As it turned out, they were subjected to forms of re-election which were more offensive to them than anything Narkompros had intended. Very few educational soviets were in operation, and so the re-election was usually conducted by the local Soviet of Deputies, who often took the opportunity to present the teachers with what was in effect a loyalty oath to the Soviet government. According to provincial reports gathered by Narkompros, in Smolensk 'pedagogues were allowed to perform teachers' duties only after filling in a questionnaire containing a statement of the candidates' political and educational views'; in an *uezd* of the Orlovskaya *guberniya*, teachers were readmitted to the schools only on condition of ideological sympathy with Soviet power, 'non-membership of the exploiting classes' or 'documentary proof of revolutionary activity'; in an *uezd* in Yaroslavl the local education department confirmed teachers' appointments only on condition of their resignation from VUS; and in Tverskaya *guberniya* 'a statement of sympathy with the Soviet government' was required. Only a few cases of lenient implementation of the decree were reported, as in the Penza *uezd* where re-election was conducted by an educational soviet and only two teachers were rejected, and in Olonets, where re-election was regarded as 'a formality' and a purely educational criterion was used.[30]

Krupskaya and Menzhinskaya were particularly critical of the way in which the decree had been carried out. It was 'a most unjust form of the principle of local re-election of teachers', Krupskaya told the State Education Commission in May. 'The teachers are being cross-examined about their beliefs in the most detailed way, which is an inadmissible violation of freedom of conscience.' Ludmila Menzhinskaya pointed out that 're-election of teachers—undertaken only in relation to that category of employed person and no other—puts the teachers in a humiliating position'. Lunacharsky commented that the teaching profession saw in the decree 'a wish to demoralize the teachers by individual submission of petitions to Sovnarkom' [sic].[31]

VUS was of course violently opposed to the decree, and would have opposed it no less if it had been carried out, as Narkompros intended, as a form of popular re-election rather than official scrutiny. The Northern *Oblast'* branch of VUS resolved that

> Lunacharsky's decrees, violating the basic principles of the autonomy of the school, giving the school into the power of outside authorities and framed without regard for the elementary bases of democratic law...are on principle unacceptable to VUS.[32]

Narkompros was divided in its attitude to VUS. A splinter union composed of ex-members of VUS was organized by V. M. Pozner of Narkompros under the name of Union of Teacher-Internationalists. Pozner, putting the case against VUS to the State Education Commission, said that VUS had opposed the Soviet government in every way, and its leaders had joined the counter-revolutionary Committee for the Salvation of the Motherland and the Revolution. Then, losing hope of a quick collapse of the Soviet government, VUS had begun to negotiate with it, 'but only on the understanding that no mention is made of recognizing Soviet power'. VUS was now exploiting its negotiations with Narkompros for agitational purposes in anti-Bolshevik publications like *Novaya zhizn'*.* Pozner's conclusion was that the union of teacher-internationalists should be recognized as the only legitimate teachers' union.

Lunacharsky gave Pozner qualified support in the debate that followed, expressing suspicion of VUS' intentions in negotiating with Narkompros and pointing to 'an attempt being made at the present time to take the school into [VUS'] hands without consideration of the plans of Narkompros, but using its funds'. He thought that the teacher-internationalists were 'the only group on which Narkompros can rely'.

But Krupskaya and Ludmila Menzhinskaya were critical of the internationalists. 'VUS cannot be annihilated', said Krupskaya; and Menzhinskaya thought the activity of the teacher-internationalists in Petrograd harmful 'because it sets the democracy against the teachers'.[33]

In June, Krupskaya published her views on VUS and the teacher-internationalists:

> I, like comrades Pozner and Lepeshinsky, wanted to tear VUS from the influence of its present leaders, but I am an old splitter [*raskol'nitsa*], and thought it more appropriate to break up VUS from within. In my opinion it was necessary to persuade all teachers supporting Soviet power...not to leave VUS, but to attend its Congress as delegates, and there form a compact group and develop their programme to the full. Then it would have been clear what the real strength of the internationalists was...[34]

* *Novaya zhizn'* had recently published some particularly unflattering remarks about Pozner, and also misspelt his name.

In the debate on 23 May—the eve of the Moscow conference of the union of teacher-internationalists, the State Education Commission resolved in Pozner's favour, recommending 'the closest cooperation with the union of teacher-internationalists as the nucleus of the new teaching body' and stating that 'the State Commission rejects any kind of agreement with VUS as an organization, and will appeal to teachers leaving it to create teachers' unions on new foundations, parallel with the trade unions and in association with them'.

But the teacher-internationalists had the disadvantage, from the government point of view, of being both sectarian and highly unpopular with other teachers. This sectarian tendency was unfavourably noted by Lenin, in an otherwise sympathetic speech to the conference of teacher-internationalists on 5 June, 1918. The union, Lenin said, 'must not close in on itself...must not be afraid that undesirable elements are agitating in its midst; it must go forth with propaganda to the mass of teachers, being convinced that this mass will soon stand on the side of Soviet power'.[35]

After Lenin's speech, the balance of opinion in the State Education Commission moved against Pozner and the internationalists. On the eve of a Moscow conference of VUS, which was to be attended by 2,000 delegates, Pozner prepared a root and branch attack on VUS for publication in *Izvestiya*. Krupskaya protested against the article. It was only the leadership of VUS, she said, that was actively against the government:

> the village teachers are petty-bourgeois, close to the people, and fertile soil for socialist propaganda...It is a mistake to put the teacher-internationalists in a privileged position. It provokes a hostile reaction to them, and will induce reactionaries to join them hypocritically and out of calculation. We ought to recognize the professional teachers' union [VUS], which is changing from a militant to an organizational union.

On this occasion the commission supported Krupskaya, and resolved that although VUS' tactics were to be condemned, the mass of its members remained 'fertile soil for internationalist propaganda'. The teacher-internationalists were instructed that their union 'must not organizationally oppose itself to the professional union, but must be its ideological nucleus around which the progressive elements will group'.[36]

The ideological battle between Narkompros and the leadership of VUS continued at the First All-Russian Teachers' Congress held in Moscow in July. VUS was represented, and indeed put up a vigorous defence. Lenin spoke, as he did at most important educational conferences in the first years. Pozner described the various counter-revolutionary activities of VUS. Lunacharsky gave a spirited rhetorical performance in which, as was often the case in his public speeches, he ignored the reservations expressed in private. 'Comrades!' he exclaimed:

I am a peaceable man, but I understand those cries of indignation which were uttered during the speeches of the previous orators [from VUS]... These gentlemen ask why they were not allowed to work. After a strike? After they had said 'Let's see how the peasants will manage without us!'? And yet we would have taken them if they had come in good faith. But they did not: they came only for their wages. (Laughter) The people's power, represented by the dictatorship of the proletariat, will not be kind to you. You went against us, you set traps for us. But whatever you did, you had no luck. The real teachers are coming to us all the time, but as for these gentlemen—there's not a smell of their attitude among the mass of Russian teachers...We can't now believe in the possibility of working with them after their sabotage. Therefore we are for the re-election of teachers...We believe that better educationalists will come from the people.

Surprisingly, Bogachev of VUS, who had already spoken, seems to have been given the last word at the meeting. He said:

VUS is a professional organization including within it all teachers—even Bolsheviks and left S-Rs, although in fact there are not many of them. At the same time VUS is an educational organization. It sets itself the goal of full autonomy of the school. If the government agrees with VUS' educational principles, then we are for it; when it quarrels with our opinions we part company...They have put the schools under the systematic surveillance of the Soviets. They have conducted re-elections of teachers. They say that the teacher is unreliable, and so has to be re-elected. But one might point out that the old bureaucratic officials are sitting in the present commissariats without re-election. It means that even in the distant future there will be no autonomy. Freedom of education will perish...Science does not surrender to politics. VUS is for objective science.[37]

Bogachev's speech might be taken as the last testament of VUS, and Lunacharsky's as a promise that the union would shortly be forcibly dissolved. Indeed, as Krupskaya informed the collegium of Narkompros in August, some members of VUS were arrested by the Cheka, together with one Shanurenko, who appears to have been a member of the union of teacher-internationalists. The collegium decided to ask the Cheka why the members of VUS had been arrested, and 'to ask the Cheka to conduct their examination of Shanurenko immediately and, if no definite accusation is to be made, set him free'.[38] But still Narkompros made no move to disband VUS; and it was not until the middle of December that such a decision was taken.[39]

The question of the dissolution of VUS came before VTSIK on 23 December, with Pozner and Pokrovsky representing Narkompros.[40] The feeling of the meeting was strongly critical of Narkompros for having tolerated the existence of VUS for so long. 'Better let the schools be temporarily closed', said Yaroslavsky, 'than that they were stuffing the children's heads with nonsense.' Tomsky of VTSSPS* said that the unions disclaimed all connection with VUS and supported its dissolution. There was a heated exchange between Pokrovsky—giving a sarcastic and rather eccentric defence of Narkompros policy which failed to win the sympathy of his audience—and Mezhlauk, War Commissar for Kazan, where VUS had recently and notoriously supported the Czech insurgents. 'Comrades!' Pokrovsky said:

I am afraid of disappointing those people who may think they are killing a dragon. That union is made of paper, does not represent any real danger, and could not organize anything serious...The psychological moment has come when it is necessary, not to kill it,—because essentially it is not alive and has no power of action—but to drive an aspen stake into its grave...

If we had done this a year ago, when all the intelligentsia took an anti-

* All-Russian Central Council of Trade Unions.

Soviet stand, we should have added an extra martyr against us. But now these people are long dead and ought to be buried—I mean, of course, politically. We must put an end to their political existence out of psychological considerations, so that this spectre stops disturbing the peace of the living.

These psychological arguments particularly annoyed Mezhlauk, not only because of his experiences in Kazan but because he himself had been a teacher and, he said, well knew the reactionary spirit of the teaching profession, which had been an enslaved but privileged group under the old regime.

There is no doubt that this union should have been dissolved long ago, [Mezhlauk said] and we are going to dissolve it now. Narkompros vainly objects that it is driving in an aspen stake and killing a paper dragon—no, it is driving a paper stake into a real dragon. That is a mistake; we must wage determined war, we must go into real attack against that union, and not think that we have already dealt with it...In Narkompros things are far from healthy in this respect...I have investigated what they are doing in the lower and higher schools in Kazan, and I must tell you that the secondary and higher schools are still serving capitalism and creating lackeys and people remote from the real world [*lyudi v futlyare*].

Pozner completed Narkompros' discomfiture by making a quite extraordinary claim for one clause in his 'Statement on the United Labour School' which included instructors in physical labour among the school teaching staff. 'It sounds modest,' he said of this clause, 'its content is hidden, but its sense will be disclosed by events...The instructors in physical labour...will be conscious proletarian workers, who will come into the school and bring into it the genuine spirit of collectivism, carry in that reality of productive labour which will give new life to the school...'

No wonder that some of his audience felt that Narkompros had lost touch with real life, or that the VTSSPS (as Pozner complained) had so far refused not only to recognize VUS but also Pozner's union of teacher-internationalists.

VTSIK'S decision to dissolve VUS was, of course, a foregone conclusion. It was done with the assurance, for what it was worth, that members of VUS 'will not be subject to any victimization or restriction for membership of the union'.[41] On 26 March 1919, the collegium of Narkompros decided that the property and funds of the union should go to Shatsky's colony 'Children's Labour and Rest'. The property of local branches was given to local education departments 'for the professional and educational needs of the teaching profession'.[42] None of the property of VUS—at least officially—went to the union of teacher-internationalists.

With VUS dissolved, Narkompros had the choice of sponsoring a new, broad professional organization of teachers or a narrow Communist union on the basis of the teacher-internationalists. The internationalists, represented by Pozner and Lepeshinsky in Narkompros, strongly urged their claim. It was opposed (in Krupskaya's absence through illness) by Pokrovsky, Ludmila Menzhinskaya and L. G. Shapiro. The argument against unqualified support for the internationalists was reinforced by the unwillingness of VTSSPS to recognize their union; and, as the Narkompros journal observed, local sympathy with the teacher-internationalists remained minimal, only Party members being prepared to join it.[43]

In January 1919 the teacher-internationalists took the initiative by organizing a meeting of Communists* which declared itself the constituent assembly of a new, and exclusively Communist, teachers' union. This meant, in effect, that the basis of the new union would be the union of teacher-internationalists. Pozner, who made the key speech at the meeting, took the occasion to express his lack of sympathy with the union movement as a whole, as insufficiently committed to the Communist Party and the Soviet government. 'The professional workers' movement, of course, is not acceptable to us—revolutionary Marxists—in all its forms', he said. The new teachers' union must be so constituted that 'it can be transformed not only into an organ of social life, but an organ of *State power*'.

After intervention by Lunacharsky on 14 January, the congress of teacher-internationalists, continuing in session, was persuaded to modify its position to admit that although 'the urgent task is self-organization of Communist workers', this was only a precondition for the necessary creation of a broad professional union.[44]

* Formally a joint meeting of the Communist fractions of the Congress of *guberniya* education departments and the congress of the union of teacher-internationalists; with other invited representatives of various institutions.

But this was a verbal concession, which scarcely altered the old heresy-hunting spirit of the teacher-internationalists. VTSSPS remained hostile—understandably, in view of Pozner's attitude of holier-than-thou—and refused to affiliate a teachers' union which proposed not only to operate as 'an organ of State power' but to impose Party loyalty tests on its members. Lunacharsky, perhaps with some embarrassment, described the conflict with VTSSPS in an article for the Comintern journal:

The trade unions in Soviet Russia are regarded as non-Party organizations. As well, however, there is a paragraph in their constitution emphasizing that only workers recognizing the dictatorship of the proletariat as a necessary means of achieving socialism may be members of a trade union.

The worker-comrades [of VTSSPS] pointed out that a teacher's acceptance of this paragraph was quite sufficient to count him as a worthy participant in revolutionary work in the school.

The worker-unionists were even against the name we suggested—'Union of workers in education and socialist culture'.

They wanted to throw out the word 'socialist' as a political word. However in the end they agreed that, under the circumstances, it was useful to keep it...[45]

The union of workers in education and socialist culture (Rabpros) was finally constituted in the summer of 1919, electing a central committee entirely of Communists. But its president was not one of the former teacher-internationalists but their persistent critic, Ludmila Menzhinskaya. By October 1919 it claimed an enrolment of 70,000, and was thus well on the way to becoming a mass union (VUS at the time of its dissolution had 50,000 members); in the autumn of 1920, the union was said to number 250,000.[46]

THE NEW EDUCATIONAL SYSTEM IN PRACTICE

To put its educational principles into practice, Narkompros needed the cooperation of local educational authorities. But these authorities, which formally owed a dual subordination to the local Soviet executive committee (*ispolkom*) and the central commissariat, were for practical purposes in much closer contact with the local *ispolkom*. Narkompros had two possible levers of control: finance and inspection. Educational finance came from the *ispolkom* (for local needs) and the centre (for 'general state' requirements): in effect this seems to have meant that the primary schools were locally financed. Officials of local education departments appear to have been paid by NKVD through the *ispolkom*,[47] which put them in a strong position to resist any disciplinary action Narkompros might wish to take. Inspection had at first been repudiated by Narkompros, as reminiscent of tsarist methods; later it was hoped that the educational soviets would fulfil this function; and it was not until 1920 that the centre began to send inspectors (called 'instructors') to the provinces in any systematic way.

Under the structure of local finance adopted at the end of 1918,[48] the *gubernii* distributed central credits to the city, *uezd* and presumably *volost'* departments. Narkompros made its first major attempt to distribute credits to the *gubernii* in January and February of 1919. In March, having received no acknowledgement from the *gubernii*, Narkompros complained to the Commissariat of Posts and Telegraph and (remembering the experience of a year earlier)* asked the Treasury to send out reply-paid telegrams to the *guberniyi*, 'indicating that if necessary Narkompros will pay for the telegrams'.[49] But it turned out that the fault lay with the *guberniya* education departments, which had received the credits without bothering to acknowledge them or inform the centre of how they were to be used.

Even in April 1918 Lunacharsky had drawn attention to 'peculiar local interpretations of the slogan "All power to the Soviets"' which might deprive the central commissariats of influence in the provinces; but he had nevertheless insisted that local authorities be given 'maximum autonomy'.[50] Sixteen months later Krupskaya travelled through the Volga region and found that the absence of central direction left schools and local education departments either bewildered or subject to the dictation of the *gubernii*, which 'instruct the *uezdy* very insistently, and because of these instructions the good work that is done in the *uezdy* is destroyed, all initiative is

* See above, p. 21.

destroyed'. 'All my impressions lead to the conclusion that we are unforgiveably alienated from provincial work,' Krupskaya wrote.[51]

The most openly intransigent of local education departments, and the most powerful, were those of Petrograd and Moscow. Narkompros could ignore the situation in the provinces, and indeed was usually in no position to do anything else, but it could not ignore the capitals. Nor, on the other hand, could it control them since the Moscow and Petrograd education departments were appointed by and responsible to the Moscow and Petrograd Soviets.

Until the beginning of 1919, Lunacharsky was in personal charge of education in Petrograd as Commissar of the Union of Communes of the Northern *Oblast'*, with a collegium including Vera Menzhinskaya, D. I. Leshchenko, E. P. Poletaev and Z. G. Grinberg. Towards the end of 1918 a rival district [*oblastnoi*] commissariat of education was organized in Petrograd by the engineer F. F. Shu. This was presumably done with some support from the local administration. Shu rejected Narkompros' polytechnical school in favour of the 'United Technical School', which would provide specialized professional training from the beginning of secondary school.[52]

Lunacharsky left Petrograd early in 1919. The *oblastnoi* commissariat remained in occupation. Almost at the time of Lunacharsky's departure, the Union of Communes of the Northern *Oblast'* was dissolved and replaced by a Petrograd Soviet administration—headed, as the Union of Communes had been, by Zinoviev. In March the collegium of Narkompros in Moscow made a bid to re-establish control in the Petrograd area by organizing a Petrograd *okruzhnoi* commissariat of education, which would serve not only the city and *guberniya* of Petrograd but the surrounding *gubernii* of Novgorod, Cherepovets, Pskov, Olonets and Petrozavodsk. Its collegium—Lunacharsky, Vera and Ludmila Menzhinskaya, Leshchenko, Grinberg, B. S. Yatmanov and I. V. Kimmel—was taken over from Lunacharsky's Petrograd commissariat of 1918. It was to hold monthly joint meetings with the Moscow collegium of Narkompros, and to be financed by the Petrograd *guberniya* Soviet and the Commissariats of Finance and State Control.[53]

The *okruzhnoi* commissariat had achieved a precarious existence, and held its first joint meeting with Moscow on 7 May, when its establishment was countermanded by VTSIK.[54] This was evidently the result of pressure from the Petrograd Soviet, which intended to appoint its own education department independently of Narkompros. Skirmishing continued throughout the summer, with Narkompros making a further unsuccessful effort to maintain a bridgehead by establishing a 'filial' organization in Petrograd. It was argued that this was necessary because of 'the presence in Petrograd of a huge number of all kinds of cultural, educational, scientific and artistic institutions of a general state character'.[55]

In September the *ispolkom* of the Petrograd Soviet appointed an education department under Ya. Zelikson.[56] Shu, the anti-polytechnicalist, was in charge of professional and technical education. The dominating figure in the collegium was Zlata Ionovna Lilina, Zinoviev's wife, who was in charge of school education: 'our "conqueror" ', as Gorky's wife Andreeva described her to Lunacharsky.[57] In terms of educational policy, the threat from the new Petrograd collegium seems to have been less on the polytechnical issue—on which Lilina and Shu disagreed—than on the general issue of treatment of the non-party intelligentsia. The Petrograd administration was tough; Narkompros was tolerant. Lunacharsky's criticism of the Petrograd education policy, guardedly expressed in the autumn of 1919, was directed against 'the attempt to put extra pressure on the teaching profession, the attempt in general to sharpen the action of the Government and proletariat on school staff'.[58]

The Moscow education department (MONO), after a radical start in 1918 when it had been strong in support of the school-commune, later moved to the opposite extreme. Unlike Petrograd, which was too hard on the teachers, Moscow proved to be too kind. MONO's programme for the 1919–20 school year contained, in the opinion of the Narkompros collegium, 'completely inadmissible concessions to the reactionary teaching profession'. After an unsuccessful attempt to put an announcement to this effect in *Pravda* or *Izvestiya*, Narkompros found that its only method of combatting this 'deviation from the principles of the Labour School' was to circularize all departments subordinate to MONO on the errors of MONO's policy.[59]

Presumably this had little effect, for the trouble recurred in the summer of 1920, when MONO published theses 'On school policy in the coming years'. The theses, which had been approved by the presidium of Moscow Soviet, recommended increased discipline in schools, re-establishment of individual instead of collegiate control, employment of experienced teachers—'not only as consultants, as has been the case until now, but as organizers of affairs in responsible posts'—and payment of these experienced teachers as highly qualified specialists. The schools were no longer to have the right to appoint or dismiss staff without permission from MONO.[60]

Narkompros, which had not been consulted on the theses, gave 'extraordinary political significance to MONO's action in abandoning the Communist line in education' and threatened to take the matter to higher authorities.[61] A full-scale battle over the theses seems to have been averted by P. G. Smidovich, newly-appointed head of MONO and an old friend of Lunacharsky, who persuaded the Narkompros collegium that 'disagreements on principle [with MONO] do not exist'.[62] But since there was no public revision or recantation of the MONO theses, it seems a clear case of failure on the part of Narkompros to intimidate a subordinate department which had the backing of the local soviet.

The disputes between Narkompros and the Moscow and Petrograd education departments belong to the world of inter-departmental politics. The implementation of Narkompros' educational policies had to go on, if at all, at a much lower level of the educational system—in the *uezd* and *volost'* departments and the schools themselves. Here Narkompros was dependent on the comprehension, energy and goodwill of small-time officials and country schoolteachers, and on the resources which local soviets were prepared to give to education.

The 'Declaration' and 'Statement on the United Labour School' required secularization of parish schools formerly maintained by the church, provision of clothing and hot meals for children, and equipment of school workshops. All this had to be carried out by the local education department, which was also responsible for re-allocating school buildings.* Schools had to drop religious instruction and classics from the curriculum, and introduce labour and aesthetic training and physical education; abolish homework, punishment, examinations and possibly textbooks; democratize the internal administration of the school; and adopt activity methods of teaching.

'Many well-intentioned educational workers are agonizingly seeking some sort of instruction, especially practical instruction, for the conduct of everyday routine work', reported *Petrogradskaya pravda* on 4 December 1918. In May the conference of teacher-internationalists, showing a rather uncharacteristic interest in the outside world, suggested that 'if only for the partial realization of the new educational ideas' Narkompros must arrange for the urgent issue of new textbooks, equipment for practical work, and 'full, simple and clear' instructions for teachers on the ideas and methods of the labour school.[63] But Narkompros remained even more permissive in practice than it was in principle. Only the kindergarten department seems to have sent out a substantial number of programmes, instructions on teaching methods and lists of necessary equipment to its schools and teachers. The department of The United Labour School did not issue instructions but waited for guidance from below. In 1919 it circularized teachers as follows:

> Comrades, we would like to know what innovations you have managed to bring into the school.
>
> 1. Does life there go on just as it used to? Are the same subjects taught in the school?
>
> 2. Are the children as strictly divided into groups (classes)? Or has something new perhaps come into your life? Is new work being done? (but what kind of work?)...
>
> 3. Is the partition between classes perhaps already crumbling, and the groups acquiring a more fluid character? (but how did this happen?)

* This was made necessary by: (1) the introduction of coeducation; (2) the division of the United Labour School into a 'first level' of 5 years and a 'second level' of 4 years. The existing elementary schools normally had 3 of the 5 years required for the new '1st level' school, while existing 'higher elementary' and trade schools were normally 3 years on a basis of 3 years' elementary schooling and thus approximated neither to the 1st nor the 2nd level of the new school.

4. Perhaps the lessons themselves are conducted differently; perhaps there is no division between lessons and between subjects; perhaps all kinds of work are concentrated around labour processes (but what kind of work exactly, and how do you organize it?)
5. Perhaps the school has already become a living organism and lives a single life; perhaps there is a common aim and common tasks (but what kind of aim is it and what steps do you take towards realizing it?) Perhaps [the school], like a single collective, works on its own Soviet or private economic enterprise. Has it perhaps taken on other responsibilities (sawing and carrying wood, clearing snow from bridges and roofs, organizing a Library Week, a Hygiene Week and so on)?
6. Describe the course of a school day.
7. What are your plans for the future?

Comrades, we expect concise descriptions of life and work in your school from you. We think that by continual mutual endeavour we will together overcome the difficulties ahead of us and create the labour school in real life.[64]

As one teacher later recalled, the information on the United Labour School which he received at this time was 'extremely obscure' in content, and so badly printed as to be almost unreadable: 'you had to read by guesses, working it out letter by letter, and often whole dozens of lines remained undeciphered'.[65]

Narkompros had its own network of children's colonies and experimental [*opytno-pokazatel'nye*] schools—its pride and (in effect though not in intention) its Potemkin villages.* Lunacharsky, Krupskaya and Lepeshinsky were particularly closely involved in the work of the experimental schools. It was here that the principles of the United Labour School were most nearly realized, and methods for their adoption in ordinary schools worked out. 'Each of these institutions gave special attention to the solution of some particular problem', writes V. Dyushen, sometime head of the Narkompros department of experimental schools.

Thus A. A. Lunacharskaya's children's colonies and the children's town 'Third International' investigated how best to set up children's homes—whether to make them of one or various age-groups, whether to educate the children from the children's home separately or together with

* See statement of Narkompros collegium quoted below, p. 165.

children from families. The children's town 'Third International' gave particular attention to the political education of children: it experimented with the organization of Pioneer groups attached to the school...The Narkompros school-communes conducted an interesting experiment on linking the school with production...The Shaturskaya experimental station [run by the wife of the director of the local construction works] did a very great deal of cultural work among the surrounding population ...[66]

There were also experimental schools specializing in the arts (including Isadora Duncan's school in the early '20s) and in methods of labour training. S. T. Shatsky, a disciple of Tolstoy, ran a children's colony under Narkompros auspices called 'The Good life' [*Bodraya zhizn'*]. Lepeshinsky, of the collegium of Narkompros, established his own school-commune. Makarenko in the Ukraine organized his first children's colony under the Ukrainian Narkompros.*

There was a great variety of experiment going on in the Civil War years, and this was, of course, as Narkompros intended. It was not looking for any single blueprint of the future school. What it valued in its experimental schools was a spirit of freedom, of community activity, and perhaps above all of hope. In the worst period of the Civil War Lunacharsky, Krupskaya and on occasion Lenin visited the kindergartens and the children's colonies and felt that they saw the beginning of a new world: these were 'corners full of joy, full of the morning light portending future socialism; light grains of the future for which we struggle against the twilight, cruelly battle-coloured backdrop of our suffering land'.[67]

But even these 'corners full of joy' were part of a harsh environment. The children in the experimental colonies were *besprizornye* who had lost their homes and families; they took part in the running of the colonies not only because of the labour principles of the United Labour School but because of poverty and shortage of manpower. Lepeshinsky, who believed that labour skills must be taught 'by life itself', had no difficulty in making a virtue of necessity.

* Makarenko's later colonies were under the GPU, as was the Petrograd *Shkola imeni Dostoevskogo* immortalized in Belykh and Panteleev's *Respublika Shkid* (1927). On the GPU and child welfare, see ch. 9, pp. 230–6.

The following passage evidently describes the experience of his own school-commune:

> Life *forced* the creation of boarding-schools (because there was nowhere to put homeless orphans, children of the streets, or it was not possible to send children from neighbouring villages home in the evening)...The building *had* to be cleared of rubbish. Provisions are being given out somewhere: they *must* be brought or dragged home, otherwise in a few hours painful hunger will be felt. It is not very pleasant to lie on the bare floor with nothing to lie on, so beds *must* be set up. Shirts are dirty, insects are nesting on the body, so washing of shirts is *on the agenda*. The school has received cloth, which means great rejoicing and a lot of work: it is *necessary* to sew and sew and sew. There is no wood and the school is freezing—so it is necessary to *drop everything* and mobilize all forces in the search for firewood...
>
> And in this way the circumstances of the children's psychological rebirth emerge. *Social* labour and *communal* conditions of life are doing their great educative work...So what is the matter? You say there are no exemplary programmes for the secondary school teacher? You say that these teachers are...going back to the old textbook and the old learning? But really these are trifles. If any teacher...succeeded even to a small extent in approaching a comprehension of the tasks of the Labour school,...he can never become a backslider, because he has already discovered the educational secret which makes all his future teaching work of uncommon creative joy...[68]

Lepeshinsky's was one version of the United Labour School; another was represented in the Znamenskaya school-commune, organized beside an electric power-station and a *sovkhoz* in a former convent in the Vyatskaya *guberniya*. Here the emphasis was not on labour but aesthetic education; the teachers were of the old intelligentsia and knew literature, foreign languages and progressive educational theory; and their pupils were '400 exhausted children from gloomy orphanages'. The revolution had created the school, but it belonged in spirit to the nineteenth century: a chapter from some pre-revolutionary utopia. Sofia Sukhoretskaya, the singing teacher, recalled these as the best years of her life—'years full of boiling activity, initiative and the strongest feelings...My music and my songs began to subdue and delight people...I realized that people needed me, that I could do something useful and pleasant for them; and I began to sing and play more bravely and to teach others...'

The most memorable day in the history of the Znamenskaya school was the third anniversary of the revolution, 7 November, 1920. The celebration was to be held, for the first time, by electric light, but the generator failed to start:

We had to hold the meeting, as before, by the light of kerosene lamps. The loud pulsing of the generator coming up from below excited the audience all the more. The first part of the performance of 'Judgment on the old school' was conducted in semi-darkness. The producer had for some reason decided to begin in a mystical tone. Someone in a grey cape poked his head through the curtains and pronounced in a tragic voice, to the accompaniment of a 'sobbing' violin: 'I am a living human soul. I beg your sympathy. I was long tormented in the old school' etc.

Then the public accuser came on with a fiery speech directed at the audience...'The school-*bourse* has turned into a corpse and you, comrade judges, must burn it on the bonfire of revolution, carrying out a verdict of "guilty" on the social structure which gave birth to the old school...'

The second half of the spectacle began. It was devoted to the new labour school. There was a scene of harvesting—and in that instant the long-expected happened: all 'Ilyich's little lamps' sprung to life, lighting up the auditorium, the buildings and the grounds of the settlement and the neighbouring *sovkhoz*.

There was an outburst of tumultuous applause. Everybody cried out ecstatically 'Hurrah!', and got up from their seats and burst into comradely singing of the *Internationale*...[69]

Information of what went on in the ordinary Russian school is harder to come by: here the historian, like Narkompros at the time, is working in semi-darkness. How many teachers puzzled over Narkompros instructions, or read the endless columns of small print in which the 'Declaration' and 'Statement on the United Labour School' were published in *Izvestiya*? How many officials of local education departments had any idea other than getting rid of the priests and the 'old priests' wives' from the schools?

A. S. Tolstov, who was working in the Ranenburgsky *uezd* from 1918–20, remembered that the first impact of the revolution on the local school was that its premises began to be extensively used for meetings and theatrical performances, because 'this was what the population and the *volost'* and *uezd* administrations wanted'.

If a teacher gave a report at a meeting, he was first of all confronted with the stern question 'Do you have performances [*spektakli*]?' And if the teacher gave an evasive answer to the effect that they didn't have performances or were only intending to arrange them, he got a thorough dressing-down. School business and the school buildings suffered from this a great deal. In a rush of enthusiasm, they broke down all the partitions in the schools to widen the 'concert-hall'. They acted badly, without rehearsal. There was a fashion of relying on the prompter—it was considered shameful to know the part. They only put on very stupid vaudeville, like 'The battle of the gramophones', 'The boy-friend under the bed' and so on...

In Tolstov's school the attempt to organize hot lunches failed for lack of support from local authorities; and as for provision of clothing 'in three years the schoolchildren only once received cloth (for everyone) and shoes (two pairs for the school)'. Labour training was introduced, if at a rather low level: 'They invited a local villager, usually a joiner or a carpenter, to teach his trade to the children, but the whole equipment of the "workshop" consisted of a bag containing a plane, saws, an axe and so on which he brought with him...'[70]

In Trubchevsk, a small town near Bryansk, the 'Statement on the United Labour School' was not only read by the teachers but on the whole approved, except that the teachers objected to the 'pedagogically-unacceptable' principle of the school-commune, and to the abolition of homework and punishments, because it gave ammunition to sceptics ('of whom there were not few' in Trubchevsk). Elementary-school teachers complained that they could not understand what was meant by a 'children's encyclopedia...centred on labour processes' recommended by the 'Declaration'.[71]

In Karelin the teachers showed an equally high degree of consciousness. A teacher of history and geography suggested that 'the history of Tsars and military commanders be replaced by a history of the people, a history of labour and culture'; and the handicraft teacher, whose hour had come at last, 'spoke on the Labour School, dreaming of school-palaces where labour was on the boil from morning to night'. The local education department discussed whether punishment was compatible with the free school, whether pupils should stand up when addressing the teacher and whether textbooks should be kept 'or thrown out as an attribute of the old school'.[72]

But there were those, even in Narkompros, who doubted that the policy of the labour school could be realized. Shulgin quotes Pokrovsky as saying that what was needed was not so much the labour school as any school at all, and comments with disapproval that 'there was no labour school, in [Pokrovsky's] opinion, and could not be'.[73] Lebedev-Polyansky was also critical of the labour school, at least in practice, for he thought what it amounted to was *samoobsluzhivanie**—that is, the children doing their own washing and cleaning.

> They made the little children wash their own linen, clean rooms, carry buckets of soup through the frost and so on; and naturally the children were not really helping or doing 'productive labour', but getting themselves dirty through being in unsanitary conditions.[74]

The best of all sources on the condition of education in provincial Russia at this period is Krupskaya's diary of a six-week journey through the Volga–Kama region in the summer of 1919.[75] Krupskaya was well-fitted to be a reporter of provincial life—observant, shrewd, immune to flattery, suspicious of pretensions, fonder of small people than great ones. In 1917 she had given up local educational work in Petrograd unwillingly to join the collegium of Narkompros. She disliked being in the public eye, and already, in her late '40s, was beginning to dress like an old woman; a decade later she sulked when forced to meet Bernard Shaw and Lady Astor, and conducted an enormous correspondence with children—reading their letters aloud at Party congresses to yawning politicians. Lenin trusted her judgement and always supported her on educational questions. Lunacharsky called her 'the soul of Narkompros'.

She set out on the Volga trip excited and, as often, in rather bad health. 'Don't expect my speedy return', she wrote to her deputy at Narkompros, Krzhizhanovskaya, on 17 July.

* Literally, 'self-service'.

> Think, Zinusha, after so many years of emigration I have finally got to the provinces. Indeed emigration puts a definite heavy mark on the soul, and one has to clean it off with living impressions, otherwise there is much that will always be alien.

At Nizhny, the port of embarkation, Krupskaya found that in a gathering of 400 teachers of elementary and secondary schools, 'only two of the teachers spoke in favour of the Labour School'. Many of the teachers had been members of VUS. One S-R attacked the five-year '1st-level' labour school, saying that the peasants found it difficult enough to afford to give their children three years' schooling. The audience listened to him sympathetically.

In Sormovo and Cheboksary, the labour principle in the school 'ends up being *samoobsluzhivanie*', mainly in the form of cutting wood and carrying water up hill. This was said to be a great strain on the younger children: 'No time is left for work. Because of this, many parents are taking their children away from school.' In the village of Rabotka, Krupskaya met a former actor who was in charge of the *volost'* education department. He was waiting for instructions from a higher authority, but had received none and had no ideas of his own.

Kazan had recently been retaken from the Whites and was in chaos. 'The War Commissariat occupies literally all the schools and children's hostels—and the most important thing is that there is no need for it, the barracks nearby stand empty.'

The population of Rybnaya Sloboda 'hates the word "school-commune" ', and when the education department gave the children cloth for shirts, the parents refused to accept it without a guarantee that their children would not be forced to work in a commune.

In Chistopol Krupskaya took a strong dislike to the Communist head of the education department because he told her they had made no attempt to organize an educational soviet and considered it unnecessary.

> At a meeting of the local intelligentsia, one university teacher got up and said that he agreed with the principles of the United Labour School; but went on to weep 'crocodile tears' about arrests, the Cheka and press censorship, and appealed to the teachers not to join the new Soviet teachers' union but to stay in VUS. The audience applauded him.

During the whole trip, Krupskaya found only one local branch of the new Soviet teachers' union,* and no educational soviets (although she thought that Votkinsky *zavod* might organize one, after she had explained its significance). She was, on the whole, not impressed by the education departments and thought them alienated from their surroundings and out of touch with local needs. The labour principle was applied either as *samoobsluzhivanie* or lessons in modelling and woodwork: Krupskaya disapproved of the first, in so far as it was physical labour without any educational purpose, and thought the second harmless, but tending towards genteel abstraction from real life. Like Tolstov, she feared that the schools were being swamped by the current passion for the theatre. Everywhere she went, she found a great shortage of books and newspapers.

The dominant impression Krupskaya took from her journey was that the existing goodwill towards school reform was being wasted, because teachers did not know how to go about creating the labour school. Narkompros did not instruct them, and the instruction they received from local education departments was often unreliable. The education departments were cut off from the population, and unable to understand that the labour school could only exist with popular cooperation. Krupskaya wrote to Krzhizhanovskaya on 29 July:

> Literally nothing is coming from the United Labour School, it is all rubbish...They [the teachers] understand 'democratization' as a desire for parents' committees and independence of the teaching profession from the Soviet...The basic principle of the United Labour School—that it must take into account local conditions, and be *built by the teachers together with the population*—is completely ignored. The teachers don't even suspect that there is such a principle, and take all the weight of realization of the United Labour School on themselves. They are trying to realize some sort of 'programme' supposed to have been sent out from the centre; and what emerges is the same sort of deadness there was before.

Another disquieting impression which Krupskaya gained from her journey was that local Party organizations were indifferent to education. 'Education is a kind of stepson', she wrote to Krzhizhanovskaya on 17 July. 'Everything gets taken away from it, and the

* Union of workers in education and socialist culture—see above, p. 43.

Party people think it below their dignity to be concerned with education.'

In 1919, probably after her return from the Volga, Krupskaya and Pokrovsky addressed a letter to the Central Committee of the Party stating that 'local Party comrades, not receiving any directives from the Central Committee of the Party, consider the work of the People's Commissariat of Education to be of secondary importance and therefore will not undertake it'. They asked the Central Committee to direct Party workers into the education departments, and especially into extramural education.[76] But there is no record of the Central Committee taking any action, and *Izvestiya TSK* contains no important directive to Party committees on education either in this or the following year.

By the middle of 1920, there was considerable pressure outside and inside Narkompros for changes in educational policy. The new Chief Committee on professional-technical education under Narkompros, Glavprofobr,* was unsympathetic to the polytechnical principle of the United Labour School and, like F. F. Shu in Petrograd, wanted the secondary school to provide training in specific technical skills. MONO,† and within the collegium of Narkompros, Pokrovsky, called for more instruction, supervision and support for teachers, and greater inducement to the old teaching profession to return to the schools.

Krupskaya was relatively sympathetic to Pokrovsky's position, but still believed that the solution to Russia's educational problems was to draw the population into participation in school affairs—'and here I go back on my hobbyhorse, educational soviets', she wrote to Pokrovsky. 'They are the best means of drawing the masses into the problems of building the labour school, making it clear and comprehensible to them.'[77]

In spite of pressure to change, Narkompros decided to reissue the 1918 'Declaration on the United Labour School', adding only a 'circumstantial introduction' to be written by Lunacharsky, Pokrovsky and Ludmila Menzhinskaya, which 'must again emphasize the principle of the United Labour School and suggest that, in

* See next chapter, p. 64 ff.

† See above, p. 47.

principle, a concrete plan for the actual realization of the school revolution within a specified time should be prepared'.[78] This resolution hardly suggests a settled intention to reform the methods of school administration from the centre. Nevertheless, on the evidence of Tolstov, 'correct and vital leadership of school reform' by Narkompros began in August and was reinforced by the establishment of a central inspectorate [*instruktorskaya kollegiya*] under the department of the United Labour School.[79]

In September, at any rate, Lunacharsky was prepared to admit that Narkompros had been more successful as a formulator of policy than as a practical organizer. He told VTSIK that

> Narkompros... made a mistake which was perpetuated for perhaps a year, a completely natural mistake, but one which we acknowledge. We worked out a declaration and said—'Look, that is your school and this is ours.' And we proved to everyone with a living heart and mind that our school is of a higher type... But the department of the United Labour School mistakenly thought that this declaration would be realized by 'life itself'. And by life they meant youth with its Komsomol organization, the proletariat which would help us, the teachers who would seek out new paths and the local education departments. But it turned out that 'life itself' accomplished nothing. We have had to start to demonstrate the steps towards the realization of our ideal in practical terms...[80]

1*a* Lunacharsky (centre), wearing a fur coat presented to him by Red Army soldiers, in front of decorated 'agit-train'

1*b* Lunacharsky and Lenin at the unveiling of a monument to 'Liberated Labour', 1 May 1920. Front row (from left): Olga Kameneva, D. P. Shterenberg (head of IZO, Narkompros), Lunacharsky, Lenin

2a Lunacharsky and V.M. Pozner, organizer of Union of Teacher-Internationalists, 1918

2b Narkompros delegates at meeting for reform of higher education held at Moscow University in the summer of 1918. From left: Professor M.A. Reisner, Lunacharsky, Professor P.K. Shternberg, M.N. Pokrovsky

3*a* A.V. Lunacharsky

3*b* P.I. Lebedev-Polyansky

3*c* Nadezhda Krupskaya

3*d* E.A. Litkens

4*a* Lunacharsky playing chess with his brother-in-law, I.A. Sats, 1924

4*b* Presidium of meeting held in State Academy of Artistic Sciences, 1925, to celebrate Lunacharsky's fiftieth birthday. Standing: on extreme left, the poet Bezymensky; sixth from left (with beard), O. Yu. Schmidt. Group on far right: Zinaida Raikh (wife of Meyerhold), V.E. Meyerhold, A.M. Granovsky (director of State Jewish Theatre). Sitting (from left): P.I. Lebedev-Polyansky, M.N. Pokrovsky, N.A. Lunacharskaya-Rozenel (wife of Lunacharsky), Lunacharsky, the philosopher L.I. Akselrod ('Orthodox'), P.S. Kogan, Kseniya Kudasheva (later, wife of Romain Rolland), K.S. Stanislavsky, actress Alexandra Yablochkina, literary historian P.N. Sakulin

4

TECHNICAL AND HIGHER EDUCATION

TECHNICAL EDUCATION

In theory, Narkompros' educational policy excluded the possibility of specialized technical training for school-age children. The schools department of Narkompros drew the obvious conclusion, and announced the slogan: 'Close the professional schools and use their equipment for the creation of the Labour School.'[1]

The collegium of Narkompros was more cautious. On the one hand it stated on the question of trade schools that 'this circle of hell for the children of the poor must be destroyed once and for all'. On the other hand, it added that so long as a popular demand for trade schools persisted, 'we are obliged to maintain [the trade school] where it exists; and where it does not, create it'.[2]

The real position was that Narkompros had not yet established control over technical schools and institutes. The majority of these had arisen before the revolution under the patronage of interested Ministries—Trade and Industry, Finance, Agriculture, Communications—and had never been within the jurisdiction of the Ministry of Public Education. The first steps towards the transfer of technical schools to the Education Ministry had been taken under the Provisional Government, but—like so many of its undertakings—the transfer was not completed before October. The new Soviet commissariats inherited technical schools from their respective ministries, and showed no greater willingness to hand them over to education authorities.

Narkompros took the view that all educational institutions should be collected under a single commissariat and subject to a single policy—that of Narkompros. Sovnarkom supported this claim, and in May and June of 1918 decreed that all educational institutions (except naval and military schools), together with their buildings and equipment, should be transferred to Narkompros.[3] But in September a representative of MONO told Narkompros that the list of technical institutions which the Commissariat of Trade and

Industry had offered Narkompros included 'not one substantial commercial school in Moscow. They are giving us 10 to 15 of the most insignificant educational institutions to get rid of us.' Lunacharsky called it 'sabotage on the part of the Commissariat of Trade and Industry'.[4]

Narkompros met resistance not only from the commissariats but from the staff of technical (particularly higher technical) schools and from Vesenkha.* Olga Anikst, who became deputy head of the Narkompros section of professional education in 1919, later wrote:

> When the more active members of the former Russian Technical Society learned of the need to transfer professional education to Narkompros,... they opened a campaign against transfer and began to look for ways into Vesenkha. Before this Vesenkha had paid very little attention to this question. It had no educational institutions under its control. A memorandum of a group of specialists on the need to create a single centre of professional education in Vesenkha, given to its scientific–technical department [NTO], had its effect. At any rate it helped to slow down the actual transfer of educational institutions from various commissariats to Narkompros. Comrade N. P. Gorbunov, who was then head of NTO, took up the idea and composed a project for the organization of such a centre under NTO of Vesenkha...[5]

The unions, the economic commissariats and the engineers and technical school staff believed that Narkompros lacked the technical expertise to organize professional education, and that its polytechnical policy presented a threat to the existence of professional schools. These fears had some justification. It *was* the policy of the schools department to sacrifice the junior technical schools to the United Labour School, and this policy was, at least, not clearly opposed by the collegium of Narkompros. In 1918–19, according to a trade union spokesman writing in 1921, more than 200 well-equipped technical schools were closed and destroyed. The educational historians Hans and Hessen give figures for 1918–19 of 475 professional schools with 33,259 pupils, compared with 1,500 schools with 170,000 pupils before the war in European Russia.[6]

* Supreme Council of the National Economy.

Added to this was the fact that traditionally educational institutions had been better placed under other ministries than under the Education Ministry, so that transfer to Narkompros appeared to be a move from a privileged to a disadvantaged position. This fear was also, as it turned out, a reasonable one.

In Petrograd the threat to the junior technical schools was less than in Moscow and elsewhere, since the Petrograd Narkompros directed that no professional or technical schools should be reorganized into United Labour Schools without the consent of F. F. Shu's department of professional–technical education. As a result of the vigilance of his department, Shu wrote in 1919, 'there was no need for especial concern about the fate of the professional–technical educational institutions in the [Northern] *oblast*'.[7]

Early in 1919 a section of professional education was established in Narkompros. The president, F. V. Lengnik, was a member both of Narkompros and the bureau of Vesenkha; his deputy was Olga Anikst, of Narkompros and the Commissariat of Trade and Industry; and the members were V. I. Ledovskoi of the Commissariat of Communications, A. I. Skvortsov of the Commissariat of Agriculture, N. I. Chelyapov and A. M. Rendel representing the trade unions, and F. F. Shu of the Petrograd department. The section, with the support of the institutions represented in it, urged the collegium of Narkompros to adopt a more positive policy of maintaining and strengthening the technical schools. The collegium found itself under pressure: there were rumours that an independent Commissariat of Technical Education was to be established outside Narkompros, and it was reported to the collegium that 'the Presidium of VTSSPS was considering the question of a Committee on Professional Education without informing Narkompros'.[8] Some of the proposals of the technical lobby were directed not only against Narkompros' neglect of technical schools, but against its whole educational policy. Shu, for example, had 'a general plan for...the establishment of a United Technical School' to replace the United Labour School: only primary school would have 'a general educational character'; in secondary school 'there will already be a division into specialist studies'; and higher education 'will consist of the existing higher specialist technical educational institutions', with the non-technical faculties of universities banished to an undisclosed limbo.[9] As Russia's shortage of skilled workers and technical specialists became apparent—particularly after the ending of the Civil War—such proposals became increasingly attractive. It seemed to many people working in industry and the economy that Narkompros' bias towards general (albeit 'polytechnical') education was a luxury the country could not afford.

But Narkompros nevertheless won the first battle. In June, Sovnarkom issued a decree on the Narkompros section of professional–technical education which in effect confirmed Narkompros control over the section: it was to have a collegium of 11 members, 6 of them including the president from Narkompros, 2 from VTSSPS, and 1 each from Vesenkha and the Commissariats of Agriculture and Communications. Sovnarkom repeated its earlier instruction that all technical educational institutions should be transferred to Narkompros; and that other than in 'exceptional cases' all commissariats should liquidate their education committees.[10]

At the end of 1919, the technical lobby gained a powerful ally in Trotsky's commission on labour conscription. The commission was set up by Sovnarkom on 27 December 1919 to plan a quasi-military mobilization of labour to cope with the urgent problems of industrial collapse. The commission was created at the highest level: its members were Trotsky (president and War Commissar), the Commissars of Labour, Internal Affairs, Food, Agriculture and Communications, and the presidents of Vesenkha and VTSSPS. The Commissar of Education was not a member, and Narkompros was not represented on the sub-commission appointed to investigate the position of professional education and formulate 'immediate practical measures designed to ensure the production of qualified workers'.[11]

Although Narkompros was not officially represented on the sub-commission, Lengnik, the head of its professional-education section, was a member* and reported to Narkompros on its activity. After hearing Lengnik's report, the collegium decided that the sub-commission intended to recommend that professional–technical

* Lengnik acted, 'as a private person, and not on the instructions of Narkompros'. (Statement in the collegium of Narkompros, Jan. 17.)

education be removed from Narkompros control and distributed among the appropriate economic commissariats. It resolved that such a move would be 'a rebirth of narrow professionalism and departmentalism [which] Narkompros considers a great step backwards' and an attempt 'to re-establish the undesirable aspects of professional education under the old regime'.[12]

But shortly after this protest, an agreement was reached between Trotsky and Lunacharsky, and Lunacharsky told the collegium that the theses approved by Trotsky's commission on the recommendation of the sub-commission were 'completely acceptable' to Narkompros.[13] It appears that Lunacharsky had conceded that professional education might begin in the senior classes of the secondary school in return for an undertaking that control of professional–technical education should remain with Narkompros. The theses of Trotsky's commission, published in *Pravda* on 22 January, 1920, stated that

measures for the professional training of the young generation, starting at the age of 14, must be undertaken on a large scale, so as to secure the necessary production of qualified labour forces. To this end a sufficiently strong and powerful organ, including representatives of all interested departments and institutions, must be created under Narkompros.

The project for the establishment of a 'strong and powerful organ', as recommended by Trotsky's commission, was prepared by Shu. According to Shu's project (in the form approved by the collegium of Narkompros), the Narkompros section of professional–technical education was to become a Sector of Narkompros headed by the Commissar of Education. The Sector was to have the 'full powers [*polnomochie*] of military and security organizations' and to receive maximum cooperation and material support from all institutions of the RSFSR. Individuals and institutions refusing such cooperation 'will be punished with all the severity of the law of a military–revolutionary period'. The Sector was to be given a yearly fund of one milliard roubles, over and above its normal budget. A permanent assembly representing 'interested departments and trade unions' was to be set up under the collegium of the Sector.[14]

Although the project contained no mention of the minimum age of transfer from general to specialized education, or of the organization of technical schools under commissariats other than Narkompros, concessions had implicitly been made on both points: on the second point, Lunacharsky informed the collegium that Lenin 'had instructed Narkompros urgently to formulate regulations for the opening of professional–technical schools by other authorities'.[15]

Shu's project was issued as a decree by Sovnarkom, published in *Izvestiya* on 6 February. There were some changes. It had lost the tone of military urgency characteristic of Trotsky's commission, and contained no reference to 'punishment with all the severity of the law of a military–revolutionary period' nor to the ambiguous 'full powers of military and security organizations'. The Sector was now more impressively styled 'Chief Committee of professional–technical education', and was no longer 'under' [*pri*] Narkompros, but 'within its structure' [*v sostave*]. This suggested that it was to have a quasi-autonomous status, since it was to have its own budget and independence in financial and administrative direction. The Commissar of Education was, as in Shu's project, president of the Chief Committee; but his deputy was to be appointed directly by Sovnarkom and would take an *ex officio* position in the collegium of Narkompros.

The collegium of the Chief Committee (Glavprofobr), announced in *Izvestiya* on 12 February, consisted of Lunacharsky as president, O. Yu. Schmidt as deputy president, F. V. Lengnik, Olga Anikst, B. G. Kozelev of VTSSPS and A. V. Skvortsov. The key figure was O. Yu. Schmidt, a young man trained as a mathematician and formerly a left Menshevik, who had previously worked as a member of the collegium of the Food Commissariat. He seems to have had no previous connection with the technical education lobby, but now put his considerable energy at their disposal. Kozelev, the other new member, was also a strong and articulate supporter of technical education.

Glavprofobr's task, as formulated by Trotsky's commission, was to undertake large-scale reform of professional training, beginning at the age of fourteen, in order to increase the output of skilled workers. This implied both reform of higher technical education* and the introduction of specialized professional training in the secondary school.

For two reasons, this was a difficult task to accomplish. First, the secondary school was not under the control of Glavprofobr but of the Narkompros department of the United Labour School which, with the support of the majority of the collegium of Narkompros, was against professionalization of the school. Secondly, the collegium of Glavprofobr was itself divided on the question of professionalization. Shu, who had been its most energetic advocate, quarrelled with the Muscovites on the old question of Petrograd's status *vis à vis* Moscow, and was not only left out of the central Glavprofobr collegium but passed over for the presidency of its Petrograd branch.[16] Lunacharsky, the president of Glavprofobr, was against professionalization. The technical lobby may have hoped that his presidency would be nominal, but in fact he dutifully presided over one of Glavprofobr's two weekly meetings throughout 1920 and held a weekly reception at its premises at Povarskaya 14. He was under pressure from 'Party circles', he wrote to M. F. Andreeva, to devote most of his time to Glavprofobr.[17]

Another factor working against the supporters of professionalization was that the initial momentum of the labour conscription movement had been lost, and the idea itself partly discredited by Trotsky's political opponents. When war with Poland broke out in the summer, labour conscription lost a good deal of its relevance, since it had been designed as a policy for post-war reconstruction. Glavprofobr still had a solid body of support from the economic commissariats and the trade unions, but by the summer of 1920 it had lost its high priority rating—that is, its potential capacity to effect radical changes in the education system. Without this priority the forces of inertia, which in the given situation were represented by Narkompros and the United Labour School, were likely to hold their own.

The argument on professionalization of secondary education continued throughout 1920. In April Kozelev of Glavprofobr presented theses on professionalization to the Third All-Russian

* See below, p. 80 ff.

Congress of Trade Unions, and the collegium of Narkompros sent Krupskaya and Ludmila Menzhinskaya (now head of the department of the United Labour School) to oppose them. Krupskaya told the congress that

> from our point of view, professional education must not cripple a man by making him a narrow specialist from an early age, must not narrow his horizon, but must help all aspects of his whole development. And professional education must now prepare not only the executant, the mechanical worker—it must also prepare the worker to become the master [*khozyain*] of industry...
>
> The main weakness of comrade Kozelev's theses is that their approach to questions of professional education coincides with the approach of the specialist, who is only interested in industry and not at all interested in the worker...
>
> Comrade Kozelev proposes putting all general education on the lowest priority and giving all attention to professional–technical education. However he forgets that professional–technical education at any depth requires a certain general educational preparation on the part of the student: students must be properly literate, know at least elementary mathematics, and have a more or less basic knowledge of history and geography.[18]

In June, O. Yu. Schmidt and F. V. Lengnik (both members of the collegium of Narkompros) failed to persuade Narkompros to change its United Labour School policy, which the collegium endorsed by a majority of 4 to 2.* In the autumn, Glavprofobr professionalizers scored a victory, though not a decisive one, at a meeting of the Glavprofobr council. The council's functions were to work out the 'general direction' of Glavprofobr policy and to coordinate the activity of government organs and trade unions in the field of professional education, and it was so constituted as to give Narkompros (with 5 representatives) a minority on any block vote where it was opposed by Vesenkha (8 representatives) or the trade unions (10 representatives). At the October meeting Lunacharsky spoke—as reported, in guarded and somewhat ambiguous terms—of the dangers of radical professionalization of the secondary school,

* See above, pp. 57-8.

and suggested that delegates should turn their attention from the reorganization of the United Labour School to problems of adult education and the raising of workers' technical qualifications. But the meeting allied itself 'wholly with the point of view of Glavprofobr as expressed in O. Yu. Schmidt's theses', and resolved to ask the collegium of Narkompros 'to review the question of the United Labour School and the place of professional education in the general system of education'.[19]

At this time Schmidt visited the Ukraine, where an independent Commissariat of Education under G. F. Grinko had been in operation since the beginning of the year. In the summer of 1920 the Ukranian Narkompros had established a department of professional education, and Grinko himself was a strong supporter of the professionalization of secondary and higher education.[20] The technical lobby was clearly gaining ground on Narkompros, but slowly. In November Schmidt told the collegium of Glavprofobr that it was now time to work out detailed plans for the professionalization of the United Labour School.[21] But he had yet to overcome the institutional barrier presented by Narkompros' continued control of school administration and policy, and at the end of 1920 the actual situation in the field of professional education was not substantially different from the situation in January.

For Narkompros, there was an important principle at stake in the argument over professionalization. It was a principle on which, in 1929, Lunacharsky resigned from the Commissariat of Education and (it is said) Krupskaya and Pokrovsky offered resignations which were refused. Its essence was that the Communist Party, having taken power in the name of the workers, was obliged to provide them and their children with an education. It was not enough to teach them to read and write and put them through a trade apprenticeship, because this qualified them only to become semi-skilled workers and not, in Krupskaya's phrase, 'masters of industry'. 'The people thirst after education', Lunacharsky had said in his first statement as commissar; and he believed that it was the function of Narkompros to see that they were not cheated of it. He recognized the economic rationale of early professional specialization, but concluded that the human sacrifice was too great.

We understand that the ruined Russian economy needs specialists [Lunacharsky wrote in 1920]. [But] we, as socialists who defended the rights of the worker's identity against the factors which tried to stifle it under capitalism, cannot help protesting when we see that the new Communist factory is showing, in these hard years, the same tendency.

So it is inevitable that there should be a kind of struggle between those Marxists who understand all the difficulties of the present time, the necessity of straining all our forces, of retreating from our ideals in the face of present demands,—and those other Marxists who, in spite of everything, cannot let this hard time trample the flowers of the first hopes of the proletariat and proletarian youth, their first chance of many-sided human development...[22]

THE ACADEMY OF SCIENCES AND THE UNIVERSITIES

'There was nowhere that the reforming work of Narkompros met such a thick wall of inertia and "tradition" as in the academic world, and especially in the universities', Narkompros reported in 1919. 'And on the other hand, in no sphere of Narkompros reform was so much caution and care for autonomy shown, so many concessions made from the original plan of educational reform, as in relation to the higher school.'[23]

In dealing with the academic world, Narkompros found the intelligentsia at its most entrenched and most militant. Academic institutions were prepared to accept nothing less than full autonomy, and were not prepared to cooperate with Narkompros on any plan of internal reform. Narkompros was willing to meet these conditions in dealing with the Academy of Sciences, but not with the universities. The distinction was made both on principle and in response to circumstance. In principle, Narkompros respected the independence of scholarship, but wished to limit the influence of anti-Bolshevik and non-Marxist professors on students of the universities. In practice it found the Academy of Sciences more willing to enter into negotiations than the universities.

Correspondence with the Academy began as early as January 1918, when schoolteachers were still on strike and the greater part of the intelligentsia were avoiding all contact with Soviet institutions. This was all the more surprising for the fact that the Academy's chief negotiator—its permanent secretary, S. F. Oldenburg—had been a member of the Central Committee of the Cadet Party and Lunacharsky's predecessor as Minister of Public Education under the Provisional Government. In the second half of January L. G. Shapiro, of the scientific department of Narkompros, wrote to Oldenburg proposing that the Academy should take the lead in mobilizing Russia's scientific forces, registering and classifying scientific personnel and institutions, and continuing the investigation of Russia's natural and productive resources begun during the war by a commission of the Academy (KEPS). Shapiro also suggested that the Academy should 'investigate separate themes which may urgently arise', having in mind the establishment of special commissions of enquiry into particular industries or branches of agriculture.[24]

These proposals were considered by a special commission of the Academy headed by Oldenburg. Its conclusions were that the Academy should offer general cooperation without committing itself to undertake separate projects which might be suggested by the Soviet government. The Academy's reply to Narkompros, drafted by the commission and approved at a general meeting of the Academy on 20 February, stated that the Academy 'is always prepared, on the demand of life and the state, to undertake energetic scientific and theoretical investigation of scientific problems put forward by the needs of national development', and affirmed the Academy's role as 'organizational centre and centre for recruitment of the country's scholarly forces'.[25] Academician Fersman, secretary of KEPS, added a note with the comment that research into 'separate questions and branches of industrial life', as suggested by Shapiro, lay outside the scope of the Academy and would be 'difficult to realize within its walls'.[26]

Narkompros interpreted this as agreement on principle to cooperate, and negotiations moved to a senior level—between Lunacharsky and Karpinsky, president of the Academy. On 5 March, Lunacharsky wrote a long and very respectful letter to Karpinsky on the proposed cooperation. 'In the present difficult circumstances,' he concluded, 'perhaps only the Academy of

Sciences, with its traditions of pure and independent science, would succeed in overcoming all difficulties and grouping the learned forces of the country around that great scientific task'—the task of re-establishing the national economy.[27]

Karpinsky replied, on 24 March, in terms of elaborate politeness which did not prevent him from conveying that he wrote *de haut en bas* and thought the Bolsheviks were probably barbarians. He mentioned the anti-intellectualism of the mob—'that deeply false conception of qualified labour as privileged, undemocratic'—and hoped that it would be resisted by all enlightened men, including Lunacharsky. He was cautious of making too firm a commitment to the Soviet government (which after all might not last), thought it unwise to go too deeply into 'broad generalizations' about the Academy's future role, and suggested that immediate and concrete problems should be tackled first. An enclosed memorandum signed by Oldenburg proposed that among the problems which the Academy might immediately investigate were mining and metallurgical research; use of natural forces (wind, air and water); and investigation of agriculture (statistical surveys, soil-research, fertilizers, stock- and crop-breeding).[28]

The Soviet historian I. S. Smirnov has pointed out that the Academy responded to Narkompros approaches with less than the enthusiasm it had shown to the Provisional Government when, in March 1917, it had unanimously resolved 'to offer its knowledge and abilities to serve Russia to the government enjoying the trust of the nation'.[29] This is, of course, true; and as Smirnov implies the Academy did not begin negotiations with Narkompros out of political sympathy, but in order to protect itself from what Karpinsky (in his letter to Lunacharsky) called 'those explosions which are the misfortune of Russian life'. In this it succeeded admirably, as will be seen by comparing its position for the next decade with that of the universities.

Early in April, Lunacharsky and Oldenburg went to Moscow to formalize the agreement. The news was published in *Izvestiya* on 5 April, on the basis of an interview with Lunacharsky; and on 17 April *Izvestiya* reported Lunacharsky's speech to Sovnarkom on the negotiations with the Academy:

The meeting [of 12 April]...heard a report from Narkompros on the offer by the Academy of Sciences to give academic service to Soviet power through research into the natural riches of the country. It was resolved to welcome this offer; to recognize on principle the necessity of financing such work; and to indicate to the Academy, as a particularly important task, the solution of the problems of correct distribution of industry in the country and the most rational use of its economic resources.

The Academy submitted its first financial estimates to Sovnarkom, bypassing Narkompros. Karpinsky explained that 'the Academy thought...that it was important to keep the right, which it has had since its establishment almost 200 years ago, to appeal in especially important cases direct to the highest organ of government'.[30] The estimates were forwarded to Vesenkha. Lunacharsky deplored this, because it raised the possibility that the Academy would come under the competence of Vesenkha instead of Narkompros. 'It would be desirable', he told the State Education Commission,

that all mobilization of scientific skill should go exclusively through Narkompros and not through Vesenkha...Lunacharsky again points out the pressing necessity of taking all work of a scientific character from Vesenkha and, in justification of this intention, points out that Vesenkha's extremely uneconomic spending of money could be ruinous for Soviet power.[31]

Narkompros won its point in regard to the Academy, and presented the Academy's estimates to Sovnarkom in May and June 1918. But its claim that all scientific work should come under the auspices of Narkompros was not accepted: Smirnov estimates that in the first six months of 1918 Sovnarkom allocated 10 million roubles to scientific research under the auspices of various government bodies, of which less than 3 million (including the 2.2 million allocation to the Academy of Sciences) went through Narkompros.[32] Vesenkha, through its scientific–technical department (NTO), was the main sponsor of scientific research. M. M. Novikov, sometime Rector of Moscow University and a member of the Scientific Commission under NTO until his expulsion from Russia in 1922, thought that NTO was successful in attracting scientists because of the relatively liberal approach of Gorbunov, who was head of the department, and his deputies:

A few irresponsible circles suggested the proletarianization of the Commission through the introduction of representatives of Party organizations. But the collegium of the Scientific–technical department of Vesenkha... categorically rejected these proposals. I remember at one of the meetings of the collegium when such a proposal was under consideration a young Communist member of the collegium not yet graduated from technical school, the student Flakserman,* whose attitude to science was as respectful as Gorbunov's, whispered to me—'They will spoil all your work. Don't agree, and we will support you.'

Most wounding of all to Narkompros was the belief, which Novikov shared with many others, that Vesenkha was a more desirable employer than Narkompros:

It was a fortunate circumstance that just at the time when Narkompros was already beginning to put a heavy hand on the schools, Vesenkha, like the former Ministry of Trade and Industry, offered the learned institution subordinate to it comparative freedom and supplied it quite generously with funds.[33]

An implicit condition of the agreement with the Academy was that it should not be subject to administrative interference or reorganization by Narkompros. In spite of this, the scientific department of Narkompros prepared a plan for the reorganization of the Academy into an Association of Sciences incorporating other scientific societies and institutes. Responsibility for the project has been variously attributed to Pokrovsky, L. G. Shapiro and P. K. Shternberg,[34] and no doubt all three had a hand in it. A preliminary condition, which Lunacharsky remarked on somewhat wryly, 'was, of course to pull down the existing building [of the Academy] and build a model academic city'.

Nothing came of the plan because Lenin, as well as Lunacharsky, opposed it. Lunacharsky later recalled that Lenin 'warned me in so many words that there should be no "mischief-making" around the Academy', and insisted on the need to deal with it cautiously and tactfully. 'If some brave fellow turns up in your establishment, jumps on to the Academy and breaks a lot of china, then you will

* The same Yury Flakserman who had been appointed by Lunacharsky to the Palace Ministry. He later moved from administration into scientific work on his own account.

have to pay dearly for it,' Lenin told Lunacharsky.[35] The Academy remained unreformed and autonomous until the end of the '20s.

The formidable *espirit de corps* of Moscow University seems to have so intimidated Narkompros that it made almost no approach to the university until the middle of 1918. The Moscow academic world, like that of Petrograd, was dominated by liberal professors, many of whom had been prominent members of the Cadet Party. But the Moscow liberal scholars were a less flexible breed than the Petrograd academicians. The dominant group in Moscow had resigned from Moscow University in 1911 in protest against the repressive policies of Kasso, the then Minister of Public Education, and returned in triumph after the February Revolution of 1917. The few Bolshevik sympathizers among the Moscow academics—the astronomer Shternberg, the veteran biologist K. A. Timiryazev—were ostracized by their colleagues. The students were, for the most part, no less hostile than the professors.

> How sad and terrible it was for us, builders of the new Russia, [Lunacharsky wrote] to go into a lecture-room and see the young student faces indifferent, blank, reserved, hostile, ready to break into furious grimaces, and to feel as if young Russia was against us and we had no roots.[36]

It has been argued, and by a Soviet historian,[37] that Narkompros wilfully alienated the 'progressive' members of the universities by proposing excessively radical reform in 1918. It is, nevertheless, difficult to imagine the universities cooperating with Narkompros in any reform: they were determined to manage their own affairs. There was a political antagonism between Moscow University and Narkompros which no fortuitous coincidence of educational principles could have removed. The liberal majority did not simply disagree with the minority of Communists but persecuted them, encouraged students to boycott their lectures, removed the chalk from their classrooms and their classes from the timetable, and even lodged complaints against them with Narkompros. University positions were offered to distinguished anti-Communists like Peter Struve, who had not previously been members of the university. The professors fought not only for university autonomy, but to maintain a centre of anti-Communist enlightenment, as they saw it, or of conspiracy, as the Communists saw it.

Throughout the period of the Civil War, Moscow University continued to conduct examinations and award degrees, although this was forbidden by Narkompros and by Sovnarkom decrees. The motive for this, in the opinion of Narkompros, was the expectation of White victory by professors and students, in which case students would need their professional qualifications and professors their political reputations as non-collaborators. In this period a number of professors died of hunger, cold or grief. The university was nevertheless one of the best-heated buildings in Moscow, and considerably warmer by all accounts than the Commissariat of Education.

One of the more curious factors in the situation was that Narkompros was not on principle opposed to university autonomy or to the autonomy of scholarship. Its attitude to university autonomy was compounded of emotional attachment to the principles of academic freedom, indignation with the liberal professors, and a desire to reform the universities first and give them autonomy afterwards. In 1918 Narkompros threatened Moscow University but failed to attack it, and for the next two years continued to irritate its members without molesting them. Novikov, who was Rector of the university in this period and had earlier been a Cadet member of the Moscow Duma, described the situation accurately in his memoirs:

> True, the principle of university autonomy in its very essence was untouched as yet. And more than that, the boundaries of independence on the university's side were widened, in the sense that neither elections, nor new professors, nor members of the presidium were sent to the Commissariat for confirmation. But then instructions often came from Narkompros, breaking off normal teaching work...[38]

In the early months of 1918 various projects for the radical reform of the universities were considered in Narkompros. There was no feeling of respect for the universities comparable to the respect with which Narkompros had approached the Academy of Sciences. This was a time, as Pokrovsky later remarked, when Lenin's advice to 'break less' in reforming higher education sounded 'quite old-fashioned, and conservative to the point of indecency'.[39] Pokrovsky himself was hostile to the old academic world in all its manifestations, but faced with a choice he preferred research institutes to universities because he thought the people in them did more work. Once a protégé of the historian Klyuchevsky and the youngest member of the Moscow University history department, he disliked and despised almost all academics and had renounced an academic career under the old regime.

Even Lunacharsky saw little worth preserving in the existing universities. He himself had studied for two years at the University of Zurich without taking a degree, because he would accept no limitation on his freedom to become the Universal Man.[40] 'Our higher school needs a complete reform', he said in April 1918.

> ...The university as it has been up to this time does not exist as a learned institution. It is a 'diploma factory', necessary for the careers of future state *chinovniki* who are educated there.[41]

When a plan of moderate university reform was proposed to Narkompros by the Petrograd chemist Chugaev, Lunacharsky rejected it at once as 'a quite moderate and opportunist plan on the whole, infinitely surpassed by our plan of reform'.[42]

The Narkompros plan was presented by Lunacharsky, Pokrovsky, Shternberg and M. A. Reisner to an assembly on university reform held at Moscow University in July 1918. It proposed that the university should consist of three free associations: for research, undergraduate teaching and popular education. Professors were to be elected for a term of seven years, with no minimum academic requirement. Education in the university was to be free. Students were to be admitted without examination or minimum educational requirement, and degrees would no longer be awarded. The university was to be administered by a 'university soviet' consisting of the staff of the three associations and students; but above this was projected a higher authority, the 'People's Soviet' [*narodnyi sovet*], consisting of representatives of all organizations represented in the local Soviet of Deputies, political parties, trade unions and cooperative societies, together with five representatives of the local education department and twenty-five representatives of the *guberniya*

Soviet of Deputies. In the social sciences, study programmes were to be revised 'to accord with the principles of the United Labour School'.[43]

The proposal for the division of the university into three associations was rejected outright by the assembly. Pokrovsky wrote unkindly:

What turned out impossible to bear was the creation of a special *scholarly* association in the university, where the professors would not be occupied with lecturing...but with independent scientific work...—that was too much for the unburied corpses of official [*kazennaya*] science. Well, really! To force a man to show that he is working every 10 years, or perhaps every 7! To stop him sleeping quietly with his head on the doctoral thesis he wrote 20 years ago! It will be the death of Russian universities...[44]

The assembly criticized a number of other proposals, but did not reject the plan as a whole. A commission was elected to review the plan, consisting of 6 Narkompros representatives, 6 professors, 6 students and 1 representative of the technical staff of the university.[45]

The commission reached agreement on some issues, notably the principle of university entrance without examination, which was approved on condition that the faculties retained the right to limit enrolments in special classes and for laboratory work. But it failed to agree on an overall plan; and finally two separate projects were drafted by the Narkompros group and the professors, each having three student supporters. These projects were circulated to all Russian universities in preparation for a second assembly on university reform which was to be held in Moscow in September.

K. A. Timiryazev, who was not present at the July meeting, was one of the few professors who welcomed the Narkompros plan, including even its most radical proposals for the three associations and the People's Soviet. In support of the idea of a People's Soviet he quoted the example of Switzerland, where representatives of the cantons had power of inspection and financial control over the universities. He anticipated that this idea would be bitterly attacked by the defenders of 'academic freedom' but, he wrote, he himself rarely used this term 'because experience has taught me how often in our universities it is translated into "self-administration", where either the whole body of the university or, worse, a distinct pre-arranged handful takes control'.[46]

Before the September assembly met, Sovnarkom introduced the principle of university entrance without examination. The decree stated that the universities were open 'to any person, regardless of citizenship or sex, who has attained the age of 16'. University fees, entrance examinations and minimum educational requirements for university entrance were abolished.[47]

Publication of the degree was followed by a dramatic increase in enrolments at Moscow University. Before the decree, the university had received 2,632 applications for entry from graduates of secondary schools. After the decree it received 5,892 applications, mainly from persons without a full secondary education. Most of the enrolments were in the medical and physical–mathematical faculties where, according to M. A. Menzbir, Rector of Moscow University in 1918, '9 times as many applications have been made to us as are permitted by the university constitution'.[48] The typical new applicant seems to have been a junior employee in a government department. 'The proletarian masses did not come to us,' Professor Reisner said, 'it was the intelligentsia that came.'[49]

Professor A. A. Kizevetter suggested to the Moscow University Council that the September assembly on university reform should be boycotted in protest against the August decree. But a majority of the Council voted against the proposal. Menzbir said that the August decree was acceptable to the university, on the condition established by the commission of the July assembly 'to admit everyone to lectures, but to admit to laboratory work only such students as have received adequate preparation'.[50]

The September assembly turned out far more hostile to Narkompros than the July assembly had been. 'The whole business had the character of sabotage', Pokrovsky said. 'Systematic opposition to government projects was shown, and there was a clear wish to bring about the failure of the projects and make their realization morally impossible.' The more radical proposals, like the People's Soviet, were not even raised at the meeting 'because it was clear that nothing would come of it'.

Pokrovsky added that, in spite of the professors' hostility, the Narkompros project could still be implemented: 'We have heard the opinion of that assembly and now, it seems to me, we can do what we like.' But it was generally admitted in the State Education Commission's debates that Narkompros had suffered a defeat, that implementation of the proposals as a whole had become, as the professors intended, 'morally impossible', and that the plan to publish a general 'Statement on Russian universities' would have to be abandoned. The only course left open to Narkompros—other than a show of force against the universities, a weapon which Narkompros was not prepared to use—was 'to put through some of the basic and most important points in separate preliminary decrees'.[51]

According to this new strategy of piecemeal reform, two decrees were issued by Sovnarkom in October. The first declared all chairs occupied by professors for more than ten years vacant, and to be filled by election in the faculty concerned. The second gave lecturers the status and title of professor. It was hoped in this way to exploit the ambitions of junior faculty members; but 'these hopes were realized in the minimum degree . . . The scholar-adjutants did not decide to stand against their generals, and the "lords of the kafedra" almost all stayed in their places.'[52] Elections were held only in Moscow and (perhaps) the provinces, since Lunacharsky had given the Petrograd professors a special exemption from the decree. In Moscow ninety out of ninety-nine professors vacated their chairs, and almost all were re-elected. Among the very few incumbents to be defeated was the Communist P. K. Shternberg, a member of the collegium of Narkompros. (He died at the front in 1920 without returning to the university.) K. A. Timiryazev, sympathetic to the Communists, was re-elected with 'a very insignificant majority'.[53]

The law faculty and the historical section of the historical–philological faculty of Moscow University were closed down at the end of 1918. It was decided to create a faculty of social sciences (FON) in their place. A pitched battle began between the Dean of the law faculty, S. N. Prokopovich, who insisted that all members of the law faculty be transferred to FON, and Narkompros, which proposed its own candidates—including Bukharin, as an economist, and Yu. Steklov (editor of *Izvestiya*) as an historian—for the new faculty. 'I know of no such economist', said Prokopovich when Bukharin's name was submitted to him. 'Please list his scholarly works.'[54]

The battle ended in a compromise: 'not all of the former members of the law faculty entered FON, and up to 50% of FON's members were persons without qualifications, for whom only the revolution could open the way to a professional position', the Narkompros journal recorded.[55] But the Communists appointed to FON had other work and little time to devote to the university. The old professors and the students regarded FON without enthusiasm:

> In the days when Denikin was advancing on Moscow and Yudenich on Petrograd, the students were afraid of enrolling in the 'seditious' faculty, and the professors were expecting Orders of the Red Banner for giving lectures in it...[56]

The decree of August 1918 had opened the universities to all applicants, but it had not removed the basic disadvantages of the newcomers: their lack of educational preparation, and their estrangement from the rest of the students. To solve these problems, the 'workers' faculty' (*rabfak*) was devised as a means of bringing worker-students up to the normal standard of university entrance.

The first of the *rabfaks* opened at the Zamoskvoretsky Commercial Institute on 2 February 1919. It originally offered courses including accounting, physics, economic geography and commercial law; but soon found that its students needed more elementary teaching and introduced Russian language, arithmetic, nature study, geography of Russia, elements of politics [*politgramota*], writing and drawing. Subsequently, the normal entrance requirements for *rabfaks* came to be the ability to read and write fluently, knowledge of the four basic arithmetical processes, and an elementary knowledge of society and politics.[57] The student usually spent three to four years in the *rabfak* before entering the university proper.

Moscow University opened a *rabfak* on 8 October 1919. Its establishment, and particularly its physical presence in the university was greatly resented by staff and students. A. Ya. Vyshinsky,*

* Head of Glavprofobr in 1928–9; later Chief Public Prosecutor of the USSR.

then a teacher at the *rabfak*, recalled the humiliations of its early days:

How much condescension, contempt and mocking disregard the rabfaks met from some of the professors and the old student body! It was a time when there were many cases of 'shortage' of lecture-rooms for the rabfak students, of tables, benches, electric light globes, chalk for the blackboard...[58]

The attitude of the old professors to the *rabfak* is indicated by the (apocryphal) story, related by Novikov on Prokopovich's authority, that the original idea had come from the former proprietor of a cramming school, who had persuaded Pokrovsky that he could prepare workers for university entrance in two or three months.[59]

In response to this situation, the soviet of the Moscow University *rabfak* (of which Vyshinsky was a member) developed the theory that the *rabfak* was the basis of a future workers' university which would completely replace the old university. The soviet recommended that the process of replacement should begin from the 1920–1 academic year.[60] There were also suggestions that bourgeois students should be completely excluded from the university by making graduation from the *rabfak* a condition of university entrance. The *rabfak* students, Lunacharsky wrote, 'regard the professors unfavourably and without the slightest confidence, as if to say: "Go on, lie. We know you—you are a bourgeois agent." '[61]

Following the recommendations of Trotsky's labour conscription commission at the beginning of 1920, there were moves to increase the efficiency of higher technical schools, which were transferred from Narkompros control to Glavprofobr. (The universities remained under the Narkompros department of higher schools until February 1921.)

On 19 March 1920, Glavprofobr established a commission for the reform of the higher technical school, headed by O. Yu. Schmidt, and including F. V. Lengnik of Glavprofobr and Professors A. D. Arkhangelsky and Dimo among its members. The reforms proposed by the commission were the elimination of 'general educational' subjects which Narkompros had introduced into the curriculum of the higher technical schools; drastic reduction of vacations ('We suggest that vacations for their own sake or because they are traditional cannot exist now; that it is necessary to establish the minimum of free time that is essential and recognize that as the maximum that can be given', said Schmidt sternly); the introduction of extensive periods of student practical work in factories, both at labour and managerial level; and the financial maintenance of students, who were to be considered as government employees subject to penalties for absenteeism or unsatisfactory performance, by the state.[62]

These proposals were approved by Glavprofobr, GUS (the State Academic Council under Narkompros) and the April session of the Glavprofobr Council. They were the basis of the decree on higher technical schools issued by Sovnarkom, and published in *Izvestiya* on 9 June 1920. The decree stated that 'all teaching in higher technical institutions must strictly correspond with the present needs of the RSFSR'; that instruction must be based on practical study of industrial processes and organization; that the course of instruction should be three years; that students of higher technical schools 'are counted as being in government service and are under study conscription [*uchebnaya povinnost'*]'; and that they were to receive the same rations as pupils of military schools and may be deprived of rations for absenteeism.

The key point of this decree was the introduction of 'study conscription', which was clearly intended as part of a general policy of labour conscription. In August, the medical faculties of all universities were 'mobilized'. This meant that not only were students under study conscription, but that former students who had not completed their studies were ordered to return to the universities from all civil organizations and (with some exceptions) divisions of the Red Army. Medical students were not only to receive rations equal to those of military school students, but were to be issued with uniforms, shoes and linen from central supply.[63] In September the *rabfaks* were placed under study conscription. Narkompros, drafting the decree, included a guarantee of rear army rations to students; but it was omitted by Sovnarkom in the final version.[64] In fact rear army rations seem to have been given only to the students of the chemical department of the Moscow University *rabfak*.

Study conscription turned out to be a policy without teeth—on the one hand, the labour conscription policy of which it was a part disintegrated; on the other, payment of rear army rations to students was too expensive, and had to be abandoned. What was left of the study conscription policy (in economic terms) was that some categories of students in a few privileged higher schools received special rations.

The professors, perhaps unexpectedly, did better than the students in terms of rations. Students received rations according to their potential usefulness to the state, medical students coming first and students of the humanities last. No criterion of utility was applied to scholars, nor any criterion of political reliability; and the 'academic ration' was predictably unpopular in the street and among Party members. As Oldenburg points out,

> it needed the limitless authority of Lenin and the enormous popularity of Gorky to carry off the issuing of an 'academic ration'. For this exceptional ration was created before the eyes of the hungry masses who had set themselves the task of destroying all privileges and hierarchies.[65]

Narkompros did not initiate the academic ration. It was on V. D. Bonch-Bruevich's suggestion that the first 'Sovnarkom' ration was issued to scholars, literary men and artists in the capitals in the spring of 1919; and in practice it reached only to Moscow because the Zinoviev administration in Petrograd disapproved of it.[66] In July 1919, Gorky came from Petrograd to discuss the organization of an official body for the protection of scholars with Lenin. His project was passed on to Narkompros, which drafted a proposal for the establishment of a 'Commission for improving the life of scholars' in December. The academic ration was suggested by Lenin, evidently as an extension of Narkompros' proposal.[67] A resolution 'On the improvement of the life of scientific specialists' was passed by Sovnarkom on 23 December. The number of rations made available to scholars was 1,800, later increased to 2,000.[68] They were allocated by the 'Commission for the improvement of the life of scholars' (KUBU), which in Moscow was headed by A. B. Khalatov of the Food Commissariat, and in Petrograd by Gorky and M. P. Kristi of Narkompros.

If the professors were, for the time being, receiving rations without discipline, the students under study conscription seemed threatened with the opposite situation. One of the consequences of study conscription was to do away with the idea that university education must be available to all, and that its purpose was to broaden the horizons of individuals and not to train specialists of various types for the state. The priority given to medical and technical students emphasized the role of universities as professional training schools. The September decree on *rabfaks* almost excluded the possibility of free, individual entrance to the *rabfaks* (although the *rabfaks* had originally been created to secure the right of free, individual entrance to universities) by the provision that students would normally be delegated to the *rabfak* by unions, factory committees and local Soviet and Party organizations.

In the wake of study conscription, and the stricter discipline of students which it demanded, Narkompros announced a reorganization of university administration: it was the long-expected rape of university autonomy.

Pokrovsky had anticipated reorganization and even 'militarization' of the universities since the introduction of labour conscription at the beginning of 1920. He had written that

> in the present circumstances a military type of control may be necessary—that is, the replacement of collegiate organs...with one-man administration by a person temporarily entrusted with military powers: the political commissar of the given higher school. Of course this commissar who is put in charge of the higher school must not be a professor or a student. He will probably be one of the responsible Communist workers from the front.[69]

But Pokrovsky—since Shternberg's death the only member of the Narkompros collegium to have taught in a pre-revolutionary university, and the most belligerent towards the academic world—had been making threatening gestures towards the universities since 1918, and nothing had come of them.

Lunacharsky had also threatened the universities, but when it came to the point of action he was less resolute than Pokrovsky. He was evidently in two minds even in September 1920, when he described the impending university reorganization to VTSIK—although the reorganization, like the dissolution of VUS eighteen months earlier, must have struck many members of VTSIK as long overdue. 'Indeed there was a time when we ourselves, being students, fought for the autonomy of the higher school,' he said, 'and it would have been hard to send a commissar to act just as Bogolepov and Magnitsky* used to do . . .'[70]

The university reorganization initially applied only to Moscow, and was announced in a statement 'On the temporary presidium of Moscow State University' signed by Pokrovsky on 29 September 1920.[71] The temporary presidium, replacing the old university council, consisted of 3 representatives of university staff including 1 from the *rabfak*, 1 representative of non-academic staff, the 'military commissar of the faculties'† and 3 representatives of Narkompros. The president of the presidium (Rector of the university) must be approved by Narkompros, and was given extensive powers. Decisions of all faculty boards, except for the 'militarization commission' of the medical faculty, had to be approved by the president of the presidium before implementation, and the president was responsible to Narkompros for the proper conduct of the whole university.

Together with this statement, Narkompros issued a statement 'On scientific workers of the university'.[72] Professors, who had previously been elected by the faculties, were to be appointed by GUS of Narkompros. Other teaching staff were to be appointed by the temporary presidium.

M. M. Novikov, as incumbent Rector, led a deputation of protest to Narkompros.

We were received by Lunacharsky in the presence of some members of Narkompros including the deputy commissar, M. N. Pokrovsky. I was asked to speak... The character of my speech was quiet, objective and strictly business-like. But, remembering the insistence of my companions that I should abandon the mildness which was (so they said) my innate

* N. P. Bogolepov (1846–1901), Minister of Public Education, assassinated. M. L. Magnitsky (1778–1855), reactionary guardian of Kazan University in the later years of Alexander I.

† Probably the Military Commissar of the Medical Faculty, appointed to carry out 'mobilization' of the faculty.

quality and speak sharply and decidedly, I ended my speech with the following statement: 'If, in spite of our arguments, the new Statement is nevertheless put into effect, I fear that history will have to record that the destruction of the higher school which was not achieved by Pobedonostsev and Kasso* was achieved by Lunacharsky and Pokrovsky.

I had scarcely finished when Pokrovsky, as if losing all self-possession, jumped from his place and, without asking permission of Lunacharsky, who was in the chair, began to shout that he would not tolerate Cadet speeches and that my reliance on the safety of the building of the commissariat might turn out to be mistaken...

In his concluding remarks, Lunacharsky stated that the disagreements on principle existing between the commissariat and the Rector could not be reconciled by any compromise, and that the commissariat would continue to hold its point of view.[73]

A new rector was elected by the temporary presidium in November 1920. By unfortunate coincidence he, like Nicholas II's Minister of Education, was a Bogolepov—Dmitri Petrovich Bogolepov, Party member since 1907 and lecturer in financial law at Moscow University. Although not assassinated, D. P. Bogolepov made himself extremely unpopular and held the position only for six months.

Moscow University was outraged but not subdued by the violation of its autonomy which, as soon became clear, was not harsh enough to give Narkompros effective control. The temporary presidium of 11 members contained only 4 totally reliable votes for Narkompros (its 3 appointed members and the military commissar). The 2 *rabfak* representatives were presumably intended to give Narkompros the necessary 6 votes, but in fact 'as a result of the strong opposition of the representatives of the reactionary part of the student body and the professoriate, the Communists did not always manage to collect the required majority',[74] and Bogolepov was driven to the tactical mistake of creating a 'small presidium' of 3 persons to replace the unmanageable presidium of 11. This step caused such resentment in the university that it had to be abandoned. At the end of 1920, the membership of the presidium was increased

* K. P. Pobedonostsev (1827–1907), Chief Procurator of the Holy Synod under Alexander III and Nicholas II. L. A. Kasso (1865–1914), Minister of Public Education under Nicholas II.

to 12—7, as before, elected by professors, students and non-academic staff of the university, and 5 appointed by the scientific sector of Narkompros.[75]

In defiance of the Narkompros statement 'On scientific workers of the university',

> the reactionary élite of the physical–mathematical, philological and in part the medical faculties continued to conduct elections for the posts of professors and teachers in faculty meetings, to award degrees, which had been abolished by Soviet power, and so on...[76]

Decisions of the presidium were ignored in the faculties and the deans' offices [*dekanaty*] of the university. The *rabfak* was a target of reactionary reprisals, and repeatedly appealed to the presidium to protect its right to use university class-rooms and lecture-halls. Olga Lepeshinskaya—a Communist, wife of P. N. Lepeshinsky, and later under Stalin a great figure in the scientific world—was appointed to the medical faculty by the presidium; but the faculty refused to let her take up the appointment because they claimed (although Soviet historians deny) that she was unqualified. She began teaching, apparently after having gathered some student support, at the beginning of the 1921–2 academic year.

The concept of the university as a professional training institution was gaining ground. Rabkrin (the Commissariat of Workers' Inspection) conducted an investigation of FON, the social science faculty of Moscow University, and recommended that new courses be introduced

> establishing a much closer correspondence between the new study plans of the departments of the faculties and the functions of those commissariats for which they were providing specialists. For this purpose, the university had to circulate the new programmes to interested commissariats, which were instructed to give Narkompros their conclusions.[77]

Lunacharsky had believed in 1918 that the university must cease to be 'a "diploma factory", necessary for the careers of the future *chinovniki* who are educated there' and become a purely scientific institution. Times change but images remain. He now spoke with approval of the university 'like a factory, turning out socialists on the orders of particular government departments'.[78]

Narkompros described the future university, as envisaged at the end of 1920, in the following terms:

The *rabfaks* are the foundation, giving a 2-year course of *general* education and the technical skills necessary for following courses in the higher school. The higher school itself is divided into two: (1) a school for the preparation of mass specialists for Soviet construction, subdivided into departments or faculties corresponding to the divisions of the organs of Soviet construction (departments of applied economics—corresponding to Vesenkha and the Commissariats of Food and Labour—statistics, external trade and diplomacy; an administrative department training workers for the Commissariat of Internal Affairs; an institute of modern European languages etc.) and (2) a school for the preparation of highly-qualified specialists (teachers for the higher schools, workers for scientific institutions etc.) divided into institutes according to scientific speciality . . .'[79]

At this time, after some months of inconclusive struggle with Moscow University, Narkompros was still uncertain whether the 'temporary presidium' was to become a permanent instrument of Soviet control over the university. Both alternatives—university autonomy or control by People's Soviet—were felt to have been discredited: the first by the arrogance and hostility of the professors, and the second on the basis of experience in the provinces, where

the local working masses revealed an enormous and touching naiveté in the university question. Each big workers' centre wanted to have its own university, inviting indiscriminately professors of theological academies, secondary school teachers, local semi-Cadet journalists—in a word, all kinds of people, alike only in that none of them possessed genuine scientific or minimum political qualifications...[80]

The only question which remained, Narkompros thought, was

whether it was necessary to proceed directly to a system of one-man administration through the appointment of deans and rectors, or whether, in the early period, it was possible to confine ourselves to introducing the more Soviet type of collegiate administration...

In its report at the end of 1920, Narkompros again described the appointment of the presidium of Moscow University as a temporary measure; and the reference to 'more Soviet types of collegiate administration' indicated uneasiness at the prospect of maintaining unpopular commissars (as Bogolepov in effect was, in spite of his university connections) in office indefinitely. The report concluded with the noncommittal remark that 'the future will show whether this system turns out to be a workable one'.[81]

5

PROLETKULT

Lunacharsky's first declaration as Commissar of Education contained a virtual abdication of the powers of Soviet government institutions in the direction of cultural affairs:

> The people themselves, consciously or unconsciously, must evolve their own culture...The independent action of...workers', soldiers' and peasants' cultural–educational organizations must achieve full autonomy, both in relation to the central government and to the municipal centres.[1]

In one sense, this declaration pointed the way to the educational soviets which Narkompros tried unsuccessfully to establish.* In another sense, it pointed the way to Proletkult: the association of proletarian cultural organizations which Narkompros sponsored and subsidized as an independent body.

On 29 October 1917, when Lunacharsky's declaration was made, he had been Soviet Commissar of Education for three days and a supporter of proletarian culture for almost a decade. Among the assumptions he carried with him into Narkompros were those of the *Vpered* group on proletarian culture, and in particular Bogdanov's concept of the autonomy of the spheres of politics, economics and culture. As a member of the government, he now represented the political spheres of proletarian organization; but as a Vperedist, he was bound to resist his own encroachment as commissar on the cultural sphere.

This may have been a logical *impasse*, but since Lunacharsky was an enthusiast he refused to recognize it; moreover he knew himself to be a man of goodwill. It was only after some years as a member of the Soviet government that he became conscious of institutional determinants of behaviour: in 1917 he thought of institutions as neutral, given a correct ideological and class position.

The first conference of proletarian cultural–educational organizations was held in Petrograd from 16 to 19 October 1917. It was called

* See above, p. 26 f.

by Lunacharsky, as president of the cultural–educational commission of the Petrograd Party Committee;[2] and according to his recollections the initiators, other than himself, were F. I. Kalinin, P. K. Bessalko, P. I. Lebedev-Polyansky, P. M. Kerzhentsev, A. I. Mashirov-Samobytnik, I. I. Nikitin and V. V. Ignatov.[3] All of these men later played a prominent part in Proletkult: the first three had been associated with Lunacharsky in the *Vpered* proletarian culture movement in emigration, Kerzhentsev was a Bolshevik theorist of proletarian culture who had not been associated with *Vpered*, Mashirov-Samobytnik and Nikitin were proletarian writers, and Ignatov is described by Lunacharsky as 'half-proletarian, half-actor'. The conference, in short, was organized on a largely Vperedist initiative but authorized by an organ of the Bolshevik Party.

The conference was attended by 208 voting delegates representing the Petrograd Party Committee, soviets, trade unions, factory committees, youth, army and peasant organizations, city and *raion* dumas and the Petrograd Committee of the Social-Revolutionary [S-R] Party.[4] Lunacharsky estimated that three-quarters of the delegates were workers, and either Bolsheviks or Bolshevik sympathizers, but added that there were some Mensheviks among the intellectuals.[5] Of the former Vperedist group, Gorky and Desnitsky were in Petrograd at the time of the conference but took no part in it; Bogdanov and Pokrovsky were in Moscow.

The conference elected a central committee of proletarian cultural–educational organizations of Petrograd which included Lunacharsky, F. I. Kalinin, Krupskaya and Larisa Reisner; and appointed Krupskaya organizer of a school department and Lebedev-Polyansky of a literary department.[6] A week later, the Bolsheviks took power.

Of the officers elected by the conference of proletarian cultural–educational organizations, Lunacharsky, Kalinin, Lebedev-Polyansky and Krupskaya became members of Narkompros immediately after the October Revolution, and Krupskaya thereafter had no part in the proletarian culture movement. But the conference had created an organization, Petrograd Proletkult, which was distinct from Narkompros and chose to remain so. The Proletkultists were jealous of their autonomy, and although some argued that Proletkult should submit itself to Party directives, all were agreed on the necessity of independence from Soviet government institutions.

Jealousy was at first only on the Proletkult side. Since the intelligentsia as a whole boycotted the Bolsheviks after October, Petrograd Proletkult was the first and for some time the only cultural organization to have dealings with the new government, and Narkompros was prepared to give it the status and facilities of a department of the commissariat without prejudice to its right of independent organization and policy. When the former officials of the Ministry of Public Education were finally evicted, the Bureau of the Central Committee of Petrograd Proletkult (secretary V. Ignatov) moved with Narkompros—though perhaps in a separate motor-car—to the building on Chernyshev bridge.[7] The November decree on the State Education Commission provided for 'a department of aid to independent class enlightenment organizations';[8] and in January this department was formed under the name of 'department of aid to independent proletarian cultural–educational organizations', headed by F. I. Kalinin. This department was not Proletkult, but a department for liaison with it, which would work 'in full contact with the Central Committee of Proletkult'.[9] In March the department moved with Narkompros, leaving behind Lunacharsky and the Central Committee of Petrograd Proletkult.

By this time Moscow also had its Proletkult, whose central figure was Bogdanov. Bogdanov, unlike Lunacharsky, Pokrovsky and Lebedev-Polyansky, had not rejoined the Bolshevik Party. But there seems no evidence to suggest that the Moscow Proletkult had a smaller proportion of Bolshevik members than the Petrograd one. The first Moscow conference was held in February 1918, and mustered 288 delegates, the largest groups coming from factory committees and trade unions. The conference, like the Petrograd one, declared itself to be an independent mass class organization with full autonomy (quoting Lunacharsky's declaration of 29 October 1917 and the Sovnarkom decree of 9 November 1917 on the State Education Commission), 'on an equal footing with other forms of the workers' movement—the political and economic'. Separation from Soviet cultural–educational organizations was justified by the claim that they 'do not completely reflect the class point of view of the proletariat'.[10]

In Petrograd, the germ of future disagreement had been evident even at the October conference, when it was argued by some

> that all culture of the past might be called bourgeois, that within it—except for natural science and technical skills (and even there with qualifications) there was nothing worthy of life, and that the proletariat would begin the work of destroying the old culture and creating the new immediately after the revolution.[11]

The adherents of this point of view were opposed to all cooperation with 'bourgeois specialists' in the cultural field, and by the same token were opposed to a major part of the policy which Lunacharsky adopted as commissar.

Early in 1918, members of Petrograd Proletkult refused to participate in a 'theatrical soviet' including bourgeois specialists organized by Lunacharsky. At a meeting held to discuss the issue Lebedev-Polyansky, head of Petrograd Proletkult, claimed that since the State Education Commission invited the cooperation of bourgeois specialists and was therefore not representative of proletarian interests, 'full power in cultural questions' should be transferred to Proletkult. It was decided to ask Lunacharsky to prepare a report on his views on proletarian cultural organization and, if they were found to be in conflict with the aims of the Petrograd proletariat, 'the Central Committee of Proletkult would raise the question of a break with Lunacharsky'. Lunacharsky left the meeting abruptly without waiting for the end.[12]

Petrograd Proletkult also refused to take part in a conference proposed by the Narkompros department of extramural education in Petrograd. Reporting this to the State Education Commission in Moscow, Krupskaya said: 'In regard to Proletkult, there has been a definite decision in Petrograd: it must not exist as an autonomous organization.'[13] The decision must have been Lunacharsky's, and it indicates a probably painful revision of his earlier attitude to Proletkult. He agreed that Proletkult had a right to independence. But Petrograd Proletkult was no longer simply claiming independence: it was asking for 'full power' in the cultural field, in effect an organizational monopoly at Narkompros' expense. Furthermore, Petrograd Proletkult was encroaching on the educational field, and apparently trying to sabotage the Petrograd extramural department of Narkompros. 'Because of Proletkult's opposition,' Lunacharsky told the State Education Commission, 'the attempt [by the Petrograd extramural department] to find grassroots support did not succeed. Proletkult thought there was an intention to disband it. In fact there was an attempt to unite its work with that of the extramural department.'[14]

In April, still resentful of Petrograd Proletkult's attitude to Narkompros, Lunacharsky expressed 'a doubt that Proletkult is a real manifestation of spontaneous proletarian activity', since 'the enrolment of intellectuals deprives [the proletkults] of a purely class character'. Narkompros departments and Proletkult were working in the same field, and he 'found it inappropriate that two competing organizations should exist'. He suggested that Proletkult should be subordinated both to Narkompros, the organ of the Soviet government, and to the Communist Party:

> Proletkults, as organs for the elaboration of a strictly class ideology and purely proletarian culture, must be accountable to the Central Committee of the Communist Party...The sole bearer of proletarian culture can be the Communist Party, which stands on the position of class war.[15]

Lebedev-Polyansky, speaking in the debates of the State Education Commission, accepted the idea of Proletkult's accountability to the Communist Party, but not to Narkompros, whose proper relation to Proletkult he compared with the relation of the Commissariat of Labour to the trade unions. F. I. Kalinin said that although the Soviet government 'is no less democratic than Proletkult...it is not in a position to work out the problems of proletarian ideology, since it cannot refuse to educate the bourgeoisie'.

Krupskaya was firmly on the side of subordination of Proletkult to Narkompros. She thought that Proletkult had set itself up as an opposition centre to Soviet power for left-wing intellectuals—'if you don't work with the Soviets, you go and work for Proletkult'. Lunacharsky added that to admit any special claims of Proletkult to speak for the proletariat 'means to lose faith in Soviet power and recognize its bureaucratic character'.[16]

But in spite of the arguments of Krupskaya and Lunacharsky, the State Education Commission did not reach a firm decision to subordinate Proletkult either to Narkompros or to the Party. Instead, it tried to separate the spheres of activity of Narkompros and Proletkult, giving Narkompros the educative and Proletkult the creative function:

> The State Commission, considering the question of the Proletkults, states its opinion that these organizations must exist in the future as strictly class organizations, giving all their strength exclusively to the business of developing purely proletarian, socialist culture on completely autonomous bases. Soviet power takes on itself the task of broadly acquainting the proletariat, together with the whole working population, with the conquests of culture; and sets itself the aim of further developing [the cultural inheritance] in a socialist spirit.[17]

There was no mention of subordination of Proletkult to the Party in the commission's resolution, probably because of the objections of the left S-Rs expressed by Dora Elkina at the meeting of 8 April.

The view that Proletkult should be subordinated to Narkompros and its local organs was held by the Moscow education department (MONO) and by *Izvestiya*. MONO particularly resented Moscow Proletkult because, unlike other local Proletkult organizations, it was financed directly by Narkompros and not through the local education department.[18]

Pravda, under Bukharin's editorship, was sympathetic to Proletkult and Proletkult autonomy. Bukharin, reviewing the first number of the journal *Proletarskaya kul'tura* on 23 July 1918, noted that the journal 'makes an extraordinarily favourable impression'; and although he found some 'exaggerations and distortions characteristic of A. Bogdanov' in some contributions, he praised Bogdanov's article as well as those by Kerzhentsev and Nikitin. Bukharin thought that Proletkult's independence of Soviet government organs was on principle acceptable—although Lebedev-Polyansky put the case too strongly—and welcomed the idea of Proletkult as 'a laboratory of pure proletarian ideology'.

The first All-Russian Conference of proletarian cultural-educational organizations met in Moscow on 25 September 1918.[19] Here the attitudes of suspicion of Narkompros and rejection of all previous culture, which Lunacharsky had already encountered in his dealings with Petrograd Proletkult, were widely and emphatically expressed. Many delegates were impatient at the idea that the proletariat had to master the culture and science of the past in order to create their own. 'We are entering the new life with a load of proletarian consciousness', cried one speaker from the floor. 'They want to load us with another excessive burden—the achievements of bourgeois culture. In that case we will be like an overloaded camel, unable to go any further. Let us throw away bourgeois culture entirely as old rubbish.' (Kalinin at once rebuked the speaker for 'anarcho-individualism'.)

Narkompros was subjected to a good deal of criticism, especially on the point of its class allegiance, which was felt to be diluted by its obligation to educate the whole population and not only the proletariat. K. A. Ozol, of Petrograd Proletkult, was anxious to sever connections with Narkompros and the government, while at the same time strengthening relations with the Communist Party—Ozol indeed called for an exclusively Communist membership of Proletkult.

The concepts of Proletkult as 'a laboratory of proletarian ideology' and as a mass educational organization were freely used without regard to their seeming incompatibility. Thus Lebedev-Polyansky described Proletkult as 'a laboratory in a well-equipped factory [Narkompros], conducting energetic and intensive creative work to improve the organization of production', but added that 'proletarian culture must be worked out in the process of independent activity at the grassroots, among the working masses'.

Bogdanov spoke on the 'Workers' University', with reference to the experience of the Capri and Bologna schools, and on the 'Workers' Encyclopedia'. It was no use, he said, simply sending proletarian students to bourgeois universities, as Pokrovsky intended to do, since they would succumb to the bourgeois ideology of the university. The proletarian university must be an institution *sui generis*, instilling proletarian consciousness into the worker-student, enabling him to acquire the methods of scientific research, and offering 'comradeship, cooperation, vital collective work illumined by the spirit of free critical thought'. The body of knowledge accumulated by the bourgeoisie was useful to the proletariat only when reformulated in proletarian terms as the basis of a monistic, all-embracing 'organizational science'. 'History shows that each great class created its encyclopedia', Bogdanov said, meaning that each class had reinterpreted knowledge in the light of its own class consciousness. The Workers' University must do for the proletariat what Diderot and the *encyclopédistes* had done for the French bourgeoisie in the eighteenth century. 'Our general slogan in the philosophical field', Bogdanov concluded, 'is the socialization of science. Our scientific-organizational slogans are "a *Workers' University*, a *Workers' Encyclopedia*".'

Kerzhentsev, one of the most iconoclastic of the Proletkult intellectuals, spoke on proletarian theatre. The theatre, he said, needed a new repertoire and new companies of non-professional actors. Existing theatres must be nationalized and handed over to proletarian companies. Bourgeois theatre companies must be broken up and their members redistributed to serve the needs of the whole population (by this Kerzhentsev apparently meant that bourgeois actors should be sent off to bring culture to the provinces, while proletarian companies would take over the big city theatres).

Although Pokrovsky and Krupskaya spoke at the conference, and Lenin sent a greeting on being elected its honorary president, their opinions on the cultural and educational tasks of Proletkult were clearly less popular with delegates than those of Bogdanov, Lebedev-Polyansky and Kerzhentsev. Lenin, in his message to the conference, suggested that the most useful work Proletkult could do was to help bring the proletariat into participation in government; but although the Proletkultists were delighted to receive his greeting, they managed to ignore its substance completely in the debates. Proletkult, with its eyes fixed on the imminent cultural revolution, had little interest to spare for participant political democracy.

Pokrovsky suggested that 'the first step in the creation of proletarian culture is the complete conquest of that culture which has already been created, at least in its technical aspect'. But, as he said himself, the suggestion sounded old-fashioned to Proletkultists, who did not in any case regard him as one of their supporters: *Proletarskaya kul'tura* had commented in August that

as is well known, there are two different views on proletarian culture among our educational leaders. Some, including the People's Commissar of Education, A. V. Lunacharsky, think with us that the proletariat must create its *own* culture, qualitatively different from the former bourgeois culture, in the fields of science, art and daily life [*byt*]. Others, like M. N. Pokrovsky, deny this: allowing, for example, a special proletarian view in science only in the field of the social sciences (and there only in part, with the exclusion of all the formal side) and for the rest recognize only culture and science outside class.[20]

Lunacharsky was to have attended the conference and spoken on 'The proletariat and art', but at the last minute was called to Petrograd. Although he did believe that the proletariat would create its own culture, and was to that extent Proletkult's supporter, the theses he had prepared were primarily directed against proletarian iconoclasm. Had he attended the conference, he would probably have found himself arguing the conservative point of view with Pokrovsky and Krupskaya, against Bogdanov, Lebedev-Polyansky and Kerzhentsev who had the support of the majority of delegates.

Lunacharsky's theses, which were not discussed at the conference, argued that the best art of all classes and all periods is part of the 'human treasury' of art; art is moulded by its class origin, but a single class may produce different types of art mirroring its rise and fall in artistic terms; the intelligentsia may play a part in the development of proletarian culture; and the proletariat must draw on the art of the past in order to produce its own.[21]

These theses were in plain contradiction to the spirit of Kerzhentsev's paper on proletarian theatre, and also with Lebedev-Polyansky's claim (made in his opening speech at the conference) that only the proletariat could participate in the creation of proletarian culture. (It is not clear how Lebedev-Polyansky, as an intellectual, justified his own position in Proletkult.) In Lunacharsky's absence, theses on proletarian art were presented by Bogdanov, whose position seems to have been somewhere between those of Kerzhentsev and Lunacharsky. Bogdanov did not deny the value of past culture for the proletariat, but he saw it less as a 'human treasury' to be drawn on by all than as an armoury, whose weapons might be turned against their makers:

The treasury of old art must not be taken passively...The proletariat must take the treasury of old art in the light of its own critical analysis, in its own new interpretation, uncovering their [*sic*] hidden collectivist elements and organizational sense. Then they will be a valuable heritage for the proletariat, a weapon in its battle against the very world which created them...[22]

The conference elected Lebedev-Polyansky president of the Central Committee of the Council of Proletkults, with F. I. Kalinin and Mashirov-Samobytnik as deputy presidents and V. Ignatov secretary. It also took the unorthodox step of electing the members of Narkompros' department of aid to proletarian cultural organizations (confirming Kalinin as its head). Bogdanov was elected a member of the Central Committee and of the editorial board of *Proletarskaya kul'tura* (with Kerzhentsev, Kalinin, Lebedev-Polyansky and Mashirov-Samobytnik).[23]

There were a number of different types of Proletkult organization and activity in the Civil War period. The largest Proletkult organizations, in the big industrial towns and the capitals, set up an administrative apparatus similar and in many respects parallel to the local Narkompros department. Thus Moscow Proletkult had an administrative apparatus divided into departments of literary publishing, theatre, music, art, finance and clubs.[24] The Moscow Proletkult had no department of adult (extramural) education as such; but there were, nevertheless, frequent suggestions that the big Proletkults were actively in competition with Narkompros departments in the field of extramural education.

Another type of Proletkult organization, which probably appeared as a threat more to local Party committees than to Narkompros, was the factory cell. A correspondent from the big industrial town Ivanovo-Voznesensk wrote in 1919 that 'Proletkult has its cells in every factory'.[25]

The third basic unit of Proletkult work was the studio, where workers learned and practised the arts. This was the Proletkult activity which Narkompros was most anxious to encourage. Lunacharsky urged that Proletkult

> should concentrate all its attention on studio work, on the discovery and encouragement of original talent among the workers, on the creation of circles of writers, artists and all kinds of young scholars from the working class, on the creation of various kinds of studios and vital organizations in all fields of physical and spiritual culture.[26]

The studios of necessity employed 'bourgeois specialists' as instructors. In Petrograd, Gorky was one of the lecturers at the Proletkult literary studio; in Moscow—Vladislav Khodasevich and Andrei Bely. But in other aspects of Proletkult studio work an aggressively proletarian policy was often more strictly applied. Applications for the Proletkult choir in Petrograd, for example, were invited only from persons 'with Party recommendations';[27] and the Tula *guberniya* Proletkult commissioned the composition of proletarian marches, as well as supporting a symphony orchestra, a brass band, an 'orchestra of chromatic harmonies' and an ensemble of folk instruments.[28]

The artistic influences on Proletkult were as varied as its activities. A concert, organized by Moscow Proletkult for the first anniversary of the revolution and attended by Lenin, included the obligatory performance of the *Internationale* and recitations from the proletarian poet Demyan Bedny, together with Brutus' speech from *Julius Caesar*, scenes adapted from the French poet Verhaeren ('Rebellion' and 'Uprising'), and choreographic representations of 'Darkness', 'Outburst' and 'Marseillaise' performed by workers 'from the factory bench'.[29]

In literature, Bogdanov recommended that models be sought not in 'the *reklamist* Mayakovsky' nor in the decadents Severyanin, Leonid Andreev, Balmont and Blok, but in the 'simplicity, clarity and purity of forms' of the Russian nineteenth-century classics—Pushkin, Lermontov, Gogol, Nekrasov and Tolstoy.[30] But in spite of Bogdanov's advice, the proletarian poets continued to be attracted by the *reklamist* Mayakovsky, and were to be found listening with fascinated disapproval to the dramatic recitations by Mayakovsky,

Shershenevich and Balmont at the Moscow Poets' Café. In the Moscow literary studio of Proletkult, lectures by the symbolist poet Andrei Bely were particularly well attended by young proletarian writers.[31]

'We were never disciples of the block of leftists,' Bessalko wrote in an article on 'Futurism and proletarian culture', 'still less advocates of union with those who, in our opinion, are *to the left of common sense*.'[32] Yet there was a great deal in the futurist and constructivist movements in art to attract Proletkultists—iconoclasm, revolutionary fervour, enthusiasm for technology and the images (or myths) of the mechanized life of the contemporary city. Gastev, disputing Bogdanov's recommendation to learn from the classics, wrote: 'We do not wish to be prophets, but in any case *we must bind the stunning revolution of artistic methods with proletarian art*.'[33] And Bogdanov himself seemed to give some encouragement to proletarian admirers of the constructivists Rodchenko or Tatlin when he advocated the use of new techniques in proletarian art—'photography, stereography, cinematography, spectral colours, recording etc.'[34]

According to Lunacharsky, the futurist influence was increasingly noticeable among proletarian artists, especially in the visual arts and the theatre. He explained this by 'the great readiness of the futurists to work hand in hand with the workers, the absence of a similar readiness on the part of the "realists", and the influence of a few more or less outstanding Proletkult workers: Mgebrov, Smyshlyaev* and others'.[35]

In Petrograd, the influence of the futurists on Proletkult appears to have attracted the critical attention of Zinoviev himself, who wrote in greeting to a conference of proletarian writers meeting in Petrograd in the autumn of 1919:

> At one time we allowed the most nonsensical futurism to get a reputation almost as the official school of Communist art. We let doubtful elements attach themselves to our Proletkults. It is time to put an end to this. We must give the promising worker-writer the chance to study in earnest.

* A. A. Mgebrov and V. S. Smyshlyaev were leading directors of Proletkult theatre in Petrograd and Moscow respectively.

Dear comrades, my wishes to you are that we should bring more proletarian simplicity into our art.[36]

According to the State Education Commission's resolution of 1918, Proletkult's sphere was that of proletarian creativity, while education belonged to Narkompros. Proletkult formally accepted this demarcation, but thought its duty was, in the words of a Moscow Proletkult resolution of 1919, 'to exert its ideological influence' on educational work as well as proletarian creativity.[37] This was most notably attempted in the formation, on Proletkult initiative, of a Proletarian University in Moscow in 1919.* This 'new temple of proletarian science' (as *Izvestiya* called it in its 25 March report of the opening ceremony) was unveiled by Lebedev-Polyansky, with Pokrovsky representing Narkompros and Bukharin the Eighth Congress of Soviets.

Bogdanov, reporting on the Proletarian University to the Congress on extramural education in May 1919, said:

The Proletarian University dedicates itself completely to the elaboration and development of proletarian science, and its work has partly the character of laboratory experiment.

All its work is conducted on a basis of practical work, seminars and excursions. Lectures serve as an introduction to practical work.

There are 450 delegates [students] at the university, mainly from Soviet institutions, and primarily coming from the working class and the peasantry, with an insignificant number from the working intelligentsia.

N. V. Rogozinsky, president of the Proletarian University and a member of Narkompros' extramural department, seemed less optimistic of the university's prospects than Bogdanov. He told the Congress that 'it is in embryo the form of a genuine proletarian university, but because of its short courses, its well-known emphasis on practical work and its one-sided approach, the basic idea of the proletarian university is not developed as it should be'. He praised, evidently in contrast, the proletarian essence of the Central School

* An earlier Proletarian University, founded under the auspices of the Moscow Soviet in 1918, collapsed after a three-cornered battle for control between the Moscow Commissariat of Education (predecessor of MONO), the extramural department of Moscow Soviet and the Narkompros department of aid to independent proletarian cultural organizations.

of Soviet and Party work, established on Sverdlov's initiative in 1918 for the training of Communist organizers and propagandists. The impression given by Rogozinsky's speech was that he was not in sympathy with Bogdanov or with the Bogdanovist concept of the 'Workers' University'.[38]

In fact, as some of the delegates to the extramural education congress may have known, plans were already being made for the reorganization of the Central School of Soviet and Party work and its merging with the Proletarian University. In March 1919, the Presidium of VTSIK had instructed Narkompros to find premises for the proposed Sverdlov Proletarian University'.[39] In the summer of 1919 Rogozinsky—without, it was claimed, consulting staff or students of the Proletarian University—submitted to the Central Committee of the Party a plan for the merging of the Central School of Soviet and Party work and the Proletarian University.[40] According to his plan, the new institution was to be known as the 'Sverdlov Communist University', to be divided into two faculties of Soviet and Party work, and to be under the administrative control of Narkompros and the political control of the Communist Party. Proletkult was to have no part in it.

When this plan of reorganization became known to the Proletarian University, there was considerable indignation. Leaving aside the question of control, Rogozinsky proposed to change the character of the Proletarian University from that of an institution concerned with the broad perspectives of proletarian science to that of a mere training school for government and Party officials. Members of the Proletarian University appealed for a third 'general-scientific' faculty to be added to the faculties of Soviet and Party work envisaged in Rogozinsky's plan. This request was refused.

On 17 July, *Izvestiya* published an article contrasting the principles of a 'proletarian' and 'Communist' university. A proletarian university could only teach 'a Marxist revolutionary *outlook*', the article claimed, whereas a Communist university would teach its students to be Marxist revolutionaries in practice. In other words, the Soviet government and Communist Party were interested in training agitators, propagandists and local organizers. They were not interested in sponsoring 'laboratory research' into proletarian science and ideology or in producing a 'Workers' Encyclopedia'—especially if this work was to be done under Bogdanov's leadership.

Maria Smit, a professor of the Proletarian University, wrote a reply to the *Izvestiya* article defending the Bogdanovist concept of the university. The proletariat, she argued, needed not only local organizers [*vozhaki*] but leaders [*vozhdi*] with a thorough grasp of Marxist revolutionary ideology. It is perhaps not surprising, if this was the Proletarian University's view of its function, that the *vozhdi* of the Communist Party regarded it with suspicion. *Izvestiya* declined to publish Smit's reply, which appeared in extract in the journal *Proletarskaya kul'tura*.[41]

The merger of the Proletarian University and the Central School of Soviet and Party work was raised again in the Central Committee on 3 July, and the previous resolution confirmed. Bukharin, who was both a professor of the Proletarian University and a member of the Central Committee, claimed that the decision did not involve a rejection of the principles of the proletarian university, and was motivated only by the urgent immediate need for trained Soviet and Party workers.[42] But his was not an impartial judgement.

The collegium of Narkompros seems to have been sympathetic to the Proletarian University. At the beginning of September the collegium noted a Central Committee instruction, dated 5 August, that the Proletarian University be closed 'from the present moment', but made no resolution to act on it. The *rapporteurs* on the question were Zinaida Krzhizhanovskaya, of the extramural department of Narkompros, and Smit, of the Proletarian University. At the beginning of October, Smit again addressed the collegium on the Proletarian University, and it was decided that, pending 'a final clarification of the question of principle' of the existence of the Proletarian University, it should be transferred to the control of Proletkult.[43] This appeared to be acting in direct defiance of the Central Committee's decision. But Narkompros support was not enough to save the Proletarian University, although it may have prolonged its life. The Sverdlov Communist University seems to have come into operation early in 1920.

During the period of the attack on the Proletarian University,

Moscow Proletkult was under similar attack from MONO. At the March 1919 conference of Moscow Proletkults S. I. Mitskevich, for MONO, suggested that Moscow Proletkult should be merged with the extramural department of MONO. He won the support of some delegates from the *raiony*, but not of the conference as a whole.[44] 'All [Proletkult's] work is parallel with the work of the education departments', Mitskevich wrote in *Izvestiya* on 22 March. 'It disperses our forces, which are small enough anyway, and spends public money received from the same source—that is, from Narkompros—and for the same purposes as the education departments.' MONO had the support of the Moscow Soviet in its campaign against Proletkult. But it was unable to take any action as long as Moscow Proletkult enjoyed the support of the Moscow Party Committee, which had decided after hearing an appeal from Moscow Proletkult that 'at the present moment it is inappropriate to merge Proletkult with the extramural department of MONO'.[45]

Pravda was, as usual, sympathetic to Proletkult. On 15 April 1919 it published a defence of Proletkult as an independent laboratory of proletarian culture. Unfortunately not all Proletkultists were prepared to accept a defence on these grounds. Kerzhentsev, for example, doubted the 'laboratory' justification of Proletkult, and suggested that it should concentrate on extending its work among the masses.[46] Lunacharsky, who deplored the attempt to 'destroy' Moscow Proletkult, nevertheless urged Proletkult 'to concentrate all its attention on studio work'; and on 13 April *Izvestiya*—a declared partisan of MONO and Moscow Soviet on the Proletkult question—conceded in an editorial note to Lunacharsky's article that if Proletkult 'would limit its activities to the "studio" boundaries which comrade Lunacharsky suggests, and not try to change and impede the work of Soviet organs, which it has neither power nor ability to do', its independence might be tolerated.

Krupskaya, like Mitskevich, saw Proletkult as a mass organization in direct competition with the extramural department of Narkompros. She wrote in 1920 that

> in so far as Proletkult could not be isolated from the surrounding environment, it could not sustain its laboratory character...But, turning into an organization working among the masses, Proletkult was not in a

position to protect itself from the wave of intellectual and petty-bourgeois elements calling themselves bearers of proletarian culture.

And Proletkult turned into the most ordinary educational [*prosvetitel'naya*] organization, little differing either in method of work or class composition from the organizations of Narkompros...The laboratory turned into a factory competing with the Narkompros factory... —everyone knows from experience that nine-tenths of Proletkult institutions do not have a laboratory character.[47]

This was also the conclusion of a rank-and-file member of Proletkult who supported its subordination to Narkompros:

Not only are the aims and tasks of the extramural department and Proletkult the same, but they are in practice run by the same people. That is known to anyone who has worked in these organizations... [Proletkult] played its role, and in a certain sense quite successfully, only it was not as a laboratory but as a fighting force thrown up by the time. Its direct aim at the beginning was political struggle and not laboratory work.[48]

The status of Proletkult was argued at length at the First All-Russian Congress on extramural education which opened on 6 May 1919. On the evidence of a questionnaire circulated among delegates at the beginning of the congress, there were 576 voting delegates of whom 156 were Communists, 70 Communist sympathizers, 200 non-Party and the rest (150!) 'anarchists, Social Revolutionaries, Bundists, Independents, left Social Revolutionaries, Maximalists etc.' This estimate was later amended to give the more respectable figure of 229 Communists and 189 Communist sympathizers.* 'The representation should have been bigger,' Krupskaya wrote later, 'but the mobilization of Communists prevented us from fully realizing it.'[49] Even on the revised estimate, the percentage of Communists at this congress compared poorly with the March conference of Moscow Proletkults, where 55% of the delegates were Communists and 30% Communist sympathizers.[50]

After the opening speech by the president of the congress,

* The first estimate appeared in *Izvestiya* on 8 May; the second in *Izvestiya* on 13 May. The likely basis of the revision was a paper transfer of the 70 Communist sympathizers of the first estimate into the 'Communist' category, and a corresponding widening of the category of 'sympathizer'. The first estimate gives 350 non-Party and other delegates; in the second, this number drops to 176.

Lunacharsky, Lenin made a short speech. His main themes were the inadequacy of library work and the campaign against illiteracy but he made a passing thrust at Proletkult, referring to

> the abundance of escapees from the bourgeois intelligentsia, who often looked on the newly-created workers' and peasants' educational institutions as the most convenient field for their own personal fantasies in the sphere of philosophy or culture,...and smuggled in something supernatural and foolish under the guise of pure proletarian art and proletarian culture.[51]

On the morning of 8 May, Lebedev-Polyansky spoke for Proletkult. He 'agreed that where the work was being done on a government scale and was serving the interests of the whole population, it was necessary that the organizational plans [of Proletkult and Narkompros extramural department] should coincide'. But, he said, 'where strict creative work—laboratory work—is going on, there cannot be strict definition and regulation of work. Proletkult organizations must have great freedom and great independence.'[52]

After the opening speeches, the congress divided into various sections and commissions, two of which met jointly to discuss 'the creation of a basic state system of extramural education and Proletkult'. Bogdanov, Kerzhentsev and Lebedev-Polyansky were the spokesmen for Proletkult. Their opponents were Krupskaya, Ludmila Menzhinskaya, Rogozinsky and P. G. Smidovich (representing Moscow Soviet). The Communist fraction of the congress put forward a resolution that 'the Congress finds that Proletkult work must be a part of Narkompros and be closely tied to the work of the extramural department, entering it as one section of the central and local *apparat*'. It was carried on a vote of 166 for, 36 against and 26 abstaining.[53]

This vote was an undoubted victory for the extramural department of Narkompros and a defeat for Proletkult. But on two other questions, the congress supported a Proletkult point of view: first, on the question of the Proletarian University, where its resolution was in the spirit of Bogdanov's paper rather than Rogozinsky's; and second, on the theatre, where a resolution (probably proposed by Kerzhentsev) was passed that audience participation should be encouraged in order to create 'the theatre of collective action which the proletariat are waiting for', and that 'the repertoire of this new theatre will be the result of the creation of plays by a process of collective improvisation'.[54]

On the last day of the congress, Lenin made a second and unscheduled* speech 'On the deception of the people by slogans of freedom and equality'. The speech, lasting an hour and a half, was an attack on the anti-Communism of the socialist and liberal intelligentsia. Presumably Lenin chose to speak on this theme to the congress because of the large number of Social-Revolutionaries, anarchists, Bundists and non-Communists who were present. He also used the occasion to comment unfavourably (but, as in his first speech, only in passing) on Proletkult:

> I have shown you that the dictatorship of the proletariat is inevitable, necessary and undoubtedly obligatory in order to escape from capitalism. Dictatorship means not only force—though it is impossible without force—but also a higher level of labour organization than before. That is why, in my short welcoming speech, I underlined this basic, elementary and most simple task of organization; and that is why I regard all intellectual fantasies of 'proletarian culture' with such ruthless hostility. To these fantasies I oppose the ABC of organization. The task of proletarian discipline is to distribute bread and coal in such a way that there is a careful attitude to each unit of coal and each unit of bread...If we solve this very simple, elementary problem, we shall win...The basic task of 'proletarian culture' is proletarian organization.[55]

Lunacharsky had had to leave the congress after the opening day, and was therefore spared the necessity of taking sides either with the Proletkultists or with his own extramural department. In his absence, as has been described, the congress passed a resolution directing that Proletkult should enter the extramural department of Narkompros as a section within it at central and local levels. This resolution was not discussed in the collegium of Narkompros until Lunacharsky's return early in June. The basis of discussion was a report by Lebedev-Polyansky; and the conclusion of the collegium

* Both *Pravda* and *Izvestiya* were taken by surprise and had no room to print the speech. Both promised to print it in full later, but never did so. It was published as a pamphlet by Gosizdat.

was that Proletkult, both in the centre and locally, was to be regarded as one of the sections of the extramural department of Narkompros, but that it 'conducts its work independently, with its own separate budget'.[56]

This last phrase made the Narkompros resolution significantly weaker than the resolution of the congress, and was evidently the result of Lunacharsky's conciliatory presence. The collegium decided to publish the resolution over the signatures of Lunacharsky (Commissar of Education), Krupskaya (head of the extramural department of Narkompros) and Lebedev-Polyansky (president of the Central Committee of the Council of Proletkult). It does not, however, appear to have been published in any of the major daily papers.

Since the much stronger resolution of the congress on extramural education had been published in the national press, many local Proletkultists believed that Proletkult had finally lost its independence. 'We—proletarians, factory workers—are thunderstruck by this decision', wrote a Proletkultist from Ivanovo-Voznesensk. '...To us the truest explanation seems that the people at the congress were chiefly heads of education departments, their deputies and instructors—people who are far from being proletarian elements.' It was reported that in Smolensk there was strong support for Proletkult autonomy from Proletkultists who 'evidently confuse the organ of proletarian power—Narkompros—with Kolchak', and that their relations with the extramural department were deteriorating. 'Who can object on principle to the existence of a creative laboratory of proletarian art, which Proletkult must essentially be [?]' asked one of the Smolensk Proletkultists. 'In any case, not us.'[57]

The journal *Proletarskaya kul'tura* tried to reassure its readers by publishing the resolution of the collegium of Narkompros, which gave the extramural department only nominal control over Proletkult. For further comfort, it added a quotation from an article written by Lunacharsky shortly before the May congress on extramural education:

> ...Perhaps the Proletkults have not always clearly understood their tasks; perhaps they have sometimes conducted work parallel with the work of Soviet organs. But what of it? All the Soviet organs get entangled with each other, and it is impossible to avoid interdepartmental friction.

But no-one thinks that it follows that when two institutions—for example the Council of the National Economy and the Food Commissariat—clash, that one of them should be abolished. There is a quite unique place for Proletkult. I completely support Proletkult's right to a separate existence and to broad state subsidy.[58]

6

THE ARTS

FIRST CONTACTS WITH THE LITERARY AND ARTISTIC WORLD

In dealing with the arts, Narkompros confronted a world which was both hostile and amorphous. There were few institutional channels by which it could be approached, and almost all its members—writers, actors, artists and musicians—were determined to boycott the new government.

Most of the artistic institutions which had formerly been under the Palace Ministry came under Narkompros jurisdiction from October (the rest being officially transferred to Narkompros only after the dissolution of the Commissariat of Property of the Republic in the middle of 1918), but for some months remained virtually untouched by Soviet power. The administrators and commissions of reform established by the Provisional Government continued work.

There were few outright strikes in the artistic world. Some theatres stopped work after the October *coup*, but all had resumed normal activity by the end of November. The artists' and writers' characteristic tactic was to ignore Narkompros on the official level, while at the same time attacking it in the non-Bolshevik press—treating it with the hostility due to a Soviet government organ, but also with marked disrespect, because of its conciliatory intentions.

For Lunacharsky, the most mortifying attacks came from Gorky's social-democratic internationalist paper *Novaya zhizn'*. He was on friendly terms with its editors—Gorky, Sukhanov, Stroev-Desnitsky (the former Vperedist) and A. N. Tikhonov—and with its literary and artistic correspondents, who included V. Bazarov (Lunacharsky's friend and companion in exile twenty years earlier), A. N. Benois, the artists Petrov-Vodkin and Natan Altman, and Mayakovsky. Before October, Lunacharsky had headed the cultural department of *Novaya zhizn'*. He had protested against the Central Committee's instruction to leave the paper in August, and again early in October, when he had submitted a statement to the Central Committee explaining that he was unwilling to abandon his work there because 'a number of the staff of the cultural department of *Novaya zhizn'* intended to leave if Lunacharsky gave up the editing of the department'.[1] This gesture of solidarity was not reciprocated by his friends after October.

In the first months of Soviet power, *Novaya zhizn'* 's line was not only hostile to the government but—with the special malice of familiarity—to Lunacharsky. Gorky described him as 'lyrically-minded but muddle-headed', a satirical poem on his November resignation from the government referred to 'our soft-hearted Anatoly', and in January Desnitsky made an entirely negative assessment of the achievements of his commissariat.[2] At the same time, *Novaya zhizn'* was giving thorough and sympathetic coverage to the activities of VUS, the Arts Union, Countess Panina and other of Narkompros' public opponents.

Lunacharsky, who had never lived for long in Petersburg before the revolution and had returned from a decade of emigration only six months before October, had only a slight acquaintance with the Petrograd artistic world when he became commissar. In August or September he had had one meeting with leading figures of the Petrograd theatres. This was arranged by Y. M. Yuryev, an actor in the Petrograd imperial theatres and friend of Gorky and Andreeva, through whom Lunacharsky probably met him. Yuryev had invited Lunacharsky to debate with the Cadet leader Nabokov on cultural policy because, he said, 'I am convinced that we theatrical workers will find ourselves under the leadership of one or other of you in the near future.' Lunacharsky knew few of those present at the debate. 'At that time, I...had no direct connection with the theatre', he wrote. 'I was very little acquainted with the then leading circle in the theatre.'[3]

In Petrograd, the bases for Bolshevik organization in the arts were almost non-existent. In the educational field, the nucleus of Bolshevik organization had been formed before October in the Petrograd municipal administration and its cultural–educational commission. But the Petrograd Bolsheviks had no equivalent foothold in the arts, unless they had the support of Gorky and Maria Fedorovna Andreeva, who headed the administration of Petrograd municipal theatres under the city Duma; and Gorky and Andreeva were estranged from the Bolsheviks for some months after October. The only cultural organization to which Lunacharsky could turn was the newly-formed Petrograd Proletkult. But the Proletkultists had no influence or standing among the Petrograd intelligentsia.

Until the government moved to Moscow in March 1918, Moscow was effectively outside the scope of the central commissariats. But in relation to the organization of the arts, the Bolsheviks were initially in a better position in Moscow than in Petrograd. In April 1917, the Moscow Soviet had formed an artistic–educational commission (later department) in which the Bolsheviks P. P. Malinovsky and his wife Elena were the leading figures.[4] Both were old Party members who had been active in cultural affairs for many years: Malinovsky was an architect, and his wife had worked in the field of popular theatre. Before October, Malinovskaya had already established a working relationship with leading figures of the Moscow theatre like A. Ya. Tairov and F. F. Komissarzhevsky.

In January 1918 Lunacharsky delegated control of the state (formerly imperial) theatres in Moscow to Malinovskaya,[5] who continued to work in the artistic–educational department of the Soviet. P. P. Malinovsky became head of the Commission for the Preservation of Artistic and Ancient Monuments in Moscow, and Civil Commissar of the Kremlin. At the very beginning of 1918—before any agreement, or even basis for negotiation, had been reached with artists in Petrograd—Malinovsky persuaded the Moscow artists' union, Izograf, representing mainly the older generation of realist artists, to cooperate with his commission in 'the protection of artistic monuments and...the working-out and consideration of all questions of artistic life in Moscow'.[6]

The arts were, of course, a secondary problem for Narkompros, which was in any case not trying to set up a government administration of culture but to establish contact and enter into discussion with the artistic world. Narkompros was immediately concerned only with the institutions formerly administered by the Palace Ministry—the imperial theatres (Aleksandrinsky, Mariinsky and Mikhailovsky in Petrograd; Bolshoi and Maly in Moscow), the Academy of Arts [Akademiya Khudozhestv] in Petrograd and Moscow, and the imperial palaces—and with the protection of art collections and historical monuments. In the case of the institutions formerly under the Palace Ministry, Narkompros had the problem of displacing the administration and commissions set up by the Provisional Government, and it was this factor which gave some urgency to its approaches. As for the protection of art treasures and historical monuments, the urgency of the task was dictated by the circumstances of war and revolution which put them under constant threat of destruction.

It was suggested that a separate Commissariat of the Arts should be established outside the Commissariat of Education, with Lunacharsky at the head of both, P. P. Malinovsky as his deputy for the arts and M. N. Pokrovsky deputy for education.[7] Narkompros was opposed to the idea. 'A Ministry of the Arts is an inheritance from a purely despotic regime,' Lunacharsky said, 'a survival of the time when art was completely under the control of the Palace.'[8] Olga Kameneva, head of the theatre section in Moscow, also denied rumours that a separate Commissariat of the Arts was to be set up: this, she said, would mean that the Soviet government intended to direct [*rukovodit'*] art and creative work, which was inadmissible. 'While art is in the Commissariat of Education, the government has one aim—an educative one, to demonstrate and explain. Russia is in the stage of development when it has to be educated in art.'[9]

However, the artistic world, especially in Petrograd, was bent on autonomy and took little account of the actual intentions of the Soviet government towards art. For artists, as for universities, the February Revolution had removed controls and for the first time created the possibility of autonomous corporative organization. The Petrograd state theatres wanted to become self-administering on an autonomous basis. The Arts Union [Soyuz Deyatelei Iskusstv] wanted to reform the Academy of Arts and assume sole responsibility for all artistic institutions.

Lunacharsky described these aspirations as 'syndicalist' and—especially in regard to the theatre—impracticable because of the need for state subsidy.[10] The Arts Union decided in November 1917 to appeal to the Constituent Assembly for funds to support artistic schools, state theatres and museums, and declared itself 'the only organ which has the right to direct the artistic life of the country'. (This claim was in evident conflict with the state theatres' intention to administer themselves.) 'It is necessary to separate [art] from the state', the poet F. Sologub told the Arts Union. 'Our attitude to Golovin [head of the Palace Ministry under the Provisional Government] and to Lunacharsky is identical.'[11]

The Arts Union, founded in May 1917, was informally divided into three groups—the 'left', including V. V. Mayakovsky, O. M. Brik and N. N. Punin; the 'non-party centre'; and the right or '*delovoi blok*', led by Sologub. The left group was the closest to the Bolsheviks in politics, but for the time being the most violent in defence of the autonomy of art.

On 12 November 1917, N. N. Punin informed the union of Lunacharsky's proposal for the establishment of a state soviet on art affairs, half of whose members would represent the arts and half the Soviets of workers', soldiers' and peasants' deputies. The union rejected the proposal unanimously—even Punin, Lunacharsky's intermediary, voted against it. The union objected both to the intrusion of the commissar in its affairs, and to the suggestion that non-artistic delegates (from the Soviets of Deputies) should have a voice in the organization of artistic life. Their reaction was similar to that of the professors of Moscow University, confronted with Narkompros' plans for university reform six months later.

After the rejection of his first approach to the Arts Union, Lunacharsky made a second, more limited, proposal for cooperation between the union and Narkompros in the protection of art treasures. This also was rejected, sixty-eight voting against and two abstaining.[12] One of the abstainers was motivated by concern for the art treasures; the other, Mayakovsky, was registering a political position (he thought that the protection of art treasures could be easily accomplished by stationing a few units of soldiers around the imperial palaces, and in March 1917 had criticized Gorky and Benois for compromising their artistic independence by joining a state commission set up for this purpose by the Provisional Government;[13] his abstention in this vote indicated a greater general willingness to cooperate with the Bolsheviks than the centre and right-wing of the Arts Union).

In April 1918, when the Academy of Arts was liquidated by decree,[14] Lunacharsky had still reached no accommodation with the Arts Union. The union, which had its own commission for the reform of the Academy of Arts (established under the Provisional Government), protested because the reorganization of the Academy into 'free artistic studios' was entrusted to Punin, a left-wing member of the union, and not to the union's candidate Romanov.[15] By this time Punin, Mayakovsky and others of the left were on bad terms with the majority of the union, and subsequently left it altogether. The leading figure remaining in the union was Sologub, of the *delovoi blok*.

On 19 April Lunacharsky addressed a meeting of the Arts Union. *Novaya zhizn'*, reporting his speech unsympathetically on 21 April, noted that it was of some interest in having the character of 'a government declaration'. The government, Lunacharsky told the union, stood for the complete separation of art from the state, for complete liquidation of all diplomas, titles, honours and exclusive privileges; and opposed state support of any single artistic group or organization on the grounds that it would inhibit the development of other groups. The Academy of Arts had been abolished because to maintain it meant giving state support to one privileged artistic group. (This argument was perhaps not entirely convincing, since the government continued to maintain the state theatres.)

Members of the union, *Novaya zhizn'* reported, criticized various actions of 'irresponsible' commissars, whose offences Sologub listed as 'liquidation of the Academy, juggling of votes and "searches" at the meeting of the conference of artistic institutions, police attacks on freedom of assembly itself..., the barbarian and illiterate decree* on the taking down of monuments'.

All this, in the opinion of F. Sologub, is in direct contradiction with the assurances which Lunacharsky gave in his time, and can be explained only by Lunacharsky's ignorance of what his subordinate commissars are doing. In the opinion of the Executive Committee [of the Arts Union] there can only be one way out of the *impasse*—the resignation of the

* Sovnarkom decree 'On the taking down of monuments raised in honour of the Tsars and their servants', 12 April 1918.

existing government 'collegium on art affairs'* and the transfer of control of art affairs to the hands of the Executive Committee of the Arts union...

Lunacharsky, for his part, was 'astonished that the union, ...which stands for the principle of the autonomy of art, can pretend to the conquest of government power'. He admitted that the government had failed to come to terms with the greater part of the artistic intelligentsia but, he said, 'we are not the first to go against the democracy', and the experience of Europe and America had shown that the majority was bourgeois. 'We stand for the policy of the active minority and, in art, for union with separate outstanding talents.' The Constituent Assembly of artists proposed by the union would be nothing more than a congregation of the untalented.

On this provocative note Lunacharsky left the hall, accompanied (*Novaya zhizn'* reported) by cries of protest from the assembled artists. After this meeting the Arts Union decided to break off all relations with Lunacharsky.

Before October the Petrograd state theatres were administered by the liberal professor F. D. Batyushkov, appointed by the Provisional Government. Under Batyushkov, a project for self-administration of state theatres had been discussed, and had gained widespread support in the theatres. Lunacharsky's first major statement on the state theatres dismissed the plan for full independence of the state theatres as 'hopeless, because the theatres cannot manage without their losses being covered by the Republic,...and harmful, because it amounts to an attempt to leave the theatres unchanged, still finding its support among the same bourgeois public...in a completely changed country'. The alternative plan which Lunacharsky offered provided for the administration of the state theatres through a state soviet of theatrical and government representatives which would issue general instructions on membership of theatre companies, repertoire and so on. Within the framework of these general instructions, the company of each theatre had 'full autonomy': 'it works out its own internal constitution, elects a directorate and manages the artistic side of affairs'.[16]

Early in December there was a clash between theatre workers and

* Probably the collegium of the Narkompros art department, IZO.

Bolsheviks when a big Bolshevik meeting was held in the Aleksandrinsky theatre without prior consultation either with the theatre or Lunacharsky. In the recriminations that followed, Lunacharsky took the opportunity to point out (in *Izvestiya* of 12 December) that the artists of the Aleksandrinsky theatre had 'so far not regulated their relations with me', and therefore were in no position to complain to him or seek his protection from intruders. On 10 December he had written to Batyushkov requiring him 'to regulate the relations of the democracy and the theatres of the Republic'—that is, to enter into negotiations with Narkompros. Batyushkov refused, pointing out that he had the almost unanimous support of the theatre companies, whose artists 'insist on the independence of art from political parties and the recognition of the administrative autonomy of artistic collectives'.

Lunacharsky then dismissed him. 'It is sad', he wrote to Batyushkov, 'that so many socialists including you, Fedor Dmitrievich, so definitely turned out on the opposite side of the barricades from the people.' Lunacharsky considered that Batyushkov, as a state-appointed official, had no right to pose as a defender of artistic autonomy, and the demand for autonomy was in itself a partisan political act on his part. 'Perhaps a demand from the popularly-established government to a person bearing the title of representative of the Provisional Government constitutes political interference in the life of the theatre,' Lunacharsky suggested sarcastically, 'while the appointment of such a representative by Golovin* and Kerensky is an act of defence of theatrical autonomy?'[17]

Since Batyushkov did not recognize the Bolshevik government, he did not recognize his dismissal. Instead, he instructed that the 160,000 roubles remaining in the treasury of the state theatres should be distributed among actors and employees of the theatre. Lunacharsky, exceedingly indignant, wrote that until the money was returned to the state, the theatres would receive no state subsidy, and threatened 'the person giving contrary instructions' with the Revolutionary Tribunal.[18] Batyushkov, who was no less indignant, challenged Lunacharsky to arrest him.[19]

* F. A. Golovin headed the former Palace Ministry after the February Revolution.

Batyushkov was not arrested. But there was a notorious arrest in the theatrical world: that of the pianist A. Ziloti, appointed administrator of the Mariinsky theatre by the Provisional Government. Ziloti refused to hand over the keys to the imperial box, unless to 'the representatives of a legal government'. He was arrested at his flat by young Flakserman, flanked by two Red guards from the Cheka. A day later he was released with a fine, after being rebuked by Dzerzhinsky for making a 'pointless demonstration'. The theatrical world was outraged, and Flakserman's name briefly acquired connotations of unbridled Bolshevik intimidation of the arts. These were not forgotten even after the actors of the Petrograd imperial theatres had made a reluctant peace with Lunacharsky. Some time later Flakserman attended a performance of Gounod's *Faust* at the Mariinsky theatre, and in the interval exchanged greetings with the actress Vladimirova.

'Who was that who greeted you?'
'Flakserman', answered Vladimirova.
'What?' exclaimed one of the artists. 'So young, and already Flakserman!'

For a long time 'so young, and already Flakserman' was my nickname in those circles.[20]

Batyushkov and Ziloti expressed the feelings of a majority of the artists of the Aleksandrinsky and Mariinsky theatres. 'If the People's Commissar Lunacharsky enters the Mariinsky theatre during a performance,' the conductor Albert Coates announced, 'I will immediately put down my baton and stop conducting.'[21] There was an attempt to sabotage the work of the Aleksandrinsky theatre by offering all its artists employment in the café-chantant 'Aquarium' for 30,000 roubles a month. Most of the company accepted this offer, but performed both at the 'Aquarium' and the Aleksandrinsky—enriching themselves, but at the same time, the Soviet historian Zeldovich points out, 'upsetting the plans of the counter-revolutionaries'.[22]

On 23 December, Lunacharsky wrote to his wife that the situation in Petrograd was improving: 'The *Narodnyi dom*,* Mikhailovsky

* Literally, 'People's house', normally including a theatre, reading-rooms etc. The Petrograd *narodnyi dom* was under the municipal administration.

theatre, the technical personnel of the state theatres and the soloists of the Mariinsky theatre have recognized me.'[23] But this still left the Aleksandrinsky theatre and most of the Mariinsky company outside the sphere of Soviet influence. In this crisis, as in the occupation of the Ministry of Public Education a month earlier, Lunacharsky turned to the left S-R Bakrylov, whom he appointed Commissar of State Theatres in Petrograd. 'His firm hand,' wrote Lunacharsky, 'even though it pressed rather painfully at certain points, turned out —at least in the initial period—to be appropriate.'[24]

Lunacharsky had told the Arts Union that the government's policy in the arts was 'union with separate outstanding talents'. This, of course, was a policy *faute de mieux*. But among the few who offered their cooperation to the Soviet government in the first months after October were three men of outstanding talent—the poets Mayakovsky and Blok, and the producer Meyerhold.

In December Rurik Ivnev (a poet not of outstanding talent) had the idea of organizing a pro-Bolshevik rally of the intelligentsia, and invited Lunacharsky, Kollontai, Blok, Meyerhold, Esenin, Petrov-Vodkin and others to speak.[25] Blok accepted 'at once without any hesitation' according to Ivnev's account. The meeting apparently went off reasonably well, although in the midst of a snowstorm and consequent transport failure which caused Ivnev himself to arrive more than an hour late, though not before the end of Lunacharsky's introductory speech. Most of the audience—whose size is not indicated by Ivnev or the report of the meeting in *Izvestiya* of 28 December—were sympathetic, although there was a small group of hecklers. *Izvestiya* reported that Lunacharsky, Kollontai, Blok and Petrov-Vodkin spoke; and hailed the meeting as an important sign that part of the intelligentsia had decided 'on the necessity of working under the direction of Soviet power'.

Ivnev, piqued at being ignored by the *Izvestiya* report, wrote a letter to the editor (published on 4 January, 1918) pointing out, first, that he was the initiator of the meeting, and second, that he and those like him had no intention of recognizing 'artistic direction' from the government. 'If poets and artists recognize any sort of "direction",' Ivnev wrote, 'it is only the direction of their own poetic and artistic taste. Art, from my point of view, is free and cannot "serve anything earthly and transient".' His motive in organizing the meeting had been his 'deep conviction that now, this minute, it is necessary to force the broad circles of the intelligentsia out of the inert condition they are in...'

Among individuals who offered their support to the Soviet government, those of outstanding talent were at least balanced by those who were ridiculous or disreputable in the eyes of the intelligentsia. In this second category were the writer Ieronim Yasinsky, who visited Lunacharsky in the Winter Palace to read him poems on Nietzsche;[26] Ivan Rukavishnikov, the eccentric son of a rich merchant family who was the organizer of the 'Palace of arts'; and perhaps Ivnev himself.

The first group conversion to the Bolshevik side was that of the futurists, who had earlier been on the left wing of the Arts Union. The leader of the group, Mayakovsky, described his decision very simply: '*October*. To accept or not to accept? For me (and for other Moscow futurists) such a question did not exist. My revolution. Went to Smolny.'[27]

In fact Mayakovsky behaved more cautiously than this would suggest. He did go to Smolny, and did not break off relations with Lunacharsky when the Bolsheviks took power.[28] But in November he told the Arts Union that he agreed with Sologub's opinion that 'Lunacharsky is not the people, but only a "gentleman in a jacket" from whom it is necessary to protect art, which is the property of the whole people'; and differed with Sologub only in thinking that the best way to protect the people's property was 'to turn to the government, to welcome the new power'.[29] Instead of voting for Lunacharsky's proposals to the Arts Union he appears to have voted against them on the first occasion, and abstained on the second.

For Mayakovsky the conflict seems to have been between the principle of the complete autonomy of art, which he had warmly advocated before the Bolsheviks took power, and the practical advantages of securing government support for left or 'futurist' art. After publicly associating himself with the Soviet government in Petrograd, but not actually committing himself to its service or joining the Bolshevik Party ('they would have sent me to catch fish in Astrakhan', he remarked in his autobiographical sketch *I myself*), he went to Moscow and spent six months reciting his poems in the Poets' Café and working for the private film company 'Neptune'.[30] It was not until the autumn of 1918 that he returned to Petrograd, 'finally understanding that the struggle for the new art could only be waged within Soviet organizational forms', and began work in the art department (IZO) of Narkompros. In the words of his friend O. M. Brik, he 'saw in the Soviet government the strength that could and must break the power of the "old aesthetic junk" [*esteticheskoe staryo*]'.[31]

Another left artist to join Narkompros at this time was Nikolai Punin, an art critic on the journal *Apollon* (and later second husband of the poetess Anna Akhmatova). Punin belonged to the left, both in the political and the artistic sense. The political views which led him to sympathize with the Bolsheviks were anti-liberal, and indeed in retrospect might be described as proto-fascist. They were expressed in a book published by Punin and Evgeny Poletaev, then head of the Narkompros department of middle schools in Petrograd, under the title of *Protiv tsivilizatsii* [*Against civilization*]. The civilization which Punin and Poletaev attacked was of the effete English and French variety. They admired the 'will to grandeur and power over dry chaos' embodied in contemporary German 'state capitalism', and their book celebrated the virtues of discipline, mass organization, harshness, mechanization and scientific regulation of life. It was these Germanic qualities (as they regarded them) which Punin and Poletaev recommended to Russian Communism, and partly observed in it. *Protiv tsivilizatsii* appeared in 1918 with a preface by Lunacharsky, who appeared puzzled, but on the whole not displeased, at finding 'typical intellectuals' advocating order instead of anarchy.

Punin had first met Lunacharsky towards the end of 1917, when he and the avant-garde composer A. S. Lourie went to the Winter Palace to ask Lunacharsky's permission to stage a play by the futurist poet Khlebnikov in the Hermitage theatre. Punin was greatly struck by the commissars' isolation both from the life of the intelligentsia and from the old bureaucracy, which was still occupying the ministries.* 'There are few people', Punin wrote, 'who knew and felt the loneliness of the Bolsheviks in the first few months'. Lunacharsky greeted Punin and Lourie enthusiastically (Punin's account suggests that before their arrival, time had been hanging heavy on Lunacharsky's hands) and

> willingly and at length talked to us of art, of the tasks of the Communist Party and the position of the intelligentsia. Soon our little project of staging in the Hermitage theatre was left far behind. The question under discussion was of the organization of a new administrative apparatus in all fields of art.[32]

Punin joined the Petrograd collegium of IZO; and Lourie became a member of the music department of Narkompros (MUZO) and later its head.

The dominance of the artistic left, which became characteristic of the arts departments of Narkompros, was particularly marked in IZO [*otdel izobrazitel'nykh iskusstv*]. The Moscow branch was headed by the constructivist V. E. Tatlin. The head of the Petrograd branch and overall head of the department was D. P. Shterenberg.

Lunacharsky had first met Shterenberg and admired his painting in Paris in 1914. When Shterenberg returned from emigration after the October Revolution, Lunacharsky saw him as the ideal head of IZO, both because of his distinction as a painter and his left-wing politics. Shterenberg was a left Bundist, 'undoubtedly devoted to Soviet power', Lunacharsky wrote in 1920, '[who] only refrained from joining the Communist Party because it somehow sickened him to join it in the hour of its victory'.[33] Punin, when he met Shterenberg, was also impressed:

> I went to see him, cautiously began to talk about young Russian art and so-called futurism, and was taken aback when Shterenberg pulled out photographs of his work and began to talk about Picasso and Picabia and the new French masters...[34]

By the end of December 1917, the futurists' adherence to Narkompros was sufficiently well known to provoke cautionary comment in the Soviet press. Zalevsky wrote in *Izvestiya* on 29 December:

* This seems to place the meeting in November and not, as Punin recollected, in December 1917.

> The stronger the new socio-political structure in Russia becomes, the greater will be the number of intellectuals who try to fasten on to the proletariat. An especially abundant stream is expected from the ranks of artists. The proletariat should distinguish its own categories among those ranks...The futurists, penetrating into the proletarian milieu, could bring the putrid poison of the decaying bourgeois organism into the healthy spirit of the proletariat.

The art needed by the proletariat, Zalevsky wrote, was one in which 'beautiful form will be the reflection of rich content'. The proletariat must defend its artistic purity against 'uninvited "friends" '.

The IZO futurists were an aggressive group. Within the Soviet camp their main opponents were the Proletkultists, whose connections with Narkompros were slightly older than their own, and whom they accused of monopolizing art. Shterenberg wrote:

> You shout about proletarian culture. You have taken a monopoly on yourselves. But what have you done for all this time, when you have had every chance to act?...Nothing.
>
> You are an empty place.
>
> And if we, a group of young artists, created schools in which each proletarian could receive technical skill and show his face, we have the right to say we have done something.
>
> If we, destroying old forms of human culture, created new forms appropriate to new content, we have the right to state that we are doing great revolutionary work.
>
> And you?
>
> You are pouring new wine into old, tattered wine-skins.[35]

Outside the Soviet camp, the futurists attacked the artists of 'Mir iskusstva'—in effect the centre group in the artistic world—and the conservative academic artists with equal energy. They equated revolutionary art with revolutionary politics, and traditional art with reactionary politics. 'It is extraordinary', Punin wrote, 'that this division [between the left, 'Mir iskusstva' and the conservative artists] corresponded on the whole and with rare individual exceptions with the political division of the philistine environment of those days...'[36] In the autumn of 1918, Petrograd IZO addressed the following militant statement to traditional artists:

...Now, when the victory of the working class is clear as the day, many of the artists who a year ago were grumbling and maliciously croaking about the swift collapse of Communism have come to apologize. Now they are ready to serve the 'socialist fatherland' on an equal footing with everyone else. Good luck, belated comrades! We will work. But before we start, let us come to an agreement...

Those who come after eight months of sabotage are now shouting about the non-party nature of art, as if art could not be either reactionary or revolutionary. We must speak directly: he who is not with us is against us. Our art is revolutionary, like almost everything now. Let non-revolutionary art perish!...Protect our revolutionary art. Protect yourselves from the old, the dead, the bourgeois. Let only those who break and destroy forms in order to create new ones be with us, because they and we have a single thought—Revolution. Long live the proletariat! Long live the revolution in art![37]

What was Lunacharsky's attitude to futurism? 'I never was a futurist, am not a futurist, and will not be a futurist', he told VTSIK in 1920.[38] Indeed his own taste was for 'high seriousness' in art. Formal experimentation interested him comparatively little. But he was tolerant of it. He liked to explain and understand it. He was sometimes touched by the futurists' enthusiasm. In a preface to a futurist publication of 1918, *Rzhanoe slovo*, he wrote:

The book is written by futurists. People have various attitudes to them, and there is much that can be said in criticism of them. But they are young, and youth is revolutionary...

V. N. Shulgin's comment, though perhaps overemphasizing Lunacharsky's liking for modern art, is worth quoting:

The new which was being born filled [Lunacharsky] with ungovernable joy. But it was another joy than that which was aroused by great works of art of the past. The latter he wanted to preserve, not only because without them it was impossible to build our proletarian culture, but because they had long ago entered his life, become a part of him, and without them life would have been boring, empty, out of joint. In the new that was being born he saw another source of pleasure—it opened up tomorrow, continued life...

There was nothing monolithic in his world-view. He was excited by

Levitan and Tatlin, Picasso and the *peredvizhniki*,* the circus and Tchaikovsky.

'But it is art all the same', Anatoly Vasilevich said, looking at a canvas in whose centre was poked a needle with a piece of material hanging from it.

'Art?'

'Yes, new art. You have to be able to understand it. I understand it.'[39]

In December 1918, Petrograd IZO began publication of the journal *Iskusstvo kommuny*. Among its contributors were Mayakovsky, Shterenberg, Natan Altman, Punin, Mark Chagal (who had organized an art school under the local education department in Vitebsk) and K. S. Malevich (who taught in Chagal's Vitebsk school and later took control of it, ousting Chagal). Its tone was revolutionary, enthusiastic and irreverent. In the first issue Mayakovsky published his poem 'Prikaz po armii iskusstva' ['Order to the army of art']; in the second, the poem 'Radovat'sya rano' ['Too early to rejoice'], containing the famous lines

> And why
> not attack Pushkin
> and other
> generals of the classics?

In the fourth issue, which appeared on 29 December 1918, Lunacharsky felt that it was time to intervene—urged on, as he explained, by colleagues in the government who did not understand why Narkompros should, on the one hand, take great pains to preserve and protect Russia's cultural heritage, and, on the other, allow an official organ of Narkompros 'to describe all artistic work from Adam to Mayakovsky as a heap of rubbish which ought to be destroyed'. 'I confess,' Lunacharsky wrote, 'I am embarrassed.'

Lunacharsky himself thought that Narkompros was capable of defending Pushkin from Mayakovsky's attacks, but he was disturbed by the futurists' intolerance of other artistic schools, and by their monopolistic claims.

Tens of times I have stated that the Commissariat of Education must be impartial in its attitude to separate trends in artistic life. As for questions

* The 'Itinerants'—a group of realist artists who broke away from the Academy of Arts in the 1860s.

of form, the taste of the People's Commissar or of any government representative cannot be taken into account. To offer free development to all artists and artistic groups. Not to allow one trend, armed with either acquired traditional fame or fashionable success, to stifle another...

It would be misfortune indeed if the artistic innovators finally imagined themselves to be a state artistic school, to be official exponents of an art which, although revolutionary, was dictated from above...

The editors of *Iskusstvo kommuny* published Lunacharsky's rebuke with a note that the 'destructive inclination' which he criticized had been present only in Mayakovsky's poems; adding with tongue in cheek that they supposed 'that one of the firmest cultural achievements of European literature in recent times is the liberation of poetic works from literal interpretation'. The journal was prepared to publish works representative of all artistic groups, 'but at the same time, the editors cannot but point out the profound passivity shown by those few genuinely talented leaders of the so-called "rights" and other trends'.

Lunacharsky came in for more criticism when he allowed the futurists to decorate the capitals for revolutionary festivals in 1918, and to design monuments to revolutionary heroes of the past. Lenin disliked the cubist and futurist monuments, thinking them 'straight-out mockery and distortion' of the original notion of celebrating the revolutionary tradition, and held Lunacharsky partly to blame. Lenin was also very irritated when some futurists painted the trees in the Aleksandrovsky gardens outside the Kremlin in bright colours for the Mayday holiday, especially when the paint turned out almost impossible to remove.[40]

Lunacharsky himself thought most of the revolutionary monuments unsuccessful, but he does not seem to have felt indignant about them. In 1924 he recalled with some amusement that the sculptor Merkurov had devised a project for a statue of 'Karl Marx, standing on four elephants'; and that another monument, which was actually constructed in Moscow, represented Marx and Engels together 'in a kind of swimming-pool' and was nicknamed by Muscovites 'the bearded bathers'.[41]

Lunacharsky saw futurism as an offspring of the decay of capitalism, an artistic phenomenon parallel to the political phenomenon of imperialism. Even in 1919 he wondered whether futurism could develop into a proletarian art form:

The dynamism and methods of collective creative work which are so characteristic of futurist art certainly stand in some sort of relationship to what the proletariat may create in the artistic field. If we cannot speak of futurism as a whole as proletarian art, we can talk of individual artists of futurist persuasion as artists close to the proletariat. And we already see that this young art is winning its place in the proletarian artistic ideology ...[42]

A year later he wrote that the futurists had proved 'unacceptable to the masses, although they showed much initiative during popular festivals, good humour and capacity for work of which the "old artists" would have been absolutely incapable'.[43]

But the main reason for Lunacharsky's patronage of the futurists was that they were the first artistic group to offer cooperation to Narkompros, and they sympathized with the revolution. Lunacharsky explained this to foreign delegates to the Comintern in 1922:

In Russian bourgeois society, [the futurists] were to some extent persecuted and considered themselves revolutionaries in artistic technique. It was natural that they soon felt some sympathy for the revolution, and were attracted to it when it extended a hand to them...

It must be confessed that, above all, it was my hand. I extended it not because I admired their experiments... [but] because in the general policy of Narkompros we needed to depend on a serious collective of creative artistic forces. I found it almost exclusively there, among the so-called 'left' artists. Indeed this was repeated in Hungary; it also took place in Germany...

Yes, I extended a hand to the 'leftists', but the proletariat and peasantry did not extend a hand to them...[44]

At the opposite extreme to the futurists stood the intellectuals who cooperated with Narkompros in the protection of art treasures, historical monuments and museums. In November 1917, Lunacharsky had invited this cooperation from the Arts Union. The union refused. But a number of persons outside the union accepted: their cooperation was in almost every case expedient and unrelated to their political beliefs, and it was not accompanied by declarations of loyalty or artistic manifestos. The preservationists were anathema to the futurists, who were shocked that Lunacharsky should pay any attention to them. Brik wrote:

It was not only the 'leftists' who began to work under the direction of the Soviets. There was also A. Benois and Count V. P. Zubov, who saw in the Soviet government a 'firm power' which could preserve objects of cultural value and monuments of the art of the past. The meeting of Mayakovsky with his traditional 'enemies' in the office of the revolutionary People's Commissar threw Mayakovsky into complete bewilderment. His passionate futurist suggestions met a sharp rebuff from the side of the 'preservers of old junk'. And, strange as it may seem, the revolutionary People's Commissar Lunacharsky listened more carefully to Benois' advice on the organization of museums than to the 'arch-revolutionary' attacks of Mayakovsky.[45]

Count Zubov, who had no trace of political sympathy for the Bolsheviks, was one of the first to cooperate with Lunacharsky. 'I personally considered that once I had worked with the Provisional Government, nothing hindered me from working with the Bolsheviks', Zubov wrote in his memoirs. In October 1917, Zubov was in Gatchina, charged by the Provisional Government with the evacuation of its art treasures before the German advance. He almost immediately reached an agreement with Lunacharsky that he should continue the evacuation, now under Bolshevik auspices. Zubov found Lunacharsky kind-hearted but open to manipulation by those who, like himself, had the wit to manipulate. He was concerned not only with the Gatchina treasures, but with the fate of his Institute of the History of Art on Isaakievskaya square, Petrograd. So, when breakfasting with Lunacharsky at the Winter Palace, he took some official paper, wrote an order protecting the building from confiscation, and obtained Lunacharsky's signature.

Zubov had greater difficulty in persuading the professors of the institute not to participate in the intelligentsia's boycott of the Bolsheviks. 'As for myself,' he wrote,

I recognized the new government both in my capacity as Director of the Gatchina Palace, and in my capacity as Rector of the institute. In respect of the latter, I acted on my own initiative. When I called a meeting of professors, among whom there were not only museum workers (who behaved as I did) but other persons, and suggested that we should officially enter into contact with the new power, I met opposition...I managed to obtain my colleague's agreement that the institute would remain neutral. However, I did not take any notice of this platonic resolution, and continued to act as sole representative of the institute in negotiations with the Commissariat of Education...[46]

Aleksandr Nikolaevich Benois, who was also on good personal terms with Lunacharsky and worked with him on the building up of the Hermitage art collection, remained hostile to the politics of the Bolshevik government. He opposed the nationalization of private art collections, and reproached his friend I. E. Grabar, director of the Tretyakov gallery in Moscow, for condoning it. 'I cannot believe that you took an active part in taking Princess Meshcherskaya's Botticelli away from her', he wrote to Grabar. 'Or have you been infected with the general psychosis which has grown out of the ruins of war and utter turmoil?'[47]

Grabar cooperated with I. V. Kimmel and G. S. Yatmanov, delegates from the collegium of the Petrograd Narkompros, in setting up a museum department of Narkompros in Moscow early in 1918. But later in the year he clashed with P. P. Malinovsky's Commission for the Protection of Artistic and Ancient Monuments over the commission's decision to abolish the office of director in all museums and create an 'artistic soviet' in its place.[48] Grabar resisted, and succeeded in keeping the Tretyakov gallery under his effective control. In 1922, perhaps remembering Benois's reproaches, Grabar used his position to return property confiscated from private collectors and held in the Tretyakov gallery to its former owners.[49]

For Lunacharsky, the central figure of the Russian intelligentsia whose cooperation was desirable above all others was Maxim Gorky. Lunacharsky's relationship with Gorky between 1917 and 1921 was a paradigm of his relationship with the old intelligentsia—half lover and half commissar. Gorky disapproved of the October Revolution, and for some months held aloof from the Bolsheviks and Narkompros. But in April 1918 he was observed to be a frequent visitor at Lunacharsky's office in the Winter Palace, and in May he made his first formal offer of cooperation with Narkompros in its dealings with the scientific world.[50] In September, after the attack on Lenin's life, Lunacharsky announced to the press that Gorky intended to enter into close cooperation with the Soviet government, and that an agreement had been signed by himself and Gorky on the establishment of a publishing house 'Vsemirnaya literatura' ['World literature'], which Gorky was to organize as an autonomous department of Narkompros. The announcement appeared in *Izvestiya* on 10 September 1918.

From the moment when Gorky entered into cooperation with the Soviet government, he occupied a liaison position between the Bolsheviks and the intelligentsia, as Lunacharsky did, and became a patron and protector of the intelligentsia and a channel for the expression of its grievances. But where Lunacharsky saw his first loyalty to the Bolsheviks and to the Soviet government, Gorky's first loyalty went to the intelligentsia. This fine distinction between Lunacharsky's position and Gorky's was not always recognized. Lunacharsky was offended when, at a meeting in Gorky's flat in 1918, it was suggested that members of the intelligentsia would agree to work for him personally but not for his colleagues. This would have made him, he thought, 'a peculiar kind of hard skin or, more exactly, a tortoiseshell, behind which art was intending to sit out the unpleasantness threatened by the "barbarous revolution" '.[51] On another occasion, Lunacharsky was congratulated on being a true *intelligent*—that is, the opposite of a commissar—and astonished the company by rising 'without his usual smile' to declaim:

> No, I am not with you. You call me yours
> In vain and hypocritically.*[52]

In their second period of estrangement, which followed Gorky's departure from Russia in the early '20s, Lunacharsky was critical of Gorky's attitude to the intelligentsia. Gorky, he wrote, 'turned out completely in the camp of the intelligentsia,. . .siding with it in its grumbling, lack of faith and terror at the prospect of the destruction of valuable things under the blows of the Revolution'.[53] In his play

* *Net, ya ne s vami. Svoim naprasno*
I litsemerno menya zovyote.

Osvobozhdennyi Don-Kikhot [*Don Quixote liberated*], written in 1922, Lunacharsky depicted a character drawn partly from the writers Korolenko and Romain Rolland but largely from Gorky in his relations with Lunacharsky and Lenin between 1917 and 1921.[54] Gorky, Lunacharsky and Lenin are presented in the characters of Don Quixote, Don Balthazar and Don Rodrigo. Don Balthazar speaks these parting words to Don Quixote:

If we had not broken the plots in the rear, we would have led our army to ruin. Ah, Don Quixote! I do not wish to aggravate your guilt, but here you played your fatal role. I will not hide the fact that it came into stern Rodrigo's head to bring down the threatening hand of the law on you, as a lesson to all the soft-hearted people who thrust themselves and their philanthropy into life, which is stern and complicated and full of responsibility...

I restrained him from that...

Yet Lunacharsky—'our soft-hearted Anatoly', as *Novaya zhizn'* had called him—was himself a philanthropist. For the poet Vyacheslav Ivanov, he suggested that the collegium of Narkompros finance a trip abroad on grounds of ill-health; and later that Narkompros should send him to the Northern Caucasus to work with local cultural authorities, at the same time petitioning the Commissariat of Health to allocate places in a sanatorium for the sick members of Ivanov's family and asking MUZO to give paid work to his musician daughter. For Konstantin Balmont, Lunacharsky urged Vorovsky, then head of Gosizdat, to publish a book of his poems and pay him in advance ('It seems to me that Balmont, who has written a series of fine works, has at least deserved to have a crust of bread for his child'); and he suggested to the collegium that Balmont and the musician S. Kusevitsky should be commissioned by Narkompros to work abroad, keeping their salaries. When Kusevitsky's exit visa was held up by the Special Department of the Cheka, the collegium empowered Lunacharsky (at Lunacharsky's request) to negotiate with the Cheka on Kusevitsky's behalf. For Stanislavsky, founder of the Moscow Arts theatre, Lunacharsky wrote to Lenin appealing against an order evicting Stanislavsky from his flat. For Nemirovich-Danchenko, joint head with Stanislavsky of the Moscow Arts theatre, Lunacharsky suggested a trip abroad to finish his book *Narodnye tribuny i mucheniki revolyutsii* [*People's tribunes and martyrs of the revolution*]; and for the Petrograd publishing house 'Alkonost'* he urged Gosizdat to facilitate printing of the series *Zapiski mechtatelei* [*Dreamers' notes*].

For Count Zubov, Lunacharsky had the Petrograd Institute of the History of Art removed from the jurisdiction of the unsympathetic Petrograd education department of Narkompros. He even raised the possibility of government subsidy for Ivanov-Razumnik's Free Philosophical Academy [Volfila]—the last surviving free-thought society, whose only Party member was the anarchist Communist Victor Serge—on condition that the name was changed from 'academy' to 'society'.[55] No other member of the collegium of Narkompros came near to approaching Lunacharsky's record as a defender of impoverished artists and unhappy intellectuals. He might criticize the intelligentsia as a group, but he was completely vulnerable to their individual appeals for help. His generosity assumed an anecdotal quality; and he wrote so many letters of recommendation that their currency was quickly devalued in the eyes of other members of the Soviet government, and even those of the recipients.[56]

'Vsemirnaya literatura' was established by agreement between Gorky and Lunacharsky, signed on 4 September 1918, for the purposes of publishing translations of the classical works of European literature. It inherited the premises and many of the staff of the journal *Novaya zhizn'*, which had been closed down in July 1918. Gorky almost certainly intended 'Vsemirnaya literatura' to provide a refuge for the Petrograd literary intelligentsia, and this in practice is what it did. (Victor Serge, who was offered employment there, refused because 'the only people I met there were ageing or embittered intellectuals trying to escape from the present'.[57]) The office of 'Vsemirnaya literatura' was hung with paintings by Levitan, Benois, Kustodiev, Sudeikin, Boris Grigoryev and others from the collection of Z. I. Grzhebin (who worked for 'Vsemirnaya literatura' as well as running an independent publishing house), and tea was drunk from eighteenth-century china. Up to 350 highly qualified

* 'Alkonost' was organized by S. M. Alyansky, with the support of the poet A. Blok in 1918, and published the first edition of Blok's *Dvenadtsat'* [*The twelve*].

translators worked for 'Vsemirnaya literatura' in its heyday: they included Academicians Oldenburg, Krachkovsky, Alekseev and Vladimirtsev, translating from the Indian, Arabic, Chinese and Mongol; Blok, working in the German section; N. Gumilev and A. Levinson in the French; Akim Volynsky in the Italian; Chukovsky and Zamyatin in the Anglo-American; and Professor Batyushkov, whom Lunacharsky had dismissed from the directorship of Petrograd state theatres, advising on techniques of translation.[58]

In April 1919, Gorky concluded an agreement with Lunacharsky on the opening of a department of twentieth-century Russian literature under 'Vsemirnaya literatura'; but plans for further development were hindered by opposition from Gosizdat, paper shortage and difficulties with printing, partly caused by lack of cooperation from the Petrograd Council of the National Economy. In three years, 'Vsemirnaya literatura' issued only fifty-nine titles.[59]

The purpose of providing employment for writers and men of letters was served not only by 'Vsemirnaya literatura' but by the arts departments of Narkompros, notably its theatrical department (TEO), which employed Balmont, Bryusov, Khodasevich, Pasternak, Baltrushaitis, Georgy Chulkov, Ivan Novikov, V. Volkenshtein and Vyacheslav Ivanov among others. However, this did not solve the problem of publishing the writers' work.

Private book publishing was not formally restricted either by the 1918 restriction on freedom of the press or by the establishment of the State Publishing House (Gosizdat) in May 1919. The decree on Gosizdat put private publishers under its control and provided that they should submit manuscripts for its approval before publication. But because of Gosizdat's inefficiency, which was notorious, and the laxness of Vesenkha's typographical department, this regulation was not strictly observed: no author or publisher was prosecuted for illegal publication in the Civil War years. In 1920 there were instances of Gosizdat forbidding the publication of works submitted by private publishers, but 'this policy was mainly dictated by the typographical and paper crises, which had reached an extreme point'.[60]

The effective restrictions on private publishing were the paper shortage and the mal- or non-functioning of the printing presses, and the municipalization of the book trade, which was first introduced by the Moscow Soviet in October 1918. From April 1919, by Sovnarkom decree, free sale of new books ceased; and until the autumn of 1921 all books and other printed matter were distributed free of charge by Tsentropechat and its local organs.[61]

Lunacharsky believed that it was Narkompros' responsibility to arrange for the publication of works of all literary schools, using all available publishing resources. In 1918 he wrote in a preface to the futurist *Rzhanoe slovo* (published on one of the state printing presses in Petrograd):

> Now the workers' and peasants' state must take on itself to an ever-increasing extent the publication of literary works by all available means—directly through the state publishing house, or through Soviet publishers, or by subsidy [to private publishers].
>
> And of course the state must make it a rule to give the mass reader access to all that is new and fresh. It is better to make a mistake and offer the people something which is not now capable of arousing their sympathy than to leave a work which is rich with future possibilities hidden, because it is not to somebody's taste...
>
> Let the worker hear and evaluate everything, the old and the new. We will not impose anything on him; we will show him everything.

These were admirable sentiments, but very far from the reality of the Civil War years. A decree on state publishing, framed by the State Education Commission in November 1917 and subsequently issued by VTSIK, instructed Narkompros to undertake 'broad publishing activity' through its literary-publishing department in consultation with its other departments and invited experts. But the creation of a literary-publishing department proved extremely difficult. The nationalized printing presses were under the control of Vesenkha and not Narkompros. The literary experts invited by Narkompros were unwilling to cooperate. In May 1918 Lebedev-Polyansky called a preliminary meeting of experts, but 'the majority of those invited not only did not appear, but did not answer the invitation'. Of those who came (the writer Veresaev, Bryusov, Grabar, Sakulin, Gershenzon, the publisher Sytin and the Tolstoyan Chertkov among them), a number opposed Narkompros' policy of nationalizing the Russian classics.[62] No agreement with the writers was reached, and the literary-publishing department remained a department on paper rather than in fact. The attempt to attract the writers, Lunacharsky explained, failed because 'after a few discussions it became clear to me that a constituent-democratic tendency was emerging: we will organize, they said, and you give us part of the power and the money'.[63]

When, early in 1919, Narkompros made a second attempt to organize a literary department, Lunacharsky was at once accused of trying to turn the old anti-Soviet intelligentsia into a new bureaucracy, and of giving Gorky, Andrei Bely and Georgy Chulkov the power to suppress proletarian culture. The attack, by N. Ustinov, appeared in *Izvestiya* of 2 February. On 6 February, Lunacharsky published a sharp reply. Despite the fact that 'only educated people can educate', he wrote, Narkompros had consistently resisted pressure from its non-party specialists to put them in charge of departments. He was not intending to put 'highly-respected comrade Gorky' in charge of literature, still less of proletarian literature.

> The business is very simple. Private publishers cannot exist now without subsidy; [they receive] paper only with our permission.
>
> For writers, this is the end. Surely comrade Ustinov does not think that we can simply stop all literature... [and] that in Russian literature—which Russian society lived on until the revolution—there was nothing valuable and nothing promising. We need to take care of it, and we need to act so that even under the paper and typographical shortages those works which are most valuable from the purely artistic point of view find an outlet.
>
> For this it is necessary to create a special literary department from among the writers themselves...At the head of the literary department, I wished to see M. Gorky.

Shortly after this exchange, discussion began on the merging of Narkompros' literary-publishing department with the publishing departments of VTSIK and the Petrograd and Moscow Soviets to form a central state publishing house, Gosizdat. This was formally created by Sovnarkom decree on 14 May 1919. The first editorial collegium of Gosizdat consisted of V. V. Vorovsky (head of Gosizdat), Bukharin, Pokrovsky, V. I. Nevsky and Skvortsov-

Stepanov.[64] Gosizdat remained a part of Narkompros, but was independently organized and financed.

Lunacharsky hoped that the establishment of Gosizdat would solve the writers' problems and render a literary department of Narkompros unnecessary. By the end of the year he had changed his mind. Gosizdat did not give high priority to literary publication, by no means always followed Narkompros' recommendations to it, and for the first two years of its life was in a state of chronic organizational confusion. This last point was made in *Pravda* on 9 November 1919 by 'Communist-worker', who claimed that Gosizdat's failure to produce their works had driven such leading government figures as L. B. Kamenev and Lunacharsky to publish with the private 'adventurist' publisher Z. I. Grzhebin.* In the midst of the acrimonious correspondence that followed between Vorovsky, Gorky and Grzhebin, and the editors of *Pravda*, Narkompros after prolonged gestation gave birth to a mouse—the literary department.

LITO, which was formally constituted by Narkompros on 11 December, was intended to act as a liaison between the government and the literary world, give support to literary groups, establish norms of payment to writers for publication of their works, and cooperate with Gosizdat in allocating paper and typographical resources for the publication of artistic literature.[65] The president of LITO was Lunacharsky, deputy president the poet Valery Bryusov, members A. Serafimovich, Vyacheslav Ivanov, M. Gorky, A. Blok, Yu. Baltrushaitis and either M. Gerasimov or V. Kirillov, representing Proletkult. The candidate members were O. Brik, P. N. Sakulin, Yu. Aikhenvald, M. O. Gershenzon and I. Rukavishnikov.

Controversy now hinged on the membership of the LITO collegium. Was it representative of the literary world? Was it representative of the literary world in a sense acceptable to a proletarian government? Both Proletkult and the futurists felt themselves to be under-represented. Many Communists felt that the

* Lunacharsky's work published by Grzhebin was *Velikii perevorot* (1919), a first instalment of his political memoirs which Grzhebin apparently published without Lunacharsky's permission. The book had had something of a *succès de scandale*, so that it was particularly embarrassing to Lunacharsky to have it cited in this context.

symbolist poets in particular, and the non-Party literary intelligentsia in general, were grossly over-represented. Krupskaya, who was not present at the meeting establishing LITO, was dissatisfied both with the notion of a 'literary department' and with its present membership. Interestingly enough, in a memorandum addressed to the collegium of Narkompros she presented a more sophisticated version of Ustinov's argument that the creation of such a department put dangerously monopolistic powers into the hands of a literary clique which was, at best, neutral in its attitude to the Soviet government and proletarian literature.

The form of organization suggested by the writers [Krupskaya wrote], is hardly appropriate from the point of view of the broad masses as readers. It is inappropriate because it gives great power into the hands of a group of people, power to strengthen their own literary position... That would be permissible if the nine men [appointed to the LITO collegium] were non-controversial—if in respect of talent, literary affiliation and conscientious attitude to novice writers the nine were beyond doubt.

But where at the moment will you find a committee of nine which is not just nominal but capable of working? Where are those generally-recognized names?

Gorky? Perhaps Serafimovich? Perhaps they are proletarian writers? But who can determine that, and who can select the nine?

The mass reader might be able to determine it. He has made his attitude to Gorky quite clear, but what about the rest?...Only the reader can determine the significance of a writer. That is how it must be...

The new life will probably give birth to new writers, a new and vitally infectious trend in literature. And the nine will only involuntarily put brakes on that new literary trend. Organization is necessary, so let there be a [collegium of] nine, but let them have fewer powers. They must not take unions, associations, clubs and literary circles under their monopolistic control. All these organizations must have the right to find their own identity, the right to choose whatever literary trend they like. It is also necessary to think how to give the broad masses the chance to show their attitude to proposed literary works before the size of the edition is determined. And we need other means to decide the minimum standard of literary achievement which would give each writer the right to publish his works, even if only in an edition of 1,000...[66]

Krupskaya's fears turned out to be exaggerated, at least in the short term. It was one of the many occasions when Communists, in honest indignation, sounded a false alarm about threatened monopoly in the arts. Perhaps, as in the story of the boy who cried 'Wolf!', people grew tired of responding to the alarm, and so ten years later let the real monopolists in indifferently and without protest.* LITO, at any rate, turned out to be not a monopolist but a mouse—a place for the employment of literary intellectuals, capable of distributing small benefits among the writers it approved (as, for example, a grant for medical treatment to Andrei Bely from 'the special fund at the disposal of the commissar, A. V. Lunacharsky')[67] but not powerful enough to force its views on Gosizdat or even to compete against the strident voices of Proletkult and the futurists in the world outside Narkompros.

The result of Narkompros' first contacts with the artistic and literary world was not, in the normal sense, the establishment of an administration, but of a framework of cooperation with disparate and mutually intolerant groups. Lunacharsky's policy was one of open-handed goodwill, subject only to the qualification that he had little to offer except employment, arbitration and small bonuses to individuals in particular need. His policy was to open channels of communication with the literary and artistic intelligentsia, to encourage equally all groups which were sympathetic or accommodating in their attitude to the Soviet government, and to outmanœuvre those which showed it blatant hostility.

The organizational structure devised for this purpose was administratively and economically irrational to a high degree. It was wasteful of manpower and resources at a time when both were scarce.

But the most common objection to Narkompros' organization in the arts was not to its irrationality but (*pace* Krupskaya) to its impartiality, and came not from outside the artistic world but within. Almost every literary and artistic group regarded itself as having overriding and even exclusive claims on Narkompros'

* At the end of the '20s the associations of proletarian writers (RAPP), artists and musicians established a three-year monopoly in the arts before being dissolved by Stalin in 1932.

goodwill. The most aggressive claimants, as will be seen in the second part of this chapter, were Communist members of the artistic left, and their main battleground was the theatre.

The first calls for a tendentious administration of the arts, an end to the weak-kneed policy of cooperation and tolerance, came not from the Party or the government but from the artists themselves.

THE THEATRE

The two organizational issues confronting Narkompros in the theatrical field were administration of the state theatres and the status of private theatres. In regard to the state theatres, the question Narkompros had to decide was whether to give the companies administrative and artistic autonomy. This raised the second question of whether their artistic traditions were worth preserving, as Narkompros believed, or should be sacrificed to the revolutionary experimenters of the theatrical left: to give the state theatres autonomy was in effect to protect them against intrusion by the theatrical avant-garde as well as by the government. In regard to private theatres, the issue was whether they should be nationalized, municipalized or allowed to remain under private ownership. The theatrical left supported nationalization—again in the hope that, being nationalized, the theatres would be more accessible to avant-garde penetration.

Lunacharsky was not unsympathetic to the artistic revolutionaries, so long as their experiments were not conducted at the sacrifice of other artistic groups. He believed that the state theatres had a tradition worth preserving and, in order to assure its continuation, created a special department of state theatres separate from the Narkompros theatre department, TEO. Lunacharsky himself was in charge of the department of state theatres in Petrograd in 1918, and his deputy in Moscow was Elena Malinovskaya.

This arrangement was obviously unsatisfactory to the Moscow head of TEO, Olga Kameneva. In June 1918, she suggested to the State Education Commission—Lunacharsky being absent—that the state theatres were thus encouraged in their 'tendency to isolate themselves from the democracy', and that they should be transferred to the democratic jurisdiction of TEO. The commission refused to do this without Lunacharsky's approval.[68]

One of Lunacharsky's great personal successes was to win the confidence of the grand old men of the Moscow theatre—Stanislavsky and Nemirovich-Danchenko, of the Moscow Arts, and Yuzhin-Sumbatov of the Maly theatre. To Kameneva and the theatrical left, this association of Lunacharsky and the old theatrical establishment was highly suspect: it seemed to them that the traditional theatres were in fact using Lunacharsky as a 'tortoise-shell' to shield them from the barbarous revolution, both in the political and artistic sense. Certainly the confidence of the traditional theatres was given to Lunacharsky personally rather than to the government he represented. During the nationalization debates of 1919, Yuzhin—a public opponent of nationalization—wrote privately to Lunacharsky that if the private theatres must be nationalized, 'above all, *only you* must keep the highest government authority' in theatrical affairs.[69] Stanislavsky, an accomplished flatterer of the powerful, had the same thought:

> To understand art means to feel it.
>
> This capacity is by no means given to all.
>
> To the great good fortune of the Russian theatre, it is possessed by our leader, Anatoly Vasilevich Lunacharsky.
>
> Anatoly Vasilevich understands...that it is necessary to give artists and the old art time in which to be reborn and create new forms, to penetrate deeply into the essence of great events...
>
> Finally, our leader understands that the plane of our art is the aesthetic plane; and it is impossible with impunity to transfer art into the other plane of politics or practical life, which is alien to it by nature, exactly as it is impossible to transfer politics into the plane of pure aesthetics...[70]

Before the October Revolution A. I. Yuzhin (Prince Sumbatov), director of the Maly state theatre in Moscow, had begun to prepare a project for the autonomous self-administration of the Maly theatre. The Maly, under his guidance, did not join the boycott of the Bolsheviks or go on strike because, 'as an institution serving the eternal tasks of public enlightenment', its activity 'must continue irrespective of political upheavals and changes of state power'.[71]

He was nevertheless suspicious of the Bolsheviks and expected them to reject his project for the autonomy of the Maly theatre.

Early in 1918 Yuzhin, armed with his project, met Lunacharsky for the first time. He behaved, Lunacharsky recalled affectionately,

> with all his superficial cunning...One felt in him a genuine Oriental;* he was improbably cautious, as if treading on ice, suspecting an underhand trick in almost every paragraph. He kept thinking that he was going to be tricked into some sort of condition which he himself would sign, and which must then be sacredly observed, but which would destroy the theatre and permit it to be put to some use that was base—that is, anti-artistic,—in Yuzhin's eyes.[72]

Lunacharsky was prepared to give a measure of autonomy to the state theatres. In Petrograd his strong-arm man, Bakrylov, was soon removed from the charge of the state theatres and replaced by a moderate autonomist, I. V. Ekskuzovich of the Mariinsky theatre. Lunacharsky and Ekskuzovich were responsible for the drafting of the 'Statutes of the autonomous state theatres' of March 1918, according to which the state undertook to finance the theatres, retaining some rights of financial control, and entrusted their administration and artistic direction to a 'Soviet of state theatres' consisting of representatives of the artists, technical workers of the theatres, Narkompros and invited specialists from the Narkompros arts departments. In token of the continuing hostility of the state theatre companies to the government, a clause was included stating that the autonomous collectives of the state theatres stand 'outside politics'. Yuzhin's project for the administration of the Maly theatre was accepted by Lunacharsky, with only slight amendment, in May.[73]

Nationalization of the private theatres was urged by the theatrical activists of Proletkult, led by Kerzhentsev. It was not the immediate policy of the central government. In 1919 the short-lived revolutionary government of the Hungarian Soviet Republic nationalized the theatres the day after taking power. Lenin thought this odd, and asked a Hungarian Comintern delegate whether they had no more important business to attend to.[74] Kameneva, in October 1918,

* Yuzhin was born in Tiflis.

disclaimed any intention to nationalize the private theatres in the immediate future: TEO, she said,

is against hasty nationalization, and struggles against such tendencies in the [local] Soviets. This is not because private ownership is in principle the best form of theatrical organization, but because the theatre is a complicated organism—it may either be destroyed, if a Soviet representative who does not understand theatrical affairs is put at the head of an enterprise, or crippled, if it is taken over by some actor showing Soviet colours and conducting business correctly in the commercial sense, but in the cultural and educational sense giving nothing.[75]

In spite of this attitude at the centre, nationalization—or, more exactly, municipalization—was widely practised in 1918. The initiative was purely local: municipalization was the spontaneous policy of Soviets all over the country. It took place, Kameneva commented, 'partly against the wishes of the centre'. It has been suggested that, because of economic conditions of the time, municipalization was often favoured by local theatrical companies and entrepreneurs. The Leningrad historian Trabsky writes:

For the majority this was not at all a theoretical issue, but a vital and essential question connected with the need to conclude a contract for the coming season. To be employed by the Soviets was more reliable and, for the entrepreneur, more profitable. Letters poured into Narkompros demanding an answer to the question—'What is happening about nationalization?'[76]

Thus Narkompros was pushed into nationalization partly against its will, and against an outcry from leading members of the Moscow theatres, whose objection to the principle was not softened by any prospect of material advantage. In June 1919, at a meeting held to discuss the nationalization project, only Yu. Slavinsky (president of Rabis, the union of art workers) spoke in favour of nationalization because, he said, 'it has already been carried out by local Soviets in various distorted forms'. Yuzhin, in 'a pathetic speech', as *Izvestiya* reported on 17 June 1919, 'demanded absolute freedom for the theatre' and held this to be incompatible with wholesale nationalization of private theatres. Another speaker 'permitted himself to make coarse and incorrect attacks against TEO of Narkompros and its leaders', after which the Communists present left in protest.

In July Yuzhin, Stanislavsky, Nemirovich-Danchenko, Tairov of the Kamerny theatre and E. M. Novomirsky of the Bolshoi issued a statement on behalf of the state theatres and the associated Kamerny and Moscow Arts theatres claiming that nationalization was both impracticable and 'irreconcilable with the principle of freedom of creative work'.[77]

Within the government, support for nationalization came from A. V. Galkin and S. I. Kanatchikov of Maly Sovnarkom.* Their campaign for nationalization was, at the same time, a campaign for 'proletarianization' of the theatres and reversal of Lunacharsky's policy towards the state theatres and theatrical tradition. In 1919 Galkin called for an end to subsidization of the state theatres in their present form, saying that 'it would be better to use the stage of the Bolshoi theatre for agitation and propaganda'.[78] Galkin and Kanatchikov proposed a resolution to Maly Sovnarkom obliging Moscow theatres to include plays 'of revolutionary content' in their repertoire.[79] On both these occasions, Lenin intervened in support of the traditional theatres and the proposals were rejected. A project for the nationalization of the theatres was twice accepted by Maly Sovnarkom in 1919 and twice rejected by Bolshoi Sovnarkom.[80] Again, the rejection of the projects was initiated by Lenin. They had originally been drafted by TEO, under Kameneva.

In July, Kameneva left TEO, with evident reluctance, and went to work in the cultural section of MONO. At her farewell party the symbolist Vyacheslav Ivanov recited a poem dedicated to her. Her successor at TEO was Lunacharsky.[81]

The spontaneous movement of municipalization, together with political pressure from the left, had created a situation in which some reorganization of theatrical administration was inevitable. It was Lunacharsky's task to formulate it in terms which would be acceptable to the theatrical leaders as well as the politicians, and at the same time do as little as possible to change the *status quo*.

At the beginning of August, Lunacharsky called a meeting to

* Maly Sovnarkom—an office of (Bolshoi) Sovnarkom whose function was to prepare material and projects for Sovnarkom's consideration.

announce his project for 'concentration of theatrical affairs' and the creation of a central organ of theatrical administration, Tsentroteatr. According to his project, as reported in *Izvestiya* of 3 August 1919, theatrical property (buildings and inventory) was to become the property of the state, to be put at the disposal of theatre companies and associations on conditions to be determined by Tsentroteatr. Theatres were to submit financial estimates and would be financed in various categories by the state; but 'theatres able to exist on their own resources, and not regarded as harmful, may be left completely outside the attention of the state'. Theatres under reliable direction, 'whose cultural value is recognized as incontrovertible' would be 'recognized as autonomous', although Tsentroteatr reserved the right to make certain demands on them in respect of repertoire and 'in the direction of bringing the theatre closer to the popular masses [and] to the socialist ideal'. Private theatres would have the use of theatrical property, on condition that their administrative boards included representatives of Tsentroteatr or the local education department; but they would not be regarded as possessing autonomy. Tsentroteatr, being anxious to encourage the growth of independent artistic activity, would progressively transfer 'all theatres whose artistic collective is sufficiently strong' to the category of autonomous theatres.

There was to be no change in the administration of the state theatres, Lunacharsky's project continued, but both TEO and the department of state theatres were to be subordinate to Tsentroteatr and would function as its technical apparatus. Tsentroteatr's jurisdiction included state, municipal and private theatres. Its president would be the People's Commissar of Education (Lunacharsky), and the deputy president would be appointed by Narkompros. The collegium of Tsentroteatr would have 7 members, 4 of them appointed by Narkompros and 3 by the union of art-workers.

The first notable feature of Lunacharsky's project was that it maintained the *status quo* in the administration of the state theatres—neither diminishing their autonomy nor removing the protective barrier of the department of state theatres—and gave other theatres the chance to achieve the same privileged status and administrative autonomy. The second feature of the project was that it put

Tsentroteatr, as well as TEO and in effect the department of state theatres, under Lunacharsky's personal control, and that the composition of the Tsentroteatr collegium was such as to exclude persons not acceptable to Narkompros or the art-workers' union. The third feature was that private entrepreneurship in the theatre was not excluded, and the regulations imposed on the private theatres were undoubtedly less burdensome than the *ad hoc* practices of many local Soviets.

The project apparently made such a favourable impression on the theatrical world that Lunacharsky almost immediately found it necessary to correct the illusion that he was offering autonomy plus subsidy to one and all. Apart from the state theatres and the Moscow Arts theatre, he thought it probable that in fact only two Moscow theatres would initially qualify for autonomous status, he wrote in *Izvestiya* on 7 August.

On 26 August, Sovnarkom passed Lunacharsky's project with only one substantial amendment: the collegium of Tsentroteatr was to have 10 members instead of 7, of whom 7 were to be appointed by Narkompros and 3 by VTSSPS. This was a blow to Rabis, which had supported Lunacharsky in introducing the project, but had no particular significance for Narkompros. The Sovnarkom decree also gave Moscow and Petrograd Soviets the right to send voting representatives to Tsentroteatr. The Sovnarkom decree, under the title of 'Decree on the unification of theatrical affairs', was published in *Izvestiya* on 9 September.

The acceptance of Lunacharsky's project was a victory for him and the state theatres, and a great disappointment to the theatrical left. K. N. Malinin, who had defended the state theatres against Kerzhentsev's attacks at the Proletkult conference of September 1918, was appointed deputy president of Tsentroteatr. The first Narkompros appointees were D. I. Leshchenko (of the original Petrograd collegium of Narkompros), P. M. Kerzhentsev, Vyacheslav Ivanov, I. V. Ekskuzovich (director of state theatres in Petrograd), Elena Malinovskaya (head of the department of state theatres in Moscow), the musician L. L. Obolensky and A. I. Yuzhin—Nemirovich-Danchenko having the right to deputize for Ekskuzovich when the latter was in Petrograd.[82] This representation overwhelmingly favoured the state theatres. There was only one representative of the theatrical left (Kerzhentsev of Proletkult), no futurist and no representative of the private theatres. The status of the Moscow Arts theatre, represented by Nemirovich-Danchenko, was effectively that of a state theatre.

In December 1919, in token of their role as repositories and teachers of theatrical art invulnerable to revolutionary attack, the state theatres and the Moscow Arts theatre were given the title of 'academic' theatres.[83]

The battle over ideology was a constant accompaniment to the struggle over organizational forms, and in the winter of 1919–20 Lunacharsky was under persistent attack from the left for his defence of the traditional theatre and (as his opponents claimed) neglect of the revolutionary and experimental theatre. His chief opponents were P. M. Kerzhentsev and Bukharin.

Kerzhentsev saw Lunacharsky as in sinister alliance with the theatrical reactionaries Yuzhin (of the Maly theatre) and Tairov (of the Kamerny theatre). He believed that proletarian theatre would be created through rejection of the past, and not—as Lunacharsky thought—through mastery and development of traditional forms. The bourgeois theatres should be kept only as museums, Kerzhentsev wrote, 'still protecting the monuments of the past for us and keeping them from dust and decomposition—but nobody would claim that art is created in the quiet of museums'.[84] There could be no compromise with the ideological enemy in the theatre because 'the present is not a period of peaceful construction in any field, including the theatre, but a period of cruel struggle, of bloody struggle'.[85]

Lunacharsky, replying to Kerzhentsev 'in the name of the proletariat', argued that the proletariat actually preferred the classical theatre to the 'revolutionary'. This fact, he added, was more important than the ideas of 'any intellectual publicist, even if he is a member of the Party'.

And imagine, comrade Kerzhentsev, I have not only seen how bored the proletariat was at the production of a few 'revolutionary' plays, but have even read the statement of sailors and workers asking that these revolutionary spectacles be discontinued and replaced by performances of Gogol and Ostrovsky!*[86]

Lunacharsky further rebuked Kerzhentsev for his behaviour at a recent conference on the worker–peasant theatre when, in defiance of the Party line on the relations of proletariat and peasantry, he had done his best to create antagonism between proletarian and peasant playwrights.

The first of Bukharin's attacks appeared in *Pravda*, of which he was editor, on 16 October 1919. He criticized 'the production of pure tedium' at state expense in the traditional theatres, and reproached Narkompros for its neglect of Proletkult, 'which cannot get a *decent theatrical building* for the production of a militant play'.

In the days of this greatest of revolutions, to enjoy *The cherry orchard* (not even *The cherry factory*) is the most supernatural stupidity. It is just *barbarianism*, which becomes simply sad and ridiculous. The working-class public, which comes to such plays and yawns from boredom,... steels itself to 'understand' all the 'value' of these nice things—that is, to adapt his militant psychology to the psychology of our grandmothers. The remnants of slavish respect for aristocratic culture are deepened by the preaching of some of our ideologists who support this corruption of the proletariat.

The title of Bukharin's article was, characteristically, 'Struggle with the whites in the theatre (a business proposition)'. It was prompted by a Proletkult studio production of the play *Krasnaya pravda* [*Red truth*], written by a wounded Red Army commander and submitted to a competition for the best original melodrama organized by Gorky and Lunacharsky. Bukharin admitted that the play was crude (although he put the word in inverted commas), but said that it suited the militant psychology of Red Army soldiers: 'It will make them *tremble* with excitement, and it is useful. And that is all that art can achieve.'

Bukharin struck again in *Pravda* on 16 December. The occasion for his second article was a production of the play *Mstitel'* [*Avenger*], adapted by the Proletkultist V. F. Pletnev from a story by Paul

* The 'statement', mentioned elsewhere by Lunacharsky, came from the Kronstadt sailors.

Claudel on the last days of the Paris Commune. It was put on by the Proletkult theatre in a hall accommodating 300–400 people. Why, Bukharin asked, was it not playing to audiences of thousands? 'Because the leaders of our theatres are in the captivity of bourgeois ideologists.' Writing of the traditional theatres, Bukharin allowed that 'flowers may grow even on a corpse. But these are not the flowers which the proletariat needs.' The audience reaction to *Mstitel'*, according to Bukharin, had been overwhelming. Everyone had participated in a collective emotional experience:

> Comrades came up to me one after the other, and each said in the same words: 'I am shaking from head to foot'...
>
> We must smash the old theatre. The person who does not understand that understands nothing.

Lunacharsky was happy enough for Bukharin to praise proletarian melodrama (*Mstitel'*) and proletarian agitational drama (*Krasnaya pravda*), for on principle he too supported these genres. But he was infuriated that Bukharin, a prominent politician, should throw his weight against the traditional theatres in a way that was perhaps 'suitable for a journalist, but scarcely appropriate from the state point of view'.[87]

Lunacharsky wrote a long reply to Bukharin's second article, sending copies of it to government and Party leaders.[88] He was an older supporter of proletarian culture, he wrote, than Bukharin, and he was not prepared to see its future compromised by exaggeration of its present achievements. Proletarian plays were not popular with a broad public, nor even with a proletarian public; and for the time being their proper setting was the studio and the small theatre.

> To put on *Mstitel'* in front of 300 comrades of definite sympathies, using amateur artists who put not much artistry but a great deal of revolutionary élan and sincerity into the play is a fine thing. But it is another thing to put it on as a finished production with professional actors who are not well disposed to it, in a theatre which has to attract an audience of 2,000 every day...
>
> So long as I remain People's Commissar of Education, my first concern will remain the introduction of the proletariat to the mastery of all human

culture. No primitive ABC of Communism* will swerve me personally from that path...If the leaders of the Russian revolution wished to take another path, they would have to appoint another People's Commissar, who would be able to ride off on a white—sorry, red—horse and liquidate the universities,† and silence the unfortunate bourgeois Beethoven, Schubert and Tchaikovsky at all concerts—ordering the musicians to play only one 'hymn' (not of course 'God save the Tsar' but the 'Internationale'), albeit with variations.

There the debate rested until the autumn of 1920. Meanwhile the administration of theatrical affairs remained, somewhat precariously, in the hands of the traditionalists. Lunacharsky's problem was that, apart from himself, there was no prominent Party member of moderate views to take charge of the theatre. With the formation of Glavprofobr at the beginning of 1920, Lunacharsky had even less time than before to devote to the theatre. He remained head of Tsentroteatr, but in February was forced to hand over TEO to Vera Menzhinskaya[89] who, as a schoolteacher of mild disposition and no theatrical experience, had little authority. Kameneva sulked in the arts department of MONO and—perhaps only by the logic of interdepartmental warfare—began to patronize the theatrical left.‡

The one possible candidate seemed to be Maria Fedorovna Andreeva in Petrograd. Andreeva was certainly not lacking in experience in the business of defending the traditional theatre from the onslaught of the left. As head of the department of theatres and spectacles of the Northern Commune, she had effectively dealt with the competing authority of Meyerhold who, as head of Petrograd TEO, was a supporter of the left; and after his departure for the south in May 1919 had consolidated the administration of Petrograd theatres (other than state theatres) under her own authority. She had waged a relentless campaign against the Petro-

* A reference to Bukharin and Preobrazhensky's *ABC of Communism* [*Azbuka kommunizma*], recently published.

† A paraphrase of the passage in Saltykov-Shchedrin's *Istoriya odnogo goroda* describing Major Perekhvat-Zalikhvatsky, Governor of the town of Glupov, who 'rode into Glupov on a white horse, burned down the gymnasium and abolished learning'.

‡ In his memoirs Khodasevich, writing of the mutual antagonism between Andreeva and Kameneva, comments that Kameneva 'called Meyerhold to her aid' in self-defence.

grad IZO futurists appointed by Lunacharsky; and on one occasion they had complained—to Zinoviev, of all people—of her 'administrative suppression' of their right to free creative labour. Zinoviev, who disliked the futurists only less than he disliked Andreeva, promised them his support.[90]

Andreeva was, undoubtedly, more aggressive than Lunacharsky would have wished in her battles with the left, but she was capable and understood the theatre. In January 1919, Lunacharsky nominated her as his deputy as head of the arts sector [*khudozhestvennyi sektor*] of Narkompros in Petrograd.[91] Unfortunately Andreeva, who had originally been appointed not by Narkompros but by the Petrograd administration, was no longer *persona grata* to the Petrograd Soviet, which refused to confirm her appointment to the arts sector of Narkompros and, early in 1920, tried to appoint another candidate to the position. The attempt failed, and Andreeva was confirmed as head of the arts sector in Petrograd, only as a result of Lenin's intervention on her behalf.[92]

In the spring of 1920, Lunacharsky appears to have offered Andreeva the position of head of TEO in Moscow,[93] but the offer was not taken up. The position in Moscow deteriorated under continued pressure from the left. Then, unexpectedly, Lunacharsky found a solution. In the second half of August 1920 he was sent to the Kuban on the agitation train 'October Revolution'. In Rostov he met Meyerhold, recently released from imprisonment by the Whites and now a candidate for Communist Party membership.[94] Without further ado, Lunacharsky brought him back to Moscow and announced his appointment as head of TEO.[95]

Meyerhold's appointment was greeted by the theatrical left as a sign that at last the theatre was to be revolutionized. Lunacharsky may have hoped otherwise. In 1918–19 Meyerhold—unlike Mayakovsky and others of his friends—had not been a polemicist of the left, although he was a major theatrical innovator in his own right. Before the revolution he had served for a decade in the Petrograd imperial theatres, and this may have led Lunacharsky to hope that he would have at least some tolerance of theatrical tradition.

But Meyerhold had returned from the south a changed man

'possessed', as his friend Ehrenburg wrote, 'by the spirit of iconoclasm'.[96] In October, against Lunacharsky's wishes, he liquidated the state model theatre [*pokazatel'nyi teatr*] and gave its premises to Proletkult.[97] Then in association with Kameneva, he announced the slogan of 'Theatrical October'—revolution in the theatre.

'Theatrical October', according to the *Izvestiya* report of 27 October, meant full nationalization of theatres, liquidation of the state theatres, introduction of revolutionary plays according to the directives of a general repertoire plan, struggle against false ideology in the theatre, and the development of theatrical technique. Its artistic imperatives were 'the abandonment of literature, psychology and representational realism' in the theatre, and use of the techniques of cubism, futurism and suprematism.*[98]

Leaving aside the artistic programme of 'Theatrical October', its slogans were wholly unacceptable to Lunacharsky because they were directed against theatrical tradition, against his theatrical administration and against tolerance of any theatrical group except the avant-garde. 'Theatrical October' was an unqualified bid for a theatrical monopoly of the left.

In November one of Meyerhold's supporters claimed that Sovnarkom was about to grant this monopoly by reorganizing Tsentroteatr, introducing full nationalization and abolishing the autonomous and semi-autonomous status of theatres approved by Tsentroteatr.[99] Whether or not this was the case, Lunacharsky found the situation serious enough to take defensive action. In November he announced that the state theatres (Aleksandrinsky, Mariinsky, Mikhailovsky, Bolshoi and Maly), the Moscow Arts theatre with its first and second studios, the Kamerny and the new Children's theatre were and would remain outside the jurisdiction of TEO and thus outside the sphere of the theatrical revolution.[100]

As far as the state theatres were concerned, Lunacharsky's announcement was only confirmation of the administrative situation which had existed since 1918. To argue that because TEO existed all theatres without exception should be subordinated to it, Lunacharsky wrote in an explanatory article published with his announce-

* 'Suprematism' was the term used by Malevich for his geometric style of painting—e.g. his 'White on white' of 1918.

ment, was 'a childish and childishly bureaucratic objection'. The exemption of the Moscow Arts and Kamerny theatres could also be justified in terms of the 1919 decree 'On the unification of theatrical affairs'. It was harder to justify the exemption of the Children's theatre—whose organizer, Natalya Ilyinichna Sats* was seventeen years old—but Lunacharsky explained disarmingly that

> Comrade Meyerhold does not like the direction of the [Children's] theatre, but I like it...How can that theatre stay under the control of comrade Meyerhold when, according to his own conscience, he cannot answer for it?

The effect of Lunacharsky's announcement was to limit the sphere of 'Theatrical October' to those theatres which were already revolutionary and the smaller and less successful of the traditional private theatres. It was understood by the left as an emasculation of 'Theatrical October' which must be fought with every available weapon.

Among the weapons available to the left were Lunacharsky's own activities as a dramatist. Two of the plays which Lunacharsky wrote in the Civil War years—*The Magi* [*Magi*] and *Ivan goes to Heaven* [*Ivan v rayu*]—were symbolic poetic dramas in the manner of Maeterlinck.[101] He wrote them at night as a form of relaxation from his political and organizational duties, simply wanting, as he explained, 'to forget myself and go away into the kingdom of pure images and pure ideas'.[102] The images which came to him in these curious waking dreams were religious and mythical: they served not only as an escape from his working life but as comforters against the immediate violence of the revolution and Civil War.

A third play, *Oliver Cromwell*, belonged to a different dramatic genre—that of historical melodrama. Following Romain Rolland,† Lunacharsky saw melodrama, the drama of high passions, as the only medium through which the writer could speak directly to a broad public. It was therefore the most appropriate dramatic form

* Niece of Natalya Aleksandrovna Rozenel (née Sats), who became Lunacharsky's second wife in 1922.

† Rolland's theory of melodrama is set out in his *Théatre du peuple*, published in Russian translation by 'Znanie' in 1910, and in a new translation by Vyach. Ivanov by TEO, Narkompros, 1919.

for a period of popular revolution. Melodrama, Lunacharsky wrote in 1919,

> will not be a simplified, coarsened and degraded form, as aesthetes think, but will be a transformation from our capricious, refined, hyper-cultural experiments...to a form that recommends itself to healthy, monumental, simple, clear and strong taste...[103]

The historical melodrama *Oliver Cromwell* was written with the intention of producing a 'revolutionary' play which would be acceptable to the traditional theatres and to professional actors,* as well as being accessible to a broad public. It set out to explore the nature of Cromwell as a successful revolutionary, and implicitly to compare his revolutionary leadership with that of Lenin.

On 20 November 1920, at the height of the struggle over 'Theatrical October', Kerzhentsev launched a violent and essentially political attack on Lunacharsky as playwright. It was published in *Pravda* under the neutral heading of 'Bibliography'. Kerzhentsev wrote:

> In recent months, Gosizdat has published three plays by A. V. Lunacharsky.
>
> What is their content?
>
> *Oliver Cromwell* is a historical play. The author praises the Danton of the English revolution—Oliver Cromwell—and condemns its Marats—the Levellers...It is a real hymn to political compromise and a stern [dismissal] of the communist aspirations of the epoch.
>
> *Magi* is a mystical and philosophical play. Under the occult and mystical veneer, its essence appears to be an affirmation that 'everything in the world is one', that God and the Devil are equal, that high and low are the same. If we decipher its symbolism, we find a typical petty-bourgeois anarchist philosophy which is ready to accept the whole world, and to praise equally the right and the left, Communism and the Whiteguards, Lenin and Wrangel.
>
> *Ivan goes to Heaven* is a religious play. In it Jehovah and Christ, angels and archangels, hell and heaven, are introduced as living, genuine realities. Its content is that under the influence of the Bolshevik propaganda of Ivan, who has landed up in heaven, the revered Jehovah and Christ

* *Cromwell* was produced by the Maly theatre, with Yuzhin in the leading role, in 1921. The Maly thus became the first of the state theatres to take a 'revolutionary' play into its repertoire.

themselves repent their sins and renounce their divine power in favour of the people. The heavenly king was ashamed of his mistakes and kindly gives the people a constitution.

It is strange that the People's Commissar in charge of the Communist education of Soviet Russia can preach reactionary ideas in poetic form, and that these plays were published by Gosizdat and are not passed round in manuscript as material for entertaining reading.

But the most interesting thing is that A. V. Lunacharsky states that the ideas which he preaches in his plays are not normally elements of his world-view (see the preface to *Magi*). This is really a sensational discovery! It turns out that A. V. Lunacharsky considers it necessary to be faithful to Communist ideas so long as he is acting as a politician; but finds it quite permissible to preach completely contradictory ideas as soon as he picks up his pen as a dramatist. Here you have a typical model of disorganized individual creative work. I think that if, before publishing his plays, comrade Lunacharsky had sought the advice not of his friends (who, he writes, like *Magi* very much) but of a genuine proletarian audience, he would have heard bold and sharp criticism, which might have been able to direct even his poetic inspiration into the Communist and not the present individual and [hazardous] channel.

It has long been time to bring the fantasy of a few of our Communist poets into the strict but necessary limits of Party discipline.

As Kerzhentsev assailed Lunacharsky from the left, Krupskaya was attacking from the right. The first object of her disapproval was Meyerhold's avant-garde production of Verhaeren's *Les Aubes* [*Zori*] at his First Theatre of the RSFSR. The play had been partly rewritten and given a Russian revolutionary setting. Krupskaya, writing in *Pravda* on 10 November, criticized both the futurist decorations and the modernization of the play, which she found incongruous and—as a representation of the Russian Revolution—inaccurate. Since Lunacharsky had appointed Meyerhold to TEO, allowed him to organize the First Theatre of the RSFSR, and introduced the première of the Verhaeren play with the statement that he in principle approved 'the reworking of plays and their adaptation to our revolutionary reality',[104] Krupskaya reproached him in the collegium of Narkompros (though not in print) for his patronage of Meyerhold and his encouragement of the theatrical left.[105]

Lunacharsky was therefore in the unhappy position of being

attacked from the left for his support of the traditional theatres, from the right for his tolerance of the left, and by *Pravda* for the unorthodox ideology of his plays. The attack on his plays, although apparently irrelevant to the central theatrical issue of futurists versus traditionalists, was particularly damaging because it revived all the old Bolshevik doubts of Lunacharsky's political and ideological reliability. As *The Times* (London) commented on 23 December, quoting at length from Kerzhentsev's article under the heading 'Reds at variance: a heretic poet',

It is a curious fact that in *Der Materialismus* [*Materializm i empiriokrititsizm*], published in 1909, Lenin attacked Lunacharsky for 'coquetting with religion', and said that it was enough to make one laugh, just as in 1915 he publicly attacked Trotsky as 'a bourgeois opportunist'.

The joint effect of Krupskaya's and Kerzhentsev's articles was to force the theatrical controversy into the political arena. Kerzhentsev—probably with Bukharin's support, since his article appeared in *Pravda*—threatened Lunacharsky with 'Party discipline', and appeared to be trying to mobilize support for political intervention on behalf of the left and against Lunacharsky's policy of tolerance in the arts. Krupskaya made no threats or accusations of alien ideology. But, since she was Lenin's wife and Lenin was known to share her views on art, her article was treated by the theatrical left as an authoritative political challenge and a sign that futurism was on political trial. The left expected a political battle in the arts and hoped to win it. Lunacharsky hoped to avoid it, but prepared to defend himself against political attack from both sides.

The left attack on Lunacharsky was based on the premise—directly opposed to Krupskaya's—that Lunacharsky was not a friend of the avant-garde but an opponent. This seemed to be borne out by his contribution to the public debate on Meyerhold's production of *Les Aubes*, when he denied that 'revolutionary' art had any necessary connection with revolutionary politics and criticized futurism in stronger terms than he had ever done before:

'Futurism has dropped behind', he said. 'It already stinks. I agree that it has been only three days in the grave, but it already stinks, and there is no need to look for any Picasso for the proletariat. You say that they [the proletariat] are the captives of the old theatre, but really they have seen little of it. It is you who are captives of the Paris cafes.'[106]

This provoked Mayakovsky, one of the most active defenders of the left, to publish an 'Open letter to A. V. Lunacharsky' suggesting that Lunacharsky was now retreating from an earlier position of support for the left. Mayakovsky recalled Lunacharsky's praise of his own *Misteriya-buff*,* pointed out that Lunacharsky had appointed left artists as heads of TEO (Meyerhold), MUZO (Lourie) and IZO (Shterenberg), and—for polemical purposes—claimed that Lunacharsky's play *Ivan goes to Heaven* was itself a work of left art, though presumably not of a type which Mayakovsky approved since he described it as using 'the abstruse language of twisted minds'. 'Won't you find it rather awkward to "explain away" so much that is compromising?' Mayakovsky asked.[107]

On 26 November, a confrontation between Lunacharsky and Kerzhentsev was arranged at the *Dom pechati* [house of the press].[108] The theme of the debate was Kerzhentsev's attack on Lunacharsky's plays. The underlying issue was whether left art should or should not receive exclusive state support.

The defence Lunacharsky offered for his plays was based on the principle of individual creative freedom. Kerzhentsev rejected the principle. Other speakers for the left—Mayakovsky and Viktor Shklovsky—ignored it. In 1920, the principles of creative freedom and mutual tolerance in the arts were defended only by artistic traditionalists and 'reactionaries', and by Lunacharsky. They were attacked by the artistic left in expectation of Party support which, in the event, was not forthcoming; for although *Pravda* published Kerzhentsev's article and Bukharin probably approved it, there was no editorial endorsement of the article and no follow-up, except for the publication of a reply by Lunacharsky (also without editorial comment) on 28 November. In the absence of any government or Party statement to the contrary, Lunacharsky remained the official spokesman on the arts, and the principle of individual creative freedom remained—if only by default—officially sanctioned. 'It must be said', writes a Soviet historian,

* Produced by Meyerhold, décor by Malevich, in Petrograd in 1918.

that the demand to annihilate the opponent and wipe him from the face of the earth, the appeals to the government to deprive that opponent of the possibility of creative work and even to subject him to measures of a repressive character, came only from the camp of the 'leftists'.[109]

In his original preface to *Magi*, Lunacharsky claimed the poet's right 'to put forward any hypothesis and dress it in the most poetic colours, because one of the tasks [of poetry] is the limitless widening of human perceptions and ideas'. Replying to Kerzhentsev in *Pravda* on 28 November, Lunacharsky restated this idea and announced his opposition to those Communists who for political reasons wished to discipline, and thus to diminish, creativity in the arts:

Comrade Kerzhentsev considers himself called on to defend Party discipline in the field of poetic creativity. I consider that one of my own functions, on the basis of the office which I hold, is the defence of the rights of free culture against Red sycophancy...

And when Mayakovsky, during the debate in *Dom pechati*, accused Lunacharsky of persecuting the futurists, he replied:

I, as People's Commissar, have forbidden nothing to the futurists: I say that there must be freedom in the cultural field. Other Communists wrongly imagine that we are censors, police. No. We are obliged not to permit freedom of the press because we are in the midst of civil war; we are also limiting printing because we have no paper. Kerzhentsev knows that we are establishing a state dictatorship so as to send the state itself to the devil. So we should not get carried away by police activities [*politseishchina*], and I will fight their excesses in every way.

Kerzhentsev, restating his attack in the *Dom pechati* debate, said that Lunacharsky's psychology was that of 'the wavering Communist needing special comfort'. He added that 'neither in his plays nor in his political life does Anatoly Vasilyevich wish to wage ruthless war for the creation of the new. He follows the line of least resistance, which produces an opportunism in which there are Communist elements, but also many bourgeois cultural elements.' Lunacharsky was unmoved. 'Perhaps I have sinned,' he said in his concluding speech, 'but I stubbornly will not repent.'

As well as stating his principled position, Lunacharsky offered specific defences of the three plays under attack. He did not retreat, as he might have done, from discussion of the political implications of his plays. In defending *Cromwell*, he made a quite explicit comparison with Lenin although no such comparison is to be found in the text of the play (and was not made, even implicitly, in the Maly theatre production of 1921, which appears to have presented *Cromwell* as heroic costume drama and not as a play of ideas). Cromwell, like Lenin, impressed Lunacharsky above all by 'the particular quality of his attitude to the masses, to actuality, and to the inward idea'. In his speech at *Dom pechati* Lunacharsky compared the confidence which Cromwell derived from Biblical inspiration to the confidence which Marx and Lenin had in their scientific (but also moral) premises. In a great leader, Lunacharsky said, opportunism is not lack of principle but an uncommonly keen sense of the real world—shown, for example, in Lenin's attitude to the peace negotiations in 1918. The Levellers, whom Kerzhentsev admired, were dismissed by Lunacharsky in his letter to *Pravda* as counterparts of the anarchists of the Russian Revolution.

In his preface to *Magi*, Lunacharsky had written that its philosophy was not one which he would defend theoretically. Nevertheless he did defend it, and his defence has a peculiar interest because—as Gorky said of the play—it 'was written at a time of intensive terror by a member of the Soviet government'.[110] The philosophical concept of the play, as stated in Lunacharsky's letter to *Pravda*, was that conflict and its resolution are a necessary part of life, and that its inherent violence is justified 'by the consciousness of the inner unity of all life'. Through the historical perspective of Marxist relativism, Lunacharsky told his audience at *Dom pechati*, we realize that men come into conflict with each other through inescapable historical circumstances. The Marxist fights his enemy without hatred, understanding that each is performing his historical role.

Kerzhentsev accused Lunacharsky of equating Lenin and Wrangel. Lunacharsky denied this in his letter to *Pravda*, but in the debate at *Dom pechati* he had in a sense admitted it:

> The comrade criticizing me has claimed that I virtually consider Wrangel and Lenin as one and the same...We have terrible ruin, colossal mutual

destruction. Well, are all of those whom we ruthlessly destroy really necessarily scoundrels?...In the first place, they are not all scoundrels, and in the second place the scoundrel is not to blame for being a scoundrel ...We know and everyone knows that they kill a regiment not because it is evil but because it is fighting against them. We may say: 'He is a fine man, we justify him, but he is a Whiteguard hero'—and we shoot him. Do we really regard the oppressors with 'hatred'? We state only the historical fact [that they are oppressors]...

Within a week of the debate on Lunacharsky's plays, Lunacharsky and the left were the joint victims of a Central Committee letter 'On the Proletkults', published in *Pravda* on 1 December, condemning futurism and criticizing Narkompros for encouraging it.* It could be argued that this was the Party intervention in art which the left had tried to provoke, only (from their point of view) wrongly directed. There is, all the same, an important difference between Party or government intervention in support of a group claiming monopoly and intervention against such a group. At the end of the 1920s, the Party gave its support to the association of proletarian writers—a lineal, if debased, descendant of the Proletkult left of the Civil War period—and thereby secured them a monopoly of power in the literary world which was freely and predictably abused. In December 1920, the intervention of the Party was against the would-be monopolists, and its end effect—though perhaps not its intention—was rather to perpetuate a situation of coexistence of various artistic groups than the reverse.

After the publication of the Central Committee's letter, according to Lunacharsky, some of the futurists appealed to him against this unwarranted external interference and asked 'if it was not possible to preserve the autonomy of art'. 'They were the very same comrades', Lunacharsky commented wryly, 'who were extraordinarily indignant at all shades of autonomy in relation to those big historic institutions [the state theatres] which have justified themselves from the artistic point of view.'[111]

Meyerhold himself was not yet discouraged. 'To the attack, dear comrades!' he wrote after the publication of the letter. 'And

* The Central Committee letter 'On the Proletkults' is discussed in detail in ch. 7, pp. 186–7.

Lunacharsky with us!'[112] Announcing that 'the left group of Communists active in the arts does not think of abandoning its position', Meyerhold looked forward to the establishment of 'first general principles on art' by a conference of responsible Party workers in the arts, and the incorporation of these principles into the Party programme.[113]

This conference—the All-Russian Conference of Heads of Sub-departments of the Arts—opened in Moscow on 19 December.[114] The two questions before the conference were the creation of a separate Commissariat of the Arts (otherwise described as a separate Chief Committee, or *glavk*, equal in status with Glavprofobr), and Meyerhold's proposed reform of the state academic theatres.

The creation of a separate Commissariat of the Arts was supported by delegates of the left and the right, and especially by delegates from the provinces. Among those who spoke for it were Yu. Slavinsky, head of Rabis, the artist Kandinsky, the composer M. F. Gnesin and Lunacharsky's friend D. I. Leshchenko of Narkompros. Gnesin, representing the Donskaya *oblast'*, expressed an opinion generally held at the conference when he said:

> In the local education departments sit people who are alien or hostile to art, and to whom it is impossible to entrust our work. We strongly insist on the independence of the central arts sector and its local organs.

Lunacharsky was not reported as expressing an opinion on the creation of a separate commissariat, but the conference, warmly welcoming him as 'the leader of Communist culture and art', hoped that he would remain at its head. The resolution on the creation of a Commissariat of the Arts was taken without a dissenting voice.

Papers on the reform of the state and academic theatres were read by Meyerhold and his supporter V. M. Bebutov. The conference resolved accordingly that

> the bourgeois association of academic and state theatres under Narkompros has turned out incapable of coping with its tasks and ought to be abolished. All its administrative apparatus, and the working studios of the academic and state theatres, must immediately be transferred to the control of TEO...

But it was already too late for the realization of the conference's resolutions. The crucial decision against the artistic left had been taken by the Central Committee of the Party. Narkompros, guilty by association and almost equally in disfavour, was about to undergo a radical reorganization which was intended not to increase but to reduce the relative weight of its arts sector.

7

TOWARDS REORGANIZATION OF NARKOMPROS

Sometime—I am almost sure that it was on the eve of the October revolution, and in any case not later than the evening of the first day—someone said: 'But Narkompros is doing nothing.' And to this very day, whenever one of our journalist comrades picks up his pen to write a few lines about education in Soviet Russia,...he simply remembers this axiom, with which Soviet geometry on the Narkompros problem begins. Narkompros is doing nothing—thus spake our forefathers, who were wiser than we...M. N. Pokrovsky, 'Old news of Narkompros', *Pravda*, 10 July 1920.

In 1918 Narkompros debated universal educational principles, and claimed responsibility for the whole of Russian educational and cultural life. But as the geographical area under Moscow control contracted during the Civil War, so did Narkompros' aspirations.

Problems of local physical survival replaced general principles and national plans on the agenda of the collegium. From the winter of 1918–19 until the autumn of 1920 Narkompros did nothing but survive. Its preoccupations were firewood, food rations, the health of its workers and the upkeep of the building at Ostozhenka 53.

Ostozhenka 53 was not only the administrative centre of Narkompros but an unofficial hostel for homeless members of its staff. The latter function developed spontaneously, and first came to the notice of the collegium when V. M. Pozner—one of the more or less legitimate inhabitants of the building—complained of persons living there without authorization. He named Sofia Azanchevskaya who, since her dismissal from the finance department in 1918, was no longer an employee of Narkompros. Following his complaint, Azanchevskaya and two others were evicted. It was decided at the same time to 'empty the rooms occupied by workers who have left for the front, setting aside two rooms in case of their return'. The condition of the building deteriorated, and a month after Pozner's complaint an outbreak of typhoid was reported among inhabitants of the basement.[1]

Welfare of individual members of staff took up a good deal of the collegium's time. Special allowances of firewood were voted for the scholar K. A. Timiryazev, and for Lebedev-Polyansky, in view of his wife's serious illness and 'the impossibility of recovery with the temperature at 1 degree above freezing point'. A. I. Yuzhin, head of the Maly theatre in Moscow, and Aleksandrov of the professional education section of Narkompros were given orders for issue of fur coats by the Moscow Consumers' Society to replace those 'stolen from them in the execution of their official duties' (Yuzhin's order was for 18,000 roubles; Aleksandrov's for less than half that amount).[2]

Narkompros complained of discrimination against it in the official supply of food rations and fuel, and claimed that because of this it was impossible to recruit or retain staff—'not a day passes without responsible workers...coming to one of the heads of department to announce that they are moving to another government department where they will get rations, where it is warm...' The dining-room of Ostozhenka 53, where food rations were issued to employees of Narkompros, belonged to a low ration category and was supplied from the Khamovnichesky *raion*. In December 1919 its situation was described as 'catastrophic'. The collegium decided to petition the Moscow Consumers' Society for immediate transfer to a higher category and central supply, in view of 'the impossibility of maintaining a minimum of labour discipline among employees with such incredibly meagre nourishment'. Only a small proportion of the staff of the central commissariat received a food ration, and there were reports of 'death from exhaustion, on a basis of undernourishment' among Narkompros employees.[3]

Unofficial sources of supply existed, but Narkompros had little success in tapping them. Agents were sent to the provinces in search of fuel and food. Many of them absconded, leaving Narkompros poorer but not less hungry. Early in 1920, for example, Lenin ordered local authorities in the Belebeisky *uezd* to search for a missing Narkompros agent sent to the *uezd* to acquire cattle for children's colonies; and in October of the same year the Cheka was asked to trace an agent of the Narkompros Food Bureau 'sent on a trip to buy unrationed products for Narkompros employees' and failing to return.[4] The supply department of Narkompros, according to M. M. Novikov (then Rector of Moscow University), was inferior to that of the university, which was organized by a member of the merchant family Azarkh on a basis of former trading connections with villages in the Moscow *oblast'*. Novikov recalled that in the winter of 1919–20, when the temperature of Moscow University lecture-rooms was kept at a luxurious 7–8 degrees centigrade, Narkompros tried unsuccessfully 'to discover our secret of obtaining fuel'.[5]

Narkompros could offer some protection to workers in the central commissariat, since it received special rations for its senior employees as well as for scholars and some categories of student. But teachers had no special rations. In February 1920 the collegium of Narkompros stated that

> the teachers...are without clothes and without shoes, and all reproaches on the ground of sabotage are a bitter mockery of their position; because to work lacking food and provision of the most necessary requirements is something nobody, not even a hero, could do...The peasants give nothing for money, and except for money the teachers have nothing left. Terrible cases of poverty among teachers, suicide from want, have been reported...

In February and April 1920 Narkompros asked for special rations for teachers, but unsuccessfully. Stories of privation and misery among teachers continued to reach Narkompros. 'Who goes along the village roads without a cap, in a torn jacket and cotton trousers, with sandals on his bare feet? The teacher.' In the autumn of 1921 a Gomel teacher reported begging, prostitution, madness and death from starvation among his colleagues. His letter ended with a desperate appeal:

> Comrade, dear friend, help, save us! Already there is no school. No new school, no old school, nothing.
>
> I have taught for twenty years and I cannot take it in, cannot comprehend it.
>
> For we can only build the future on the education of the people. What will an illiterate generation say to us?[6]

Towards Reorganization of Narkompros

In February 1920, near the end of the second winter of hunger, cold and mobilization, Narkompros morale reached its lowest ebb. The collegium resolved

> urgently to call the attention of VTSIK, Sovnarkom and the Central Committee of the Party to the grave material position of educational workers which—if Soviet power does not take extra measures for the improvement of the position of educational workers, for the return of mobilized workers to educational work etc.—threatens a cultural collapse.

A document setting forth Narkompros' grievances was signed by Lunacharsky, Pokrovsky, F. V. Lengnik, Z. G. Grinberg and Ludmila Menzhinskaya (for the union of workers in education and socialist culture)* and dispatched to VTSIK, Sovnarkom and the Central Committee.[7]

The document described the difficulties of staffing the central commissariat because of inadequate heating and poor rations, the poverty of teachers and the collapse of schools after the mobilization of their staff. 'At the present time', the document stated,

> not a day goes past without the Commissar of Education being obliged to give an interview to some foreign journalist. Europe sends its observers, and the Commissariat of Foreign Affairs immediately sends such people—as it will send the official commission of the League of Nations—to Narkompros, to show what great work is being done in the field of education. That work really was done. We can normally show a few model colonies, a few model children's homes built—even if approximately—according to the enlightened type devised by Soviet educationalists. We can show a few deeply comforting figures, but we know perfectly well that behind all that gapes the abyss of destruction, and that a deeper and more careful insight into educational affairs in Russia would make it clear to each foreigner what essentially needs to be done for education—not by Narkompros, but by the central government...

The essential need, as Narkompros saw it, was not for money (since 'no financing can be adequate at the present time, as money does not meet real needs') but for goods: food rations and clothing for teachers, writing equipment for schools. If these demands could not

* All those present at the meeting of 26 February (when the document was discussed) signed except O. Yu. Schmidt. Krupskaya was absent.

be met by the Soviet government 'to any significant degree', the collegium of Narkompros, with the support of the union of workers in education and socialist culture and MONO, and 'in full agreement' with the presidium of Moscow Soviet,

> is obliged to shed all responsibility for the progress of education in Soviet Russia; and at best will be able, by desperate struggle for the survival of education, to preserve its weak remnants until better times.

The response to this *cri de cœur* was small. VTSIK, which had established a commission of investigation into Narkompros earlier in the month, no doubt felt it had done its duty by the commissariat. It took no further action. On 14 April, the Politburo of the Party Central Committee heard 'a statement by Narkompros on the need to take measures to improve the position of educational workers',[8] but took no action. No educational question was included in the agenda of the forthcoming Ninth Party Congress. Sovnarkom issued instructions for improving the supply of rations to teachers[9] which appear to have been ignored by local authorities.

The Ninth Party Congress met in Moscow in April. Lunacharsky was not a delegate, and lobbied unsuccessfully to have education put on the agenda. He was given permission only to hold a meeting on education immediately after the congress, in the hope of attracting a substantial number of its delegates. The meeting was announced by Lunacharsky on the front page of *Izvestiya* on 6 April, and took place on the same day.

Although Lunacharsky had hoped that 50–60% of the delegates to the congress would attend his educational meeting, it seems likely that few did so. *Izvestiya*'s report (on 7 April) suggests that in the event it was not a meeting of delegates to the Party Congress anxious to acquaint themselves with educational problems, but a meeting of Moscow teachers and educational officials rehearsing familiar grievances to a narrow and familiar audience. For what they were worth, the meeting's resolutions were sympathetic to Narkompros. It was resolved that all educational work conducted by other (including military) authorities should be transferred to Narkompros; that an 'Education Week' should be organized in the near future; and that 'a number of measures concerning food, finance and other things necessary for the fruitful work of Narkompros, proposed by comrade Lunacharsky, should be conveyed to the Central Committee'.

On 3 April, *Pravda* had published an article by V. Lukin on education under the title of 'The forgotten front'. Lukin pointed out the weakness of Narkompros and its local departments, and commented on the small numbers of Communists employed within them. 'Narkompros is naturally beginning to attract some attention to itself', noted Lunacharsky in *Izvestiya* on 6 April. He cited the appearance of articles on Narkompros in the press, the establishment of the VTSIK commission, educational questions raised at the recent plenum of VTSIK, and 'the demands of some of the delegates to the Party congress to put the question of education on the agenda'. He thought the revival of interest in Narkompros salutary, but at the same time viewed it with some apprehension: 'of course,' he wrote, 'this interest may at first be manifest only in a certain feeling of pain, both for the whole Soviet organism and for a neglected organ such as Narkompros...'

The VTSIK commission on Narkompros was to have reported in the summer, but the report, although prepared, was not presented. It was argued, according to Lunacharsky, that 'all criticism of Narkompros' activity would be fruitless because, notwithstanding the many deficiencies in its work, its needs cannot be satisfied while we are still in the throes of military activity and while the Soviet government has almost no chance to strengthen the extremely inadequate reserves at the disposal of Narkompros'.[10] Apparently Narkompros was crowded out of VTSIK's agenda by the Polish war.

Investigation by the VTSIK commission was followed by a number of smaller inspections by Rabkrin, the Commissariat of Workers' and Peasants' Inspection. Narkompros had perhaps welcomed the VTSIK investigation, even if it did immediately inflict, in Lunacharsky's words, 'a certain pain'. But Rabkrin's attentions were unlikely to offer any future benefit to compensate for present discomfort. During 1920, according to a report published by Rabkrin in *Izvestiya* on 7 November, Rabkrin's investigations in the educational and cultural field had covered Moscow primary schools, kindergartens, the organization of summer amusements, Gosizdat, Tsentropechat (the agency for the distribution of books and printed matter), ROSTA, the Moscow Experimental theatre and the Narkompros departments of MUZO and FOTO-KINO. The report noted that 'especially great results were obtained through the revisory supervision of MUZO and FOTO-KINO, where significant reform was undertaken on Rabkrin's initiative'. (Within Narkompros, the greatest impact was made by Rabkrin's investigation of MUZO in the last quarter of 1920. The head of MUZO, A. S. Lourie, was currently answering charges before the Revolutionary Tribunal.[11]

In July 1920 the collegium of Narkompros agreed to the presence of a Rabkrin representative with advisory voice at its meetings 'on condition that it leads to the prevention of all kinds of misunderstandings between the two institutions and makes it easier for Narkompros to undertake a preliminary reform'.[12] A. M. Rossky, representing Rabkrin, attended meetings of the collegium from 24 July.

In September, with the autumn session of VTSIK approaching, Narkompros became anxious lest Rabkrin was intending to present a companion report to that of the VTSIK commission. If Rabkrin presented a report, Narkompros assumed that it would be severely critical. An extraordinary meeting of the collegium was held, in which it was resolved to make an urgent appeal to VTSIK for advance copies of any Rabkrin report 'so that Narkompros will have the opportunity to give a sufficiently exhaustive explanation'.[13]

There was, however, no Rabkrin report. The only report on Narkompros at the September session of VTSIK was that of the VTSIK commission appointed in February, headed by V. I. Nevsky.

Lunacharsky, who spoke first in the VTSIK debate on Narkompros,[14] had the difficult task of defending Narkompros from criticism which had not yet been made. He told the meeting that

> without a change in the position of education in the purely economic sense, no internal measures can in any way move us from the miserable condition in which we find ourselves...
>
> I gratefully accept critical comments made by competent comrades on

our blunders and shortcomings. But even if these blunders and shortcomings remained uncorrected we might—with proper supply, more Communists participating in our work, better feeding of children and teachers, more school buildings—immediately show results which could be counted among the objects of our justified pride before Europe . . .

Lunacharsky referred more than once—perhaps disingenuously, in view of Narkompros' earlier remarks on its dealings with foreign journalists*—to the admiration for Narkompros and its educational policy expressed by foreign observers. Narkompros had achievements to be proud of. But, Lunacharsky said,

we do not have administrative scope...My insistent request is that Narkompros should be strengthened with administrators...Without such people in the collegium of Narkompros, we cannot sustain our own existence. We have nobody of pure working-class origin in our collegium ...When the late F. I. Kalinin [d. February 1920] was in the collegium of Narkompros, we felt how he grew in that environment. We would welcome in his place even the most powerful worker-organizer in our midst at Narkompros...

The speeches following Lunacharsky's were briefly reported in *Pravda* on 28 September. Krupskaya repeated Lunacharsky's claim that with greater economic backing and an influx of Communist workers the educational crisis would solve itself. V. I. Nevsky, himself a member of Narkompros since his appointment as commissar of *rabfaks* in June as well as head of the investigating commission, gave a fairly sympathetic report on Narkompros, although including detailed criticisms of the 'shadowy side' of its work. Another member of the commission, N. V. Krylenko, criticized Narkompros' failure to issue practical instructions to local departments and teachers. Criticisms of the administration of higher education were made by various speakers, and indignantly rebutted by Pokrovsky. At the end of the discussion (*Pravda* reported), VTSIK instructed a commission of Lunacharsky, Nevsky and Krylenko to prepare a final formulation of the resolution on educational affairs proposed by Lunacharsky.

The resolution which emerged from this commission was a

* See p. 165, above.

triumph for Narkompros and, in particular, for Lunacharsky. It contained no censure of Narkompros, and instead listed the respects in which its material position must be improved: provision of experienced administrators for the central apparatus, improvement of food supply to children, priority for Narkompros in supply of essential materials, return of requisitioned buildings, return of mobilized educational workers and former workers currently employed in other government departments, and improvement in teachers' rations. It promised, in effect, satisfaction of all the grievances set out by the collegium of Narkompros in February.

Lunacharsky was justifiably proud. The day after delivering his speech to VTSIK, already convinced of a happy outcome of the debate on Narkompros, he gave an exuberant reading of his latest play to the company of the Nezlobin theatre. When the actors complimented him on his theatrical talent and invited him to join their company, he cheerfully declined with the remark that 'judging by the victory I have just won at the plenum of VTSIK, it seems that I am also in the right job as People's Commissar of Education'.[15]

By misfortune, or the normal apathy of the press in reporting educational questions, VTSIK's resolution was not immediately published either in *Pravda* or *Izvestiya*. Ten days after the debate, Lunacharsky pointed this out to the collegium of Narkompros, which instructed him to make representations to the editors.[16] The resolution was published, but in *Izvestiya* only, on 10 October.

There was a further flaw in Lunacharsky's victory. The VTSIK resolution outlined the measures necessary for improving the material position of Narkompros and education in general, and recommended that they be implemented by various authorities (Vesenkha, the Commissariat of Internal Affairs, PUR* etc.) or, in some cases, given legislative form by Sovnarkom. The crucial point was whether VTSIK's instructions would be followed. They were not.

'VTSIK promised Narkompros many fine things', wrote Plyusnin-Kronin, a member of Narkompros, in *Pravda* on 6 March, 1921.

* Politicheskoe Upravlenie Revvoensoveta Respublika—the political department of the army, whose responsibilities included agitation propaganda and political education in the army.

'We were overjoyed and began to wait. We are still waiting. In spite of frequent prompting and reminders, we actually got nothing or almost nothing. Often they simply wave us away like troublesome flies.' This failure of implementation had already been noted by the *Pravda* journalist V. Esipov on 11 January, in an article headed 'And this front is still forgotten'. When VTSIK, as Esipov put it, 'finally turned its benevolent attention' to education and passed a resolution,

> that resolution did not improve matters and gave no results because it was not put into practice...Already two months have passed since the day of publication of the VTSIK resolution, and there has not been one decree to carry it out. Sovnarkom and other institutions evidently obey VTSIK's instructions poorly...

Esipov also found weaknesses in the substance of the resolution.

> It says—'return all qualified workers of Narkompros to educational activity', but, the qualification follows 'if they are not irreplaceable'. That qualification brings the whole resolution to nothing.
>
> You find cases when, for example, a former educational worker has a job somewhere in a food committee or a forest committee. But they will not get him out because the committee, thinking him irreplaceable, will not let him go, and he himself will resist moving because in the food committee and the forest committee he gets a ration...

Of the clause in the VTSIK resolution giving teachers priority in accommodation equal to that of doctors and engineers, Esipov remarked tersely: 'That resolution might be carried out only on the moon.'

It was not quite true that Sovnarkom had done nothing to implement the VTSIK resolution. In March 1921, Narkompros reported the following measures taken in accordance with the resolution by Sovnarkom: a decree of 27 January 'On the improvement of the position of aged and invalid pedagogues', a decree of 8 February on food supply to hospitals and children's institutions, an instruction on the organization of food supply to rural schools, a resolution on the improvement of the position of *rabfaks* (dependent on the cooperation of the Commissariat of Internal Affairs in providing accommodation for *rabfak* students) and a resolution of Maly

Sovnarkom 'On the providing of premises for cultural–educational institutions'.[17]

But on two major issues Narkompros and the VTSIK resolution suffered substantial defeat. The first was on the issue of increased rations for teachers. In an open letter in *Izvestiya* of 12 February 1921, the Soviet teachers' union claimed that 'not one resolution on concrete measures for the feeding and supply of educational workers had been carried out', and charged the Food Commissariat with failing to carry out the instructions of VTSIK and Sovnarkom in this respect. A. B. Khalatov of the Food Commissariat countercharged (in *Izvestiya* of 23 February) that Narkompros had failed to supply the Commission for Workers' Supply with the data necessary to carry out these instructions. What appears to have happened is that Sovnarkom had, on 6 November, resolved to move a number of categories of educational workers into a higher ration group, and instructed the Food Commissariat accordingly. But this instruction, in the opinion of the Food Commissariat, had been nullified by a later decision of Sovnarkom forbidding the rationing of state employees at a higher level than manual workers. In any case (Khalatov explained in *Izvestiya*) the Commission for Workers' Supply had decided against taking further measures to improve supply to educational workers, as recommended by VTSIK, because of the general food crisis in the country and earlier measures taken to improve the rations of students on study conscription.

The second issue concerned supply of manufactured goods to Narkompros. Narkompros' experience of supply through other government departments was so discouraging that it had already repeatedly sought permission to undertake manufacture on its own account. At the beginning of 1920, the collegium of Narkompros had resolved to ask for the transfer of certain pencil- and ink-manufacturing enterprises.[18] Later in the year Glavprofobr decided to petition for the right to produce equipment needed by its schools.[19] Neither request was granted, but Lunacharsky raised the question again in his speech to VTSIK in September 1920. After describing Narkompros' failure to obtain cloth, shoes, pencils and so on for its schools, he said:

> You yourselves understand that Narkompros can do nothing. We say 'Give us the right to produce all this...' They say to us that Vesenkha produces it. That means that nothing is produced. Centralism says 'Don't do it yourself, I will do it for you', but in fact does nothing. Perhaps we need to do some decentralizing. Then you can consciously and ruthlessly berate me and every other People's Commissar, if you will only give us the right to produce things ourselves. Do not give us any money or resources. Just give us the right to begin production of this equipment...

But VTSIK, instead of giving Narkompros the right to undertake its own manufacture or deal directly with the factories, left the onus of supplying Narkompros on Vesenkha, the Commission for Workers' Supply and the Food Commissariat. It resolved

> to oblige Vesenkha to increase the production of educational equipment, teaching aids and essential goods for school children...to oblige the Commission for Workers' Supply to work out concrete plans, to be agreed with Narkompros, for improving the supply of food and goods to educational workers [and] to oblige the Food Commissariat to renew the issue of manufactured goods for the preparation of work-clothes [*prododezhdy*] for educational workers.

Vesenkha was scarcely more cooperative in carrying out VTSIK's instructions than the Food Commissariat and the Commission for Workers' Supply. Early in 1921, Narkompros introduced a project in Maly Sovnarkom

> to give Narkompros all the manufactured products of the former Balkashin glass factory, whose work should be conducted according to Narkompros specifications; to transfer the former Zalesskaya globe factory into the control of Narkompros, instructing Vesenkha to supply it with all necessary materials...[and] to suggest that Vesenkha urgently undertake mass production of slates and slate-pencils...

This project was on the agenda of Maly Sovnarkom nine times in the first ten weeks of 1921, and was eight times postponed because Vesenkha failed to present its report. At the ninth attempt, on 10 March, the Vesenkha report was presented, and Maly Sovnarkom decided that VTSIK's instructions in regard to Narkompros had been satisfactorily carried out. The Narkompros proposal was shelved, and Vesenkha was asked only to take 'more energetic measures' to provide Narkompros with stationery requirements, and to report to Sovnarkom on the situation once a month.[20]

VTSIK's recommendation on the return of mobilized teachers to educational work narrowly escaped a similar fate. In March, it was reported that the project of a resolution on this question had been passed from STO (Council of Labour and Defence) to Maly Sovnarkom to the War Council, so far without any result. But in July the Narkompros journal was able to report that the project had successfully passed from the War Council (in March) back to Maly Sovnarkom and through a commission of Bolshoi Sovnarkom to emerge as a decree on 9 May[21] almost eight months after the passing of VTSIK's resolution.

In terms of material gain, the victory of the VTSIK resolution was illusory. But in one respect it was a real victory for Narkompros, since VTSIK recognized that the basic weakness of the commissariat was economic and not of its own making. VTSIK did not recommend—as Narkompros had feared it would—either internal reform or changes in educational and cultural policy. It accepted a resolution drafted by Lunacharsky. Momentarily, at the end of September 1920, Narkompros seemed absolved of blame for its 'blunders and shortcomings' and promised better times ahead.

The promise lasted scarcely more than a week. On 7 October Lunacharsky committed an indiscretion which cost Narkompros all its hard-earned moral capital. It was the first in a series of events leading to the radical reorganization of Narkompros from outside.

The occasion of Lunacharsky's indiscretion was, perhaps predictably, a conference of Proletkult, held early in October 1920. Lenin had instructed Lunacharsky to tell the conference that Proletkult must lose its autonomy. Lunacharsky in fact told the conference that it must keep it. The incident stirred the Party as no stories of the poverty of provincial teachers could do. For four months, Narkompros was repeatedly discussed in the Politburo and Central Committee. The creation of Glavpolitprosvet (Chief Committee for Political Education) on a basis of the Narkompros extramural department was put on the agenda of the Tenth Party Congress. Narkompros had earlier complained of neglect. Now it had publicity, but it was publicity of the wrong kind. The subject of discussion was not Narkompros' economic and financial difficulties, but its 'bureaucratic character' and the political irresponsibility of its leaders. The moral advantage which Narkompros should have gained from the VTSIK resolution was swamped in a high tide of Party indignation and the cross-currents of political manœuvre.

Three problems involving Narkompros occupied the attention of the Central Committee at the end of 1920: the subordination of Proletkult to Narkompros, the conversion of Narkompros' extramural department into Glavpolitprosvet and the administrative reorganization of the whole commissariat. Had the first issue not risen in acute form, it seems likely that the second would have interested the Party less, and the third perhaps not at all. The tolerance Narkompros had shown towards Proletkult over the past three years was seen to be characteristic of its policies in general. A number of Party leaders were confirmed in their suspicions that Narkompros was politically unreliable, administratively disorganized and intimidated by the non-party intelligentsia.

Lenin's attention had been drawn to Proletkult in the late spring of 1920. In May, he re-read Bogdanov's *Kratkii kurs ekonomicheskoi nauki* [*Short Course of Economic Science*], which had just been issued in a second edition by Gosizdat, and noted its 'serious deficiencies'. He raised the matter at a meeting of the Politburo.[22] In August, he wrote to Pokrovsky asking for information about the status of Proletkult. Pokrovsky replied that it was 'an autonomous organization working under the control of Narkompros and subsidized by Narkompros'.[23] In September Lenin told Bonch-Bruevich of his intention to put out a new edition of his *Materializm i empiriokrititsizm.** He 'emphasized that this was especially necessary in connection with the strengthening of propaganda for A. A. Bogdanov's anti-Marxist views under the guise of "proletarian culture"'.[24]

Reorganization of the extramural department of Narkompros was proposed in the summer of 1920. S. I. Mitskevich, an old opponent of Moscow Proletkult recently appointed second deputy head of the extramural department under Krupskaya, raised the question in the

* See above, pp. 5–6.

collegium of Narkompros on 13 July. The collegium agreed that on principle the extramural department should be reorganized 'for the unification and systematic coordination in one centre of all political-educational work among adults in the Republic', and proposed that the department should become the 'political-educational sector' of Narkompros. Mitskevich then suggested that the sector should be up-graded to a Chief Committee (Glavpolitprosvet) which, on the pattern of Glavprofobr, would be a part of Narkompros having a separate budget and distributing its own credits. The suggestion was accepted. In August the collegium of Narkompros, on Mitskevich's proposal, approved a collegium of Glavpolitprosvet headed by Lunacharsky (president), Krupskaya (deputy president) and Mitskevich (deputy to Krupskaya). Its members were to be P. M. Kerzhentsev, D. I. Leshchenko, L. G. Shapiro and I. P. Brikhnichev.[25]

Mitskevich's reorganization of the extramural department of Narkompros was a domestic one. No outside authority was involved and no outside appointment made to the new collegium (Leshchenko and Shapiro were foundation members of Narkompros, Kerzhentsev represented ROSTA, Mitskevich was from MONO and Brikhnichev from the Gomel education department). The only untoward feature of the reorganization was Krupskaya's absence from the crucial meetings of the collegium of Narkompros, and the non-appointment of her friend and deputy at the extramural department, Zinaida Krzhizhanovskaya, to the Glavpolitprosvet collegium. But the explanation, in both cases, was probably ill-health. Almost certainly Mitskevich hoped to subordinate Proletkult to the new Chief Committee. He—and the collegium of Narkompros—must also have intended to reach some agreement with PUR, whose political–educational network served the civilian as well as military population in areas near the front and was evidently larger and better financed than either the Proletkult or the Narkompros extramural network.

In September, VTSIK's resolution on Narkompros approved the formation of Glavpolitprosvet, and proposed that it should absorb the political-educational apparatus of PUR, except for political-educational work among soldiers at the front. No agreement had yet been negotiated with PUR or Proletkult.

On 5 October, the First All-Russian Congress of Proletkult opened in Moscow. Lunacharsky was scheduled to speak on 7 October. According to Lunacharsky's later recollection, already 'measures were being taken to pull [Proletkult] towards the Party', and Lenin had decided that at the same time Proletkult must be pulled 'towards the state'. He therefore instructed Lunacharsky to go to the congress 'and say definitely that Proletkult must be under the control of Narkompros [and] must regard itself as an organ of Narkompros'.

On 7 October, Lunacharsky spoke as President of the International Bureau of Proletkult, which had been formed on his own initiative after the Second Congress of the Comintern.* 'I phrased the speech I made...in a fairly evasive and conciliatory way', Lunacharsky recalled. 'It seemed to me wrong to launch into some sort of attack and disappoint the assembled comrades.'[26]

Izvestiya of 8 October reported Lunacharsky's speech as follows:

> Touching the relations of Narkompros and Proletkult, comrade Lunacharsky said that Proletkult must be given a special position, the fullest autonomy...
>
> The spheres of Narkompros and Proletkult must be distinguished with profound attention to the problems of each. Educational affairs and, for the most part, the education of working youth is in the hands of Narkompros, the affairs of proletarian culture in the hands of Proletkult. Both the extramural departments and Proletkult [may] organize their own clubs, and there must be no friction but competition. There must be a Proletkult representative in Glavpolitprosvet...
>
> In conclusion, comrade Lunacharsky again emphasized that Proletkult must keep its character of autonomous activity, and congratulated the congress on the extension of Proletkult's work to world scale.
>
> Now, concluded comrade Lunacharsky, even the sceptics are convinced that the good seed of proletarian culture has been sown in endlessly favourable soil.

On 8 October, Lenin read the *Izvestiya* report and noted indignantly that 'comrade Lunacharsky said *exactly the opposite* of what I arranged with him yesterday'.[27] Lenin 'sent for me and

* Members of the bureau included Harry Quelch, J. Humbert-Droz, John Reed, Raymond Lefebvre, Lebedev-Polyansky (secretary) and Lunacharsky (president).

scolded me', Lunacharsky wrote in his recollections of the incident in 1924. Lunacharsky claimed that his speech had been misreported, and even wrote to *Izvestiya* explaining what he thought he had really said:

I said that Narkompros had finally begun to give proletarian (Communist) tasks in school and extramural work first priority...[and that since] Proletkult had grown numerically into a significant cultural force, it was necessary to have a formal rapprochement. To this end, I suggested that the president and a representative of Proletkult be included in Glavpolitprosvet and in the artistic sector [of Narkompros], so that Proletkult should be coordinated as a whole with the work of government organs without losing its creative autonomy...[28]

However, the reports of Lunacharsky's speech in *Kommunisticheskii trud* (8 October) and *Proletarskaya kul'tura* (nos. 17–19) correspond closely with the report in *Izvestiya*.

Lunacharsky was aware that Lenin's views on Proletkult did not exactly match his own. In the first place, Lenin thought Proletkult misdirected its own energy and that of its students by theorizing about the creation of 'proletarian science' and 'proletarian culture' instead of facing the urgent problems of turning a semi-literate country into a working democracy. 'He was very much afraid that Proletkult intended to occupy itself...with the elaboration of proletarian science and, in general, with the whole volume of proletarian culture', Lunacharsky wrote in 1924. 'Firstly that seemed to him premature and a task beyond its strength. Secondly he thought that the proletariat shut itself off from study and from the assimilation of the already-existing elements of science and culture by such fantasies, which were naturally for the time being precocious.'

Lenin's second objection to Proletkult was political. 'Vladimir Ilyich was evidently rather afraid that some sort of political heresy was nesting in Proletkult. He had quite a hostile attitude, for example, to the large part which A. A. Bogdanov then played in Proletkult.'[29] Lunacharsky left his own opinion on this point unexplained. But as he would certainly have acted differently had he believed that Proletkult was harbouring serious 'political heresy', he presumably thought that Lenin was misled by the memory of his bitter political conflict with Bogdanov in emigration before the revolution.

Immediately after reading the report of Lunacharsky's speech to Proletkult, Lenin decided that Proletkult must be formally subordinated to Narkompros. A resolution to this effect must be put through the Central Committee, sent to Narkompros, and presented to the Proletkult congress for confirmation before the end of its session. The resolution, drafted by Lenin on 8 October, stated that

...The All-Russian Congress of Proletkult most definitely rejects as theoretically incorrect and practically harmful all attempts to think up its own special culture, to shut itself up in its own isolated organizations, to draw boundaries between the spheres of work of Narkompros and Proletkult or to establish the 'autonomy' of Proletkult inside the institutions of Narkompros...On the contrary, the Congress charges all organizations of Proletkult to observe their undoubted obligation to regard themselves as subsidiary organs of the network of institutions of Narkompros, and to perform their tasks, as part of the tasks of the proletarian dictatorship, under the general leadership of Soviet power (especially Narkompros) and the Russian Communist Party.[30]

The Politburo discussed the Proletkult question on 9, 11 and 14 October. Krupskaya and E. A. Litkens (representing Glavpolitprosvet) were invited to the Politburo's meetings, but not Lunacharsky. The most frequent speakers were Lenin and Stalin.*[31] It was proposed that Lenin's resolution, approved by the Politburo, should be conveyed to the Proletkult Congress by Bukharin. But Bukharin himself greeted this proposal without enthusiasm. In a note to Lenin evidently written during the meeting of the Politburo of 9 October he explained his principled disagreement with some parts of the resolution:

I personally think that to 'master' bourgeois culture as a whole, without destroying it, is as impossible as to 'master' the bourgeois state [Bukharin wrote]. The same thing happens with 'culture' as with the state. Since culture is an ideological system, it is assimilated by the proletariat in a *different* arrangement of its constituent parts. In practice, the thing is that if you take up a position in favour of mastering [bourgeois culture] as a whole, you get, for example, the *old* theatres and so on. The new

* Stalin's interest in the question is unclear. He was at the time both a member of the Party secretariat and Commissar of Rabkrin.

[theatre], which is considered 'coarse', is not given a chance (analogy: the fear of 'breaking the machinery' in the economic sphere and so on).[32]

As a result of Bukharin's intransigence, Lenin dropped the theoretical attack on Proletkult from the resolution. The resolution, as conveyed from the Politburo to the Proletkult Congress, dealt only with the organizational relations of Proletkult and Narkompros. But the earlier draft probably reached Proletkult as well, since Narkompros apparently received Lenin's resolution on 8 October—before its amendment in the Politburo—and resolved, without comment, to pass it on to the Communist faction of the Proletkult Congress.[33] On 11 October, after 'heated debates', the Communist faction of the congress resolved that Proletkult should enter Narkompros as a department and submit itself to Narkompros' direction.[34] This resolution was then put to the final plenary meeting of the Proletkult Congress where, as *Izvestiya* reported on 17 October,

a resolution was taken on the entry of Proletkult into Narkompros as a department preserving its existing organization. In the near future, concrete forms of organization will be worked out. Until that time, so that the reorganization may be conducted painlessly, Proletkult exists on its former basis, of which local departments have been informed.

As a result of the Proletkult affair, the plans for the creation of Glavpolitprosvet ceased to be a domestic concern of Narkompros and became a concern of the Party. A new project for a Sovnarkom resolution on Glavpolitprosvet was presented to the collegium of Narkompros by E. A. Litkens on 24 October. Litkens, who had not been proposed as a member of the earlier Glavpolitprosvet collegium, was a newcomer to Narkompros, having previously worked in the extramural department of MONO, with the 5th Army, and as NKVD representative in the Crimea. He was young (thirty-two years old) and a Party member of only one year's standing. But he was a childhood friend of E. A. Preobrazhensky and a protégé of Trotsky. It was Litkens who, at the end of 1920, was charged with conducting the reorganization of Narkompros under the supervision of Lenin and the Central Committee.

The scope of Litkens' project on Glavpolitprosvet was much

broader than Mitskevich's earlier project. Glavpolitprosvet was to include—as institutions 'retaining their administrative identity but implementing the instructions of Glavpolitprosvet'—Proletkult, the arts sector of Narkompros, Gosizdat, Tsentropechat, the circus and the political-education apparatus of PUR. This was ambitious enough. But even more striking was the inclusion—as an institution 'completely subordinate' to Glavpolitprosvet, transferring to Glavpolitprosvet all its staff and equipment—of the *agitprop* department of the Central Committee of the Party. Transfer of the *agitprop* department, according to Litkens' project, was to be arranged by negotiation with the Central Committee.[35]

The *agitprop* department of the Central Committee was currently still in the process of organization. It was headed by R. Katanyan, and did not (at this stage) carry big guns in the Central Committee. The *agitprop* department, like Glavpolitprosvet, aspired to the leadership of all comparable organizations. In September 1920, Katanyan named the extramural department of Narkompros, ROSTA, Tsentragit, Tsentropechat and the nationalities' sections under the Central Committee as institutions which 'would have to be closely linked with the *agitprop* department of the Central Committee of the RKP, some retaining a separate identity and others becoming part of the departmental apparatus'.[36] But Katanyan's plan, like Litkens', needed authoritative political support for its realization.

Litkens' project on Glavpolitprosvet was accepted by the collegium of Narkompros. Narkompros thus put itself in the curious position of bidding for control of the Party's ideological department immediately after the exposure of its own lack of ideological vigilance in regard to Proletkult.

Narkompros' previous relations with the Central Committee had been neither close nor cordial. No member of the collegium belonged to the Central Committee. Except for Lenin, members of the Central Committee had shown little interest in educational questions. There had been little contact between the new *agitprop* department of the Central Committee and Narkompros. Narkompros resented the mobilization of educational workers by the Central Committee, and retaliated with the weapons which came to hand. Twice in 1920 Narkompros refused with hauteur to send a consultant on a Central Committee mission, explaining to the Orgburo on the second occasion 'that the Central Committee's systematic refusal to return mobilized workers to Narkompros or to send the local workers needed by Narkompros to the centre has created conditions for Narkompros under which it is completely impossible to prepare any number of qualified educational consultants'. In each case, Narkompros had eventually backed down, informing the Central Committee after a decent interval that it had 'succeeded, although with the greatest difficulty' in finding a suitable candidate. The Central Committee, for its part, placed only 45 graduates of the Sverdlov Communist University at Narkompros' disposal in 1920, instead of the entire class of 240 which Narkompros rather unrealistically demanded.[37]

At a local level, relations between educational officials and Party workers were no better than at the centre. This had been noted by Krupskaya in her tour of the Volga region in the summer of 1919; and had prompted Krupskaya and Pokrovsky to write a letter of protest to the Central Committee.* Later in the same year, Krupskaya complained again of the lack of coordination between Party cells and education departments in rural areas, and argued the need for one basic instrument of rural educational [*prosvetitel'naya*] work. The reading-rooms [*izby-chital'ni*] set up by Narkompros were deprived of resources and support. The local Party cell, on the other hand,

> sets up its own library, which has all the latest pamphlets and a fair collection of political literature. The library is used by 5 to 10 people—and the countryside, thirsting for literature and in terrible need of it, cannot even use one book. A Party club is set up (even with a dining-room, to the general irritation of non-Communists) where members of the Party amuse themselves; but the mass of the population remains outside the influence of the Communists, who have isolated themselves in the club...[38]

The proposal that Glavpolitprosvet should take over the *agitprop* department of the Central Committee came from Litkens, but Lunacharsky—who on most issues was not an ally of Litkens—took

* See above, p. 57.

it up with enthusiasm. The task of the Party, as Lunacharsky understood it, was the enlightenment of the people. Party propaganda was propaganda of enlightenment. 'Were we, Communist propagandists, ever really concerned with anything other than the education of the people?' Lunacharsky asked.[39] In 1923, he reminded students of the Soviet Party schools that before the revolution those who joined the Party did so sacrificing all thought of careers in order to further the work of enlightenment, and that their work among the masses had traditionally been above all educational [*nauchno-prosvetitel'naya*] work. 'For us, the political propaganda of our Party was in no way distinct from the general work of raising the cultural level of the whole country.'[40]

Given this view of Party propaganda, it would have been difficult to argue against the closest coordination of the work of Narkompros and Party *agitprop*. The question that remained was whether the senior position in this partnership should go to Narkompros or the Party.

Lunacharsky took the view that 'the Party must be everywhere, like the Biblical spirit of God',[41] but that organizational and administrative responsibility properly belonged to the organs of the Soviet government. In November 1920, he told a meeting of political-education departments that the VTSIK resolution on Narkompros did not go far enough on the political-education question:

> The business of the near future is the prohibition of cultural–educational work to all bodies except Narkompros, and a more decisive attack on the problem of uniting the work of Narkompros and the Party.
>
> Our political education must become all-embracing, saturated with the spirit of the most militant direction of the creative will. As long as the proletariat of Russia trusts the Communist Party, only the Party will direct education. Thus the question of the rapprochement of Narkompros and the Party becomes acute. The Party is giving the greater part of its work and strength in the educational field to Glavpolitprosvet. Such is the will of the Party. Perhaps such a definite Communist character will frighten many people, but we must state that, at the present time, even the bystanders must march with us [*dazhe te, kto ne nazvalsya gruzdem, dolzhny lezt' v nash kuzov*].[42]

A similar expectation of imminent agreement between the Party and Narkompros was expressed by the political-education department (formerly extramural department) of Narkompros in September 1920. Under the heading 'Experience of cooperation (Party and Narkompros)', the department stated that 'the Party is moving towards wide use of government organs in its *agitprop* work. The government organs will stand more and more clearly on the path of self-transformation into organs of Communist propaganda.' Cooperation between the Party and Narkompros had already been achieved in the agitation campaign on war with Poland, and the recent food campaign, whose origins were described as follows:

In connection with the bad harvest predicted to the political-education departments, Narkompros approached the Central Committee at the beginning of August with the suggestion that a big agitational food campaign should be organized among the peasantry. This proposal, supported by the Food Commissariat, was accepted by the Central Committee.[43]

The agitation campaign on the Polish war was launched in a circular 'On the organization of short agitational schools on the question of war with Poland' addressed to all *guberniya* Party committees and extramural sub-departments of *guberniya* education departments, and signed by Preobrazhensky (secretary to the Central Committee) and Krupskaya (extramural department of Narkompros) in May, 1920.[44] A similar circular on the food campaign was published in *Pravda* on 26 August.

Litkens' project for Glavpolitprosvet was put before the Politburo on 28 October 1920. The Politburo met its proposal for the unification of *agitprop* and Glavpolitprosvet with reserve. Lenin drafted a resolution stating that

the exact formulation of the VTSIK resolution speaks of 'uniting *all political-educational work*' in the RSFSR. The Politburo, completely acknowledging the need for such unification, states first of all that this resolution may be understood only in the sense of preservation, strengthening and broadening not only of the independence of Party organizations, but of their directing, leading and pre-eminent position in relation to all spheres of Narkompros work without exception.[45]

In other words, Narkompros was in no circumstances to be the senior partner in any joint enterprise with the Party.

The Politburo delegated Bukharin and E. A. Preobrazhensky to prepare a project on Glavpolitprosvet, paying particular attention to 'the organizational interrelations of the *agitprop* institutions of the Party and the educational institutions of Narkompros subordinate to their direction'. Bukharin opposed the idea of transferring Party *agitprop* to Narkompros. He was afraid, Lunacharsky wrote, 'that I wanted to dissipate the Party in Soviet anarchy [*razboltat' partiyu v sovetskoi stikhii*]'. Lenin, according to Lunacharsky, took a milder view. 'Vladimir Ilyich laughed that, as he said, Bukharin had taken fright in case Narkompros should eat up the Party.'[46]

The Sovnarkom decree, based on Bukharin and Preobrazhensky's revision of Litkens' project on Glavpolitprosvet and published in *Izvestiya* on 23 November 1920, omitted any mention of the inclusion of the Party *agitprop* apparatus in Glavpolitprosvet. But equally the *agitprop* department of the Central Committee had so far failed to extend its authority to Narkompros. The question remained open.

The collegium of Glavpolitprosvet held its first meeting on 11 November 1920, under the presidency of E. A. Preobrazhensky. Those present were Preobrazhensky, Krupskaya, Litkens and V. I. Solovyev of PUR. The collegium's second meeting was also attended by Lunacharsky and L. G. Shapiro (who, with Krupskaya, was the only survivor of the collegium originally proposed by Mitskevich in August).[47] Preobrazhensky, who was currently a member of the Central Committee and its Orgburo and Secretariat, was responsible for overseeing the establishment of Glavpolitprosvet on its new basis. He had not previously been involved in Narkompros work.

The position of Proletkult in Glavpolitprosvet, according to the Sovnarkom decree, was as it had been in Litkens' original project: that is, an institution retaining separate administrative identity but acting on the instructions and overall plans of Glavpolitprosvet. But by November, Lenin had lost some of his October belligerence towards Proletkult. Thus on 10 November, when the plenum of the Central Committee considered an instruction prepared by Glavpolitprosvet on the status of Proletkult, it recommended on Lenin's suggestion that the instruction should undergo final revision by the Politburo

> for a more exact expression of the important point that Proletkult's work in the field of scientific and political education is merged with the work of the *guberniya* education departments and Narkompros, [but] remains autonomous in the artistic field (music, theatre, art, literature); and the leading role of the organs of Narkompros, closely scrutinized by the Russian Communist Party, is retained only for the struggle against clearly bourgeois deviations.[48]

At the time of the Politburo's discussions of Proletkult in October, Lenin had agreed to remove the ideological attack on Proletkult from his resolution because of Bukharin's opposition. The Politburo had then appointed a commission to prepare an exhaustive ideological statement on Proletkult. Bukharin was not a member of the commission. The result of the commission's work was a document, apparently drafted by Zinoviev,[49] published as a letter of the Central Committee 'On the Proletkults' in *Pravda* on 1 December. It is clear from the wording (and length) of the letter that the Central Committee was anxious to conciliate the proletarian followers of Proletkult and convince them that they had been exposed, not through any fault of their own, to the pernicious influence of certain bourgeois intellectuals. The letter stressed that although Proletkult was to be subordinated to the organs of Narkompros, 'full autonomy of the reorganized workers' Proletkults in the field of artistic creativity has been assured'; and the Central Committee wished only to encourage proletarian activity in the arts.

On the other hand, both futurism and 'non-Marxist' ideologies of proletarian culture were condemned in the strongest terms. The claims of 'futurists, decadents, supporters of idealist philosophy hostile to Marxism and...mere idlers, renegades from the ranks of bourgeois publicists and philosophers' to determine the nature and direction of proletarian culture were rejected. The letter explained that the years of reaction between 1905 and 1917 had given birth to various perversions of Marxism, notably 'Machism' (the philosophy attacked by Lenin in *Materializm i empiriokrititsizm* in 1908) and Lunacharsky's synthesis of religion and socialism, 'God-building'.

Since the revolution, the letter continued, decadent tendencies had reappeared not only in Proletkult but in Narkompros.

> The Central Committee...recognizes that up to the present time Narkompros itself, in the artistic sphere, displays these same intellectual trends which have been the corrupting influence in Proletkult. The Central Committee is managing to get rid of these bourgeois tendencies in Narkompros as well...

Obviously 'On the Proletkults' was effectively an attack not only on Bogdanov and the futurists but on Lunacharsky. Lunacharsky's responsibility was more than that of a commissar under whose jurisdiction abuses had flourished. As a former Machist, God-builder, head of the arts sector of Narkompros and protector of futurists, founder of Proletkult and recent defender of its autonomy in defiance of Lenin's instructions, Lunacharsky came near to personifying the evils which the Central Committee proposed to purge. The inference which might well have been drawn from the Central Committee's letter was that among the bourgeois elements to be removed from Narkompros was the People's Commissar himself.

8

REORGANIZATION

On 24 November, the Politburo of the Central Committee appointed a commission to prepare a plan for the reorganization of Narkompros. Lunacharsky, who was appointed to the commission, took no part in its work. The dominant figure was Litkens, supported by V. I. Solovyev. On 26 November Litkens (drawing on the work of a commission, of which he had also been a member, set up inside Narkompros earlier in the month) submitted a project for the reorganization of Narkompros to Lenin.[1]

The main principles of Litkens' project were that Narkompros should be divided into three 'basic administrations' (also called 'chief administrations' or 'chief committees') dealing with technical and higher education, school education and political education respectively; that unity of policy should be maintained by an 'Academic centre' directing 'theoretical, scientific and aesthetic work' throughout Narkompros; and that unity of organization should be maintained by an 'Organizational centre' dealing with supply, finance and information throughout Narkompros. 'The basic task before any administrator,' Litkens wrote, 'is the organic unification of the parts of Narkompros, which must become a single organism with a single head and a single will.'[2] The unifying forces in Litkens' project were the Academic and Organizational centres. The executive arms were the three basic administrations: Glavprofobr, Glavsotsvos* and Glavpolitprosvet.

Litkens' project departed in a number of significant respects from the existing structure of Narkompros. It made no provision for an arts sector. It gave some of the present functions of the collegium to an 'Academic Centre' without executive power. It remodelled Glavprofobr as the basic administration for 'preparation of workers [that is, professional–technical education] and higher educational institutions', incorporating the former Narkompros department of higher schools. It dropped the title of 'United Labour School', and

* Glavnyi Komitet (Glavnoe Upravlenie) Sotsial'nogo Vospitaniya.

turned its department into the basic administration for 'social education and the polytechnical education of children', dealing with both primary and secondary education. The whole project could—as Litkens himself foresaw—be attacked for its strict separation of policy-making and executive powers.

Krupskaya found Litkens' project 'completely unacceptable'. 'It is not a plan for the reorganization of the existing Narkompros,' she protested, 'but a bare scheme, a construction on the empty place of a commissariat.' Lenin also disliked the project, and criticized it severely on both occasions when it was submitted to him (once with Litkens' signature and a second time, substantially unaltered, with the signature of V. I. Solovyev).[3] 'In my opinion, [Litkens'] and comrade Solovyev's projects are artificial', Lenin wrote to Lunacharsky. The only one of Litkens' innovations which Lenin accepted without qualification was the 'Organizational Centre' (although he called it 'Organizational sector'). He rejected the 'Academic Centre' as coordinator and maker of policy, and proposed instead that GUS (the State Academic Council) be revived, with a membership of 'all members of the collegium [of Narkompros] + the best *specialists*, even if bourgeois'. He rejected the plan of three 'basic administrations', and proposed instead a reform in the opposite direction: dissolution of Glavprofobr and Glavpolitprosvet, and division of Narkompros into six sectors for pre-school work, primary school, secondary school (incorporating Glavprofobr), extramural work (incorporating Glavpolitprosvet) and the arts. The arts sector, which Litkens proposed to abolish, was retained by Lenin with the proviso that ' "politicians" from among the Communists' should be placed in all its main departments.

The bias of Litkens' project was towards the technical lobby, as was indicated by its transfer of the universities to Glavprofobr control. The bias of Lenin's proposals was in the opposite direction. Lenin proposed to liquidate Glavprofobr and merge it with the secondary school sector, on condition that this did *not* mean the professionalization of the secondary school, that existing professional training schools should become polytechnical, and that 'the general educational and polytechnical subjects in the secondary school are increased'.[4]

Among Lenin's suggestions for the reorganization of Narkompros was 'to create the office of *pomnarkom* [assistant to the People's Commissar], giving the *pomnarkom* all administrative work'. But the original idea of this office seems to have come not from Lenin, but from Litkens or the Central Committee. It may have emerged as a compromise between Lenin, wanting to keep Lunacharsky as commissar, and the majority of the Central Committee (including Zinoviev and Preobrazhensky) wanting to get rid of him. The *pomnarkom* was to have powers overriding those of the commissar and his deputy in all matters relating to the organization and administration of Narkompros. The Central Committee's candidate for the office was Litkens.

On 8 December, in the presence of Lunacharsky, Pokrovsky and Litkens, the plenum of the Central Committee considered the question of the reorganization of Narkompros, failed to reach a decision on Litkens' project as a whole, but recommended the appointment of Litkens as *pomnarkom*. The Orgburo was instructed to provide Glavpolitprosvet with Communist workers as quickly as possible. A final decision on the reorganization of Narkompros was left to a Party meeting on education which was to follow the session of the Eighth Congress of Soviets at the end of December.[5]

The Central Committee's resolution of 8 December was drafted by Lenin, but one clause, on the office of *pomnarkom*, was added to his draft. Lenin proposed 'to create the office of *pomnarkom* in Narkompros, concentrating all administrative work in its entirety in the hands of the *pomnarkom*'. The clause added by the Central Committee provided that

> direction of the work of Narkompros in the organizational–administrative sphere, both on the national scale and within the apparatus of Narkompros itself, is to be *realized by the Commissar only through his assistant.*

This meant that in all organizational matters—an area which could be very widely interpreted—Lunacharsky would have to defer to Litkens. Lunacharsky communicated this ominous fact to the collegium of Narkompros on 9 December, together with news of the candidature of Litkens for *pomnarkom* and the information that on

11 December Sovnarkom was to be asked to authorize the creation of the office of *pomnarkom*.[6]

Sovnarkom was indeed asked to authorize the office, but declined to do so. On 25 January 1921, Goikhbarg (deputy president of Maly Sovnarkom) wrote to the Central Committee pointing out that 'it is impossible to authorize this decision through Soviet channels since, according to the constitution, Commissars occupy a position sharply at variance with the position which the Commissar of Education would occupy according to this resolution'.

The Soviet historian I. S. Smirnov, quoting this letter, remarks that 'for V. I. Lenin, A. G. Goikhbarg's arguments were completely convincing'.[7] Lenin, by virtue of his position as president of Sovnarkom, was a member of Maly Sovnarkom; and he was the only one of its members who belonged to the Central Committee. Thus it seems possible that Lenin was all the more convinced by Goikhbarg's arguments for having helped to frame them.

On 31 January 1921, Sovnarkom appointed Litkens second deputy commissar of Narkompros. The appointment was announced in *Izvestiya* on 12 February.

Litkens' first major task—still, pending Sovnarkom's decision, using the title of *pomnarkom*—was the organization of the Party meeting on education, which met from 31 December 1920, to 4 January 1921. The meeting was attended by 134 voting delegates, representing the unions (VTSSPS, Rabpros, and Rabis), the Komsomol, the Russian Narkompros, the Ukrainian Narkompros, and such heads of provincial education departments as had attended the Eighth Congress of Soviets. The presidium of the meeting consisted of Zinoviev (for the Central Committee), Kozelev (VTSSPS), G. F. Grinko (Commissar of Education for the Ukraine), Lunacharsky and Lilina (Petrograd education department).[8]

Krupskaya later claimed that the Party meeting was unrepresentative, being overweighted with supporters of technical education from the unions, the Ukraine and Glavprofobr and lacking adequate representation of the Central Committee. 'It was supposed to be a meeting of the Ukrainian and Russian Commissariats of Education with the Central Committee', she wrote. '...[But] the Central Committee's part in the meeting was quite small. It was limited just to Zinoviev's introductory speech and Preobrazhensky's attendance at one of the meetings.'[9]

It was certainly true that the technical lobby was very strongly represented at the Party meeting. Lunacharsky tried to convince the delegates that the educational principles which Narkompros had followed since 1918 were still valid, although inadequately realized in practice. But the meeting was inclined to repudiate all that had been done by the Russian Narkompros in the past, and to approve instead the policies of the Ukrainian Narkompros which were outlined by the Ukrainian Commissar, Grinko.[10]

Grinko explained that in March 1920, on his initiative and against 'sharp protests' from the Russian Narkompros, the Ukrainian Narkompros had adopted new policies. Work had been divided between the department of social training [*sotsial'nogo vospitaniya*], Glavprofobr and the political education department (later Glavpolitprosvet). The department of social training had taken the children's homes [*detskii dom*] instead of the school as its basic educational unit, in order to counteract the corrupting influence of the family, and conducted the education of children up to fifteen years 'according to the labour principle'. Glavprofobr was responsible for professional training from the age of fifteen. It was in charge of all higher education, and rejected the old-fashioned concept of the single university in favour of separate specialized institutes, strictly organized for the rapid production of specialists needed by the state. The political education department had from the beginning incorporated all work in the arts.

In contrast to the purposeful technical orientation of the Ukrainian Narkompros, the Russian Narkompros had, as Litkens expressed it to the meeting, 'drowned completely in general cultural enterprises, utterly failing to set itself the task of giving practical service to Soviet construction'. The commissariat as a whole had failed to learn the lessons of the Civil War. 'Military practice', Litkens said, 'has put forward completely new methods of approach to cultural–educational work among the masses...Military practice has taught us how to plan work.' Only Glavprofobr, which had tried to meet the demands of the economic commissariats for trained specialists, had been responsive to the needs of the state. Indeed 'the rebirth of

Narkompros began...from the moment of the organization of Glavprofobr'. The arts had been allowed to develop in an anarchic manner, giving birth to 'ugly forms of artistic activity and artistic propaganda' which had been properly condemned by the Central Committee's letter 'On the Proletkults'. The present task in the arts was to subordinate them to the practical problems of political education: Litkens, like Grinko, believed that the arts should be entirely contained within Glavpolitprosvet. In the universities, Narkompros had tolerated 'a woolly-liberal [*rasplyvchato-liberal'nyi*]' kind of work, but this would be remedied by their transfer to Glavprofobr control. 'With the transfer to Glavprofobr, higher educational institutions are regarded exclusively as institutions preparing highly qualified workers necessary to the state.'

O. Yu. Schmidt, speaking for Glavprofobr, supported Litkens' criticisms of Narkompros. It had been justly reproached with excessive theorizing, he said, and 'in three years the slogan of the polytechnical school put forward by the commissariat has not in the slightest degree been transformed from a cloudy ideal into concrete reality'. The present secondary school—'in my view an extremely artificial and pedagogically irrational form', said Schmidt—must be destroyed. The two junior years of the secondary school would be added to the primary (or 'social training') school, and the two senior years converted into technicums. Professional education would begin at the age of fifteen instead of seventeen. This change was dictated not only by the economic needs of the state, but by 'a series of pedagogical and sociological considerations' (in Schmidt's words), including the possibility of enrolling adolescent workers, now outside the normal educational system, into technicums, and the enthusiasm of fifteen and sixteen-year-olds for practical work. In its policy towards higher schools, Schmidt said, Glavprofobr 'unmasks the false pretensions of the former universities to give a pure scientific education', when in fact the majority of their graduates become teachers or take up some other profession for which they have no practical training.

Litkens' project for the reorganization of Narkompros was accepted almost without debate by the meeting, in spite of Lenin's disapproval of it. Two clauses only were controversial. These concerned the office of *pomnarkom* and the future of the arts sector of Narkompros. The meeting decided that a second deputy commissar should be appointed to Narkompros instead of a *pomnarkom*, thus differing from the Central Committee and anticipating the decision of Maly Sovnarkom. One deputy commissar (Pokrovsky) would have charge of the Academic Centre, the other (Litkens) of the Organizational Centre. 'Leadership of the work of Narkompros in the theoretical and political field is conducted directly by the People's Commissar',* the meeting resolved, but work 'in the field of organization and administrative management' at all levels may be conducted by him only through the second deputy commissar. This meant that the meeting took the side of Litkens and the Central Committee on the point of substance, although taking an independent position on the point of terminology.

The arts question provided the meeting's liveliest debate. The report issued by VTSIK comments that

> not one of the points of the reorganization of Narkompros called forth such sharp and stubborn objections as the question of the abolition of the independent arts sector...The representatives of Vserabis [Union of Art-Workers] directly accused the reformers of wanting to slaughter all art, of spitting on art, so to speak, because when their projects were put into practice art would immediately die a sudden death.

The Rabis representatives, supported by members of the arts sector of Narkompros, demanded the creation of a separate commissariat or a separate chief administration of the arts. But 'none of the other participants of the conference shared this point of view'. The meeting decided that 'art, like science, must be subordinated to the general tasks of the state', and accepted Litkens' statement that 'the whole active mass of artistic work must be organically bound to Glavpolitprosvet'. The only concession to the arts was the proposal to establish a Chief Artistic Committee [Glavnyi Khudozhestvennyi Komitet] within the Academic Centre. There was no discussion of the functions of the committee.

The question of the relations of Narkompros and the Party was

* The word '*komissariat*' and not '*komissar*' appears in the text, but it is clear from the sense of the passage that this is a misprint.

raised in general terms by Lunacharsky; and, more specifically but briefly, by Litkens. Lunacharsky said:

Narkompros is above all a laboratory which works out and organizes the whole system of beliefs which, as Lenin has said, is the basis on which the enforcement of proletarian dictatorship rests. Narkompros is the organ of the Party...

So far the Party has concentrated propaganda and agitation in Party organs, but now it is laying them on Soviet organs, that is, on the organs of Narkompros.

The oddness of this lies in the first sentence, which seems to suggest that Narkompros should be responsible for *formulating* Party propaganda rather than carrying it out. Moreover, Lunacharsky had inadvertently described the situation of Narkompros *vis-à-vis* the Party in the heretical terms which Proletkult had used to describe its own position. But this, fortunately, passed unnoticed. Litkens' statement on the question was odder still: he suggested that the organs of Glavpolitprosvet should be responsible for 'all theoretical organization, leaving a general directing and leading role to the agitprop departments of the guberniya Party committees'.

The relations of Glavpolitprosvet and Party *agitprop* were the subject of a separate meeting of delegates to the Eighth Congress of Soviets, summoned on the initiative of the Central Committee on 31 December 1920.[11] Katanyan spoke for the *agitprop* department of the Central Committee and L. G. Shapiro for Glavpolitprosvet. Katanyan said that the formation of Glavpolitprosvet had cut deeply into the sphere of *agitprop*. Among the work which he claimed was already performed by his own department was control and supervision of ROSTA, the theatres, cinemas and the circus. (This, in any normal division of spheres between *agitprop* and Glavpolitprosvet, would have been unhesitatingly assigned to Glavpolitprosvet.) Preobrazhensky, giving the key speech on behalf of the Central Committee, said that there were two points of view in the Central Committee on the relations of Glavpolitprosvet and *agitprop*: 'some of the members of the Central Committee think that it is necessary to concentrate all the Party's agitational and propaganda work in Glavpolitprosvet; others think that this can be done only after decisions of the Congress or a Party conference'. Preobrazhensky himself appeared to take the second point of view. Until the congress, which was to meet in spring, Preobrazhensky recommended the consolidation of Glavpolitprosvet through the transfer to it of the political-education networks of PUR, the Komsomol and the unions; and of the Soviet Party schools, which had so far been shared between Narkompros and Party *agitprop*. The opinion of local delegates, as expressed at the meeting, was almost universally against any transfer of work from Party *agitprop* departments to Glavpolitprosvet.

Since a separate meeting had been held on Glavpolitprosvet, the main Party meeting on education passed no resolution on this topic. A good deal of the attention of the Party meeting was centred on the two issues of the *detskii dom* and its place in the educational system, and the professionalization of secondary education.[12]

Grinko's defence of the *detskii dom* as 'the institution most fully embracing the life of the child and capable of counteracting the harmful influence of the family, which is disintegrating in the process of social revolution' was strongly opposed by Lilina of the Petrograd education department. Lunacharsky took a rather ambiguous position between the two. The meeting, in its final resolution, expressed its approval of the institution of the *detskii dom*, but concluded that for the time being there was no possibility of its replacing the school as the basic educational unit in Russia.

On the issue of professionalization the two Central Committee representatives, Zinoviev and Preobrazhensky, seemed to differ in their interpretation of the Central Committee's position. *Pravda* reported on 5 January that 'Zinoviev, speaking of the principled point of view of the Central Committee...noted that as before the task of creating a labour *polytechnical* school stands before the educational authorities'. This meant that Zinoviev in effect declared his support for the polytechnicalists of Narkompros against the professionalizers. (The same position had been taken by his wife Lilina, in a series of articles on the polytechnical school published in *Petrogradskaya pravda* from 31 December 1920, to 13 January 1921: Lilina explicitly endorsed Lunacharsky's polytechnical policy, and attacked the Glavprofobr professionalists

Schmidt and Kozelev.) But Preobrazhensky, also speaking as a member of the Central Committee, appeared to support the professionalists. *Izvestiya* reported on 6 January that 'Preobrazhensky confirmed the Central Committee's attitude on the necessity of emphasizing professional–technical education in the senior classes of the United Labour School'.

The debate on professionalization and its outcome were described in a Narkompros report in the following terms:

> From the very beginning, two lines could be ascertained. Narkompros RSFSR championed ideas of the polytechnical school according to the basic principles of the Declaration on the United Labour School. Representatives of the trade unions sharply criticized the very idea of polytechnicalism, and put forward instead the concept of monotechnicalism, in the form of the introduction of the teaching of definite trades in secondary schools.
>
> The unionists' point of view did not win the majority, but all the same the meeting came to the conclusion that it was necessary to reorganize the secondary school, temporarily lowering the level of general education and considering it possible as a temporary measure, in connection with the extreme shortage of qualified workers, to transfer to professional education not at 17 years but at 15 years of age.* Thus the United School is reduced from 9 years to 7 years...The two senior classes of the secondary school must be converted into the professional type of school, but with the proviso that general training is not discontinued in the first two years [of the professional school].[13]

Early in December, Lenin had agreed to the conversion of the two senior classes of secondary schools into technicums giving specialized professional training, adding the rider that conversion was to be delayed until facilities for practical polytechnical work could be made available to secondary schools and polytechnicalism given a fair trial.[14] By the end of December, he had abandoned the qualification—which, if taken literally, would have put off professionalization of the senior classes almost indefinitely—and agreed that professionalization was 'urgently and immediately'

* In fact the temporary nature of the change from seventeen to fifteen years was not emphasized in the Party meeting's resolutions. The new seven-year school was referred to, as if a permanent institution, as 'general-educational, labour and polytechnical,... preparing [children] for special education'.

necessary because of the extremely grave economic position of the country.[15]

The theses which Krupskaya had prepared for the Party meeting on education* approved, as a temporary measure, the professionalization of education from fifteen years. Krupskaya, Lenin and Narkompros regarded this as a temporary and regrettable expedient. The Party meeting, on the other hand, was inclined to regard it as desirable in itself.

The Party meeting left both sides dissatisfied. The trade unionists (with Glavprofobr and the Ukrainian representatives) were disappointed at the small representation of the Central Committee at the meeting, and by the fact that the principle of professionalization had not been accepted for application throughout the educational system. Lenin and Narkompros were dismayed at the strength of feeling against Narkompros and the polytechnical principle, and disappointed that Litkens' project for the reorganization of Narkompros had been accepted by the meeting almost without discussion or modification.

The unionists 'considered the defeat of their position as something accidental, the result of the improper composition of the meeting'.[16] On the suggestion of the VTSSPS representatives, the meeting announced that its decisions should be regarded as preliminary, and resolved

> to create a commission of representatives of Narkompros, VTSSPS and the economic commissariats for the summoning (with the permission of the Central Commission of the Russian Communist Party) of an All-Russian Party Conference, which would finally work out the questions of principle touched on by the meeting for the [consideration of] the Tenth [Party] Congress.[17]

The unionists, communicating this to Lenin on 14 January 1921, gave him the opportunity to correct what he (though not the unionists) thought to be the inadequacies of the Party meeting's decisions. He immediately instructed Narkompros that the resolutions of the Party meeting—'resolutions concerning the future of the

* Krupskaya was unable to attend the Party meeting through illness. Her theses were presented by Lunacharsky.

commissariat'—should not be put into effect until they had been further considered by the Central Committee.[18]

On 26 January Lenin presented a project of a 'Statement on the reorganization of Narkompros' to the plenum of the Central Committee. The Central Committee appointed a commission, headed by Lenin, to elaborate the project. The commission began work on 29 January, and considered projects and suggestions from Lunacharsky, Pokrovsky, Krupskaya, Litkens, and Schmidt of Narkompros; Kozelev and Isaev of VTSSPS; and Slavinsky, of the Union of Art-Workers. On 2 February, Lenin obtained the approval of the Politburo for his suggestion that the commission be empowered to issue 'Directives to Communist workers in Narkompros' in the name of the Central Committee.[19]

In this way, Lenin had neatly turned the tables on the trade unionists, using their appeal to reverse the technical bias of the Party meeting in the name of the Central Committee. He accomplished this in spite of the fact that a sizeable group in the Central Committee was sympathetic to the technicalists and critical of Narkompros and its educational policies.

The 'Directives' were published in *Pravda* on 5 February. As Narkompros noted with satisfaction, they 'put an end to the unionists' petitions'[20] by reaffirming the principle of polytechnical education without qualification, and acknowledging the introduction of professional education at the age of fifteen to be 'a temporary practical necessity'. The 'Directives' further emphasized the need to attract specialists to work in Narkompros, although under the direction of Communists; the undesirability of 'abstract slogans' (as put forward both by Narkompros in the past and by the Party meeting on education) in place of concrete plans; and the necessity of introducing efficient forms of accountability of workers and checks on their performance in Narkompros.

No victory for Narkompros was ever complete, and Lenin's restatement of the polytechnical principle was no exception to the rule. Both *Pravda* on 5 February and *Petrogradskaya pravda* on 6 February published the 'Directives' with a persistent typographical error—the substitution of '*politicheskoe*' for '*politekhnicheskoe*' in the phrase '*politekhnicheskoe obrazovanie*'. Since the value of political, as opposed to polytechnical, education was not in dispute, the impact of the 'Directives' on current controversy was much reduced.

Lenin, greatly irritated, wrote a long letter to *Pravda* pointing out the error and attacking the technical lobby in unambiguous terms. It appeared on 9 February. Lenin criticized the Party meeting for having discussed the issue of polytechnical education at all, since the principle was written into the Party programme. The argument on 'polytechnical versus monotechnical education' was not only misconceived but 'for a Communist, directly inadmissible'.

He went on to attack the tendency of Communists working in education to regard themselves as specialists instead of as administrators directing the work of specialists. At the same time he tried to divert the Communist attack on Lunacharsky and Pokrovsky as leaders of Narkompros.

> There are two—and only two—comrades with tasks of an exceptional nature in the commissariat [Lenin wrote]. 'These are the Commissar, Lunacharsky, who provides general leadership, and his deputy Pokrovsky, who is in the first place the Commissar's deputy and in the second place a necessary advisor (and leader) on scientific questions and on questions of Marxism in general. The whole Party, being well acquainted with comrade Lunacharsky and comrade Pokrovsky, cannot of course doubt that they are both in their own way, in the respects indicated, 'specialists' in Narkompros. The rest of the workers cannot have this sort of 'speciality'. The 'speciality' for all the rest of the workers must be the ability to facilitate the recruitment of educational specialists, to manage the work correctly, and to make use of the data of practical experience in a systematic way...
>
> At the meeting of Party workers there was no such taking account of *practical* work, no interpretations of the findings of educationalists. Instead there were fruitless attempts at 'general consideration' and evaluation of 'abstract slogans'...

With this snub to Litkens and the Party meeting, Lunacharsky and the old guard of Narkompros were to some extent compensated for earlier attacks on themselves. There were now three leading figures in Narkompros—Lunacharsky, Pokrovsky and Litkens—with Schmidt at Glavprofobr also in a position of influence, and a vacant place at the head of Glavpolitprosvet.* All of them had been somewhat discredited in the last months, but not totally. The antagonism of the old guard to the new was strong, but their forces were in equilibrium. In this ambiguous situation, Narkompros entered the new era of unified leadership and rational administration which the Party had recommended to it.

Litkens began work on the reorganization of Narkompros in December 1920, using the title of *pomnarkom*. 'The reorganization of Narkompros', he informed the commissariat, 'will proceed in an organized manner through the instructions of the *pomnarkom*.'[21] Lunacharsky was not empowered to issue instructions to Narkompros without Litkens' counter-signature. The few instructions he did issue (with Litkens' imprimatur) in 1921 were concerned with the arts.

Sovnarkom's appointment of Litkens as second deputy commissar instead of *pomnarkom* put him in an awkward position. The normal powers of a second deputy were much narrower than those the Central Committee had intended for Litkens and he himself expected. His activities were at once supported and circumscribed by Lenin, who kept a careful watch on the reorganization. 'Almost every day,' according to a contemporary observer in Narkompros, '[Lenin] asked the late E. A. Litkens for reports on the progress of the reorganization and on the principles which the Litkens commission had laid down as the basis of the building of the new structure of Narkompros.'[22]

Lenin had very definite ideas on Litkens' role in Narkompros. He was to be the prototype of the non-specialist administrator described in Lenin's 'Directives'. His sphere was not policy but organization. It seems probable that on this last point Litkens and Lenin differed. On 21 March 1921, Lenin wrote to Litkens with more than his usual wealth of emphasis:

Do not break away from *organizational–administrative* work. *Soon* (in two or three months) we will severely question you and *only* you, and the results must be serious—that is, efficient *accountability*, checks on the

* Krupskaya was head of Glavpolitprosvet, but for reasons of temperament and health did not assert herself as a political leader in Narkompros. The vacant place was that of the deputy head of Glavpolitprosvet.

work of 400,000 teachers, on their degree of organization and *their* movement in the new direction. This will be asked of you and *only* of you. *All* attention on that.[23]

Lenin shared the general unease about Litkens' precise status in Narkompros. Whether he had originally favoured the title of second deputy commissar to that of *pomnarkom* or not, he later decided that it was inappropriate for Litkens' job, and suggested instead the title of administrator [*upravlyayushchii*] of Narkompros. Otherwise, he wrote,

there will be chaos without end—Litkens will feel himself 'harassed'—we (the Central Committee, the government) will not know whether Litkens has *passed the examination* or not. Because so far he has not been given exact rights.[24]

But the suggestion was not taken up. Litkens himself was against the title of administrator, evidently thinking that it diminished his status rather than increasing it. This in some sense may have been Lenin's intention, but he was nevertheless anxious that Litkens' powers in the administrative field should be respected. Lenin in government was usually an observer of rules, and the rule in this case said that Litkens was the final arbiter on matters of Narkompros organization. When Lunacharsky contested Litkens' exclusive right to allocate special rations, Lenin supported Litkens. He informed the Politburo that

on the question of Lunacharsky's statement which was sent to me, I find that he is undoubtedly incorrect. Administrative and organizational affairs (undoubtedly including rations) cannot be dealt with by him without Litkens; and Lunacharsky's instructions cannot be considered binding on Litkens. If the members of the Central Committee do not agree on this matter,* then I ask that the question be put on the agenda of the Politburo next week when I will be present.[25]

Litkens' project for the reorganization of Narkompros turned out to have one grave disadvantage for himself. This was the distribution of power within the commissariat following its division into

* Clearly there was more in this affair then meets the eye. The Politburo at first rejected Lenin's formulation of the rights of Litkens and Lunacharsky in Narkompros because of Stalin's opposition, for reasons unknown. It was accepted on 8 September.

three chief administrations. In spite of the constitutional weakness of Litkens' position as second deputy commissar, he had some success in asserting himself against Lunacharsky and Pokrovsky, since this was what the Central Committee expected of him. But there was no Central Committee ruling on Litkens' relations with the heads of the chief administrations. This problem became acute from the time of Preobrazhensky's appointment to Glavprofobr in March 1921. Litkens owed his authority entirely to the terms of his appointment. Preobrazhensky—although no longer member of the Central Committee, the Party Secretariat and the Orgburo as he had been in 1920—was still a powerful figure in his own right. In spite of their earlier connection, Litkens and Preobrazhensky were soon, almost inevitably, at odds.

Lenin attempted to mediate between them.[26] But he did not allow that Litkens could overrule the heads of the chief administrations as, on organizational questions, he could overrule the commissar. Lenin wrote (in proposing that Litkens take the title of administrator of Narkompros), that

> the administrator deals with *everything* concerned with the chief administrations (Glavprofobr, Glavpolitprosvet, Glavsotsvos) *by agreement* with the 'chief administrators'—that is, not on his own. Of course he has the right to take questions to the collegium of the commissariat...[27]

Since the heads of the chief administrations were *ex officio* members of the collegium of Narkompros, Litkens would hardly have counted this as an advantage.

The new structure of Narkompros was formally sanctioned by a Sovnarkom 'Statement on Narkompros' published in *Izvestiya* on 15 February. The 'Statement' followed the lines proposed by Litkens and approved by the Party meeting on education. The commissar 'directs the work of Narkompros on the general bases established by the constitution of the RSFSR'. His first deputy is head of the Academic Centre, and his second deputy head of Organizational Centre. Gosizdat was to have the formal status of a chief administration, together with Glavsotsvos ('social training and polytechnical education to 15 years'), Glavprofobr ('professional polytechnical schools from 15 years and higher schools') and

Glavpolitprosvet. The Academic Centre consists of a scientific section (GUS) and an artistic section (the Chief Artistic Committee), plus a museum administration and an archive administration.

The 'Statement' represented a success for Litkens, since Lenin had always been doubtful of his plan, and Lunacharsky, Pokrovsky and Krupskaya disliked it. But serious problems remained for Litkens, and above all the problem of personnel. Most of the old staff of Narkompros regarded Litkens with hostility, but it was almost impossible to replace them. As before, in spite of numerous protests from Narkompros, only insignificant numbers of Communists were available for educational work, and those already in Narkompros remained liable to Party mobilization to other duties. V. I. Solovyev—Litkens' associate in framing the project on reorganization of Narkompros and briefly deputy president of Glavpolitprosvet—stayed at Narkompros only a few months. Apart from him, Litkens seems to have brought little new blood into Narkompros at the top level. Even his deputy at the Organizational Centre, Z. G. Grinberg, was one of the Narkompros old guard.

If it was difficult to obtain responsible workers for Narkompros, it was no easier to dismiss them. Litkens tried to remove L. G. Shapiro from the collegium of Glavpolitprosvet, but was prevented from doing so by Lenin's intervention (prompted by Krupskaya) on Shapiro's behalf.[28] He tried to dismiss N. N. Glebov-Putilovsky, head of Petrograd FOTO-KINO; but although on this occasion he had the support of the whole collegium of Narkompros, the dismissal was countermanded by the Orgburo of the Central Committee.*[29]

Glavpolitprosvet had particular need of responsible Communist workers. In its first months, it appealed repeatedly for more Communists—to the Central Committee for P. M. Kerzhentsev, L. S. Sosnovsky, V. N. Maksimovsky and N. S. Angarsky in November 1920; to the Central Committee for 500 Communists and

* Glebov-Putilovsky, who seems to have been a protégé of Zinoviev, was accused of disrupting the work of Voevodin's FOTO-KINO department in recording the Third Congress of the Comintern in Petrograd, and refusing to obey Voevodin's instructions. The Narkompros collegium decided that 'Glebov cannot be left to work in any Narkompros organ after what has happened' (18 July). But the Orgburo set up a commission of enquiry which recommended against dismissal.

to the Orgburo for Sosnovsky, N. I. Smirnov and V. I. Nevsky in December; to the Central Committee for Maksimovsky and Ya. A. Yakovlev in January 1921.[30] In December the Central Committee had instructed the Orgburo to provide Communists for Glavpolitprosvet, and accordingly in January 1921 the transfer of three senior Party members to Glavpolitprosvet was announced (A. K. Voronsky, to edit the journal *Krasnaya nov'*, V. N. Maksimovsky and B. Volin).[31]

For some months the situation in regard to the leadership of Glavpolitprosvet was confused. Krupskaya, who was president, was often absent from meetings of the collegium because of ill-health. The first deputy president (in December 1920) was Litkens, but he had to retire after his appointment to Narkompros. Then the collegium's meetings were for a short time chaired by Preobrazhensky, the Central Committee representative. From January 1921, V. I. Solovyev acted as deputy president. He was probably Litkens' candidate for the office. But the Orgburo had another candidate in V. N. Maksimovsky, who had been brought up from work in Ryazan for this purpose. Maksimovsky attended meetings of the collegium of Glavpolitprosvet from February, and for a time he and Solovyev alternated as chairmen. In March Litkens announced a temporary collegium with Solovyev as deputy president.[32] On 26 April Sovnarkom approved a collegium with Maksimovsky as deputy president, but including Solovyev as an ordinary member. The Sovnarkom resolution was published in *Izvestiya* on 18 May. It was already out of date. Solovyev had attended his last meeting of the Glavpolitprosvet collegium on 6 May; and on 12 May the collegium of Narkompros was informed that a commission of VTSIK, acting independently of Sovnarkom and apparently without consultation with it, had approved a Glavpolitprosvet collegium with Maksimovsky as deputy president and two additional members (Isaev of VTSSPS and Gusev of PUR), and without Solovyev.[33] Thus the Glavpolitprosvet collegium as finally constituted had a deputy president (Maksimovsky) appointed probably in spite of Litkens' support for another candidate, and included among its members one (L. G. Shapiro) whom Litkens had unsuccessfully tried to dismiss.

The VTSIK commission referred to above was established to review the membership of the collegiums of all commissariats. Besides its ruling on Glavpolitprosvet, it recommended a number of changes in the departmental collegiums of Narkompros. Almost all the departments concerned protested, and an appeal was made to the commission to review its decisions.[34]

No sooner had Narkompros taken evasive action against the recommendations of one VTSIK commission than another was at its gates. The second commission was set up by VTSIK in October to review the membership of the commissariats and cut down their numbers. It was headed by Yu. M. Larin; and its purpose was, in Larin's words, 'to launch a Tartar attack [*mamaevo nashestvie*] on Soviet institutions, to conduct...a pogrom'. The purpose of the exercise was to save money currently spent on official salaries and give the state 'the chance to offer workers in heavy industry more money and more food'.[35]

The first Soviet institution that came to mind in this if in no other context was Narkompros. Larin said that a preliminary investigation of Narkompros had already been made:

> My impression...is that a number of organs and institutions [of Narkompros] will be immediately dissolved because they are clearly unnecessary, or to eliminate parallelism, or because in present circumstances it is possible to do without them. Altogether 1,200,000 persons are receiving salaries from Narkompros...The commission is thinking of reducing this number to 400,000 or slightly more.

Asked which departments of Narkompros would be dissolved, Larin answered that in his opinion Tsentropechat (agency for the distribution of printed matter), Glavmuzei (museum administration), Gokhkom* (Chief Artistic Committee), Nachuchupr (administration of scientific and scientific–artistic institutions†) and Aktsentr (the Academic Centre)—'organs with names and functions mysterious to the uninitiated, but disclosed to the commission', Larin remarked —would have to go, as would most of the present expenditure on the arts. The subsidy of state academic theatres which, to Larin's

* Properly Glakhkom (Glavnyi Khudozhestvennyi Komitet).

† Larin's definition. Pokrovsky in his letter to *Izvestiya* of 30 October denied the existence of such a body.

indignation, were taking up 5% of the whole Narkompros budget was also under threat.

Lunacharsky and Pokrovsky were both deeply affected by the proposed economies—Lunacharsky because of the renewed attack on the arts and Pokrovsky because of the attack on scientific administration. Pokrovsky made the first protest in an angry letter to *Izvestiya* on 30 October accusing Larin of inadequate knowledge of Narkompros. Two days later, the collegium of Narkompros resolved that Lunacharsky should inform the presidium of VTSIK that 'Narkompros considers it necessary to present its own project for the simplification of its apparatus, which will be worked out within a fortnight'.[36]

The threat from the Larin commission affected Litkens, as architect of the reorganized Narkompros, as much as it did Lunacharsky and Pokrovsky. But in this situation Litkens was at a disadvantage. He was not a member of VTSIK; and Lunacharsky, who was a member, necessarily took the initiative in defending Narkompros on a strictly organizational question.

The agreement which the Larin commission finally made with Narkompros undid almost all the work of Litkens' reorganization. It was decided that theoretical and practical leadership should be united in each chief administration. The Academic Centre was to be abolished, and its functions in the direction of scientific and artistic work transferred to a new organ, Glavnauka, which was to have the status of a chief administration. The Larin commission agreed to 'the retention and consolidation [*uplotnenie*]' of all the arts departments of Narkompros.[37] The academic theatres were transferred to Glavnauka and remained on state subsidy, except for the Bolshoi theatre, which the Larin commission insisted should be closed.*

Thus almost nothing remained of Litkens' reorganization but Litkens himself—and that not for long, since he fell ill in the winter of 1921–2, went to recuperate in the Crimea, and was murdered by bandits in April.[38]

On the recommendation of the Larin commission, the number of salaried employees of Narkompros was fixed at 513,100.[39] This reduction, though great, was not disproportionate to the overall

* See below, pp. 268–9.

reduction in numbers of state employees. At the beginning of 1922, writing in *Pravda* of 3 January under the heading 'Too many bosses', Larin stated that the total number of state employees had been reduced by 60%. According to his figures,* both Vesenkha and the Commissariat of Internal Affairs suffered proportionately more than Narkompros. Narkompros was still, post-Larin, the third largest state employer—ranking below the Commissariat of Communications (including watchmen) and Vesenkha, but well above the Commissariats of Health, Internal Affairs (including police), Agriculture and Justice (including the GPU).[40]

At the end of 1920, the administrative deficiencies of Narkompros were so clear to outside observers that it was assumed that the introduction of rational administrative practices must have swift and remarkable results.

But the results of Litkens' reforms were negligible. His administrative system was rational but, as Krupskaya pointed out, it was a construction on 'the empty place of a commissariat'. It proved almost impossible to abolish entrenched institutions: they simply reappeared under different names or under the protection of another chief administration of Narkompros. It was impossible to purge the staff because of the lack of suitable replacements and the large number of outside persons and authorities to whom appeal might successfully be made.

The multiplicity of instructions coming from VTSIK, Sovnarkom, Maly Sovnarkom, the Central Committee, the Orgburo, the Politburo and the Council of Labour and Defence meant that Narkompros had innumerable methods of defence against instructions it did not wish to follow. Narkompros was only weak in that it could not organize positive action on its own behalf. It could resist almost anything.

The notion that with 'better administrators' Narkompros could be made efficient was, in the circumstances of 1921, fallacious. It might have been changed (though perhaps not for the better) by the appointment of, for example, Preobrazhensky as commissar—on the almost impossible condition that Preobrazhensky had con-

* The figures include central, *guberniya* and *uezd* officials, but not employees of enterprises, institutions and *volost'* and village departments of the commissariats.

tinued to hold the influence he had in 1920, while at the same time resigning from active work in the Orgburo, the Secretariat and the Finance Commissariat and devoting himself exclusively to Narkompros. Some people thought that the solution was to make Trotsky Commissar of Education. In 1922 a delegation from the Union of Education Workers approached him with the suggestion that he should take over Narkompros for a year, and reorganize it as he had reorganized transport. He refused, among other reasons because he feared that the administrative apparatus of education would prove intractable.[41]

Litkens, who was no Trotsky, failed to 'pass the examination' which Lenin and the Central Committee had set him—and this in spite of persistent coaching from Lenin himself. The goal of rational administration, in a climate of political confusion and economic collapse, turned out to be a mirage.

9

NARKOMPROS AFTER REORGANIZATION

EDUCATION

The Party meeting on education did not in so many words repudiate the United Labour School. But, as if by common consent, no speaker referred to it by name, and a number attacked the basic polytechnical principle. Ludmila Menzhinskaya resigned from her position as head of the department of the United Labour School immediately after the meeting.[1]

On 4 January, the last day of the Party meeting, *Pravda* published an article on the failure of Narkompros' school policy with the title 'Pedagogical futurism and the tasks of the Soviet school'. The author, N. Baturin, wrote that

> the two-year experience of Narkompros has shown that transition from the old school to the ideal labour school is impossible for a whole series of reasons, the chief of which are the abnormal circumstances of life at a time of acute civil war, and the absence of an adequate body of teachers prepared to implement the ideal type of the labour school in practice. Furthermore, a complete synthesis of science and labour could not, of course, be found theoretically in such a comparatively short time...At the present moment it is necessary to strive towards the creation of a school of a transitional type, from which the ideal labour school will grow in the future.

The teaching programmes of Narkompros were, in Baturin's opinion, permeated with populist idealism. The recently-issued programme on natural science was criticized as instilling no more than 'a love of nature':

> the education of sentimental 'nature-lovers'...could not have corresponded better to the tastes and ideals of the provincial petty-bourgeoisie [*meshchanstvo*]. But it is quite obvious that it has nothing in common with the comprehension of nature lying at the basis of the flourishing of heavy capitalistic industry.

Under Litkens' reorganization, the department of the United

Labour School (also referred to as the sector of social training) became Glavsotsvos. For some time after Menzhinskaya's resignation it was without a head. In this period, the polytechnical school—now usually called the 'labour polytechnical school' instead of the United Labour School—was most vigorously defended against the attacks of Glavprofobr, Litkens and the trade unions by Lenin and Krupskaya.

In February, O. Yu. Schmidt, head of Glavprofobr, addressed a meeting of primary and secondary school teachers. Exactly what he said is a matter of dispute. He may, as he later claimed, have spoken only of the conversion of the two senior classes of the secondary schools into technicums, in accordance with the decisions of the Central Committee and the Party meeting. But Ya. D. Linnik, of the Moscow *guberniya* education department, reported him in *Pravda* of 16 February as saying that there had been 'a complete collapse of the polytechnical school in Russia' and suggesting that the whole principle of polytechnical education had been discredited.

The confusion of the teachers on present educational policy was well illustrated by a conversation overheard by Linnik at the teachers' meeting while the audience waited for Schmidt (who arrived an hour late):

'But are they intending to turn our school into some sort of technicum?'

'Good heavens, we have such pitiful equipment even for the present school—but they say that the social–economic technicum does not need equipment.'

'Forgive my ignorance, but what is a social–economic technicum? I seem to have got out of touch with the latest developments.'

'No, I am not clear about it myself: the question of new trends in education is not dealt with by the press, and nobody assembles us for papers, discussion and so on. I was told that the social–economic technicum is just the old Commercial School...'

After the publication of Linnik's article (which *Pravda* labelled 'for discussion'), the collegium of Narkompros met in closed session to consider its implications.[2] The question was whether Schmidt had or had not deviated from the line of the Party and Narkompros. Three of those attending the meeting (Lunacharsky, Pokrovsky and

Z. G. Grinberg) were Schmidt's probable opponents; five (Schmidt himself, Litkens and three trade union representatives admitted to the collegium on the recommendation of the Party meeting) were his supporters. In Krupskaya's absence and with no representative of Glavsotsvos, Schmidt's supporters were in the majority. The meeting decided that Schmidt had been misreported. A rider was added that 'the collegium finds it necessary to call the attention of *Pravda*'s editors to their systematic publication of articles against Narkompros without preliminary verification, together with an almost complete refusal to publish material supplied to the paper by Narkompros itself'.

Schmidt, with the collegium's approval, wrote a reply to Linnik which appeared in *Pravda* on 21 February. He was now anxious to repudiate anti-polytechnical views since Lenin—writing after the date of Schmidt's speech to the teachers—had declared them to be 'directly inadmissible for a Communist'. Schmidt therefore explained that he had not attacked the polytechnical principle, but had simply discussed the formation of technicums on the basis of the two senior classes of the secondary school. All he had said was that labour and polytechnical principles, no doubt admirable in themselves, had been distorted in practice. The labour principle, which in purer form was incorporated in the Party programme, had attracted Tolstoyan idealists into Narkompros' work.

> The principle of the labour school, in the absence of Communist teachers, fell on receptive soil only among anarchist educationalists and narodnik intellectuals. In both cases labour, instead of being a means towards the conquest of nature and the increase of human power, became an end in itself, an ethical principle...

Linnik's version of his speech, Schmidt claimed, was 'malicious, slanderous fantasy'.

In *Pravda* 23 February, Krupskaya entered the controversy with indignant confirmation of Linnik's account of Schmidt's anti-polytechnical views. She had not attended the teachers' meeting, but had had to listen to such remarks from Schmidt many times in the past. Even Schmidt's reply to Linnik was offensive to Krupskaya, because Schmidt tries to prove that the labour polytechnical school is quite suitable for adorning the Party programme, but cannot be put into practice and ought to be decently buried. A strange attitude to the Party programme! The programme is one thing, life is another.

Schmidt had invoked the authority of the Party meeting on eduction. Krupskaya denied it, and cited instead the 'Directive' of Lenin's commission,* 'which confirmed the Party programme in the part concerning education, and only reduced the duration of the labour polytechnical school from 9 years to 7 in view of our poverty'. Krupskaya added in parenthesis that since compulsory secondary education did not exist in practice, 'that resolution has no particular significance': the real problem was to bring even the seven-year school into being.

Krupskaya dealt very summarily with Schmidt's lack of historical and international perspective. He claimed, she wrote, that it was necessary to produce technicians in the shortest possible time in the interests of the national economy, but

it is in the interests of the national economy that there should be the greatest possible number of capable people and the smallest number of people imagining themselves to be specialists and not able to take a single step. If O. Schmidt even slightly interested himself in questions of the history of the labour school, he would know that the labour school has proved in practice that it raises the general work-capability of pupils, and thanks to it the leading industrial countries have begun to compete among themselves on this common ground. But what has that to do with O. Schmidt!

Krupskaya pointed out that Schmidt's technicums were still hypothetical. Why should the technicums be able to arrange practical work in factories and obtain necessary equipment, when this had proved impossible for the labour school? 'For schools receiving the name of technicums and coming under the control of O. Schmidt, absolutely the same obstacles will exist as for the polytechnical schools.'

On 25 February, before Schmidt had time to reply to Krupskaya, the Central Committee dismissed him from the head of Glavprofobr.[3]

* See above, pp. 199–200.

He published a reply to Krupskaya in *Pravda* on 4 March. Not surprisingly under the circumstances, its tone was sharply polemical. Schmidt accused Krupskaya of abusing her senior Party position to attack a junior Party member, and of denying the authority of the Party meeting on education for no other reason than the fact that she did not agree with its decisions. This was both true, and an attack on Lenin as well as Krupskaya. There had been protests from 'responsible workers' in Narkompros (Litkens?) against Schmidt's dismissal, and the question was due for reconsideration by the Central Committee on 7 March.[4] Schmidt was presumably trying to muster an 'anti-authoritarian' vote against Lenin in the Central Committee.

In his article of 4 March, Schmidt again defended the authority of the Party meeting, 'which comrade Krupskaya tries in every way to discredit'. He reflected that 'even the most authoritative Party comrades are at the present time abusing one polemical convention—the masking of a lack of effective arguments by harshness of personal attack. Evidently a more junior member of the Party is left with only one thing to do: not to imitate them in this respect.'

Schmidt kept his shrewdest blow for the last paragraph:

> Surely the point is really that the resolutions* of the Party meeting and the Central Committee were welcomed by members of Narkompros, including myself, as benevolent and rational; but that comrade Krupskaya does not on her own account accept these resolutions? If that is so, let comrade Krupskaya acknowledge this openly, and not come out as the defender of the Party line against heretics in Narkompros.

On 7 March Schmidt's dismissal was confirmed by the Central Committee.[5] Krupskaya's reply to his article of 4 March, published in *Pravda* on the following day, was curt:

> Did comrade Schmidt have the right to speak against the labour and polytechnical school at a meeting of mainly non-party teachers of the city of Moscow, after the resolutions of [Lenin's] commission?
>
> As a Party member and a member of the collegium of Narkompros, he did not have that right.

Neither *Pravda* or *Izvestiya* carried an announcement of Schmidt's

* Both Schmidt and Krupskaya wrote as if the Party meeting had passed definite resolutions on the radical professionalization of the school. This was not so (see above, p. 197).

dismissal or of the Central Committee's appointment of his successor—E. A. Preobrazhensky.

It is unlikely that Lenin, having as it appears arranged Schmidt's dismissal, would have chosen Preobrazhensky to succeed him. Preobrazhensky's views on education were even more unpalatable to Lenin, Krupskaya, Lunacharsky and Pokrovsky than Schmidt's had been. Not only was he an opponent of the polytechnical school but also, under present circumstances, of the higher school. He regarded higher education, together with non-professional secondary education, *politprosvet* and the arts, as luxuries which the Soviet state could not for the time being afford.

Preobrazhensky, who was a member of the collegium of the Finance Commissariat and continued to work there after his appointment to Glavprofobr, saw education as an area of low financial priority. But he believed that the greater part of the money available for education should go to technical and professional training of adolescents and adult workers. The greatest need of the Russian economy, Preobrazhensky thought, was not for highly qualified technicians, but for technicians of middle qualifications and for skilled workmen.

These views were clearly stated in a paragraph of a long article on economic reform published by Preobrazhensky in *Pravda* on 16 July 1921. He wrote:

Now about Narkompros. There is no need to speak of the use of enlightenment. But it must be remembered that enlightenment exists on the basis of a definite surplus product of society. Where that product is small, then the 'fruits of enlightenment' will inevitably also be small. It is improper, above all for our socialist state, to imitate the ruined aristocrat who refuses to mend the roof so as to buy a valuable painting or an expensive library. Only that part of the national income can be spent on enlightenment which corresponds to the given level of development of socialist production. And that part which is spent must be distributed according to the importance of this or that branch of enlightenment for the whole economy of the country in general. In any case, higher education must be hugely diminished in favour of lower; and, in lower education, the general branch must be enormously diminished in favour of what is urgently important for industry and agriculture.

Preobrazhensky's bias against higher and general secondary education was reinforced by the conviction that they remained areas of bourgeois predominance.

In Narkompros, Preobrazhensky plunged into immediate political conflict with Glavsotsvos and Glavpolitprosvet, as well as organizational conflict with Litkens. From March to October 1921, Glavsotsvos was headed by Vladimir Alekseevich Nevsky.* [6] In October Nevsky was replaced by the 'bourgeois specialist'—a former member of the State Education Committee under the Provisional Government—N. N. Iordansky.[7] Throughout 1921, Glavsotsvos was the weakest of the chief administrations of Narkompros in internal political terms. But even under strong leadership, Preobrazhensky and the economic crisis would have made 1921 a dismal year for school administrators.

Before Preobrazhensky's first appearance in the Narkompros collegium as representative of Glavprofobr (31 March 1921),[8] Narkompros had discussed the question of distribution of educational work with adolescents between Glavsotsvos, Glavpolitprosvet, Glavprofobr and the Komsomol. The collegium had decided that the work should be unified under Glavsotsvos, with the cooperation of the Komsomol. Dunaevsky, representing the Komsomol, was dissatisfied with the decision and declared his intention of complaining to Maly Sovnarkom.[9]

Preobrazhensky, finding a controversy already in full swing, went one better than a complaint to Maly Sovnarkom. He complained against the decision, on behalf of Glavprofobr, to the Orgburo of the Central Committee. On 11 April, the Narkompros collegium was informed of the Orgburo's decision to transfer all work among adolescents to Glavprofobr. It resolved to complain to the Politburo on Glavsotsvos' behalf.[10] But the complaint was apparently without effect, and the Orgburo's decision for Preobrazhensky stood.

In July, Narkompros tackled the problem of the reorganization of the two senior classes of the secondary school into technicums.[11] This was a somewhat delayed reaction to a decision taken six months before, presumably stimulated by the end of the current school

* Not to be confused with V. I. Nevsky (Krivobokov), head of the VTSIK commission on Narkompros in 1920 and commissar for *rabfaks* from June of that year.

year. The speakers were Litkens, Preobrazhensky (for Glavprofobr) and V. A. Nevsky (for Glavsotsvos). The meeting decided that the 7-year school should be divided into a primary stage of 3 years and a secondary stage of 4 years. This meant that primary education was cut back to its pre-revolutionary norm of 3 years, instead of the 5 years envisaged by the United Labour School.

It was further decided that new premises should not be built for the technicums. Some of the existing secondary school buildings would remain secondary schools for the 11–15 age-group. Others would become technicums for adolescents from 15 to 19 years. 'With the beginning of the 1921–22 school year,' the collegium resolved, 'from 30% to 50% of all secondary schools possessing 3rd and 4th classes are to be closed for reorganization into technicums.'

Since few secondary schools in fact possessed 3rd and 4th classes (the 8th and 9th years of the 9-year school), it might seem that few schools were affected. But the resolution also provided that

> in each separate *guberniya* the buildings, equipment and teaching personnel of the secondary schools are to be divided between the *guberniya* departments of Glavprofobr and Glavsotsvos...so that the number of general educational schools with complete 7-year courses is in a ratio of 3 to 2 with technicums in the *guberniya*.

This meant that regardless of the existence of 3rd or 4th classes, a substantial proportion of secondary schools were to be closed for reorganization into technicums.

The debate was not and never had been really concerned with the fate of the 3rd and 4th classes of the secondary school. It was in fact a debate about whether the Soviet state could afford to offer general secondary education to the population as a whole, or whether education above primary level (formerly 5 years, now 3) should be predominantly professional. The resolution of the Narkompros collegium in July was a preliminary victory for the advocates of complete professionalization of secondary education.

Shortly after this resolution and the publication of Preobrazhensky's discouraging statement on 'the uses of enlightenment,* Lunacharsky declared war. His attack on Preobrazhensky, published

* See above, p. 215.

not in the national press but in the Narkompros journal,[12] began with the elaborate courtesies which are not intended to conciliate an opponent. Lunacharsky dealt first of all with the educational issue. Preobrazhensky, quite unwittingly in Lunacharsky's opinion, had given the impression that

middle and higher education are some sort of luxury, that these are in some way 'class' schools,...attentive to the interests of the governing classes [*sic*], which need be revived in socialist society only when there is money available to do so...

Anyone who took comrade Preobrazhensky literally would find himself not at all defending the policy of transitional Communism but, so to speak, the peasant–artisan policy, the kind of policy that a clever peasant or clever artisan might perhaps put forward...

I remember that comrade Preobrazhensky once argued at a meeting of the collegium that the number of specialists graduating from our educational institutions is too high, or at least high enough, which completely astonished me...Let us say directly that not only is it not necessary to cut down the numbers of our higher educational institutions, but we must tackle the problem of expanding their work...

Lunacharsky went on to discuss Preobrazhensky's view of enlightenment in general, and the necessity of art in particular.

It seems—this is what his article says—that we should not follow the policy of a ruined landowner who, selling some farm or cutting down his last forests, buys a fine painting for his gallery. And it is true that we should not do this...But we do not need to deviate into that sort of puritanism which announces the principle that 'man lives by bread alone'. And in this respect if, for example, we came to the conclusion that it was necessary to sell our whole museum collection abroad, exchanging it for the appropriate quantity of flour,* or to stop all artistic education or all artistic life in the country completely, we would hardly be acting rationally...

Because joyless life, deprived of all culture, ...is a hard-labour sentence ...I already see a sceptical smile on many lips—fables do not feed nightingales, it is true, but since we can scarcely feed the nightingale well even if we put a gag on all recitation of fables, ...the question is, are

* This example, of course, was not hypothetical. Russia was already exporting art in quantity (M. F. Andreeva, lately of Narkompros, was arranging its sale in Berlin), and there was sharp controversy within the government on how far this process should go.

even poor and hungry people to have the great comfort of art or are they not?

Preobrazhensky had the advantage of Lunacharsky in being able to publish his reply both in the Narkompros journal and the national press.[13] The strongest part of his case—which Lunacharsky, in his anxiety for the arts and the universities, almost overlooked—rested on the existing disproportion in the output of highly qualified technicians and skilled workers. The number of students enrolled in technicums and technical courses, Preobrazhensky stated, was two-thirds the number enrolled in higher schools, and only a quarter of the pre-war figure. Workers with middle qualifications were urgently needed in agriculture, especially in machine-building and peat-extraction, electrical engineering and school teaching. Preobrazhensky thought it would shortly be necessary 'to convert the majority of our present secondary schools' (at least their two senior classes for the fifteen to seventeen age-group) into pedagogical technicums for the training of primary school teachers.

Preobrazhensky considered that there was no need for more universities, and their number could even be diminished. Because of the lack of competent professors, even the medical faculties should not be expanded. The higher technical schools already in existence could accommodate more students. There was a general misconception of the numbers of highly trained specialists needed by the Russian economy in its present condition. Vesenkha, the main employer of graduates of higher technical schools, for example,

> offered us a demand for 4,000 engineers of various specialties in the coming year. We consider that figure exaggerated and inadequately based, taking into account the general contraction of our industry except for some individual branches.

The question of higher versus middle technical education was, in Preobrazhensky's opinion, an issue of class versus class.

> The bourgeois and intellectual strata of the population are frantically trying to maintain themselves and their children at the level of education and social position reached in the pre-revolutionary period. This, of course, is quite understandable. But the proletarian state will never allow the parents and children of the former privileged classes to decide the

question of the numbers and social origins of the future specialists we train in our schools. At the moment there is a genuine class war at the doors of the higher school between the worker–peasant majority of the country, which wants to have specialists from among its own kin in its own state, and the governing classes and strata linked with them. The proletarian state openly takes the side of its own people.

His conclusion was that it was necessary to limit the number of enrolments in the higher school as much on ideological as economic grounds.

Under Litkens' reorganization of Narkompros, higher education was administered by Glavprofobr, with GUS retaining only supervision of policy. The tough line which Narkompros had adopted towards Moscow University in the autumn of 1920 was regarded as an experiment, although for Glavprofobr—especially under Preobrazhensky—it was clearly the only conceivable policy.

Bogolepov, the appointed Rector of Moscow University, stood for unequivocal toughness. His policy was in effect to strengthen the *rabfak* to the point where it could destroy the remnants of the bourgeois university. Neither GUS under Pokrovsky nor Glavprofobr under Schmidt were in total sympathy with Bogolepov. Nor was Lenin, who was firmly convinced of the need to make maximum use of bourgeois specialists in all fields. As Pokrovsky wrote,

With the thriftiness of a good manager [*khozyain*] which was characteristic of him, Vladimir Ilyich did not in the least intend to part forever with the old and vital apparatus of Russian universities. Even in the faculty of social sciences he saw the chance of using the old teaching staff, not to mention in the higher technical school, where the slogan 'break less' [*lomaite pomen'she*] remained in force...[14]

Early in 1921, Bogolepov published a belligerent article in *Pravda* (27 February) arguing that 'only Communist "*spetsy*"* can put the economy of the country on other rails and build life anew'. In three years of Soviet power, Bogolepov wrote, the only gain for Communism in the universities had been the creation of the *rabfak*. It was time 'to put an end in the most definite way to every

* *Spetsy*—the common abbreviation for *spetsialisty* [specialists].

kind of university autonomy and freedom of teaching, and not give the professoriate any greater rights than other Soviet employees'.

Bogolepov found Schmidt too ready to make concessions to the professors, and sympathetic enough to the *rabfak*. Schmidt, in Bogolepov's view, allowed too much weight to the professors in the university administration, and relied too much on the students as a balancing force. 'Experience shows that students are too naive in the struggle with the well-organized class enemy, and lightly abandon their positions', Bogolepov wrote sadly. His suggestion was that the representation of the *rabfak* 'which the old professors hate so much' in the university administration should be increased at the expense of student representation.

Pokrovsky, although the creator of the *rabfak*, took up the argument in support of Schmidt. His answer to Bogolepov appeared in *Pravda* on 1 March. He used the typically oblique argument that students, since they were shortly to become members of a trade union, could not be denied representative rights in the management of their own 'enterprise'. He thought that the *rabfak* teachers were as a whole no more politically reliable than any other group of the intelligentsia, and so the *rabfak* 'as an *institution*' should not be given special representation and privileges.

With Schmidt's dismissal in March and Bogolepov's in May of 1921, the roles of Glavprofobr and the Rector of Moscow University were reversed. Bogolepov's successor was V. P. Volgin, Marxist historian and former Menshevik, who was relatively conciliatory in his approach to the old professors.[15] The tough line, formerly Bogolepov's, was taken over by Preobrazhensky at Glavprofobr. Immediately on taking office, Preobrazhensky appointed a new administration at the Moscow Higher Technical Institute which was unacceptable to the staff. The institute went on strike. In April, the Politburo intervened to reverse Glavprofobr's decision on the administration of the institute. A statement was subsequently issued over the signatures of Lunacharsky, for Narkompros, and Molotov, for the Central Committee (but not Preobrazhensky), instructing Communist students of the institute to behave less militantly towards the professors and the non-party students.[16]

This was a snub to Preobrazhensky, who had encouraged student militancy. He protested against the Politburo's decision. In reply Lenin read him a lecture on the proper treatment of bourgeois specialists. Reactionaries, Lenin wrote, ought to be exposed, but

> they must be exposed *in another way*. And on concrete grounds, . . . on the exact fact, action, statement. Then we can imprison them for a month or a year. It will be a good lesson.

Lenin found fault with both the stern and the permissive attitudes to specialists which were currently to be found in Narkompros. He suggested that Narkompros had something to learn from the Red Army, which had found out how to catch the old specialists in anti-Soviet acts, punish them, release them and re-employ them. The trouble with Lunacharsky and Pokrovsky was that they 'do not know how to "catch" their specialists'. But Preobrazhensky, in Lenin's opinion, did not know how to employ them.[17]

Lenin had had earlier trouble with Glavprofobr on the employment of specialists. At the time of Schmidt's polemic with Krupskaya, Lenin had asked Narkompros to provide him immediately with a list of educationalists with 'solid practical experience' both in the field of general and professional education. In answer to this, Schmidt produced a memorandum to show that not only did Glavprofobr employ specialists, but the members of its collegium were specialists themselves[18]—a point of view which Lenin had already vigorously denied in his February 'Directive', as Schmidt acknowledged in a reference to 'the opinion, recently expressed without proof in the press, that Narkompros does not employ specialists'.

Preobrazhensky was no more amenable than Schmidt had been to suggestions that he needed professional advisers, but Lenin did not give up the struggle. In June 1921 Lenin wrote to Preobrazhensky that

> *Recommendation* and *bringing forward* of specialists in Glavprofobr *must* be put on a *formal basis*. 100 to 200 people must at once be taken on to the staff and put on rations.[19]

In December he wrote again, this time to Pokrovsky: 'I am very much afraid that the absence of a major specialist as deputy head of Glavprofobr is *wrong*.'[20] Nevertheless, another Communist and non-specialist—Varvara Yakovleva—was appointed deputy early in 1922; and when she took over the presidency of Glavprofobr in March, the post of deputy passed to the Communist Rector of Moscow University, V. P. Volgin.[21]

Although it was common ground in Narkompros that the universities should submit themselves to Soviet discipline and 'proletarianization', there was no agreement about the method for achieving this. The bourgeois specialists of the academic world were approached in bewildering succession by Preobrazhensky with threats of liquidation, Pokrovsky with idiosyncratic logic, and Lunacharsky with a soft answer attempting to turn away wrath.

In June 1921 a meeting was held to approve the new university constitution, which tried to combine the elective principle with the principle of Narkompros appointment to the governing body of the university. (According to the new constitution, the governing body was to consist of three to five members appointed by Narkompros from candidates nominated by university staff, students, trade unions and local government bodies. Professors were to be appointed by GUS, on the nomination of specialist commissions[22].) Preobrazhensky was wisely absent. Lunacharsky spoke in a conciliatory tone, telling the professors that

> We do not deny freedom of science or freedom of teaching, but we cannot allow full freedom. It is a hard time, chains have to be borne, and for the time being we are bearing those chains. Youth is our future, and we cannot allow counter-revolutionary propaganda among our youth. The smallest weight might tip the scales against us, and therefore with a heavy heart we take on the role of censor. However there have to be strong arguments for this, and censorship can only be allowed in so far as it is absolutely necessary. In the social sciences, we want the voice of Marxist science to be heard. In the sphere of the exact sciences,...there are not these restrictions.

On the issue of university administration, Lunacharsky said that complete autonomy was out of the question.

> The internal life of the [higher] school must be open to the government, and then it is possible to establish cooperation. There is a practical

consideration: on being introduced into the general system of Soviet administration, the higher school finds in that system its protector...[23]

The meeting voted the Narkompros 'Statement on university administration' clause by clause. It was accepted by a majority ranging from 160 to 180 on separate clauses, with a minority of 45 to 56 against. Those present were 43 rectors, 46 professors, 71 government and Narkompros representatives and 136 students. Out of the total of 296 persons attending, 165 were Communists.[24]

The professors claimed that the meeting did not adequately represent the higher school, and protested to Lenin after the event that its decisions were invalid.[25] The 'Statement' nevertheless became law on 2 September 1921.

At the beginning of the 1921–2 academic year, Preobrazhensky came into his own with a list of universities and higher technical schools which must be closed. He presented the list to the collegium of Narkompros. There were some signs of discontent among its members, although it was admitted that a number of the institutions named scarcely existed except on paper. Volgin made a statement on the impossibility of closing all the listed institutions by 1 September, the beginning of the academic year, since it was already mid-August. Preobrazhensky's list was accepted after discussion, although the collegium ruled that the institutions offering general educational courses should not be closed but transferred to Glavpolitprosvet for use as people's universities [*narodnye universitety*].[26]

In December, Narkompros began an internal and external struggle over the budget, which was the tightest it had ever experienced. Larin's commission had allowed Narkompros a salaried staff of 513,100. Of these, the collegium of Narkompros allocated 60,000 to Glavprofobr and 76,450 to Glavpolitprosvet. Preobrazhensky told the collegium that if no further allocation for Glavprofobr was forthcoming from Narkompros, he would be obliged to protest at the budgetary meeting of VTSIK. He did so, and as a result 10,000 of Glavpolitprosvet's allocation was transferred to Glavprofobr.[27]

The budget season led directly to the season of strikes. The pattern of the previous year was repeated, except that in 1922 not only the Moscow Higher Technical Institute went on strike but also the physical–mathematical faculty of Moscow University and professors of the universities of Petrograd, Kazan and elsewhere. The strikes were directed against the new university constitution (which came into force in Moscow in November–December); against the *rabfak*, which the professors wanted abolished; and against the miserable economic position of the higher schools.[28] An exacerbating factor was late payment of salaries to the staff of higher schools in Moscow. Soviet historians have (somewhat unfairly) accused Preobrazhensky of Trotskyite provocation of the professors in this connection.[29]

Preobrazhensky's response to the strike was to move towards a policy of repression rather than one of conciliation. 'Class war' in the universities—*rabfak* and Communist students against the professors—was encouraged by Glavprofobr. But this was not the Central Committee's policy. The Central Committee intervened over the head of Glavprofobr with an offer of conciliation. Two commissions were established under the Central Committee. One, headed by Lunacharsky, was to review the economic position of the higher school.[30] The other, of which Stalin was a member, investigated Preobrazhensky's handling of the strike and recommended his dismissal from Glavprofobr.[31] Work in the physical–mathematical faculty of Moscow University began again early in February.

Preobrazhensky, unlike Schmidt, was too big a figure to be dismissed from Glavprofobr for reasons of purely educational policy. In fact, he was currently conducting a spirited attack on the NEP towards the countryside. His theses on economic policy were repudiated by Lenin in March 1922,[32] but the controversy surrounding them was one of the main topics of debate at the Eleventh Party Congress.

In the debates at the congress both Preobrazhensky and Lenin touched on educational questions, although they were ignored by almost all the other speakers. Preobrazhensky's comment on the professors' strike was:

The Central Committee of the Party has violated our Party programme ...There is a point in our programme where it says that we must attract [bourgeois specialists] into comradely relations, give them the best material support etc. But there is another point that the Party must not make any political concessions to that stratum, and it is put even more strongly. In relation to the professors, in whose hands lies the fate of our worker youth, the Central Committee allowed a political retreat at a moment when that retreat was not necessary, when it injured us and put the proletarians of our *rabfaks* in a bad position...

His only supporter on this point was S. S. Ioffe, representing the Communist students of Moscow *rabfaks* at the Party Congress. Ioffe was dismayed by the concessions made to the professors. 'Where, we ask, must this retreat which Narkompros has begun and continues end?'

Lenin, in his speech to the congress, insisted that the line of the Communist students and *rabfaks* against the professors had been too strong—'It is true that the Communist cells are fine cells, and the *rabfaks* are fine *rabfaks*, but they are not insured against mistakes, they are not sacred.' He criticized Preobrazhensky's repressive policies towards the higher school:

If the Party is directed like this, it would really lead to ruin. Not because comrade Preobrazhensky incorrectly understands politics in general, but because he approaches everything...[as] a theoretician, looking for definite, usual and accustomed limits, a propagandist who works with various measures directed towards propaganda. Everyone knows and values his strong side, but when he comes up with a political and administrative point of view, something monstrous comes out.[33]

In 1922 an impartial observer of Russian universities (Paul Scheffer, correspondent of the *Berliner Tageblatt*) noted that they were still a refuge for the liberal middle-class, and had this to say on their treatment by the Soviet government:

[The government] goes ahead methodically with the conversion and conquest of the universities, but without the high-handedness with which it treated other professional classes. It has thereby shown its respect for facts in the intellectual sphere. Most of the professors whose subjects were of political significance have had very unpleasant experiences, have suffered and are still suffering from unfair treatment, and have lain in prison. But in this the principal part has been played by the Tcheka (Extraordinary Commission) and not the governmental authorities. It must be remembered that the professors, especially the liberals, were always very keen politicians, and had a large part in the appointment of Ministers in the first revolution...

But no-one can conceal from himself the possibility that the Communist State, though it does not destroy the leaders of bourgeois intellectual life in Russia, may let them die out and fill their places with politically reliable but intellectually inadequate successors...[34]

CHILD WELFARE

From 1918, Narkompros had claimed that everything relating to the welfare of children—nurseries, kindergartens, children's homes, education of handicapped and delinquent children, feeding and clothing of children of school age—should be in its hands. This claim brought it into conflict with the health and social security authorities. Control of the children's homes [*detskie doma*] was particularly hotly contested by Narkompros and the Commissariat of Social Security, which had inherited the orphanages formerly under the administration of the Ministry of Welfare.

The very concept of an orphanage was anathema to Narkompros which, from the beginning, regarded the *detskii dom* as at least a potential alternative to the school, having the advantage of separating children from the bourgeois influence of the family and developing the habits of communal life. After inspecting the former orphanages (now 'children's colonies') of the department of social security in the Smolensk district, Lunacharsky reported that 'all the staff and all the children without exception are longing to enter the education department'.[35] The leaders of the Commissariat of Social Security, especially Lenin's sister Anna Elizarova, resisted the transfer of its children's institutions to Narkompros, but, Lunacharsky wrote, 'let them not exaggerate the potentialities of the old "welfare" personnel...There is no doubt at all that the new people whom Narkompros at once invites to work are on an incomparably higher level.'

In 1919, after the question had been repeatedly discussed in Sovnarkom, the administration of children's homes was transferred to Narkompros. This was one of the few interdepartmental battles in which Narkompros had an opponent its own size or smaller.

Anna Elizarova, head of the department of child welfare, moved to Narkompros with extreme reluctance.[36] In the course of 1920 the collegium of Narkompros was many times called on to adjudicate disputes between Elizarova's department and its own Council for the Defence of Children.

Early in 1919, Narkompros stated that

> Children's labour communes must serve as the instrument for the destruction of the institution of the bourgeois family. Organizing life on Communist bases, they not only prepare future Communist citizens, but... serve as hearths of Communism, stimulating and guaranteeing the reconstruction of adult society on new foundations.[37]

The children's commune, having its own school, club and workshops and managing its own domestic economy, was the basic type of the Narkompros *detskii dom*.

Children had ration priority, and the schools and children's homes were supposed to feed and clothe them free of charge. Despite repeated legislation little was achieved, mainly because Narkompros was unable to obtain supplies from the economic commissariats. In 1920, for example, Narkompros requested 9,298,725 pairs of shoes, was promised 550,000 pairs and received 250,000. The corresponding figures for children's socks were 5,632,000 requested, 385,000 promised, none received. Narkompros agents in the provinces were 'authorized' by the Food Commissariat to see that the schools and children's homes received food rations. But Narkompros' annual report suggests that these agents could do little but confront local authorities with their reproachful presence:

> The very fact of the presence of these agents in the provinces fixes the attention of the food authorities on the position of children, and thus achieves an improvement of food and supply.[38]

The Narkompros agency for the provision of food, clothing and accommodation for children was the Council for the Defence of Children. The task was, of course, beyond its strength. It had few practical successes on the home front, although on one remarkable occasion it achieved a foreign policy victory in rescuing a group of

Petrograd 'child-colonists' abducted (in Narkompros' view) from Siberia by the American Red Cross.[39]

The council was more successful in the field of policy. It was enlightened in its attitude to juvenile delinquency. 'We do not recognize juvenile crime. We know only sick children, spoilt by an ugly environment and education.'[40] Its policy was given legislative form by Sovnarkom in the decree 'On minors accused of socially dangerous acts',[41] which forbade trial and imprisonment of children under eighteen and directed that delinquent children be sent to reform schools under Narkompros.

It was Narkompros' misfortune that its enlightened policy towards juvenile offenders was introduced at the beginning of a period of unprecedented juvenile delinquency and homelessness [*besprizornost'*]. The gulf between the policies of Narkompros and the everyday experience of local authorities was almost unbridgeable. Moreover, the children's homes themselves presented a security problem. There were cases of indiscipline and delinquency among the children, even in the experimental school of the Institute of School Instructors of Physical Labour in Moscow in which members of the collegium of Narkompros took a personal interest.* Cases of counter-revolutionary activity among the teachers and administrators of children's homes were reported. H. G. Wells, visiting Russia in September 1920, noticed that 'many men and women politically suspect or openly discontented with the existing political conditions, and yet with a desire to serve Russia, have found in these places work that they can do with a good conscience'. Early in 1920, members of Narkompros' Committee on Minors were arrested. Lunacharsky protested to Lenin, who passed the protest on to Dzerzhinsky, head of the Cheka. Dzerzhinsky replied that there was 'serious evidence' of 'monstrous plundering, abuse and White-guardism'.[42]

A. D. Kalinina, a Narkompros worker, toured the south-eastern

* A Narkompros investigation at the beginning of 1920 revealed theft, speculation and card-playing among the children. A child accused of stealing and boycotted by his fellows committed suicide. The incident was discussed with great emotion in the collegium on 18 February, Lunacharsky recalling in distress that the dead child had once brought a message to him in the Kremlin. Clearly he and other members of the collegium felt themselves to be in a real sense *in loco parentis* to the children.

regions of European Russia for the Council for the Defence of Children at the end of 1920. She found that local officials had cordoned off the Caucasus and Don region and were not letting children through. Inside the cordon, hordes of children were running wild, starving and terrorizing the population; some of them were armed. Kalinina made a report both to the Council and to Dzerzhinsky of the Cheka.[43]

In September 1920, after hearing a report from G. F. Grinko on the position of education in the Ukraine, Narkompros decided to follow the Ukrainian example in reorganizing the Council for the Defence of Children as an interdepartmental organ of 'highly authoritative' membership coordinating the work of the Commissariats of Education, Health, Food, Labour and Workers' Inspection (Rabkrin). The project was finalized in December.[44] The new council (now 'State Council') was to be under VTSIK, with the president of VTSIK, M. I. Kalinin, at its head, Lunacharsky as his deputy, and representatives of the commissariats listed above together with the Commissariats of War and Justice. Its functions were to be the coordination of help to children suffering 'extraordinary need', and organization of world-wide publicity for the plight of Russia's children. The council was to work through existing authorities, temporarily creating its own apparatus only in exceptional cases.

But before Narkompros had formally put its project for a 'State Council for the Defence of Children' to VTSIK, Dzerzhinsky intervened. After reading A. D. Kalinina's report and consulting with Lenin, he telephoned Lunacharsky to say that he had important business to discuss. Lunacharsky later wrote an account of their conversation as follows:

> The questions on which our lines of work crossed were very few, and I could not at once guess what the creator and leader of the terrible Cheka wanted to discuss with me...'I want to put a part of my personal energy and, more important, the energy of the Cheka into the struggle with child homelessness [*besprizornost'*]', Dzerzhinsky told me, and in his eyes at once burned that rather feverish flame of excited energy familiar to us all ...'In this matter we must rush directly to help, as if we saw children drowning. Narkompros alone has not the strength to cope. It needs the

broad help of all Soviet society. A broad commission under VTSIK—of course with the closest participation of Narkompros—must be created, including within it all institutions and organizations which may be useful. I have already said something of this to a few people. I would like to stand at the head of that commission, and I want to include the Cheka apparatus directly in the work... I think that our apparatus is one of those which works most efficiently. Its branches are everywhere. People take notice of it. They are rather afraid of it...'

I could not find words to answer...[45]

Dzerzhinsky had his way, although certainly not with Lunacharsky's wholehearted support. Early in 1921, VTSIK established a Commission for the Improvement of the Life of Children.[46] On 17 February, *Izvestiya* announced the membership of the commission: Dzerzhinsky (president), Kornev of the Cheka (deputy president), Vetoshkin of Rabkrin, representatives of the Commissariats of Health and Food and of VTSSPS, and a representative of Narkompros yet to be appointed.

The announcement of the creation of a VTSIK commission on child welfare, headed by Dzerzhinsky and using the Cheka apparatus, caused a sensation. Even the Narkompros journal, in an article largely devoted to calming its readers, admitted that

> the fact that the business had been personally entrusted to the head of the Cheka created some panic in pedagogical circles, and it was necessary to establish exactly what were the commission's methods of work and its approach to children's institutions.[47]

An exchange of articles in *Izvestiya* between Lunacharsky and Vetoshkin, Rabkrin's representative on the commission, did not do a great deal to clarify the position. On 24 February, Lunacharsky outlined his own view of what the commission's tasks should be, claiming optimistically that this view 'will meet full sympathy in the commission'. The Cheka's function, he wrote, would be to discipline government supply organs. It would in no sense intimidate administrators and teachers, or put the children under harsh discipline.

> The point was not to frighten the teacher with a new Egyptian plague, to put him under extraordinary control, or to hound him for his blunders,

...but to give him material help. If Narkompros and its local organs get more food, clothing, bedding and school equipment, then it will be able to cope with everything else.

Vetoshkin, in an article published the next day, reassured readers that there were no differences of opinion between Lunacharsky and the commission, thus making it painfully clear that there were. He agreed with Lunacharsky that there was no question of intimidation of teachers and children, because

it is quite obvious that if the VTSIK commission headed by comrade Dzerzhinsky thought of introducing specifically 'Chekist' methods into its work, that would be worth little and be of no use to the children...The tasks of the commission are to bring everything possible to the help of children, using both the energy of the Cheka apparatus and the authority of the supreme legislative organ of the Republic [VTSIK] and the local executive committees.

Vetoshkin said nothing of the leading role of Narkompros.

Dzerzhinsky's instructions to the Cheka on 'urgent measures for the improvement of the life of children'[48] directed that work should be conducted 'in the closest contact and in agreement' with the government organs of supply and protection of children—that is, with local branches of the Food Commissariat and Narkompros. But his formulation of the tasks of the commission made it plain that disciplinary or 'Chekist' methods were also necessary. The commission would

investigate the position and number of homeless children in the relevant *gubernii* and the condition of all children's homes; ensure that decrees on the supply and feeding of children were exactly implemented; give continual help to the Soviet institutions of the *guberniya* in the business of children's feeding and supply; ensure that children's institutions are provided with appropriate premises, an adequate amount of fuel and equipment; *uncover every kind of squandering, abuse, cases of criminal attitude to children and slipshodness, and bring the guilty to trial before the Revolutionary Tribunal and the People's Courts.* [my emphasis]

The commission formally endorsed the position of Sovnarkom and Narkompros on the treatment of juvenile offenders, reminding its agents that 'for children in Soviet Russia there are no trials and no imprisonment', and instructing local executive committees immediately to set up commissions on the affairs of minors where these did not already exist, and to organize children's homes.[49]

The GPU (as the Cheka became after 1921) in fact maintained its own network of children's homes for juvenile offenders parallel with those of Narkompros, throughout the 1920s.*

In spite of the close contact which Lunacharsky had predicted between Narkompros and Dzerzhinsky's commission, Narkompros did not send an influential spokesman to the commission's meetings, and seemed to have difficulty maintaining any representative there at all. Its original representative—the last member of the commission to be appointed—was apparently nominated by Vetoshkin of Rabkrin. Three weeks later he was replaced, on Litkens' suggestion, by Z. G. Grinberg of the Organizational Centre. Grinberg later passed the job on to V. A. Nevsky, head of Glavsotsvos. But in October Nevsky offered his resignation from the commission in the course of a meeting of the Narkompros collegium attended by Kornev, a member of the Cheka and deputy president of the commission. Nevsky's successor was an obscure member of the Organizational Centre.[50]

In July 1921, at the height of the famine in the Volga region, two bodies were set up to organize famine relief: the non-political 'All-Russian Committee of Aid to the Starving' and a VTSIK 'Commission of Aid to the Starving Population'. The non-political committee was, in Soviet context, a most unusual body. Its members were supposed to be prominent public figures, chosen regardless of Party allegiance. The basis of choice was at least partly international reputation, since one of the committee's functions was to be fund-raising on a world scale. Besides the Communist Kamenev, Lunacharsky, Krasin and Smidovich, the committee's members included Gorky, Yuzhin-Sumbatov, the veteran narodnik revolutionary Vera Figner, and the former Cadet leaders Prokopovich, Kuskova and Kishkin.[51]

In its brief existence the committee—or more exactly Gorky,

* The '*Shkola imeni Dostoevskogo*' described in the novel by G. Belykh and A. Panteleev, *Respublika Shkid* (Moscow, 1927) was run by the GPU. So, after an early period under the Ukrainian Narkompros, were Makerenko's children's colonies.

acting on the committee's behalf—did obtain a promise of support from the Hoover Famine Relief organization. But at its third meeting, the committee was disbanded by the Cheka and a number of its non-Communist members were arrested.[52] Prokopovich, Kuskova and Kishkin were, according to a Soviet historian, using the committee as a base for international intrigue against the Soviet government. There were protests from some leading (but unidentified) Communists at the treatment of the committee and the arrest of its members, but Lenin supported the action of the Cheka.[53]

The VTSIK 'Commission of Aid to the Starving Population' created at the same time was headed by M. I. Kalinin, and included Kamenev, Smidovich and Rykov. Lunacharsky, who was not originally a member, attended meetings from 22 July and was accepted as a member on 28 July.[54]

In spite of the dissolution of the non-political 'All-Russian Committee', Lunacharsky evidently thought the moment appropriate to move against the Dzerzhinsky Commission for the Improvement of the Life of Children. His aim was to set up a non-Chekist but powerful organization for the protection of children which would work closely in collaboration with Narkompros. On 21 July, the collegium of Narkompros on his suggestion passed a resolution

> to empower the Commissar, Lunacharsky, to suggest to the Commission of Aid to the Starving Population in the name of Narkompros that all questions of aid to starving children... be taken out of the competence of the VTSIK Commission for the Improvement of the Life of Children... and that the members of the VTSIK Commission of Aid to the Starving Population should create a special sub-commission of aid to the juvenile population.

The president of the sub-commission would be Lunacharsky; and the sub-commission would use the child-welfare apparatus of Narkompros.[55]

The next day (as *Izvestiya* reported on 26 July) Lunacharsky conveyed this suggestion to Kalinin's Commission of Aid to the Starving Population—in effect inviting it to join him in a manœuvre against Dzerzhinsky's Commission for the Improvement of the Life of Children. His suggestion was accepted by the commission, which accordingly resolved to form 'a special section of aid to starving children'. But within a few days this decision was reversed. *Izvestiya* reported on 28 July that the presidium of the Commission for Aid to the Starving Population had 'decided after an exchange of opinions not to organize a new commission, but to conduct work on aid to children of the famine region through the VTSIK Commission for the Improvement of the Life of Children' under Dzerzhinsky. On 29 July, *Izvestiya* reported that Kornev, deputy president of the Commission for Improvement of the Life of Children, had been coopted on to the Commission of Aid to the Starving Population, no doubt with the aim of restoring goodwill between the two commissions.

Shortly after Lunacharsky's unsuccessful attempt to dislodge Dzerzhinsky's Commission, the commission began compulsory evacuation of children from the famine districts of the Volga. In November the commission, in consultation with Narkompros, approved a project for the evacuation of first 600 and then a further 1,000 children to Czechoslovakia through the Red Cross.[56] Neither of these measures was entirely happy in its effects. Moscow became flooded with child evacuees whom neither Narkompros nor the GPU could accommodate. Distressing reports of the indoctrination of Soviet children by Russian emigré teachers in Czechoslovakia were received by Narkompros, and publicized by Lunacharsky in an article with the alarmist title 'Wrangelites are educating our children' in *Izvestiya* of 2 February 1922. In the autumn of 1922, Dzerzhinsky's Commission began to return evacuated children to the Volga region. 'This was necessary', Dzerzhinsky's widow tells us in her memoirs, 'because many children had begun to return to their homes on their own initiative.'[57]

Dzerzhinsky's Commission survived another political challenge in March 1922 when, on the suggestion of a Sovnarkom commission under G. M. Leplevsky,* president of Maly Sovnarkom, the presidium of VTSIK decided to disband it. 'Dzerzhinsky was informed of this,' writes Sofia Dzerzhinskaya, 'and on March 24 sent the

* This was not Leplevsky's first brush with the security organs. His unpublished memoirs on the 1921 debate on the legality of actions of the Cheka are quoted in E. Drabkina, 'Winter crossing', in *Novyi mir* (1968), no. 10, pp. 82 ff.

president of VTSIK, M. I. Kalinin, a letter of protest against the decision to liquidate the Children's Commission [*detkomissiya*]. In his letter he said: "...I make a categorical protest against such a resolution, and consider that no other institution is in a condition to provide such aid to children as the VTSIK Commission has given up to now..." '[58]

Dzerzhinsky's protest was successful. In the years that followed, Narkompros continued to play a secondary and subordinate role to the GPU in the field of child welfare.

THE ARTS AND PROLETKULT

The Party meeting on education decided to abolish the arts sector of Narkompros (of which Lunacharsky was president) and transfer the greater part of its work to Glavpolitprosvet. Narkompros proper kept only a Chief Artistic Committee [Glakhkom] to supervise theoretical work in the arts. Like GUS, its counterpart in the field of research and higher education, Glakhkom was a part of the new Academic Centre of Narkompros. Lunacharsky was not a member of Glakhkom. Its organizer and first president was A. M. Rossky of Rabkrin, formerly learned secretary to the collegium of LITO. He was succeeded in May 1921 by the literary scholar P. S. Kogan.[59]

Litkens and the Party meeting intended Glavpolitprosvet to become the highest authority in the organization of the arts. In February 1921, the Glavpolitprosvet collegium gave itself 'the right of veto from the political point of view' of all current work in the arts and sciences. Glakhkom was to have no veto, although it might query any decision by Glavpolitprosvet in the collegium of Narkompros.[60]

Glavpolitprosvet did not find it easy to form an arts administration. Its first choice for the head of the Glavpolitprosvet arts sector—Davydov of the Moscow Council of Trade Unions—was not available. In February, Glavpolitprosvet requested Narkompros not to 'force the pace of transfer' of its arts departments. With the exception of P. Voevodin of FOTO-KINO, none of the former heads of the Narkompros arts departments moved to Glavpolitprosvet. David Shterenberg of IZO remained for a time in the Academic Centre, and then became head of the IZO department of Glavprofobr. Glavpolitprosvet proposed P. Kiselis, a fairly undistinguished 'revolutionary' painter, as head of its own IZO, and insisted on his appointment in spite of the objections of Glakhkom. Like Shterenberg, Valery Bryusov, formerly head of LITO, moved to Glavprofobr; Glavpolitprosvet appointed A. Serafimovich. Nadezhda Bryusova (sister of Valery, and an experienced worker in the field of popular musical organization) was invited to become head of Glavpolitprosvet MUZO, but preferred to keep her job at MONO. V. E. Meyerhold, formerly head of Narkompros TEO, was appointed deputy to Kozyrev (a Communist from the Commissariat of Agriculture) at Glavpolitprosvet TEO, but almost immediately resigned.[61]

The experience and artistic standing of the heads of the Glavpolitprosvet arts departments compared poorly both with Glakhkom and the Academic Centre—which employed the artist Natan Altman, the composer N. Ya. Myaskovsky, P. S. Kogan and Elena Malinovskaya—or the arts departments of Glavprofobr—with Shterenberg, Bryusov and the music theorist B. L. Yavorsky. Litkens' plan had, of course, not provided that Glavprofobr should have arts departments as well as Glavpolitprosvet and the Academic Centre. They were formed, almost certainly on the initiative of Lunacharsky as president of Glavprofobr, early in 1921.*

Glavpolitprosvet's arts departments suffered from absenteeism, which was partly the result of appointing Communists mainly employed elsewhere as heads of departments. Kozyrev, head of Glavpolitprosvet TEO, was not only concurrently working in the Commissariat of Agriculture but was frequently out of Moscow. His deputy, the theatrical 'specialist' V. V. Tikhonovich, offered his resignation at the end of 1921, claiming that as a result of Kozyrev's absence the department was unrepresented on all important theatrical commissions, and 'theatrical policy is made everywhere and by everyone except TEO, which has been turned into a purely executive apparatus'.[62]

* Except for the Glavprofobr department of 'artistic–industrial education', set up early in 1920.

One of the purposes of the reorganization of the arts was—following the prescripts of the Central Committee's letter 'On the Proletkults'—to remove Bogdanovists, futurists and cultural iconoclasts from Narkompros and Proletkult. But this purpose was very difficult to accomplish. It was almost impossible to replace the former leaders of Narkompros and Proletkult in the arts with persons who were not themselves Bogdanovists, futurists or cultural iconoclasts. In fact both in Narkompros under Lunacharsky and Proletkult under Lebedev-Polyansky the former leaders were closer to the Central Committee's position on the arts than were their subordinates.

Lebedev-Polyansky, president of Proletkult until December 1920, had been a member of *Vpered* before the revolution but was 'neither a philosophical nor a political disciple of A. Bogdanov'.[63] He supported Proletkult autonomy, but had worked in Narkompros and in cooperation with Lunacharsky. He was not a cultural iconoclast, and opposed futurist influences in Proletkult:

> Dissatisfied writers claim that Proletkult 'polemicizes with Comfuturists* and imaginists' and even forbids [proletarian writers] to perform at the bourgeois Poets' Café...Yes, Proletkult struggles both with futurism and imaginism, and sees the influence of the dying bourgeoisie with its perverted tastes even in the Communist futurists...[64]

The successor to Lebedev-Polyansky, appointed by the plenum of the Central Committee of Proletkult on the nomination of its Communist fraction, was V. F. Pletnev.[65] Pletnev represented a more radical and intransigent wing of Proletkult than Lebedev-Polyansky (and, unlike Polyansky, did not end his life as an Academician). The Central Committee's letter 'On the Proletkults' was not published in the following issue of *Proletarskaya kul'tura*, and was mentioned only obliquely. But the latest in a series of articles by Bogdanov on organizational sciences appeared as usual in a prominent position and without editorial criticism.[66] This was the last issue of the journal. At least part of the responsibility for its content must belong to Pletnev, who had already succeeded Lebedev-Polyansky as president of Proletkult. Pletnev was presumably also involved in

* Communist futurists.

Proletkult's issue of a special pamphlet (printed in Rostov-on-Don) containing Bogdanov's theses on organizational science, Pletnev's theses on the arts, and statements in favour of the autonomy of Proletkult.[67]

Pletnev's position on the arts closely resembled that of Bukharin, who seems to have acted to some extent as Pletnev's patron, both in a private capacity and as editor of *Pravda*. Pletnev was the author of the play *Mstitel'* (after Claudel) which Bukharin had praised in 1919.* On 12 April of the same year, an article by Pletnev arguing against 'professionalization' of the proletarian artist appeared in *Pravda*. It was also *Pravda* which, on 27 September 1922, published Pletnev's article 'On the ideological front' which became the subject of a celebrated political and literary battle. Lenin read the article, and saw it as epitomizing the spirit of proletarian iconoclasm in culture which he most disliked. He therefore commissioned Ya. A. Yakovlev of the *agitprop* department of the Central Committee to write an attack on Pletnev for publication in *Pravda*. But Bukharin took this as an attack on himself, and threatened to reply 'with all severity' in the columns of *Pravda* if Lenin insisted on his publishing Yakovlev's article in its original form. The article, according to Bukharin,[68] was revised, and *Pravda* duly published it on 24 and 25 October 1922.

Lunacharsky described Pletnev as one of those people 'full of revolutionary enthusiasm' who looked forward to 'a cultural October':

> They imagined that there would be...a taking of the Academy of Sciences or the Bolshoi Theatre by assault, like the taking of the Winter Palace, and new people would be established there, as far as possible of proletarian origins, or at any rate smiling kindly on the proletariat...[69]

Pletnev was of the theatrical left, attacked the concept of professionalism in the theatre on the grounds that it alienated the proletarian artists from their industrial environment, and was increasingly influenced by futurism. His play *Mstitel'* was produced in wholly traditional style, according to the critic of *Vestnik teatra* (1920, no. 50); but in 1921 the Proletkult studio gave futurist productions to his plays *Meksikanets* and *Lena* (S. M. Eisenstein,

* See above, pp. 147–8.

pupil of Meyerhold and later famous as a film director, was involved in both productions); and Lunacharsky, after seeing the production of *Lena*, wrote—'Alas, . . . futurism is flowing into Proletkult in great waves.'[70]

For the proletarians, futurism denoted a group and not an artistic style. Their response to the Central Committee's criticism of futurism was to call for a purge of 'persons calling themselves futurists or Comfuturists' from all Proletkult organizations. However, the influence of futurism as an artistic style did not decline in Proletkult after the Central Committee's letter but increased. Proletkult's cultural iconoclasm also increased, being no longer restrained by the literary intellectuals 'of pre-revolutionary formation' Lunacharsky, Lebedev-Polyansky and Bogdanov.

Bogdanov took no active part in Proletkult after December 1920, but this did not remove the danger of Bogdanovist philosophical and political heresy among Proletkult members. An anonymous pamphlet entitled 'We are collectivists' [*My-kollektivisty*] was circulated at the second Congress of Proletkult in November 1921. It is said to have attacked Communist policies, cast doubt on the socialist character of the October Revolution, defended Machist and Bogdanovist philosophy and declared political support for the 'Workers' opposition' group in the Communist Party.[71]

The collectivist manifesto was attacked by Bukharin in *Pravda* of 22 November 1921, and by Pokrovsky at the Proletkult Congress then in session. Following these attacks, the Communist faction of the Proletkult Congress passed a resolution declaring the formation of the 'collectivist' group within the Communist Party to be 'a most harmful disorganizing step in the objective circumstances of the given moment'. But there was no open attack on Proletkult—'I do not know into whose head the fantasy of disbanding the Proletkults could come', Pokrovsky told the congress—and the organization continued under Pletnev's presidency.[72]

The influence and scope of Proletkult activity declined very sharply from the second half of 1921, but the main causes seem to have been economic. 'There are no Proletkults left', Pelshe wrote in an article in *Izvestiya* (8 November 1921) on the general collapse of *politprosvet* with the withdrawal of central subsidy. Proletkult lost its subsidy from Narkompros early in 1922, receiving the 'Hermitage' theatre and its grounds as a parting endowment. Narkompros admitted this to be inadequate, but said that it could afford no more. Within a few months—against the intentions of Narkompros—Proletkult lost the 'Hermitage' theatre as well through the action of Moscow Soviet.[73] It was later supported by VTSSPS.

Given that Pletnev was a cultural iconoclast, a semi-futurist and probably also a semi-Bogdanovist, it might have been expected that Glavpolitprosvet would keep Proletkult under particularly close supervision in order to counteract the influences declared by the Central Committee to be harmful. But it did nothing of the kind. Instead, Pletnev himself was appointed head of the arts sector of Glavpolitprosvet.[74]

Pletnev's appointment illustrates the gulf between policy decisions on paper and the realities of departmental life. Nobody could have been less sympathetic to cultural radicalism than Krupskaya, president of Glavpolitprosvet. But she put forward no alternative candidate. In fact it was almost inevitable that once the organization of the arts was taken from Lunacharsky it would pass to a cultural iconoclast—if Kerzhentsev had not accepted appointment as Soviet ambassador to Sweden in 1921, he would almost certainly have been appointed to Glavpolitprosvet to take charge of the arts—for want of an alternative candidate. Lunacharsky was the only prominent Communist active in the organization of the arts who was not sympathetic (or not exclusively sympathetic) to the artistic left.

The collegium of Glavpolitprosvet, asking the Central Committee for the second time to send Pletnev to the arts sector, described him as 'a very valuable worker in political education'.[75]

But Pletnev's radicalism was, in practice, uncongenial to the collegium of Glavpolitprosvet and so, having secured his appointment, Glavpolitprosvet tended to frustrate his plans. When Pletnev put forward theses on the principles of theatrical policy, the collegium of Glavpolitprosvet removed their more radical elements —deleting the point 'denying all significance for the theatres except that of the school and the tribune' and weakening Pletnev's call for an entirely new repertoire for the theatre by 'recognizing the necessity of cooperating with AkTEO [the theatre department under the

Academic Centre of Narkompros], in the sense of using the classical repertoire...'[76]

Because Glavpolitprosvet was doubtful of Pletnev's theatrical policy and Glavpolitprosvet TEO lacked active leadership, the administration of the theatre tended more and more to revert to Lunacharsky. This happened in spite of the fact that Lunacharsky now held no office in connection with the organization of the arts; and it meant the defeat of another of the purposes of the reorganization of Narkompros, which was to take the arts out of Lunacharsky's control. The list of theatres to receive state subsidy was prepared in September 1921 by a commission of Lunacharsky, Litkens, Pletnev and Malinovskaya (head of AkTEO), in consultation with Avanesov, deputy Commissar of Rabkrin.[77] Most of the commission's work seems to have been done by Lunacharsky. All the subsidized theatres came under the control of the Academic Centre of Narkompros, which—as Meyerhold had complained in 1920—left Glavpolitprosvet TEO with very few theatres of importance and no financial control over the theatre at all. Early in 1922, 'in view of the critical position of [state] theatres, both in the administrative and the artistic respect', Lunacharsky took the administration of state theatres 'out of the competence of any intermediate organs whatsoever, putting them directly in dependence on me personally'.[78]

A sour but justified comment on the reorganization of the arts departments of Narkompros came from the dispossessed—Meyerhold and his supporters Bebutov and Derzhavin:

The Soviet bourgeois [*sovbury*] of the capitals are bustling around enthusiastically fulfilling the plan from above, burrowing in the labyrinthine corridors of the reorganized Narkompros.

So many chief administrations! So many centres! Before there was only one of TEO, MUZO, IZO, LITO and KINO, but now there are as many as there are chief administrations, as many as there are centres. Before, as the People's Commissar said, for him to go round his domain cost great labour in finding out the addresses of all the departments and sub-departments. But now the provincial who comes on business to the capital must spend half a year or more in the corridors of this man-made labyrinth, looking for one of the missing employees to tell him the address of the institution to which he has been sent from the provinces...[79]

GLAVPOLITPROSVET

Glavpolitprosvet had a good start, with the support of the Central Committee of the Party and the promise of cooperation from local Party committees. Preobrazhensky assisted at its birth, and presented theses on Glavpolitprosvet at the Tenth Party Congress in March 1921. This was the first time that any aspect of Narkompros had been put on the agenda of a Party congress.

The future of Glavpolitprosvet depended partly on its success in unifying the *politprosvet* networks of various authorities under its control. The largest networks had been established by the political administrations of the army (PUR) and transport (Glavpolitput). PUR reported in the first quarter of 1920 that it was maintaining 2,328 schools, 3,088 libraries and reading rooms, 1,315 clubs, 472 theatres and 320 cinemas.[80] Glavpolitput provided no comparable figures, but reported that during the month of August 1920 it organized 1,150 lectures, 1,612 theatrical performances, 726 concerts, 429 concert-meetings, 84 theatre-meetings, 6,328 meetings, 922 assemblies, 1,035 discussions, 38 conferences, 687 film shows, 10 excursions, and 12 children's mornings.[81] PUR appears to have had a large staff and been relatively well supplied with printed matter. Glavpolitput (judging from the nature of its activities) was equipped with film projectors but not books or newspapers, and employed fewer people than PUR.

There was very strongly entrenched opposition in PUR to any suggestion of union with Narkompros. In April 1920, a meeting of military delegates to the Ninth Party Congress called to discuss political education voted against uniting work in the forces with the work of the Narkompros extramural department. An official statement on PUR issued in September contained no clause even on cooperation (let alone union) with Narkompros in the field of political education. The extramural department of Narkompros reported at this time that although agreement with PUR had at one stage almost been reached, a change of leadership in PUR had wrecked the negotiations.[82]

The Sovnarkom decree on Glavpolitprosvet of November 1920*

* See above, pp. 180–5.

provided that the *politprosvet* apparatus of PUR was to enter Glavpolitprosvet, except for 'the organizationally-isolated political departments of the Army of the fronts and the reserves'. What this meant was that Glavpolitprosvet became responsible for all work in army divisions and institutions of the rear, and created a 'military section' for this purpose. The conditions of transfer were negotiated by a commission headed, on Narkompros' side, by Natalya Trotskaya.[83]*

The situation was easier in relation to Glavpolitput. In the November decree, Sovnarkom approved its absorption by Glavpolitprosvet; and in December—in connection with the political attack on Trotsky's quasi-military organization of transport—it was dissolved by decision of the Eighth Party Conference.[84]

On 31 December 1920, Preobrazhensky had told a meeting of delegates to the Eighth Congress of Soviets that the Central Committee was divided in its view on the relations of Glavpolitprosvet and the *agitprop* department of the Central Committee, some being in favour of union under Glavpolitprosvet while others thought that this would need the sanction of a Party congress. But by the time the Party Congress met in the spring of 1921 there appeared to be almost no division of opinion among speakers. The overwhelming feeling of the Tenth Congress was against any merging of Glavpolitprosvet and *agitprop*. Preobrazhensky and even Krupskaya were against it. The only speaker for it was Lunacharsky.

Lunacharsky explained that what he had in mind was not a transfer of control over *agitprop* from the Central Committee to Narkompros, but the transformation of the whole of Narkompros into an apparatus working directly under the Central Committee of the Party. The Central Committee, Lunacharsky said,

> cannot refrain from dominating [educational] work,...must undertake it and conquer the whole educational apparatus...Comrades, there are often confusions which arise here from a Soviet/Party dualism—as if state and Party work must be marked out as if on a map; as if the boun-

* Trotsky's wife, Lunacharsky's deputy as head of the arts sector of Narkompros in Moscow, head of the museum department of Narkompros. For obvious reasons, Trotskaya was more than once chosen by Narkompros to represent it in negotiation with army authorities.

daries where the Party fully transfers work to the state apparatus must be shown. That is wrong. The Party must be everywhere, like the Biblical spirit of God...We must act through the Soviet apparatus, which is the organ of the dictatorship of the Communist Party.

The organizational precedent for Narkompros' proposed absorption of Party *agitprop* was PUR: an organization outside the Party headed by a member of the Central Committee, whose Party cells were directly responsible to PUR and not to the Central Committee. For Narkompros, Lunacharsky proposed a structure like a civilian PUR. The Party's *agitprop* departments would be absorbed in Glavpolitprosvet like Party cells in PUR, owing a direct subordination to the head of Glavpolitprosvet or Narkompros. 'A comrade from the Central Committee must head Glavpolitprosvet or head Narkompros', Lunacharsky said.

If you find a comrade in the next Central Committee who can cope with this work, then I will be the first happily to submit to the direct leadership of a member of the Central Committee, so as to conduct this purely Party work in Communist education in the country.[85]

It is difficult to know what Lunacharsky's intentions were in making this offer. Perhaps he did it for rhetorical effect, rightly confident that no-one would accept. But it is more likely that he did it in good faith because he had become convinced that nothing but direct Party involvement in educational affairs would produce the resources, impetus and manpower to rebuild the schools and educate the adult population.

A number of speakers at the Tenth Congress objected violently to Lunacharsky's arguments. Krupskaya, although rejecting them, made the comparatively mild comment that his proposals were premature. 'When Glavpolitprosvet is penetrated with the Communist spirit, then will be the time to pose the question of whether it may be transformed into an organ of the Party', she said. Preobrazhensky, also opposing Lunacharsky, conveyed that there were particularly delicate areas of Party work which could not conceivably be handed over to a government organ. His examples were agitation among workers threatening a strike ('Can we in...such critical moments transfer direct action among the masses to Glavpolitprosvet?') and control of Party cells among students ('Glavpolitprosvet cannot direct these cells because they are Party cells... because their propagandist work is bound up with organizational work, and cells in that sphere can in no case and to no extent accept the direction of Glavpolitprosvet').[86] Preobrazhensky's opposition to the idea of union of Glavpolitprosvet and *agitprop* was so strong and unambiguous at the congress that his earlier position of neutrality on this issue (stated at the meeting of delegates to the Eighth Congress of Soviets on 31 December 1920) becomes suspect. It seems likely that he had personally always opposed the union, but that majority opinion in the Central Committee had swung from support for the union, or at least sympathetic consideration, to opposition in the first three months of 1921.

This change of attitude in the Central Committee may well have been caused by gradual realization of the strength of grass-root opposition within the Party to the idea of transferring Party *agitprop* to organs of Narkompros. This opposition was expressed by delegates at the meeting of 31 December, at the Tenth Party Congress, at the *agitprop* conference held later in the year, and no doubt at many local Party meetings. All the evidence suggests that the Party rank and file opposed the union because of their distrust of Soviet organs, and of Narkompros in particular. In his speech to the Tenth Congress, Lunacharsky claimed that there had been spontaneous local moves to merge *politprosvet* and *agitprop* departments. It was a claim which other speakers denied; but if it was true it still left one question unanswered: *kto kogo*? or who takes over whom? Given the relative strengths of local Party committees and education departments, it is easier to believe that *agitprop* would spontaneously absorb *politprosvet* at local level than vice versa.

At this time Narkompros seems almost to have been the bureaucratic model in the minds of Party members. A number of delegates to the Tenth Congress expressed the empirical view that the less work given to Narkompros and its organs the better, because Narkompros was an inefficient and bureaucratic organization. At the Eighth Party Congress in 1919, when Lunacharsky had intervened in a debate between Zinoviev and N. Osinsky in support of Zinoviev, Osinsky turned on him with the remark that 'we are developing a bureaucracy, and these sneers obviously come from comrades who have turned into Soviet *chinovniki*'.[87] This rebuke, and the widespread opinion it represented, partly explain the tortuous form which Lunacharsky used at the Tenth Party Congress to express his belief that the Party should work through the executive apparatus of Soviet organs rather than setting up machinery of its own in competition with them.

Preobrazhensky referred to the common opinion among Party members that transfer of *politprosvet* work from the Party to Glavpolitprosvet would be harmful because the work would lose its vital character. He denied this, saying that a limited transfer of work among the non-party masses to Glavpolitprosvet was part of the necessary process of 'Communization' of the Soviet apparatus. But in his concluding remarks, Preobrazhensky himself charged Narkompros with bureaucratism and bureaucratic empire-building.

> Comrades, [he said] this 'simplicity' which comrade Lunacharsky promises is 'worse than theft', because it amounts to stealing from the Party the most important part of its work. From this point of view, I ask you not to be led astray by what Lunacharsky suggests, because on this question he stands, if you will forgive the expression, on a position of departmental imperialism.

Another speaker, sympathetically reporting the hostility towards Narkompros felt by local Party workers, added that

> if agitation and propaganda are now taken out of the control of vital organs and given to Narkompros—an institution which has yet far from purged itself of bureaucratism—we may destroy and weaken that work.[88]

Lunacharsky proposed, as an amendment to Preobrazhensky's theses on Glavpolitprosvet, 'to merge the agitation departments of Party committees with the *guberniya* political education departments, and to transform Glavpolitprosvet into an organ fulfilling the functions of the *agitprop* department of the Central Committee'. The amendment was discussed in a commission consisting of volunteers from the delegates, and defeated by eight votes to four Lunacharsky claimed (though voices from the floor contradicted him) that his supporters came from the provinces and his opponents —out of touch with the realities of local administration—from

Moscow. Preobrazhensky commented that the very fact that Lunacharsky had introduced such an amendment 'shows that recently he has been cut off from Party work'.[89]

Although Krupskaya did not support Lunacharsky's amendment, her views on the ideal relationship of Party *agitprop* and Glavpolitprosvet were not substantially different from his. She thought that Glavpolitprosvet should work directly under the control of the Central Committee, and its local departments should work under the control of local Party committees. The Party's *agitprop* apparatus was, in Krupskaya's opinion, necessarily small. Political education of the whole population demanded a huge and complex machinery which must be organized by the government. 'The creation of such an apparatus within the Party itself would mean the unavoidable conversion of the Party into a part of the state machinery', Krupskaya said;[90] and she regarded this as out of the question.

Just after the Tenth Party Congress, Krupskaya wrote to the Georgian Communist Party urging it to support *politprosvet* work, and describing the relationship of the Russian Party and Glavpolitprosvet in the most optimistic terms:

Here in the RSFSR, Glavpolitprosvet conducts its work with the support of the Central Committee. Three members of the collegium of the *agitprop* department are at the same time members of the collegium of Glavpolitprosvet.*

It would have been very difficult for us to wage the struggle if the Central Committee had not supported us. When necessary, it supports our circulars with its own authority, and supports us in the financial sense. The Politburo of the Central Committee decided to give Glavpolitprosvet a million in gold over and above the sum which Narkompros gave it. And not long ago, with the support of comrade Lenin, the Politburo resolved to make the liquidation of illiteracy one of the chief Mayday slogans, and gave Glavpolitprosvet another extra sum for the liquidation of illiteracy.[91]

But this, of course was not the whole picture. The examples Krupskaya cited represented not so much the goodwill of the Party as the personal goodwill of Lenin towards Glavpolitprosvet. It had

* The three *agitprop* members on Glavpolitprosvet at the time were Yaroslavsky, Yakovlev and Solovyev.

been pointed out by delegates to the Tenth Party Congress that local Party committees and *agitprop* workers were hostile to Narkompros *politprosvet*. In July 1921, the Party held an *agitprop* conference refusing Glavpolitprosvet's request to make it a combined conference of *agitprop* and *politprosvet* departments.[92] *Izvestiya* of 10 July 1921, reported statements by speakers at the *agitprop* conference that 'provincial *politprosvet* departments do not enjoy the confidence of provincial Party committees, because they work among the petty bourgeoisie, leaving the workers on one side'. In spite of the presence of Yaroslavsky (a member of the Glavpolitprosvet collegium) and Preobrazhensky (a former member) at the conference, Krupskaya seems to have found herself alone in defending *politprosvet*. She tried to refute the opinion, which she admitted to be held by many Communists, that the encouragement—such as it was—given by the Tenth Congress to Glavpolitprosvet had been a mistake, since *politprosvet* departments only interfered with local Party *agitprop* work and it would be better if they reverted to the humbler status of 'extramural' departments of Narkompros.

After the *agitprop* conference, the Penza *agitprop* department decided that all political work should be removed from the competence of the Penza department of *politprosvet*, which was henceforth to be an extramural education department conducting non-political work like the campaign against illiteracy and the maintenance of libraries and reading-rooms. This was a decision on principle, and the Penza Communists produced a pamphlet justifying it. According to Krupskaya, the pamphlet interpreted the NEP as a general contraction of government (but not Party) activity implying a withdrawal of government organs from the field of propaganda and political education. Politics, the Penza Communists considered, was the province of the Party; culture could be handled by 'apolitical' organizations. Krupskaya was dismayed that, in November 1921, 'the *agitprop* department of the Central Committee, which possesses the Penza pamphlet, has not yet expressed its opinion of the "Penza theory" '.

The central Party press was unresponsive to Glavpolitprosvet's needs. *Pravda*, Krupskaya wrote, was repeatedly asked to introduce a '*Politprosvet* worker's page' to publicize Glavpolitprosvet's activity and 'put an end to the sheer ignorance in this field which rules among Party workers at the centre', and always refused. There was no refutation of the 'Penza theory' in the press, although

> it seems to Glavpolitprosvet basically contradictory to a Communist understanding of NEP. There must be complete clarity on this question. Then articles will not appear in *Pravda* with baseless assertions that the creation of political education departments was 'premature'!! (the Penza people are pleased); and there will not be preaching in the pages of *Izvestiya* on the necessity of transferring the 'apolitical' part of the work of political education departments to cooperatives.* [93]

In such an atmosphere of doubt whether Glavpolitprosvet, in Krupskaya's words, 'needed to exist', it is not surprising that its early territorial gains turned out to be illusory. S. I. Gusev, who succeeded Ivan Smilga at the head of PUR in January 1921, was opposed to the idea of transferring any of PUR's work to Glavpolitprosvet, and said as much at the Tenth Party Congress.[94] It is doubtful that under these circumstances any real transfer was achieved. In any case, at the end of 1922 'by order of the War Council of the Republic' the military section of Glavpolitprosvet was removed from it and transformed into the *agitprop* department of PUR. Glavpolitprosvet retained 'general intellectual leadership' over *politprosvet* work in the army and navy.[95] Political education of transport workers reverted formally to Tsektran (the Joint Central Transport Committee) in July 1921.[96] In February 1922, Glavpolitprosvet even lost control of work in prisons to the Commissariat of Justice.[97]

An attempt was made to stem the tide against Glavpolitprosvet in October 1921, when Glavpolitprosvet held its Second All-Russian Congress in Moscow. The congress, with Lunacharsky, Krupskaya and Maksimovsky as the main speakers from Narkompros and Glavpolitprosvet, would have passed almost unnoticed but for the fact that Lenin and—less characteristically—Trotsky took the opportunity to make major policy speeches: Lenin on the NEP and Trotsky on the Red Army. Both speeches were reported in

* The reference is to S. Agronsky's article 'Cooperation and enlightenment' in *Izvestiya* of 25 November 1921, p. 1.

full in *Izvestiya*, which also gave the general proceedings of the congress unusually generous treatment by reporting them in three separate numbers (15, 19 and 23 October).

Lenin believed that the main task of all educational workers, including workers in Glavpolitprosvet and Proletkult, was to raise both the literacy and the civic literacy of the population. This had been the substance of his appeal to Proletkult in 1919,* and of his speech to the first *politprosvet* congress at the end of 1920. 'How are we to understand politics?' he had asked in 1920. '...Our chief politics now must be the economic building of the state in order to get an extra pound of bread and an extra pound of coal and to decide how best to use these pounds of bread and coal so that nobody will go hungry—that is what our politics are now.'[98] Political education, Lenin thought, was no longer a matter of publicizing the Bolshevik platform and the Bolshevik Party and refuting the arguments of other political groups. It consisted of training the people in organizational and economic skills. Indeed, Lenin opposed the renaming of 'extramural' work as '*politprosvet*' because of the misleading political overtones of the new name.†

In his speech to the Second All-Russian Congress in October 1921, Lenin returned once again to the theme of civic literacy.

> The time when it was necessary to draw the political outlines of great tasks has passed, and the time has come when we have to put them into practice. Now we have cultural tasks ahead of us, the tasks of digesting political experience which must and will be put into practice. It is either the ruin of all the political conquests of Soviet power, or the establishment of an economic fundament beneath us...We must fight illiteracy, but literacy alone is not enough. What is also necessary is the kind of culture which teaches us how to fight red-tape and bribery...
>
> We—and, let us hope, you too—are conducting propaganda against barbarism and such evils as bribery, but political education is not exhausted by such propaganda. It needs to show people...how they—as

* See above, p. 107.

† 'At first I regarded the change of name of your organization with extreme disfavour. In my opinion, the task of Narkompros is to help people to learn and to teach others ...In the course of my Soviet experience, I have got used to regarding various names as children's jokes; indeed every name is a kind of joke. Now the new name is already confirmed—Glavpolitprosvet.' Lenin, speech of 3 November 1920, *Polnoe sobranie sochinenii* (5th ed.), vol. 41, p. 398.

ordinary citizens, more politically educated than others, not as members of the *ispolkom*,—can not only curse all kinds of red-tape (that is common with us) but how in fact they can overcome it.

In my opinion there are three main enemies which now stand before us, regardless of our professional roles: problems which stand before the political education workers if they are Communist, as the majority are. The three main enemies which stand before us are Communist conceit, illiteracy and bribes.

Trotsky's speech was on a narrower subject than Lenin's: political education in the army. His concept of political education was more conventionally centred on ideology, although he also thought it necessary to teach soldiers how to behave to the civilian population. Ideology, he said, should not be taught in generalizations, because the soldier 'does not keep general phrases about imperialism in his head...It is necessary to acquaint him with the reality of what exists on earth, beginning with Rumania and Poland'. He suggested (rather unexpectedly) the circulation of extracts from the writings of the *smenovekhovtsy*,* because he hoped that these would help strengthen the position of the professional officer corps.

Trotsky doubted that Glavpolitprosvet had a major role to play in educating the Red Army, since this could most successfully be done from within. He referred to the collapse of political education work in the army when it became known that it was to be transferred from PUR to Glavpolitprosvet,† and pointed out the danger of such a collapse during demobilization and reorganization of the army on a peacetime basis. Glavpolitprosvet, he said, must prove its ability to coordinate civil and military *politprosvet*. The military leaders, including Trotsky, would be its severe critics and taskmasters.[99]

Although the Second All-Russian Congress did something to restore Glavpolitprosvet's prestige, nothing could save it from the

* Term coined from *Smena vekh*, the title of a collection of essays by N. V. Ustryalov and other emigré intellectuals published in July 1921, advocating reappraisal of the Bolshevik government as working for the greater good of the Russian nation.

† Cf. Krupskaya, speaking to the Tenth Party Congress: 'The whole organization [of PUR] expects to be united with *politprosvet*, and so many workers are moving on various pretexts to other military jobs.' (*Desyatyi syezd RKP(b)*, p. 166.)

devastating impact of the NEP, which transferred the greater part of all educational work from central to local finance.* As early as the summer of 1921, political education work had virtually ceased in the Volga provinces affected by the famine. From November, when *politprosvet* became a charge on local authorities, it began to disintegrate in the rest of Russia: local authorities almost invariably gave it lowest priority among educational needs. 'Provincial *politprosvet* is in a pathetic and at the same time terrible condition', a Glavpolitprosvet member reported in November. 'Desperate telegrams and letters poured into Glavpolitprosvet', Krupskaya wrote. 'In the provinces, the restriction of credits led to an almost epidemic closing of clubs, schools and reading-rooms—as if the wind had blown them away.'[100]

Even Glavpolitprosvet's 'Extraordinary Commission for the Liquidation of Illiteracy'—the so-called Cheka likbez—came close to disaster. First there were suggestions, mentioned disapprovingly by Lenin in his October speech to the Second All-Russian Congress, that the Cheka likbez should be separated from Narkompros. Then, early in 1922, Rabkrin proposed that it should be abolished altogether. Narkompros protested, reminding Rabkrin of the recent increase of interest in the problem of illiteracy on the part of the War Commissariat and the Communist Party, and affirmed 'the necessity of continuing the work of the Cheka likbez at its former volume at least' and, as before, as a department of Glavpolitprosvet. Lenin, a reliable supporter of the campaign against illiteracy even in an institutional form he disliked,† probably intervened to rescue the Cheka likbez for Glavpolitprosvet; for Rabkrin dropped its proposal from the agenda of Sovnarkom a week later.[101]

One delegate to the Eleventh Party Congress (March–April 1922) raised the question of Glavpolitprosvet, which he described as 'in a condition of awful crisis, unparalleled even by the present condition of the national economy',[102] but the issue was not taken up. Few of the delegates were really interested in Glavpolitprosvet's problems.

* See below, ch. 10.

† Lenin thought that the campaign against illiteracy should be conducted, as it traditionally had been, through the schools. 'God forbid that we should part with old policies, if it means that we have to liquidate illiteracy with extraordinary measures', he told the October *politprosvet* congress.

Even at the Tenth Congress, when Glavpolitprosvet had been officially on the agenda, discussion had been cut short by the anxiety of the meeting to move on to the next paper (Stalin on nationalities).

Krupskaya showed some resilience in meeting the crisis of *politprosvet*. She had evidently not been happy with the style of work in Glavpolitprosvet during its brief heyday. Her dissatisfaction, hinted at in articles written in 1922, was expressed outright in a letter complaining of the Party's attitude to *politprosvet* and addressed to Chistov of the *agitprop* department in 1928. Chistov had apparently reproached Glavpolitprosvet with over-emphasis on general educational work. Krupskaya replied:

> Comrade Chistov, it seems to me that you do not evaluate political education work quite correctly.
>
> In the first place, political education workers were *never* on the side of 'general enlightenment'. On the contrary, the danger was always on the side of agitation. Even reading, the teaching of reading, was distorted into agitational chatter [*agitboltovnya*]. This was a terrible nuisance in the work.
>
> At first they used to link the work closely with the independence of the masses and with propaganda. The Party gave this line, especially Vladimir Ilyich, who placed enormous emphasis on the independence of the masses and dreamt of the broad development of libraries, of bringing the whole population to study, to reading aloud. The business began to develop on a big scale, but the Civil War forced us to pay more attention to agitation, particularly artistic agitation. When the Civil War came to an end, an enormous number of military workers poured into *politprosvet*, bringing all the methods of the front into its work. The independence of the population, all forms of deepening the work, were brought to nothing...[103]

The 'agitational' style of banners, music, speeches and parades which the Civil War brought into *politprosvet* was so far from Krupskaya's ideal that she greeted the collapse almost, it seems, with relief. *Politprosvet* without a popular basis did not, in Krupskaya's view, deserve to exist.

> The inadequate links between the political institutions and the population were especially sharply shown here [she wrote]. The government has not enough roubles—so the political institutions cease to exist. It is clear

that they did not put down roots among the masses, but were imposed from above.[104]

Krupskaya already knew what should replace the vanished Glavpolitprosvet apparatus: local initiative and the educational soviet. She was convinced that the thirst for knowledge was strong enough among the population to support libraries, reading-rooms and clubs organized by the people themselves. If their growth was spontaneous and irregular, there was no harm done so long as they grew. 'What is there to say about it! All that needs to be put into the educational soviets is time and energy.' Krupskaya's attitude in 1922 (and in 1928) was the same as it had been in 1918, when she first advocated educational soviets and participant democracy:

> We were not afraid to organize a revolution. Let us not be afraid of the people, let us not be afraid that they will elect the wrong sort of representatives, bring in the priests. We want the people to direct the country and be their own masters...We are always thinking in old terms, that if we do not spare ourselves and work day and night in the people's cause, that is enough. But it is nothing. Our job is to help the people *in fact* to take their fate into their own hands![105]

10

NARKOMPROS AND THE NEW ECONOMIC POLICY

In the immediate pre-war years, educational spending was divided between local authorities (*zemstvo* and municipal) and the central government. Some areas of education, like universities, were wholly financed by the central Ministry of Public Education. Primary education, however, was largely locally financed, especially in big municipal centres like Petersburg. It has been calculated that of the total pre-war expenditure on education per annum more than a third came from local authorities.[1]

Narkompros appears at first to have followed the traditional division of responsibility in educational financing between 'local' and 'general-state' needs—the first covering primary and low-level trade schools, the second gymnasia, technicums and higher schools. These are the categories suggested in the 'Statement on the organization of education in the Russian Republic' issued by Narkompros in June 1918.

But this division of responsibility could only function with a working system of local taxation and effective means of distributing credits from the centre. Such conditions did not obtain in the early post-revolutionary years. Narkompros certainly attempted to distribute credits to local education departments, but its contact with the provinces was haphazard and intermittent. Thus the collegium of Narkompros decided early in 1919 that it was impossible to make up arrears of payment to local education departments 'since neither Narkompros nor the *guberniya* education departments have any data at all from which it would be possible to estimate the amount of the debts...'[2] As for the credits allocated for the first half-year of 1919, the collegium was told in March of that year that there had been no response to telegrams sent at the end of January to inform *guberniya* education departments of their allocations. By May, Narkompros had been informed of receipt of credits by 29 out of the 35 local authorities in question—but this was after repeated enquiry by telegram; and of the 29 departments replying 23 did so by letter, 1 orally and only 5 by telegram.[3]

The available evidence suggests that during the first 18 months Narkompros did not make a substantial contribution to local educational finances, most of which came from *ad hoc* levies and taxes raised by local soviets. The Voronezh *guberniya*, for example, reported with pride in January 1919 that the local soviet had spent 4 million roubles, being an increase of 800% on the spending of the previous (S-R) administration, on education in the *guberniya*. In the same month, the Nizhny-Novgorod soviet reported allocations amounting to 965,000 roubles for educational purposes, together with a separate allocation of 600,000 roubles for the establishment of a People's University, out of a total expenditure of 8,488,000. Up to January 1919, the total amount of credits received for all purposes by the Nizhny-Novgorod soviet from the centre was 910,000 roubles.[4]

During 1919 and 1920, the situation was changed in two ways: first, by increasing budgetary and fiscal centralization, which meant that a larger part of local income was derived from central allocation instead of local levy; and second, by the collapse of the money economy. Education departments—like other departments of local soviets—were now primarily dependent on centrally-allocated rations of food, firewood, clothing and equipment. But allocation and distribution was in the hands of the Food Commissariat and other authorities, not in the hands of Narkompros. Narkompros itself had no goods nor (in this context) essential services to offer its local departments or to use in barter with the productive commissariats. It waged a perpetually losing battle with the Food Commissariat to assert control over distribution of supplies to education departments and schools. In the spring of 1921 it won the right to bypass the Food Commissariat (which in spite of its name had charge of distribution of all essential goods) and, in the case of goods 'of special significance for teaching, cultural–educational and artistic activity', to order directly from the appropriate producer, store in its own warehouses and distribute independently.[5] But this measure of control did not extend to the distribution of food and basic rations to educational workers. These rations were still distributed by the Food Commissariat and its local commissions, formally according to estimates offered by Narkompros and local education departments. Moreover, there was no guarantee that Narkompros would be able to obtain supply of the necessary special goods. From this situation arose Narkompros' desperate requests for permission to manufacture for its own special needs.*

During the Civil War, Narkompros felt itself badly treated in relation to other commissariats. It complained that it was allocated less than its share of rations and essential commodities, and that its teachers and employees starved where others did not. The comparative position is extremely difficult to establish. There seems no reason to suppose that Narkompros was worse off than the Health and Social Security Commissariats, although no doubt its expectations were higher and its sense of betrayal accordingly more acute. But Narkompros always compared itself with the great—as, if only in terms of size, it was justified in doing—and not with the small commissariats. Among the great, it perhaps did suffer from its leaders' lack of political influence. Litkens thought that Narkompros was at a disadvantage in the prevailing system of *udarnost'* [urgent priority] allocation,[6] under which all available resources were supposed to be diverted to the vital tasks of the moment. In the heyday of the labour conscription movement at the beginning of 1920, professional education briefly won an *udarnost'* rating, as did political education later in the year when Glavpolitprosvet was being put on its feet. But in Litkens' opinion Narkompros as a whole did not benefit, since Glavprofobr and Glavpolitprosvet remained in the *udarnost'* category for only a short time, while the schools sector was held on a permanent low priority. As Litkens suggested, a system in which 'government departments are endlessly fighting amongst themselves for *udarnost'* classification' was disadvantageous for Narkompros, lacking both political and economic weight. Nevertheless, the crucial disadvantages which Narkompros suffered during the Civil War were not products of the *udarnost'* system: they were the natural disadvantages of education and welfare institutions in wartime, intensified by the development of and economy of barter among central government departments.

* See above, pp. 172–3.

As the Civil War ended, Narkompros looked forward to a new deal for education, believing that its share of the state budget had so far been unnaturally low and must automatically rise in a period of peaceful reconstruction. In the Civil War years, Lunacharsky said in 1921, Narkompros' real share of the state budget had been 3%—'an undoubted scandal for a civilized state'.[7] But since the economy was no longer subject to the extraordinary pressures of civil war, it followed that distribution of state resources would shortly revert to a normal pattern more favourable to Narkompros.

This assumption turned out to be grossly mistaken although it was some time before the full significance of NEP for education became clear. During the first months of 1921, Narkompros was preoccupied with problems of administrative reorganization, and there was almost no discussion of financial affairs in the collegium. The financial policy in fact being practised was one of grudging retrenchment. Narkompros was forbidden by Sovnarkom to employ new staff (other than replacements) in its central administration; central and local departments, on Litkens' suggestion, were instructed not to open new institutions; and the collegium accepted proposals involving the temporary closing of many secondary schools and the permanent closing of a number of higher schools.[8] But in spite of these efforts to retrench, by the end of the summer of 1921 Narkompros owed teachers tens of millions of roubles in salaries[9] and had no prospect whatsoever of finding the money to pay them.

NEP appeared only in retrospect as an overall policy for the whole national economy. In 1921 it was a series of measures more or less logically following a change of government policy towards the peasants: the replacement of requisition of grain surpluses by a tax in kind which left the peasants with a surplus to trade. This meant, on the one hand, the revival of the free market and private trade; and, on the other, a sudden drop in government income and consequent contraction of the sphere of government enterprise and subsidy. As part of this contraction, the number of government employees—including employees of Narkompros—was greatly reduced;* and a large number of enterprises were transferred to a

* This was the task of the Larin Commission—see ch. 8, pp. 206–7.

self-supporting basis (*khozraschet*)* or let to private entrepreneurs. Within Narkompros, *khozraschet* was applied to Gosizdat, FOTO-KINO and some theatres. Other theatres failed on *khozraschet* and were let to private managements.

Under NEP, private enterprise was permitted and even encouraged in many areas of the economy. Narkompros welcomed it in publishing, tolerated it in the theatre, and forbade it in the schools.

No new economic policy was devised for education until the summer of 1921. Narkompros regarded the financial retrenchment which it practised in the first half of the year as an interim policy. Lunacharsky—even as late as the spring of 1922—publicly interpreted NEP as state financing of the service commissariats, including Narkompros, at the expense of the producing commissariats.

> The economic commissariats [he wrote], will be cut out of the state budget altogether, and the inheritors will be the commissariats which do not produce anything except the very important specialists and educated people without whom the economic commissariats would very quickly cease to exist.[10]

This was a logical assumption not apparently borne out by events. Lunacharsky had estimated Narkompros' real share of government expenditure in 1920 as 3% (against the official estimate of the 1920 budget giving it a share of 9.4%).† But its share in the 1921 budget, according to the official budgetary estimate, was 2.2%; and its share in the revised 1922 budget 2.9%.† The proportion of government expenditure actually received by Narkompros was almost certainly lower. It seems, therefore, that Narkompros did not gain but lost from the reorganization of public finance under NEP.

The government's return to orthodox financial practice meant that it was necessary to stabilize the currency and balance the budget, and consequently for the state to spend very little central money on anything. Health, education and social security were all largely disclaimed by the central budget in 1921–2. Schools and hospitals became the responsibility of local authorities. Social security was put on an insurance basis with a minimum of state contribution, and

* *Khozyaistvennyi raschet* = non-financing by the state, cost accounting.

† See Appendix I: 'Budgetary expenditure on Narkompros (estimates)'.

later—except for an inspectorate maintained by the state—had to become self-supporting.[11]

Charges were formally introduced on almost all public services provided by the state. The only exceptions were schools and hospitals, where charges were introduced spontaneously and illegally. Sovnarkom reimposed payment for use of 'water supply, sewerage, electricity, gas, railways and other communal means of transport, public baths, laundries, repair shops and chimney-cleaning services', medical supplies (except on prescription for hospital patients) and newspapers. The opening of private medical establishments and chemist shops was permitted.[12] *Izvestiya* published advertisements from 23 November, 1921.

The pressure to become economically self-sufficient, or to approach the ideal of self-sufficiency, led Narkompros to examine its own potentialities as a profit-making organization. A list of 'possible income from institutions and enterprises of Narkompros in 1922' was drawn up, with sections covering the potential income of Glavsotsvos, Glavprofobr, Glavpolitprosvet, Gosizdat, the Academic Centre and even the administration of supply under the Organizational Centre.[13] The document was written in terms of unconvincing optimism verging on fantasy. Only Gosizdat seemed to have a real potential income from the sale of books, pamphlets and newspapers. It was suggested that Glavpolitprosvet and the Academic Centre should share the profits from entrance charges to concerts, theatrical performances and art exhibitions (although the academic theatres were currently and for the foreseeable future running at a heavy loss). Glavpolitprosvet's profits from this source would presumably help it to meet the new charges for books and newspapers, from which it was not exempt. The most unlikely money-maker of all, Glavsotsvos, looked to an income—admitted to be of 'insignificant proportions'—from profits of concerts arranged in aid of children, and from the sale of produce from school vegetable gardens and objects made in school workshops. Glavprofobr listed 'income from workshops, laboratories, clinics and experimental stations' and 'consultations and enquiries'; but it was to have a competitor in the Academic Centre, which was to go on the market with meteorological and hydrological information, scientific reviews and consultations, analyses and expertise, and preparation of scientific instruments. The Academic Centre also proposed to conduct excursions and sell artistic reproductions, catalogues, guides and sheet-music—a Soviet equivalent, perhaps, of the ladies of the dispossessed bourgeoisie peddling their jewellery and the family furniture on street corners. Narkompros' central supply administration, having by no stretch of imagination a natural source of legitimate income, was to be given the profits from the sale of educational and artistic equipment—which, it must be said, Narkompros had not so far managed to obtain for its own use, let alone for resale—and 'a percentage charge on goods not of state manufacture'.

Narkompros' list did not include educational fees of any kind. As if to underline the strength of its principles and the weakness of its commercial instincts, Narkompros stated that it retained the right to suspend any of the itemized charges at its own discretion.

Gosizdat, which had at least potential earning-power, was currently crippled by paper shortages and printing crises. I. I. Skvortsov-Stepanov of Gosizdat reported in August 1921 that

> in the current year, and in particular in the middle of the summer, in connection with changes in forms of payment and enormous deficiencies in the introduction of collective supply,* there was a sharp fall in the productivity of the printing-presses...Their work actually stopped for weeks on end. A few printing-presses, where customers had found special funds and entered into separate agreements with the workers to secure the quick completion of particular commissions, were partially operative...

In view of the weakness of state publishing, Skvortsov-Stepanov proposed, with certain reservations, the stimulation of private enterprise in publishing: 'It is necessary to attract private enterprise,' he said, '...as long as it is capable of increasing the fund of paper and printing resources at the disposal of the RSFSR without drawing on general state resources.'[14]

Private publishing had not been outlawed during the Civil War,† but its operation had been made extremely difficult by the requisition of private and cooperative printing presses and the municipaliza-

* A system, replacing ration cards, whereby government institutions received a monthly quota of money and goods for distribution among their employees.

† See above, p. 133.

tion of the book trade. Private publishers issued 289 books in 1919, 122 in 1920 and only 23 in the period January–August 1921.[15] Among the private publishers which, nevertheless, retained their identity and managed to issue at least one book during this period, were 'Petropolis', 'Ogni', 'Kolos', 'Gelikon', 'Zadruga', 'Alkonost' and M. & S. Sabashnikov;[16] as well as the anomalous 'Vsemirnaya literatura' run by Grzhebin and Gorky as an autonomous department of Gosizdat, and Grzhebin's private publishing house. The collegium of Narkompros had given some support to private publishers, recommending 'Alkonost' to Gosizdat in January 1919, and in the same year commissioning Sabashnikov to publish books for Narkompros worth 1 million roubles, and subsidizing Gorbunov-Posadov's 'Posrednik' to the tune of 2.6 million roubles.[17]

Even the private periodical press had not been entirely eliminated during the Civil War. According to a report in 1921, it had been 'represented in Moscow by the following rarely-appearing journals: the left S-R *Znamya*, the minority S-R *Narod*, the Maximalists' *Maksimalist*, the anarchists' *Universalist* and I. I. Lazarevsky's *Sredi kollektionerov* [*Among Collectors*]...' Moreover, in spite of municipalization of the book trade, two private bookshops survived in Moscow, run by the Union of Writers and the Union of Poets respectively, and two in Petrograd—Khovin's 'Book Corner' and 'Book Point', run by the *Dom iskusstva*.* [18]

On the basis of Skvortsov-Stepanov's report, Narkompros issued a resolution calling for the revival of private publishing but limiting its access to state paper supplies. At the same time, the presidium of Moscow Soviet made the more concrete decision to allow private and cooperative publishers 'to sell the books which they publish freely at market prices without subsidy from the government'.[19]

In October a Gosizdat congress approved a project of a Sovnarkom decree 'to introduce payment for all printed works including newspapers from November 1'.[20] The congress decided that Tsentropechat, which had been responsible for the free distribution of printed matter, should be abolished.

* *Dom iskusstva*, literally 'House of Art', was the Petrograd writers' and artists' club during the Civil War.

Gosizdat was now, in the words of a Narkompros statement of November 1921, 'simultaneously the chief administration of publishing affairs and the state publishing enterprise'. In the second capacity, it was put on *khozraschet*. Narkompros claimed—although the claim may be doubted—that Gosizdat was successfully operating on *khozraschet* by the end of 1921. But in 1922, as a result of Lenin's expressed concern that the high prices of Gosizdat publications were limiting their circulation, Sovnarkom decided to give Gosizdat (in its capacity as state publisher) a subsidy to enable it to lower the prices of essential publications.[21]

Some unfavourable comments on the achievements of the revived private publishers came from Gosizdat in 1922. Gosizdat had hoped that private publishers would help with the publication 'which at the present time is of the least interest to the Soviet government, or which Gosizdat finds hard to cope with', instancing belle-lettres, children's books and technical literature. But, Meshcheryakov (president of Gosizdat) complained,

with the exception of a few private publishers, the majority appear to be extremely frivolous, ephemeral and even speculative enterprises. For the most part they publish thin volumes of poetry...There was a strong inclination towards the publication of theatrical journals of a trashy [*bul'varnyi*] type.

By May 1922, according to Meshcheryakov, 220 private publishers had registered with Gosizdat in Moscow and 99 in Petrograd. There were almost none in the provinces. Of those in Moscow, only 133 had submitted manuscripts for publication, and fewer had actually published. But some private publishers—'Granat', Knebel, Sabashnikov and 'Mir'—were said to be working in co-operation with Gosizdat.[22]

The chronicle of the journal *Pechat' i revolyutsiya*—of which Meshcheryakov, as it happened, was an editor—described the growth of private publishing and trading with considerably more satisfaction. 'There are now at least 30 bookshops in Moscow', it reported at the end of 1921, 'as well as the bazaar trade in books. Only one of them is soviet (the bookshop of the Moscow Soviet) and the rest are mainly run by writers or cooperatives;...old book publishers have come to life—"Severnie dni", the Writers' Publishing House, Sakharov and Leman, Vasilyev, Sabashnikov, "Tvorchestvo",—and new ones are springing up...' New journals had started publication: in Moscow alone *Pechat' i revolyutsiya* reported the appearance of *Teatral'naya Moskva* (edited by the left critic E. Beskin), *Ekran*, *Teatral'noe obozrenie*, *Iskusstvo i trud*, *Torgovo-promyshlennyi vestnik* and *Zhizn' iskusstva*.* [23]

In fact private and cooperative publishing was heavily concentrated in certain areas. Over the NEP period as a whole (that is until the end of the '20s), private publishers issued 33.3% of books on philosophy and psychology, 42.5% of essays, poetry and studies of literature, and 51% of books on painting, the theatre and sport. But only 20% of all books published in 1922 came from private and cooperative publishers, and 25% in 1923.[24]

NEP was more painfully introduced into the theatre than into publishing. The theatre had suffered less than publishing during the Civil War, having received comparatively generous subsidies whose continuance was threatened by NEP. The crucial issue for the theatres in 1921 was not freedom but finance. Private capital was not yet in a position to replace state subsidy. Private theatres without state protection were liable to crippling taxation by local authorities. 'The most experienced entrepreneurs, who were overjoyed by the birth of the free theatres, fell on their knees, so to speak, when they heard the conditions, and began to beg for finance,' Lunacharsky wrote, adding the gloomy prophecy that 'those who miss this boat will drown in the ocean depths'.[25]

Theatre subscriptions (sold mainly to the bourgeois public) had been abolished during the 1919–20 season, but most theatres continued to charge for admission. Cheap tickets were distributed among unions, Red Army units, schools and institutes, whose members also had first right to purchase of dearer tickets when they came on sale.[26] But this system was said to work poorly in practice. Lunacharsky, answering a complaint about theatre prices and the number of bourgeois speculators to be seen among theatre audiences,

* The Moscow *Zhizn' iskusstva*, ed. R. M. Olkhovsky, pub. 'Arion' 1921–2, is not to be confused with the Petrograd weekly of the same name, ed. Gaik Adonts, founded by Petrograd TEO in 1918 and continued under private ownership throughout the '20s.

described what happened to the cheap tickets distributed by Narkompros:

When we send out whole bunches of tickets,...those tickets by some curious fate once again fall into the hands of various well-dressed youths and young ladies. People say that these are Soviet employees of the appropriate government departments, who have filched the tickets for themselves. And I have heard worse rumours: that the Red Army comrades and workers who get free tickets sell them again at considerably higher prices...[27]

Before NEP, admission charges were perhaps less general in Petrograd than in Moscow. But in July 1921 Petrograd TEO, with the approval of the Petrograd Soviet, announced that in view of the financial crisis 'TEO had had to recognize the necessity of payment for performances and charges for admission and seats'.[28] The clear implication of NEP for the theatre was that individual theatres should pay their own way. It was suggested that this would be possible if entrance charges were made universal, and this was on occasion used as an argument against the reintroduction of private enterprise in the theatre. Thus an anonymous writer in *Vestnik teatra* (15 August 1921) believed that

it would be much simpler to establish the principle of paying for performances, and to put all the money obtained from them into a special reserved fund. That fund would not only cover the upkeep of the theatres which are necessary to the Republic, but would give a solid surplus which would guarantee both the appropriate artistic quality of the theatre and its ideological value.

This was to disregard the well-established revolutionary tradition of appropriation of theatre receipts by local authorities (which persisted in spite of central instructions to the contrary both during the Civil War and under NEP). Moreover, the experience of the state academic theatres, which had always charged entrance fees for the majority of seats as well as receiving state subsidies, suggested that fee-charging was no guarantee of solvency. In September 1921, VTSIK instructed the Bolshoi theatre—which had previously distributed 25% of places free to unions and the Red Army—to distribute only 15% of places at half the normal price, at the same time raising prices of seats in the rest of the house.[29] But the Bolshoi continued to run at a loss.

Narkompros' administration of theatrical affairs was the subject of a commission of enquiry set up by Maly Sovnarkom under the presidency of Kiselev in June and July 1921. The commission, consisting of representatives of Rabkrin, the Finance Commissariat and Rabis, had no representative of Narkompros. Lunacharsky, who had been out of Moscow at the time of the commission's establishment in the third week of June, made a very belated complaint that Narkompros had not been consulted and was not represented on the commission, but the complaint was dismissed.[30]

One of the questions within the scope of the commission's enquiry was the possibility of renting theatres to private entrepreneurs, and thus lightening the burden of state subsidy. On 20 July L. S. Sosnovsky (who was shortly to become head of the *agitprop* department of the Central Committee) wrote in *Pravda*:

> I have heard that the question of the theatres is being considered from the point of view of commercial profitability in the highest Soviet organs—the problem being which theatres to leave dependent on the state and which to give up to the merchant Epishkin...

There were familiar rumblings of discontent at the amount spent by Narkompros on the theatres. The Finance Commissariat complained to Lenin that

> artists and workers in Soviet theatres are not being paid according to the tariff scale but with bonuses which are many times larger than the tariffs; and the Narkompros budget lists expenses on the maintenance of the theatres at 29 milliard roubles, as against 17 milliard on higher educational institutions.

Lenin, who was particularly concerned about the financing of education and *politprosvet* and no great lover of the theatre, scribbled on the margin of the Finance Commissariat's memo '*BEZOBRAZIE*! !' [Disgraceful!][31]

During August and September, questions of theatrical finance were hotly argued in Narkompros, Sovnarkom, VTSIK, the

Politburo and Moscow and Petrograd Soviets. At an early stage of the discussion, Moscow Soviet seems to have been prepared to finance the major Moscow theatres through the Moscow Theatre Administration.[32] VTSIK had approved an allocation of 1 milliard roubles for maintenance of theatres, apparently directly to the Moscow Theatre Administration; but it fell through when Lenin protested that it was unconstitutional to bypass Narkompros by making direct allocation of funds to subordinate authorities.[33] As a result the presidium of Moscow Soviet repudiated its undertaking to maintain the major Moscow theatres. On 8 September, *Izvestiya* carried the presidium's announcement that with the exception of agitational and children's theatres *all* Moscow theatres were to be taken off the state budget and let out to rent. Applications were invited from 'collectives and cooperatives of stage workers already in existence, newly-organized collectives and private entrepreneurs'.

But Narkompros, which had been independently negotiating a list of theatres to remain on state subsidy directly from its own Academic Centre, salvaged a nucleus of Moscow theatres on the Narkompros budget. The list tentatively agreed in September included the Bolshoi, Maly, Children's and Moscow Arts theatres, together with the Chekhov, Gorky and Moscow Arts studios. A strong lobby for the inclusion of Tairov's Kamerny theatre came from the president of VTSIK, M. I. Kalinin, who even promised that if Narkompros refused to finance the Kamerny, 'the presidium of VTSIK would find some sort of funds for it...'[34]

The Larin commission for the review of staff and institutions of the commissariats* agreed to let Narkompros keep the academic theatres on its budget, with one exception. This was the Bolshoi theatre which, 'in view of its insignificant artistic value and the huge sums of money demanded for it', should be closed. The commission announced its decision at a joint meeting with Narkompros early in November 1921. Lunacharsky said that Narkompros would protest to VTSIK against the closing of the Bolshoi. But he was not supported by his Narkompros colleagues at the meeting. V. N. Maksimovsky, the deputy head of Glavpolitprosvet, spoke in favour

* See above, pp. 206 ff.

of closing the Bolshoi; and the rest of the Narkompros representatives seem to have given tacit approval to the commission.*

The threat to the Bolshoi came not only from the Larin commission but from the Moscow Council of Trade Unions which, as *Izvestiya* reported on 5 November, had made an independent decision to close the Bolshoi. Five days later. *Izvestiya* published an indignant letter from Lunacharsky pointing out that any decision on the future of the Bolshoi must come from Narkompros, not from the Moscow Council of Trade Unions. Narkompros, Lunacharsky said bravely, saw no reason to close the theatre.

Against all reasonable expectation, Lunacharsky won his case. At the beginning of 1922, Sovnarkom decided that the Bolshoi should be kept open on state subsidy. Lenin made a strong protest, and the Politburo instructed the presidium of VTSIK to reverse the Sovnarkom decision. But VTSIK—probably partly influenced by Lunacharsky's argument that the Bolshoi had in any case to be kept functioning for congresses, state functions and meetings of VTSIK—decided not to accept the Politburo's instruction, since the closing of the Bolshoi was 'economically inexpedient'.[35] Lenin pursued the question no further, and the Bolshoi survived.

The Proletkult theatre, in the old 'Hermitage' on Karetny ryad, was less fortunate. Proletkult had had the use of the theatre since the end of 1920. In January 1922, when Proletkult lost its subsidy from Narkompros, it was given the theatre and grounds as basic capital and instructed to become self-supporting. Some months later, a private offer was made for the 'Hermitage' and accepted; and it was rented to the Moscow Theatrical Association under the presidency of M. A. Razumny.† 'It is a disgrace,' Lunacharsky wrote, 'and I fully accept my share of the blame...We—the

* Those present at the meeting from Narkompros were Lunacharsky, Pokrovsky, Litkens, P. S. Kogan, Maksimovsky and Kozelev.

† Razumny, at the head of a group of businessmen, bought a 3-year lease on the 'Hermitage' for 500 milliard roubles, 100 milliard being immediately paid in cash. This gave the group an effective monopoly of summer entertainments in Moscow. But Razumny then went into partnership with the entrepreneur Aksarin, 'gave himself into the power of the yellow devil', and shortly left the theatre altogether and devoted himself to commerce. (D. I. Zolotnitsky, 'Theatre of revolutionary satire', in *Teatr i dramaturgiya* (Leningrad, 1967), pp. 142–3.)

Soviet government and the Moscow Soviet—drove Proletkult out of its premises...'[36]

Moscow Soviet accepted the offer for the 'Hermitage' with such alacrity because it was one of few: private entrepreneurs, even in Moscow, were slow to move into the theatrical field. In the summer of 1922, only the new 'Hermitage' theatre (which began operation on 13 May 1922) was advertising in *Izvestiya*, although there were reports of a new theatre of 'artistic miniatures' opening on Tverskaya, and of a Guignol theatre in Petrograd. The most promising offer, which was finally refused, came from foreign capitalists seeking 'concessions' on the Moscow academic theatres. It was reported in *Izvestiya* on 6 May as being under consideration by 'the highest government authorities'. The alternative courses of action, as described by E. K. Malinovskaya (currently administrator of the Bolshoi theatre), were that the state academic theatres should be closed altogether, that they should continue on state subsidy, or that concessions on them should be sold for a contractual period of twenty-five years. Malinovskaya herself thought that concessions were better than closure. Of the other theatrical leaders interviewed by *Izvestiya*, Nemirovich-Danchenko of the Moscow Arts theatre refused to commit himself, Yuzhin of the Maly theatre thought concessions quite acceptable 'on the basis of free agreement of each artist with the trust', and Tairov of the Kamerny theatre opposed the idea altogether ('after the theatres, we might as well hand over the universities, museums and libraries to the concessionaires...'). The origin of the offer was not disclosed; and no material appears to have been published on the reasons for its refusal.

Lunacharsky observed the onset of NEP in the theatre and the arts with dismay, and thought it a prelude to a general corruption of public taste.

> Where is the private market now? [he wrote in 1922]. Who has the money to buy art? Almost nobody but the speculator. That means that so-called free art will go into dependence on the speculator. He is a neo-bourgeois, tasteless, and thirsting to enjoy himself on his newly-won wealth. The danger is of an outpouring of filth, which may splash outside its own channels and dirty the completely healthy sections of the population...[37]

Theatrical private enterprise in the '20s is described in the official

Soviet history of the theatre as producing 'an abundance of all kinds of little theatres of the cabaret and farce type, whose "light" repertoire and frivolous manner of presentation were specially designed for Nepmen [the NEP bourgeoisie]'.[38] It should be pointed out, however, that this situation was not characteristic of NEP alone. In the winter of 1919–20, when theatres were unheated and almost unlit and the trams had stopped running, cabarets and 'theatres of miniatures' were reported to be 'growing like mushrooms after a good rain' in Moscow; and in one month (February 1920) the presidium of Moscow Soviet found it necessary to close down fourteen of them, in view of their 'clearly unbearable character'.[39]

A Glavpolitprosvet survey of ownership of theatres, cinemas and other artistic enterprises made at the beginning of 1923 (and excluding Moscow and Petrograd) showed that while 29% of cinemas and almost 100% of variety theatres were in private hands, the extent of private entrepreneurship in the legitimate theatre was small. 9% of theatres were privately owned, 34% owned by actors' collectives, 21% by unions, the Red Army or other public organizations, and 36% by the state. It was concluded that the theatres were not profitable for private capital; and that the high percentage of collectively owned theatres arose because 'the collectives of dramatic and operatic companies are forced to take on the role of proprietor in cases where neither state nor public nor private capital is prepared to support the enterprises'. The collectives survived only by virtue of 'wild self-exploitation of the work-force'. At least one in every three theatres existing at the beginning of 1922 had gone into liquidation during the year.[40]

The sphere in which NEP brought unmitigated disaster to Narkompros was education, and school education above all. In the summer of 1921, as a result of the famine and the financial crisis, the schools were already in such a desperate condition that it seemed (wrongly) that no lower point could be reached. The chronic delays in Narkompros payments of teachers' salaries were now so great that central subsidy of the local education system could be said to have effectively ceased. In some parts of the country, schools were reported to be maintained by the collective efforts of the local population—'amateur and disorganized measures of self-taxation in rural districts', as Narkompros described it. In other areas, including the Crimea, 'local education departments themselves transferred their institutions to private hands, establishing fees for schooling, and introducing a general tax on parents'.[41] Elsewhere it was said that the teachers were begging for alms. By the autumn, Litkens could make the generalization that 'our rural education workers directly and unequivocally depend on the most prosperous peasants, on the kulaks'.[42] 'An enormous confusion close to panic reigned in the provinces,' Narkompros reported, 'since the position both of education workers and school maintenance was continually worsening.'[43]

As the beginning of the school year approached, demands for a radical change in methods of school finance reached Narkompros from the provinces.

The final drop overflowing the cup and giving the *coup de grâce* to the last four or five months of Narkompros' work was a telegram from Kursk. This, like a number of other telegrams, gave notice that the teachers themselves in the provinces had been raising the question of seeking out local funds for the maintenance of the school and for its heating and repair, and also for the payment of teachers through a voluntary tax on the local population for the needs of Enlightenment.

Litkens read the Kursk telegram to the collegium of Narkompros on 4 July 1921, after which the collegium decided to organize a meeting of local educational administrators. The meeting took place on 14 and 15 July. Its conclusion was

that it was necessary to attract local funds to supplement state funds, but only under the necessary condition that education remained free and accessible to the possessing and non-possessing classes on an equal basis, and that overall direction should remain with the state organs. The new economic policy had called to life a petty-bourgeois element which was sufficiently powerful economically to permit a significant share of public educational expenses to be laid on it. In the field of educational economics, we must find support in private initiative, but on condition that this help should be sufficiently impersonal that the helper is not helping his own school and his own teacher, but the state school and the state educational worker. He must not have any 'owner's' pretensions to intellectual direction of educational institutions just because he helps them.[44]

In short, it was hoped that Marxist laws on ownership and control would be briefly suspended on behalf of the local education departments.

Litkens brought these resolutions back to the collegium of Narkompros, and a commission of Litkens, V. A. Nevsky and M. M. Isaev was appointed to prepare a final version. There was apparently no dissension in the collegium on the general nature of the resolution.* It was subsequently passed on to Sovnarkom, approved by other commissariats and VTSSPS, and issued as a Sovnarkom decree 'On measures towards the improvement of supply to schools and other educational institutions' on 15 September.[45]

All the evidence suggests that this decree—which was in effect the application of NEP to the educational system—was entirely the product of local initiative and the experience of local education departments, primarily in rural areas. It was not imposed on Narkompros by higher government authorities, nor thought up by the Narkompros collegium as a theoretical solution of educational problems or response to new economic policies in other areas.

The central point of the decree of 15 September was local self-taxation [*samooblozhenie*] for educational purposes. The unit of taxation was the *volost'*. Litkens explained that to take a larger unit—the *uezd*—was impossible, for

as soon as we make an *uezd* tax, that tax is at once converted in the psychology of the peasantry into a state food tax [*prodnalog*]. If it is put down to the village level, then it may easily turn into direct provision of food for the teacher by the parents of the pupils themselves—producing, that is to say, a direct dependence of the teacher on the prosperous stratum of the village which must be avoided...

Taxation was in kind, in the form of food for the teaching staff, fuel for the schools, and labour obligation for the maintenance of

* Those present were Litkens, Lunacharsky, Pokrovsky, Krupskaya, Grinberg and V. A. Nevsky. The collegium, apart from Litkens, may not have read the resolutions in advance, since it was resolved that all members should do so within two days and submit their comments to Litkens' commission.

school buildings. The method of collection of the tax in kind was not specified by the decree. Narkompros' interest was to keep collection under its own control, not that of local Food Commissions. 'We are taking care that the resources of self-taxation do not fall into the hands of the Food Commissariat,' Litkens said, 'and we are trying to organize...collection with the help of the cooperatives.'[46] A detailed instruction on methods of collection was not issued until the end of October.*

The recommendations of the July meeting of educational administrators on which the September decree was based had clearly referred almost entirely to rural areas. However, the September decree extended local self-taxation to urban areas, where its application was considerably more difficult. It was impossible to impose a tax in kind in urban areas, so the tax must be in money. But the mechanism of local money taxation as a whole had yet to be constructed.† Litkens thought the establishment of a regular money tax of the urban population, administered by the Finance Commissariat but used directly for educational purposes, was quite probable, but not before 1922. Lunacharsky more soberly described it as 'a thing of the not very near future'.[47]

In the meantime, the collection of the urban tax for educational purposes had to be improvised. The decree of 15 September suggested the establishment of 'school-economic soviets',‡ whose function was to organize 'every kind of voluntary contribution' and to introduce 'self-taxation of the parents of pupils, users of libraries, members of clubs etc.' Self-taxation of parents carried the obvious danger that school fees would be reintroduced under another name: the difference, in Narkompros' view, was that self-taxation was voluntary. 'The principle of the free [*besplatnaya*] school must

* Published with the signatures of Litkens and Frumkin (for the Food Commissariat) in *Prodovol'stvennaya gazeta*, 29 October 1921, and *Nar. pros.* (weekly), 7 November 1921.

† In 1920, local soviets had received a percentage of central taxes. The principle of local taxation was re-established by a resolution 'On local money funds' of 22 August (*Sobr. uzak.* (1921), no. 62, art. 446), but its forms were not announced until early December (*Sobr. uzak.* (1921), no. 80, art. 693).

‡ This creature of bureaucratic fantasy was to consist of representatives of local Soviet, education department, trade union organization, Rabpros, factories, teachers, parents and non-teaching school staff. ('Statement on district school-economic soviets...', pub. *Nar. pros.* (weekly) (1921), nos 87–8, 25 October.)

remain untouched at any cost', Lunacharsky wrote in *Izvestiya* on 25 September.

Urban self-taxation, as Litkens explained to a congress of educational administrators in September,[48] was only a palliative; and until the introduction of a regular money tax in aid of education it would be necessary to keep urban schools on the state budget. He added, however, that the state could not support the schools, and left his audience to draw their own conclusions. If the state must support the schools, and was at the same time incapable of doing so, the onus was thrown back onto the 'school-economic soviets', to whom Litkens assigned the almost impossible task of organizing voluntary self-taxation of parents in such a way that it was 'not converted into charges which would deprive workers of access' to the schools.

Self-taxation, which appeared in retrospect as the cardinal point of the 15 September decree, was not presented as such. It was one of the last points in a fairly long document whose general intention was to give Narkompros and its departments greater scope for economic activity, and to move some educational expenses from educational to other authorities. Schools attached to factories were to be supplied by the factories with premises, heating, lighting and food rations for teachers equal to workers' rations in the factory. Local Soviets were instructed to put aside a proportion of their income for educational needs, but the proportion 'was to be determined by themselves'. Paragraph 1 of the decree provided that

> Narkompros and local education departments are given the right to organize their own productive enterprises, sewing-shops, repair-shops and agricultural farms for the exploitation of the same both by pupils and teachers themselves, and on a contractual basis by cooperatives, artels and private persons...

According to Paragraph 6 of the decree, materials supplied to local education departments by the state might, if the departments had no direct use for them, be exchanged for other products on the free market.

In government and Party circles, the decree seems to have had more opponents than defenders. But the discussion was not primarily concerned with the self-taxation clause. Zinoviev criticized the decree for introducing 'commercial principles',[49] and the Petrograd Soviet (which he headed) failed to implement it.* Kamenev also criticized the decree,[50] and the Moscow Soviet, following his example, repudiated it as capitulation to the class enemy.† The Ukrainian Narkompros and Ukrainian Communist Party objected to the decree as weakening central control and the control of local Soviets over education.[51]

Lenin supported the decree and signed it as president of Sovnarkom because of the urgency of relieving the present misery of teachers and schools, and on the principle that 'more and more must be taken from the peasants for the maintenance of local schools'. In his reply to Zinoviev's criticism, he conceded that

> one can find something like the commercial principle, specifically the right to organize and rent enterprises for the supply of Narkompros institutions. But I also consider the project...to be completely correct, since without such measures it is impossible to improve school maintenance and lessen the starvation of teachers.[52]

He expressed concern only on two points: the possibility that charges for clubs and libraries might discourage their use; and that the right of education departments to exchange materials supplied by the state on the free market was liable to abuse.[53]

But the points raised by Zinoviev and Lenin seem peripheral to the real substance of the decree—the introduction of local self-taxation for educational purposes. Self-taxation deserved closer scrutiny. For at a time when the structure of local finance was still under discussion, the imposition of an irregular local tax irregularly collected was a doubtful procedure which the Food and Finance Commissariats were bound to disapprove. In fact the Food Commissariat later tried to suspend the education tax during the period of consolidation of the local budget, although apparently without success.[54]

* *Guberniya* education departments were instructed to present a resolution, prepared by Narkompros in the spirit of the September decree, for ratification by the *ispolkom* of the local Soviet. According to Narkompros' information up to 30 November 1921, 'nothing had been done and no resolution had been passed' in Petrograd. (Narodnyi Komissariat po Prosveshcheniyu, *K IX vserossiiskomu syezdu sovetov*, p. 16.)

† See below, pp. 278–9.

The glaring practical weakness of local self-taxation was that it could not be implemented in urban areas except as a *de facto* introduction of school fees. Only a fortnight after the promulgation of the decree, Lunacharsky reported in *Izvestiya* (on the front page of the 2 October issue) that unsettling 'rumours' of the introduction of school fees were reaching him from many quarters.

It has officially been brought to my attention by organs of the Cheka that in the Kursk *guberniya* fees have been introduced for the right of schooling almost universally. At the Komsomol Congress* notes were handed to me testifying that administrative activity in the Crimea had gone so far in this regard as to establish immoderately high fees and expel those unable to pay them...Now I have before me an official statement from Rabkrin to the collegium of Narkompros on a whole series of cases of the same nature. One of the schools of the City *raion* [Moscow] is charging 40,000 roubles per child for the right to attend school, and 30,000 roubles for heating; and then barefacedly—I cannot find another word—states that those who cannot produce 70,000 roubles can look for another school.

This situation was particularly embarrassing to Narkompros since it had not yet issued instructions on the method of tax-collection in urban areas. Lunacharsky promised in his 2 October article that the instruction would appear 'in the next few days' and would 'explain exactly what form—at any rate more or less socialist in character, and far from being payment for the right of schooling—the taxation of parents may take'. The instruction was not in fact issued for another three weeks, appearing in the weekly Narkompros journal *Narodnoe prosveshchenie* on 25 October.

A series of threats and legislative warning were published in the vain hope of discouraging schools and local education departments from introducing school fees. Lunacharsky announced on 2 October that there would be a most definite prohibition from Narkompros 'in the near future', and warned that 'if, after that prohibition, I personally come to know of such a thing, I will immediately start criminal proceedings against the guilty persons'. In fact Litkens—for once moving more quickly than Lunacharsky expected—

* Fourth Congress of the Komsomol, Moscow, 21–8 September 1921.

published this prohibition on the same day in the same paper,* also threatening legal proceedings against violators of the decree. This was reinforced at the end of October by a resolution from VTSIK forbidding any sort of fee-charging or discrimination between parents contributing voluntary payments and others; and announcing that any official or teacher condoning or practising fee-charging or discrimination of this kind would answer for it before the law.[55]

But there could scarcely be a question of prosecution when so many were guilty. The authority of the September decree was further undermined when Moscow Soviet, unrebuked, announced its refusal to observe it on the front page of *Pravda* on 6 October. Boguslavsky, spokesman for the Soviet,† reported that it had 'decided that self-taxation is not the proper way to finance the school' and resolved 'to request Sovnarkom not to publish the relevant point of the decree in the Moscow *guberniya*'. Self-taxation, Boguslavsky wrote, was another form of fee-charging. He gave a harrowing picture of its exploitation by a resurgent capitalist class:

> The scenes being played out at the 'self-taxation' meetings are almost identical. A 'parent' (almost always one of the 'Red merchant' type) comes in and 'explains' that the chief thing in life is science, and suggests that in view of the powerlessness of the state to educate children at the public expense the parents should 'tax themselves'. The extent of the tax is already worked out, and varies from 10,000 to 80,000 a month per child. 'Self-taxation' is implemented with a 'stern hand', and complaints are disregarded.
>
> The reader will imagine how a worker may react to the barefacedness of these shameless *sukharevtsy*,‡ who already see themselves as masters of the school. As well as the threat that this method of 'self-taxation' may reflect on the [social] composition of the student body, there is also the

* 'Art and culture. For the information of all workers of the RSFSR' (signed Litkens), *Izvestiya VTSIK* (1921), no. 220, 2 October, p. 2.

† The nature of Boguslavsky's connection with the Moscow Soviet is not clear. But the Soviet's decision was first made public in his article 'The policy of not making losses' (*Pravda* (1921), no. 224, 6 October, p. 1), and further explained in his second article 'To the aid of the school' (*Pravda* (1921), no. 263, 22 November, p. 2).

‡ *Sukharevtsy* = speculative traders (from the Moscow market Sukharevka).

danger of corruption of the teaching staff, who will be wholly dependent on their 'protectors'...

Moscow Soviet believed that the education system, like the Commissariat of Foreign Affairs, must remain completely state-financed and state-controlled. In place of self-taxation, the Soviet suggested a 'general tax' for educational purposes, which was evidently to be collected by the central government. All other cultural enterprises should be sacrificed in favour of the schools. Boguslavsky implied that Narkompros had resources which would be available to the schools if 'futurists, imaginists and other hangers-on [who] had found shelter in great numbers under the warm roof of Narkompros' were evicted.

Moscow had 5,000 schools and children's homes and 40,000 pupils to be supported, and at the beginning of October the presidium of Moscow Soviet announced this (as Boguslavsky reported on 22 November) as its current 'urgent task' [*boevaya zadacha*]. The daily allocation of funds to MONO was tripled, and teachers in the Moscow *guberniya* received 4 milliard roubles in back pay (350,000 to 750,000 each). Support for MONO was mobilized from other departments of the Soviet, which contributed food, firewood, shoes and clothing. A week of 'Aid to the School' was announced.

At the same time, Moscow did its best to extract money from Narkompros, petitioning in October for an extraordinary allocation of 5 milliard roubles.[56] But the fact that the request was conveyed to the collegium of Narkompros by Litkens, without the presence of a representative of MONO, suggested that Moscow had little hope of success. The request was refused. 'The *guberniya* Soviets, even the Moscow one,' Lunacharsky wrote later, 'thought that in refusing this resource [local self-taxation] they could replace it with some sort of extra subsidy from the completely empty treasury of Narkompros.'[57]

Lunacharsky perhaps exaggerated in calling the treasury of Narkompros 'completely empty'. In December, Moscow Soviet ceased to receive a direct allocation on the budget of the central government (in accordance with the new independence of local finance), and its departments became entirely dependent on their allocations from the corresponding commissariats pending the successful raising of local taxes by Moscow Soviet. The commissariats failed to respond to this crisis, and by the second half of December Moscow Soviet was penniless. The offending commissariats were called before the Finance Commissariat and ordered to pay up. Vesenkha was found to be the worst offender, and ordered to pay 30 milliard roubles to its Moscow department. The Commissariat of Agriculture also had to pay. The Health Commissariat was found to be as unmoneyed as its Moscow department, and was issued 8 milliard roubles from reserve funds.

Narkompros was not found to be in so desperate a position as the Health Commissariat, and the meeting was of the opinion that it had paid MONO less than was due. But Narkompros put up a fight. *Ekonomicheskaya zhizn'* reported on 14 January 1922, that

> the greatest difficulties at the meeting arose between representatives of Narkompros and MONO, since Narkompros, which had received 170 milliard roubles in December and spent 60 milliard of them on the expenses of the central apparatus, allocated only 7.5 milliard to MONO, although according to the number of pupils in educational institutions supported by MONO it should have got 15% of the Narkompros budget.

The Finance Commissariat decided that Narkompros should pay MONO 2.5 of the 5.5 milliard roubles remaining in its treasury, together with a further 7.5 milliard which was to be issued from reserve funds.

Thus Narkompros seems to have emerged from the struggle rather better than MONO, in that it paid from its own funds only 10 milliard of the 25.5 milliard roubles to which MONO—on the estimate of the Finance Commissariat—was entitled. On the other hand, Narkompros itself was left with only 3 milliard roubles in hand, and without the goodwill of the Finance Commissariat.

'The new economic policy', Krupskaya wrote in October 1921,

> does not mean a repudiation of our programme...The introduction of school fees, library charges, private schools and so on is a vulgar retreat from the Party programme, and if Communists take part in it we will have to raise the question of their Party loyalty [*partiinost'*] and send them to Party school.[58]

But this 'vulgar retreat' could not be checked by exhortation, but only by the successful implementation of local self-taxation, or by generous allocations from local Soviet budgets, or by an increase in the central budget of Narkompros. Lunacharsky acknowledged early in 1922 that self-taxation had been killed 'by the absence of a proper taxation structure [and] the direct refusal of some, even *guberniya*, Soviets to conduct this special tax'.[59] Allocations from local budgets in 1921 seem to have been small. Most local Soviets were (or so Narkompros frequently claimed) indifferent to educational problems. Even Moscow Soviet, which was exceptional in this regard, had to drop its campaign in aid of the school after a few months because of the catastrophic situation of its own finances.

There remained the possibility of an increase in the central educational budget. At the time of the September decree, it was believed in Narkompros that local self-taxation would not replace but supplement the central financing of education; and that the educational budget would at worst remain constant and probably rise. On 25 September, Lunacharsky wrote in *Izvestiya* that

> up to this time in the field of finance Narkompros had at its disposal 3% of the state issue, which is an undoubted scandal for a civilized state. At the present time there is some sort of brightening in this respect. Bolshoi Sovnarkom on the 20th [of September] put serious consideration of the raising of Narkompros resources to 8% of monthly state expenditure on the agenda...

A few weeks later, Lunacharsky told a congress of educational workers that 'for the month of October Narkompros will have 9 times the resources it has had up to now', according to a report in *Izvestiya* on 4 October. In November, still optimistic, Lunacharsky reported that

> the state now has available rather more funds for cultural needs, and so the times when the percentage of the state budget [for Narkompros] fell below 5 may be considered past. It has already significantly risen, and from January Narkompros' share will be fixed as 10% of the budget.[60]

In December a member of the Commissariat of Agriculture, complaining of the 8% of the proposed 1922 budget allotted to his commissariat, stated that 'ahead of it stand the budgets of Vesenkha, the War Commissariat, Communications, Food and Education'.[61]

Litkens was less hopeful than Lunacharsky of a significant budgetary increase for Narkompros. He pointed out that on past experience Narkompros could, in any case, expect to receive little more than a third of its budgetary estimate.* This, he explained, was 'the result of a lack of the appropriate prerequisites which would have made it possible to put pressure on all the other state organs'—by which he presumably meant possession of goods to exchange or political influence.

In the event Narkompros did well, though not so well as Lunacharsky had prophesied, on the first version of the 1922 (January–September) budget, receiving 8.6% of money and 6.6% of total (money and turnover) allocations.†

The basis for this first 1922 budget was the figure of 513,100 employees on state supply laid down for Narkompros by the Larin commission. Of these, 2,700 were employees of the central apparatus (compared with the actual 1921 figure of around 9,000), 37,000 were employees of local education departments (compared with an estimated 100,000 in 1921) and 323,000 were teachers and staff of schools and children's homes (compared with an estimated 501,000 in 1921). Even among the privileged 513,100 receiving central support, only 250,000–260,000 were to receive food rations as well as salary: 'the rest have to be provided with food rations by the local Soviet *ispolkom* by local arrangement'.[62]

The Larin commission seems to have assumed that the central government could provide finance for a part of almost all the activities of Narkompros, and the whole of none. It made no categorical division between the financial responsibilities of central and local authorities, implying that local authorities would seek out the gaps in central financing of education and culture, filling them to the best of their ability wherever they might be found. The gaps, as

* Litkens claimed that Narkompros received 8.9% on the estimates of the 1921 budget, and 3% in fact. This is not in accordance with the Finance Commissariat's figures (see Appendix I). He may have been thinking of the retrospective 1920 budget, compiled in 1921. (Litkens, *Nat. pros.* (weekly) (1921), nos 87–8, p. 5.)

† See Appendix I: 'Budgetary expenditure on Narkompros (estimates)'.

Litkens estimated them at the end of 1921, would probably amount to 40–50% of all educational expenses.

In December 1921, Narkompros attempted to categorize the expenses which were likely to fall on local authorities; and this process was carried further by decrees of VTSIK (10 December 1921) and Sovnarkom (18 April 1922) stating the obligation of local authorities to pay 85% of the maintenance of primary school teachers and 50% of the expenses of kindergartens, lower trade and technical schools, extramural institutions, libraries and local museums.[63]

Preparation of the Narkompros budget was complicated by the fact that there was a ceiling both on the number of employees on central supply and on the amount to be spent on them. The ceiling for total expenditure (as calculated in pre-war roubles for the first January–September budget of 1922) was 32 million roubles in money 'and not a kopek more', and 88 million turnover roubles,* with a possible variation of no more than 10%.[64] So even in the most favourable circumstances, Narkompros could only hope to balance its budget by a wage freeze. However, early in 1922 Rabpros, the teachers' union, put forward a claim for higher pay; and Narkompros, regarding this as 'a natural demand to raise the salaries of educational workers at least to the norm of payment for workers of other government departments', agreed. There was already some discrepancy between the ceiling of numbers of employees and the ceiling of total expenditure. The teachers' salary increases meant that Narkompros would spend its entire 9-month allocation under the first 1922 budget in 3 or 4 months.[65]

By February 1922 it was clear that, for all of its paper 6.6% of the state budget, Narkompros' financial position was going to get worse instead of better. Lunacharsky admitted as much in a statement published in *Pravda* on 24 February. 'So far,' he said,

> Narkompros has existed on a purely fortuitous and absurd budget. With the transfer to a state plan, it might have been possible to win a proper place in that plan. But when they worked out how much money was

* Russia in 1921 had not completed its return to a full money economy, and the first 1922 budget was calculated in terms of monetary [*pryamye*] and accounting or 'turnover' [*oborotnye*] payments.

needed to put our teachers in a barely tolerable position—not to speak of school repairs—the figure turned out to be immense. The gloomy picture that emerged was that instead of an increase in resources by 600–700% we were faced with a 300% reduction.

In March 1922, the total number of Narkompros employees on central supply was lowered from 513,100 to 420,000.[66] Maksimovsky told the collegium that he had already protested to the Larin Commission, and the collegium decided to protest 'right up to the presidium of VTSIK'. But protests had no effect, since what Narkompros was suffering was part of a general misfortune. In April, the whole state budget for 1922 was revised; and Narkompros' share fell from 6.6% to 2.9%.* The collegium hopelessly offered its opinion that the sum offered by the revised budget was not only 'quite inadequate for any sort of satisfactory financing of education', but 'even if the sum is increased as far as is possible for the Republic (which we must insist on) satisfactory financing is impossible'.[67]

In February and March—months of acute financial crisis for the government, when large numbers of Soviet employees in Moscow and Petrograd were taken off state supply—Narkompros received only 36% of its promised allocation. The collegium reported 'complete panic among the local leadership, indiscriminate flight of educational workers, poverty of the starving teachers (who despairingly decided on a strike, which has for the time being been staved off only by promises) and general outcry from the provinces at the absence of credits and the complete disruption of work in education'.[68]

The number of teachers receiving, or even being entitled to receive, salaries or rations from the central government fell sharply. In January, following the reduction recommended by the Larin Commission, Glavsotsvos had 324,500 employees (many of them teachers) on its books. By the end of April the permissible number had been so much reduced that Narkompros was petitioning for

* On 25 April, when the presidium of Narkompros discussed the revised budget, its allocation was quoted as 102 million roubles (as against the previous 120 million roubles). But its final allocation on the revised budget was only half this figure, according to Finance Commissariat statistics. See Appendix I.

'a minimum of 100,000' salary units for Glavsotsvos; but in vain, for the number fell to 45,000 in May. At this point Lenin intervened, forwarding a protest by Krupskaya to Sovnarkom with his endorsement. As a result, the number was pushed up to 103,800 on the revised budget in June.[69]

For Narkompros as a whole, the June revision left a total of 201,000 employees on central supply[70]—that is, rather less than half the figure established by the Larin commission six months earlier. In August, VTSIK published a revised version of the Larin commission's recommendations allowing for central maintenance of 365,000 employees under Narkompros, including 160,000 primary school teachers.[71] But the recommendation was remote from the real situation. Two weeks after its publication, Sovnarkom struck all primary school teachers off the central budget.[72]

The removal of all central support for primary schools led to widespread closure of the schools by local authorities. This was an acceleration of the process of collapse of the school system begun in the summer of 1921. Neither local Soviets nor local popular initiative proved capable of maintaining the schools without central subsidy.

The total number of primary schools in Russia had been increasing rapidly in the immediate pre-war years. This increase had continued, though probably at slower speed, during the Civil War years, reaching a peak in the first months of 1921, when official figures for primary education were 76,000 (82,000) schools with 6 million (6.8 million) pupils. By April 1922 the number of schools had dropped to 68,000; by December to 55,000; and by October 1923 to 49,000 with 3.7 million pupils.[73] The comparable figures for 1914–15 were 73,000 schools with 4.9 million pupils.[74] The steady decline in numbers of pupils was reversed in 1923–4, while the total number of primary schools in Russia began a slow rise in 1924–5.

For Narkompros, this experience was traumatic. Even Lunacharsky, usually so resilient, could not speak of the collapse of the school system in the first years of NEP without bitterness. 'It was, of course, an extremely wise move to take the schools off the state hook on which they were hanging and let them down onto local funds,' he said in 1924, 'but local funds were a swamp, and the schools began to sink...'[75]

In these circumstances, it was inevitable that Narkompros should reconsider its attitude to payment of school fees and to private schools. The first sign of a retreat came in February 1922, when Lunacharsky wrote that it might become necessary to introduce fees in secondary and higher schools, but on no account in primary schools. He also thought it possible that private schools teaching art and commercial schools might be permitted: indeed Narkompros 'had already allowed...the establishment of private paying schools'.[76] But a congress of local education departments in the same month found the introduction of fees even in secondary schools 'inexpedient'; and resolved that 'the existence of schools maintained by private funds is inadmissible'—adding, however, that under present circumstances private funds might be accepted if this involved no surrender of organizational rights.[77]

The local education departments had changed their attitude by October. On being informed by Lunacharsky that 'in view of the fact that payment for the right of schooling has already been introduced in the great majority of *gubernii*, we intend to suggest the introduction of school fees in secondary schools', the congress went further, and resolved that 'as a palliative and temporary measure', payment might be introduced in both primary and secondary schools. The congress also cautiously endorsed a Narkompros proposal 'to permit not only labour associations but associations of all types to open schools, on condition that the private school is under the same control by local education departments as the state school which is maintained on soviet funds'.[78]

By the last months of 1922, the battle against the introduction of school fees was already over. In November, Glavprofobr issued instructions on the procedure for collecting fees in higher schools.[79] School fees were reported to have been introduced (for both primary and secondary schools) in 24 out of the 31 *gubernii* from which Narkompros had information. On the average, 20–25% of places remained free and were reserved for children of invalids, soldiers, teachers, unemployed and low wage-earners.[80] In most *gubernii*, Lunacharsky said in December 1922, the Soviet *ispolkom* had decided to introduce school fees without asking Narkompros, but where they had refused to do this 'the schools themselves had introduced school fees without asking the *guberniya ispolkom*'.[81]

It remained only to legalize the existing situation. This was done at the Tenth Congress of Soviets in December 1922. Lunacharsky recommended the formal introduction of school fees because they already existed in fact, but proposed to exempt a number of categories of the population from payment. He estimated that, with these exemptions, income from fees would at best cover 15% of total educational costs; and asked for an increase in the central educational budget, and for the legal requirement that local Soviets should devote 30% of their budgets to educational needs.[82]

The congress accepted Lunacharsky's recommendations on the introduction of school fees, resolved that the central educational budget should be increased, and instructed local Soviets to devote 'the maximum possible percentage' of their budget to education. The congress declared itself 'categorically against the admittance of any form of private school, and for the maintenance of the school system as a whole in the hands of the Soviet government'.[83] Thus Narkompros' toleration of a measure of private enterprise within the school system was rejected.

The introduction of fees at all levels of the educational system, with exemption for certain categories of the population, was sanctioned by Sovnarkom early in 1923.[84]

This was the culmination of a progressive defeat for Narkompros and its educational ideals. The defeat was caused less by NEP than by new economic realities. In so far as NEP had an author, it was Lenin. But Lenin had tried repeatedly to save Narkompros from the consequences of the economic (and indeed the political) situation. If Lenin had not been ill, Krupskaya thought, the resolution of the Tenth Congress of Soviets on the introduction of school fees 'would probably not have passed'.[85] But Lenin, even in health, had been defeated on earlier educational issues by indifference of Party and government organs towards education, hostility towards Narkompros, inertia of institutions and, above all, by the poverty of the Soviet Republic.

Four stages might be noted in the progressive retreat from the programme announced by Narkompros in 1918. The first was the failure to organize education on a basis of popular participation and local initiative through the educational soviet. Krupskaya, in particular, never admitted final defeat on this question, and continued to regard popular participation and initiative as an essential basis of all Soviet administration. Lenin, to judge by his statements on extramural and political education,* shared this belief.

The second stage was the questioning and partial abandonment of the policy of polytechnical education in 1920–1. The policy was compromised and its application restricted. Nevertheless, it was not repudiated until 1929, when Lunacharsky resigned from Narkompros after being defeated on the issue by the Politburo under Stalin and Vesenkha under Kuibyshev.

The third stage was the withdrawal of the central government's ultimate financial responsibility for the educational system in the autumn of 1921. This meant that there could no longer be, in the full sense, an educational policy formulated by Narkompros and carried out—however imperfectly—by its local departments. The loss of financial control meant loss of the possibility of effective control of the actions of local departments. 'How is leadership of local departments to be exercised by Narkompros?' asked one Narkompros worker plaintively at the end of 1921. 'Through the sending of circulars?'[86]

The fourth and last stage was the defeat, or temporary defeat (as Lunacharsky always insisted), of the policy of free and compulsory education of the whole population. This defeat was brought about by the *de facto* and then *de jure* introduction of school fees at all levels of the educational system.

Against these defeats suffered must be set the defeats which Narkompros (in the years under discussion) escaped. It maintained a policy of tolerance in the arts, resisting pressure to conduct a 'cultural October', to give any artistic group a monopoly and licence to suppress other groups, or to take this licence for itself. In dealing with scientific research and higher education, Narkompros also on the whole resisted pressure to interfere and to intimidate, and maintained its policy of respecting the independence of science. The

* See above, pp. 96, 251–2.

Academy of Sciences, which Lunacharsky had brought into co-operation with the Soviet government, remained—again, until the late '20s—autonomous.

Nevertheless, in 1922 Lunacharsky looked at the situation in education and felt that Narkompros had lost everything.

Our comrades, Communist journalists abroad, inform us with great concern that there is a whole campaign exposing our 'barbarianism', and that there is nothing they can reply. They appeal to me to give them some sort of defensive weapon, but I, looking around, find almost no such weapon...I have already long ago lost that more or less tranquil tone in which I used to talk to foreign interviewers, showing them some of our contemporary achievements in the cultural field...NEP completely destroyed those gains.[87]

'Were we, Communist propagandists, ever really concerned with anything other than the education of the people?' Lunacharsky asked. But Litkens, a Communist of a later generation, thought Lunacharsky's concept of enlightenment outmoded—a relic of pre-revolutionary, pre-Civil War idealism. Narkompros, Litkens told the Party meeting on education at the end of 1920, had 'drowned itself completely in general cultural enterprises, utterly failing to set itself the task of giving practical service to Soviet construction ...Military practice has put forward completely new methods of approach to cultural–educational work among the masses.' Preobrazhensky (speaking to the Tenth Party Congress in 1921) added the comment that Lunacharsky was out of touch with contemporary Party work.

The Civil War put the Party into uniform, but Narkompros remained unalterably civilian—Krupskaya no less than Lunacharsky and, indeed, Lenin no less than Krupskaya. The character and policies of Narkompros were formed under the influence of Lenin and Krupskaya as well as Lunacharsky; and the old-fashioned preoccupation with enlightenment belonged to Lenin as well as Narkompros.

Lenin was not an admirer of Lunacharsky's plays, and would certainly have disagreed with Gorky's comment that *Magi* deserved publication 'because this play was written at a time of intensive terror by a member of the Soviet government'. But it might be said of Narkompros that, however its policies had been compromised or defeated by the end of 1921, it was left with a singular achievement, for which Lenin as well as Narkompros deserved credit: that these policies were formulated and partly put into practice during a period of terror, Civil War and economic collapse by a commissariat of the Soviet government.

APPENDIX I

Budgetary expenditure on Narkompros (estimates)

The basic data and the sources for the following table were supplied by Professor R. W. Davies of the University of Birmingham, to whom I am greatly indebted.

Year	Total budget estimate	Narkompros allocation estimate	% of total
	(in million roubles at current prices unless otherwise stated)		
1917	27,871[3]	328.3[1]	1.2
1918 (Jan.–June)	17,603[4]	541.5[2]	3
1918 (July–Dec.)	29,103[4]	2,463.9[5]	8.5
1919 (Jan.–June)	50,703[4]	3,920.4[5]	7.7
1919 (July–Dec.)	164,699[4]	13,323.7[5]	8.1
1920	1,215,159[6]	114,366[6]	9.4
1921	24,471,922[7]	549,526[7]	2.2
1922 (Jan.–Sept., first estimate, in roubles of 1913)			
	direct 407.4	direct 34.5	8.6
	turnover 1,469.8	turnover 88.3	6
	total 1,877.2[9]	total 122.8[8]	6.6
1922 (revised estimate, in roubles of 1913)			
	1,706.7[10]	50.6[10]	2.9
1922 (July–Sept., in million current roubles)			
	90,740[11]	3,038[11]	3.4
1922–3 (Oct.–Sept., in million gold roubles)			
	1,212.4[12]	41.2[12]	3.6

Note

The high allocations to Narkompros in 1919 (July–September) and 1920 are of no actual significance, since these budgets were adopted *post facto* in August 1921.

Appendix I

Sources

1 *Rospis' obshchegosudarstvennykh dokhodov i raskhodov rossiiskoi sotsialisticheskoi federativnoi sovetskoi respubliki po iyul'-dekabr' 1919 g.* (1921). *Obyasnitel'naya zapiska*, p. 52.

2 *Ibid. Obyasnitel'naya zapiska*, p. 53.

3 *Proposed Budget of the Empire for 1917*, part 1 (1917).

4 See R. W. Davies, *Development of the Soviet Budgetary System* (Cambridge, 1958), pp. 42–3.

5 *Rospis'...po iyul'-dekabr' 1919 g.*, p. 25.

6 V. P. Dyachenko, *Sovetskie finansy v pervoi faze razvitiya sotsialisticheskogo gosudarstva*, part 1 (Moscow, 1947), p. 186; *Narodnyi Komissariat Finansov 1917 7. xi/25 x. 1922* (1922), p. 45.

7 *Narodnyi Komissariat Finansov...*, p. 45.

8 *Rospis' obshchegosudarstvennykh dokhodov i raskhodov R.S.F.S.R. po yanvar'-sentyabr' 1922 g.* (1921), p. 36.

9 *Ibid.* p. 3.

10 *Narodnyi Komissariat Finansov...*, pp. 64–5.

11 *Ibid.* p. 70.

12 *Vestnik finansov* (1925), no. 1, pp. 160–1.

APPENDIX II

Biographical notes

ALTMAN, Natan Isaevich (b. 1889). Artist; lived in Paris for some years before First World War, painting in Cubist style. Returned to Russia on outbreak of war. Foundation member of Petrograd IZO, Narkompros. Headed art department of Narkompros Academic Centre 1921. Since 1930s working in Leningrad as theatrical designer and book illustrator.

ANDREEVA, Maria Fedorovna (1868–1953). Actress with Moscow Arts theatre 1898–1905. Worked with Bolsheviks from 1902. In 1903 separated from husband (A. A. Zhelyabuzhsky, State Councillor) to live with writer Maxim Gorky (q.v.). In emigration 1906–12. Returned to Moscow late 1912, acted with private Nezlobin theatre, etc. After February Revolution, headed administration of municipal theatres under Petrograd City Duma. Appointed Commissar of Theatres and Spectacles for Northern Commune, Sept. 1918. Simultaneously headed Petrograd dept of Commissariat of External Trade; founded and acted in Bolshoi dramaticheskii teatr, Petrograd. In 1920, against Zinoviev's wishes, appointed head of Narkompros arts section in Petrograd. April 1921 sent abroad to negotiate sale of art and antiques. From 1922 represented Commissariat of External Trade in film negotiations abroad and worked with Soviet trade delegation in Berlin. Separated from Gorky on leaving Russia. Returned Russia 1930. Director of Moscow House of Scholars 1931–48.

ANIKST, Olga Grigoryevna (1886–1959). Worked in Narkompros dept of professional education; later in Glavprofobr, heading dept of workers' education. In revolutionary movement from 1905, in emigration after 1905, joined Communist Party 1918.

AZANCHEVSKAYA, Sofia Vasilyevna (1874–1951). S-R, later left S-R. In emigration 1908–17, acquainted with Lenin. Worked in Narkompros finance dept, but dismissed at end of 1918 and evicted from Narkompros building early 1919. Later worked in finance and personnel dept of Commissariat of Foreign Affairs; then as statistician and accountant.

BAKRYLOV, V. V. (?–1922). Left S-R, employed by Lunacharsky in situations demanding show of force—the occupation of Ministry of Public Education in Nov. 1917; administration of Petrograd state theatres, Jan. 1918.

BALMONT, Konstantin Dmitrievich (1867–1943). Symbolist poet very popular before 1917; wrote hymns to Revolution in 1905, but emigrated 1921; died in Paris. Lunacharsky at one time thought well of him, and was responsible for obtaining his exit visa, but in 1928 he admitted that B. had deceived him with protestations of revolutionary sympathy and said that his poetry had not stood the test of time.

BARYSHNIKOV, A. Left S-R, worked in Narkompros from 1918. During '20s, Glavprofobr inspector of art schools. Dismissed by Vyshinsky in 1928 after newspaper attack.

BATYUSHKOV, Fedor Dmitrievich (1857–1920). Liberal professor of philology at Petersburg University. Headed administration of Petrograd state theatres under Provisional Government and refused to accept dismissal by Lunacharsky in 1918. Subsequently worked as consultant on technique of translation in 'Vsemirnaya literatura' publishing house.

BAZAROV, Vladimir Aleksandrovich (1874–1939). Real name RUDNEV. Social-Democratic propagandist from 1895. In Vologda exile with Lunacharsky and Bogdanov. Bolshevik in 1905, but broke with Lenin in 1907. Close to *Vpered* group; contributed articles (with Lunacharsky, Bogdanov, Gorky, Valentinov etc.) to collections of Marxist philosophical essays pub. 1904–9. Worked with Gorky on journal *Letopis'* (from 1915) and daily *Novaya zhizn'* (1917–18). During '20s worked as economist in Gosplan and Communist Academy. Prominent in debates on industrialization 1927–8, representing labour dept, Gosplan. Like Lunacharsky, opposed crash programmes and lowering of standards in training of cadres for Five-Year Plan. Arrested 1930 as Menshevik wrecker.

BELY, Andrei (1880–1934). Real name Boris Nikolaevich BUGAEV. Symbolist poet of strong mystical inclinations, follower of Rudolf Steiner's school of anthroposophy. Revolutionary sympathizer pre-1917; 1917–18 close to left S-Rs and member of 'Scythian' literary group, lecturer in literary studio of Moscow Proletkult. Worked in TEO Narkompros during Civil War. In emigration 1921–3, then returned to Russia. Attacked by RAPP in late '20s as decadent, but readmitted to Soviet literary life in 1932 on RAPP's dissolution.

Regarded himself as Marxist in later life, but did not abandon mysticism or messianic approach to Russia and Revolution.

BENOIS, Aleksandr Nikolaevich (1870–1960). Landscape and water-colour painter, theatrical designer, associated before the revolution with 'Mir iskusstva' group and Diaghilev ballet. Director of Picture Gallery of Hermitage 1918–25. Settled in Paris from 1926 (retaining Soviet citizenship), worked for Diaghilev and Ida Rubinstein. Active as theatrical designer in New York, London, Milan etc. until mid-'50s.

BESSALKO, Pavel Karpovich (1887–1920). Revolutionary from 1904. In 1910 escaped from Siberian exile to Paris, becoming member of Lunacharsky's proletarian culture circle and writing novel called *Catastrophe*. Joined Bolsheviks after February Revolution. One of co-founders with Lunacharsky of Petrograd Proletkult. Mobilized into Red Army 1909, died of typhoid in Kharkov, 1920.

BLOK, Aleksandr Aleksandrovich (1880–1921). Symbolist, widely regarded as greatest Russian poet of this century. One of first leading members of Russian intelligentsia to accept Soviet power (in Dec. 1917); but remained close to left S-Rs, in whose journal poem 'Scythians' first published in 1918. Worked in repertoire section of Petrograd TEO, and in Gorky's 'Vsemirnaya literatura'. B.'s political position has been bitterly disputed, controversy centring on interpretation of poem 'The Twelve' (1918). Attitude to Soviet government and to Russia itself became increasingly critical; last months of his life spent in state of physical collapse and spiritual disillusionment.

BOGDANOV, Aleksandr Aleksandrovich (1873–1928). Real name MALINOVSKY. Politician, philosopher, scientist, doctor of medicine. Social-Democrat from 1896. Central figure among exiled Marxists in Vologda, where became friend and brother-in-law of Lunacharsky. Met Lenin in Switzerland 1904, joined Bolsheviks, established himself as politician almost rivalling Lenin in ambition and authority. Quarrelled with Lenin on political and philosophical questions, expelled from Bolsheviks 1919. Leader of *Vpered* group and organizer of Capri and Bologna Party Schools. Returned to Russia 1913. During war served at front as doctor. In 1917 living in Moscow, very critical of Lenin's political tactics. One of founders of Moscow Proletkult early 1918, and involved in organization of Moscow Proletarian University; member of Central Committee of Proletkult until Dec. 1920, when dropped as a result of pressure from Lenin and the Central Committee of Communist Party. Finally abandoned Proletkult and political activity late in 1921. Devoted himself to scientific work; active in Communist Academy; in 1926 founder and director of Institute of Blood Transfusions under Commissariat of Health, Moscow. Died accidentally as result of experimental transfusion performed on himself. Bukharin and Lunacharsky spoke at his funeral.

BOGOLEPOV, Dmitri Petrovich (1885–1941). Party member from 1907; 1914–15 member of Social-Democratic fraction in Fourth Duma. Lecturer in law faculty of Moscow University. After October Revolution, worked in Finance Commissariats of Russia, Ukraine and Turkestan. From 1920 to 1921 Rector of Moscow University. Later worked in Gosplan and teaching.

BOGUSLAVSKY, Moisei Solomonovich. Acted as spokesman for Moscow Soviet on education 1921. In mid-'20s, speaker in VTSIK and Sovnarkom on educational questions, especially child homelessness [*besprizornost'*] and teachers' salaries. President of Maly Sovnarkom 1926–7. Trotskyite, member of 1927 Opposition.

BONCH-BRUEVICH, Vera Mikhailovna (1868–1918), 'Velichkina'. Wife of V. D. Bonch-Bruevich (q.v.). Doctor by profession. Active revolutionary past in Russia and emigration. Headed Narkompros dept of school health and hygiene; member collegium of Commissariat of Health.

BONCH-BRUEVICH, Vladimir Dmitrievich (1873–1955). Communist, historian, ethnographer. Active in revolutionary movement from 1896; worked on Social-Democratic archives and as Party propagandist in emigration before 1905. Made scientific study of Russian sectarians; escorted group of Dukhobors to Canada in 1899. Returned to Russia after 1905; ran legal publishing house 'Zhizn' i znanie' for Bolsheviks; organized special section for study of religious sects under Academy of Sciences. From Oct. 1917–20 secretary to Sovnarkom. Later concentrated on scientific and literary work, as chief editor of 'Zhizn' i znanie' (now a cooperative publisher), organizer of literary–historical series 'Zven'ya' etc. Founder and first director of State Literary Museum (1930). From 1946, director of Museum of History of Religion under Academy of Sciences. Wrote valuable memoirs of work with Lenin in first years of Soviet government.

BRIK, Osip Maksimovich (1884–1945). Literary critic, member of prerevolutionary formalist group OPOYAZ. Close friend of Mayakovsky (q.v.), husband of Lilia Brik. Member LEF. Worked in IZO Narkompros and ROSTA during Civil War.

BRIKHNICHEV, Iona Panteleimonovich. Head of Gomel education dept during Civil War. Responsible for lavish decoration of local buildings with revolutionary slogans. Came to Narkompros late 1920 and participated in work on establishment of Glavpolitprosvet and reorganization of Narkompros. Regarded by some Narkompros workers as an intruder.

BRYUSOV, Valery Yakovlevich (1873–1924). Symbolist poet of considerable classical scholarship. Good organizer, interested in the spread of enlightenment. On fairly close terms with Lunacharsky after October Revolution. Held various posts in Narkompros including head of LITO (1919–20) and head of Glavprofobr dept of artistic education; after leaving active administrative work in Narkompros, president of literary section of GUS. 'A *Kulturträger*' (Ehrenburg).

BRYUSOVA, Nadezhda Yakovlevna (1881–1951). Musician, sister of Valery Bryusov (q.v.). Before 1917 worked at Moscow Conservatorium and Moscow People's Conservatorium (1906–16). Disciple of musical theorist Yavorsky. Wrote widely on music in education. Involved in the organization of RAPM (Association of Proletarian Musicians) in late '20s. Worked in music departments of Narkompros, MONO, Glavprofobr.

BUKHARIN, Nikolai Ivanovich (1888–1938). Bolshevik politician of pronounced intellectual interests, especially in philosophy and sociology (where influenced by Bogdanov, q.v.), economics and the arts. Bolshevik from 1906; student of economics at Moscow University from 1907; in emigration 1911–17. After October Revolution, member of left opposition to Brest peace 1918. In '20s editor of *Pravda*, candidate member and member of Politburo, head of Comintern. In 1929 leading member of right opposition, defeated by Stalin. Edited *Izvestiya* 1934–6, without recovering political standing of pre-1929. Publicly tried and convicted of espionage and wrecking in 1938; apparently shot. One of the best minds in the Party, but judgement unstable. On the arts, B. took ultra-radical 'proletarian' position in first years after revolution, but by mid-'20s had become main Party advocate of artistic tolerance and opponent of proletarian monopoly in the arts. Similarly, hostile in early years to Narkompros and all its works, but in 1928–9 defended Narkompros position on education in Central Committee and Politburo against Stalin and Molotov. Not personally close to Lunacharsky, despite similarity of interests and sometimes of opinion.

CHAGAL, Mark (b. 1887). Painter, born Vitebsk, worked in Paris pre-war, held very successful exhibition in Berlin 1914. Returned to Russia, and in 1918 organized Vitebsk art school with Narkompros support; ousted from control of school by Malevich (q.v.) 1919. Worked with Jewish Kamerny theatre in Moscow early '20s, then returned to Paris and has since lived outside Russia; paintings not exhibited USSR.

CHARNOLUSKY, Vladimir Ivanovich (1865–1941). Educationalist, author of a number of important books on Russian educational system before revolution. In 1917 member of Central Committee of party of popular [*narodnykh*] socialists, and deputy president of State Education Committee est. Provisional Government. Worked in Narkompros throughout '20s as librarian, bibliographer and archivist.

CHULKOV, Georgy Ivanovich (1879–1939). Symbolist poet, prose writer, critic. Imprisoned and exiled for participation in revolutionary movement in youth. After 1905 close associate of Vyach. Ivanov (q.v.), advocate of doctrine of mystical anarchism, 'non-acceptance of the world' after Ivan Karamazov. Remained in Russia after revolution, but 1919 rumour that he was to head LITO, Narkompros, proved unfounded. Published critical and historical works on Tyutchev and Pushkin in 1930s.

DESNITSKY, Vasily Alekseevich (1878–1958). Also known as STROEV-DESNITSKY. Elected to Central Committee of Russian Social-Democratic Party at 1906 Congress. Member of *Vpered* group and lecturer at Capri Party School 1909. With Gorky, one of the editors of *Novaya zhizn'* 1917–18. Later became literary scholar, writing mainly on Gorky. In last years, professor of Leningrad University.

DZERZHINSKY, Feliks Edmundovich (1877–1926). Polish, member Polish–Lithuanian Social-Democratic Party, worked for Central Committee of Russian Party in Russia from 1906. Member of Central Committee from August 1917; one of organizers of October rising in Petrograd. Headed Cheka from December 1917, GPU from 1922. In addition, appointed Commissar of Communications April 1921, president of Vesenkha February 1924.

EKSKUZOVICH, Ivan Vasilyevich (1882–1942). Educated as engineer. Administrator of Petrograd state theatres 1918–24. From 1924, administrator of all state academic theatres of RSFSR.

ELIZAROVA, Anna Ilyinichna (1864–1935). Née ULYANOVA, elder sister of Lenin. After October Revolution, headed child welfare dept of Commissariat of Social Security. Moved unwillingly to

Narkompros in 1919, remaining there in child welfare field until 1921.

ELKINA, Dora Yulyevna (1890–1963). Left S-R, joined Communist Party 1919. Foundation member of Narkompros, working mainly in adult education, campaign against illiteracy. Later taught in teacher-training institutes in Moscow.

FLAKSERMAN, Yury Nikolaevich (b. 1895). Member of revolutionary family; sister Galina m. N. N. Sukhanov (q.v.), brother Aleksandr worked as Lunacharsky's secretary 1918–21. Appointed by Lunacharsky Commissar of former Palace Ministry Nov. 1917, then headed Narkompros cinema committee during nationalization of private film companies. Mobilized 1919 to political-educational and editorial work at front. From 1921, member of scientific–technical dept of Vesenkha, where tactful approach appreciated by scientists; student of Moscow Higher Technical School, from which he graduated in 1925. Then worked in Glavelektro, and as G. M. Krzhizhanovsky's deputy at Energotsentr. In mid-'30s, detached himself from administrative work and became practising engineer. Still (1969) works in Moscow as technical consultant to Ministry of Power and Electrification of USSR.

GASTEV, Aleksei Kapitonovich (1882–1938?). Poet, theorist of proletarian culture and scientific organization of labour. Metalworker by trade. Active in social-democratic and syndicalist movements in Petersburg and Paris pre-war; member of Lunacharsky's proletarian culture group in Paris 1913. From 1917 to 1918 secretary of union of metalworkers; at same time active in Proletkult and, as 'proletarian poet' choosing then fashionable cosmic themes, in literary group 'Kuznitsa'. In 1920 founded TSIT (Central Institute of Labour) under Central Council of Trade Unions for investigation of theoretical problems of organization of labour. TSIT subsequently organized short-term labour training courses instilling mastery of basic physical motions necessary for performance of semi-skilled factory work; these courses became popular in late '20s, as offering cheaper and quicker labour training than Narkompros' factory schools (which also provided general education). TSIT flourished during '30s, G. becoming Party member in 1931, until 1938, when G. was arrested and TSIT closed. Recent revival of interest in G. and scientific organization of labour in USSR.

GOLOVIN, Fedor Aleksandrovich (1867–?) Chairman of Second Duma, member of Third Duma, leader of Union of Towns during war.

Commissar for former Palace Ministry under Provisional Government. Member of Committee of Aid to the Starving Population 1921. Then imprisoned, but later released and worked as specialist for various Soviet institutions.

GORKY, Maxim (1868–1936). Real name Aleksei Maksimovich PESHKOV. Self-taught writer from the people, famous before the revolution for descriptions of Russian, especially low Russian, life. Involved in revolutionary movement pre- and post-1905, gave money to Bolsheviks, friendly with Lenin. Member of *Vpered* group 1908–9 and on terms of intimate friendship with Lunacharsky, but later broke with Lunacharsky and Bogdanov and resumed friendship with Lenin. Returned to Russia at end of 1913, edited and financed journal *Letopis'* and daily *Novaya zhizn'* in Petrograd. At first hostile to October Revolution, but made peace with new government mid-1918. Concerned mainly with protecting cultural tradition and its upholders—writers, artists, scholars—but feeling difficulties of this task left Russia Oct. 1921, ostensibly for health reasons and without breaking with Lenin. Lived outside Russia, mainly in Italy, 1922–32, sometimes writing critically of Soviet regime, sometimes himself subject of hostile articles in Soviet press (including criticism by Lunacharsky of recent plays). Visited USSR in summer of 1928 and 1930; settled there permanently 1932. Fêted on return, held court in Soviet literary world, encouraged many young writers of talent. Largely responsible, evidently with Stalin's approval, for ending period of 'proletarian hegemony' in the arts and organizing Union of Soviet Writers, which at first though misleadingly appeared to give greater freedom and tolerance to non-Party writers. Established fairly close relationship with Stalin in first years after return; did not resume personal friendship with Lunacharsky, and in 1929 publicly attacked his educational policy as out of line with Stalin's. Celebrated Soviet industrialization in journal *Nashi dostizheniya*, and did much service to Soviet prestige among foreign intellectuals. After his death, Yagoda and his doctors were accused of murdering him.

GRABAR, Igor Emanuilovich (1871–1960). Painter, art historian, critic. Guardian of Tretyakov Gallery from 1913; officially appointed director 1918 and retained post until 1925. Worked in Narkompros on preservation of art treasures from first months after October; organized museum dept of Narkompros in Moscow early 1918. Established art-restoration studios in Moscow. During Second

World War headed commission for protection of art treasures of USSR and was elected to Academy of Sciences. Edited multi-volume history of Russian art.

GRINBERG, Zakhary Grigoryevich (1889–1949). Member of Jewish Bund 1906–14. In 1919 published translation of Maurenbrecher's work on Jewish prophets. Member Communist Party 1917–22. After October Revolution member of collegium of Petrograd, later Moscow, Narkompros. Head of organizational sector 1920; deputy to Litkens (q.v.) at Organizational Centre, Narkompros, 1921. With Berlin trade commission, responsible for purchase of books and materials for Narkompros, 1921–4. Recalled from Berlin peremptorily. Then worked in administration of Historical Museum and as deputy director of Kremlin Armoury. From 1927 to 1945 engaged in teaching and research work at second Moscow University and Gorky Institute of World Literature. Published work on Gorky.

GRINKO, Grigory Fedorovich (1890–1938). Student Moscow University, pre-war member of Party of Socialist Revolutionaries. Officer during war. After October, member of Ukrainian splinter party merging with Communists 1920. Worked in Ukraine 1919–26 as Commissar of Education, president of Gosplan etc. Moved to Moscow 1926 as deputy president of Gosplan USSR. Closely involved in formulation of first Five-Year Plan. In 1929 appointed deputy Commissar of Agriculture for USSR. From 1930 to 1937 Commissar of Finance of USSR. 1938 publicly tried with Bukharin and others, accused of Ukrainian nationalism and espionage; executed.

GRZHEBIN, Zinovy Isaevich (1869–1929). Owned pre-rev. publishing house 'Shipovnik'. After October, continued as private publisher under his own name, and organized 'Vsemirnaya literatura' for Gorky. Art collector and patron. Left Russia 1921, and for some time published books in Leipzig and Berlin for Soviet market and on order of Soviet institutions, also supplying Narkompros with teaching equipment for experimental schools. Later drifted into permanent state of emigration.

GUSEV, Sergei Ivanovich (1874–1933). Real name Yakov Davydovich DRABKIN. Active in revolutionary movement from 1890s, Bolshevik from 1903. Worked in Red Army after October Revolution. In 1921 head of PUR and candidate member of Central Committee of Party. Removed from PUR on Trotsky's insistence 1922; then member of Central Control Commission, Rabkrin, Istpart. In 1926 appointed head of Press dept of Central Committee and delivered official line in literary and theatrical controversies of following years. In 1930 Trotsky called G. Molotov's adjutant and 'artiste en de nombreux domains sauf en art'—an unkind comment, as Lenin is said to have enjoyed his singing at emigré musical evenings in Switzerland before 1917. Father of Elizaveta Drabkina, author of study of last years of Lenin's life etc.

IGNATOV, Vasily Vasilyevich (1884–1938). Described by Lunacharsky as 'half-proletarian, half-actor'. Secretary of Petrograd Proletkult in 1917 and of All-Russian Council of Proletkult from Sept 1918. Organizer and administrator of Proletkult theatre in Moscow ('Arena of proletarian creativity') 1920–1. Later worked in Proletkino and Sovkino.

IORDANSKY, Nikolai Nikolaevich (1863–1941). Teacher and educational organizer. Exiled for political unreliability 1911. One of the organizers of All-Russian teachers' congress of 1913–14. Worked in Moscow zemstvo 1914–17. Deputy president of State Education Committee under Provisional Government, dismissed with other officials by Lunacharsky after October. Although not a Communist, appointed head of Glavsotsvos, Narkompros, Oct. 1921; resigned May 1922. From 1922 to 1932 professor of education at second Moscow University; then worked in various Moscow research institutes. [NB. not to be confused with Nikolai Ivanovich IORDANSKY (1876–1928), Bolshevik worker in Gosizdat and Commissariat of Foreign Affairs.]

IVANOV, Vyacheslav Ivanovich (1866–1949). Symbolist poet of considerable classical learning and mystical inclinations. In post-1905 years, held Wednesday salon at Petrograd apartment 'The Tower', attended on occasion (though not characteristically) by Lunacharsky. After October Revolution worked in TEO, Narkompros. Poetic works of this period include ode to Olga Kameneva (q.v.) on her departure from TEO. Received help on a number of occasions in early '20s from Narkompros, usually at Lunacharsky's instigation. A prolonged trip abroad undertaken with Narkompros subsidy merged into emigration. I. settled in Italy becoming a Roman Catholic, head of the Vatican library and a Cardinal.

IVNEV, Rurik (b. 1893). Real name Mikhail Aleksandrovich KOVALEV. Poet and *littérateur*, friend of Esenin *c.* 1917. Worked in Petrograd Narkompros in first months after October. Organized meeting of intellectuals accepting Soviet power Dec. 1917. Still writing memoirs.

KALININ, Fedor Ivanovich (1882–1920). Son of weaver, brother of

Mikhail (q.v.) Social-Democrat from 1902; member of *Vpered* group and participant in Capri and Bologna Party Schools; then member of Lunacharsky's proletarian culture circle in Paris. Returned to Russia 1917. One of founders of Petrograd Proletkult, head of Narkompros dept of aid to independent proletarian cultural organizations 1918–19, then mobilized to front. Died of typhoid. Regarded by Lunacharsky and Bogdanov as exemplary type of worker-organizer.

KALININ, Mikhail Ivanovich (1875–1946). Party member from 1898. President of VTSIK 1919–22, president TSIK USSR from 1922. Candidate member of Politburo 1924, full member from 1926. After apparent hesitation, sided with Stalin against the right in 1929. From 1938 to 1946 president of presidium of Supreme Soviet of USSR. Wrote and spoke on educational questions, usually as a friend of Narkompros in the '20s.

KALININA, Asya Davydovna. Wife of Mikhail Ivanovich (q.v.). Worked in Narkompros dept for protection of children until 1921, then headed MONO dept of social and legal protection of minors.

KAMENEV, Lev Borisovich (1883–1936). Real name ROZENFELD. Party member from 1901. Studied law at Moscow University. From 1908 to 1913 in emigration, one of Lenin's closest collaborators. Returned Russia 1914, editing Bolshevik paper *Pravda* in Petrograd. In exile in Siberia, 1915–17. Returned March 1917; in October opposed seizure of power, supported coalition with other socialist parties November. Resigned from Central Committee on coalition issue, but shortly reinstated. Head of Moscow Party organization and president of Moscow Soviet in first half of '20s. Member Stalin/Zinoviev Kamenev triumvirate after Lenin's death. With Zinoviev in opposition to Stalin 1925; with Zinoviev/Trotsky opposition 1926. Dismissed from leadership Moscow Party and Soviet 1926; served briefly as Soviet representative in Italy. Expelled from Party 1927; readmitted 1928. For short time headed scientific–technical dept of Vesenkha; then chief editor of publishing house 'Academia'. Expelled from Party again 1932; readmitted 1933. In 1936 tried with Zinoviev and others for organization of terrorist centre responsible for Kirov's murder; convicted and shot. An intelligent man of conciliatory disposition, editor of first edition of Lenin's collected works, author before 1917 and in later periods of political disfavour of interesting articles on literary and historical themes.

KAMENEVA, Olga Davydovna (1883–1941). Sister of Trotsky (née

BRONSHTEIN) and wife of Kamenev. Head of TEO from its establishment in 1918 to July 1919; then head of artistic–educational sub-dept MONO. From 1923 worked in field of international cultural relations, being president of VOKS from its foundation to 1929. Then president of society 'Friend of Children'. Seems to have taken no part in political opposition movements. Not popular in Narkompros, in spite of ode by Vyach. Ivanov (q.v.) on her departure.

KARPINSKY, Aleksandr Petrovich (1847–1936). Geologist. First elected president of Academy of Sciences, holding office from mid-1917 to his death at age of 89. Popular among scientists; reputedly deferred to opinion of permanent secretary of Academy Oldenburg (q.v.) on political questions.

KATANYAN, Ruben Pavlovich (b. 1881). Bolshevik from 1903, working in Russia and Georgia. Member *Novaya zhizn'* group of social-democratic internationalists March–Sept. 1917. Head of PUR 1919–20; head of *agitprop* dept of Party Central Committee 1920–1. From 1923, deputy public prosecutor of RSFSR; 1933–7 senior assistant to public prosecutor of USSR. Acted as prosecutor in many political trials in '30s. Personal pensioner since 1955.

KERZHENTSEV, Platon Mikhailovich (1881–1940). Also wrote as V. KERZHENTSEV; real name P. M. LEBEDEV. Graduate in history and philosophy, joined Bolsheviks 1904. In emigration 1912–17. After October Revolution active in Proletkult, head of ROSTA. From 1921 to 1923 ambassador to Sweden; 1923–4 president of Rabkrin Council for Scientific Organization of Labour; 1925–6 ambassador to Italy; 1927–8 deputy director of Central Statistical Administration of USSR. From 1928, deputy head of *agitprop* dept and head of cultural propaganda dept of Party Central Committee; vice-president of Communist Academy 1930, editor of various literary periodicals. From 1933 to 1936 president of All-Union Radio Committee; 1936–8 president of Committee for Art Affairs under Sovnarkom USSR. A tireless and intolerant advocate of proletarian monopoly in the arts, active both during Civil War in Proletkult and in late '20s as head of 'Litfront' group, the radical wing of RAPP. A follower of literary theorist Pereverzev, distinguished exponent of 'vulgar sociological' criticism; a consistent defender of Pereverzev, Meyerhold and others of artistic left. Narkompros and Lunacharsky only spared more damaging attack during '20s by K.'s frequent absence on diplomatic missions. Died of heart attack.

KHALATOV, Artemy Bagratovich (1895/6–1938). Born Baku; joined Party

1917 as student of Moscow Commercial Institute. Worked in Food Commissariat during Civil War; then invited by Dzerzhinsky to join collegium of Commissariat of Communications, and headed council for administration of transport of USSR from 1924. In 1927 appointed head of Gosizdat and member of Narkompros collegium. An unusually capable organizer, popular in Party and (as head of KUBU in early '20s) with non-party intelligentsia.

KHODASEVICH, Vladislav Felitsianovich (1886–1939). Poet and literary scholar, Pushkin specialist. Worked in TEO, Narkompros, from end of 1918; lectured in literary studio of Moscow Proletkult. Emigrated 1922. A witty and malicious commentator on literary events.

KISHKIN, Nikolai Mikhailovich. Cadet leader, doctor of medicine. Member of Provisional Government in its last days; arrested Oct. 1917 defending Winter Palace. Released, but rearrested 1919, charged with conspiracy imprisoned until 1921. Member of Committee for Aid to the Starving Population, 1921. Again arrested on its dissolution, then expelled from Russia.

KOZELEV, Boris Grigoryevich. Trade unionist, president of teachers' union (Rabpros) 1920–1, representative of VTSSPS on Glavprofobr collegium 1920–1 and Narkompros collegium 1921. Opposed Narkompros' polytechnical policy. Later member of VTSSPS and secretary of metalworkers' union.

KRUPSKAYA, Nadezhda Konstaninovna (1869–1939). Marxist from early 1890s. In 1891, unpaid teacher at Smolenskaya evening Sunday school near Petersburg. Joined Lenin's Union of struggle for the liberation of the working-class 1895. Arrested, exiled, became Lenin's wife 1898. Left Russia 1901; secretary to Central Committee of Party in exile 1905–7 and 1912–17. Studied and wrote on educational questions in Geneva exile. Worked in Narkompros from its foundation; briefly deputy commissar in 1918, but resigned in favour of Pokrovsky. Headed Glavpolitprosvet, Narkompros, 1921–30 and scientific–pedagogical section of GUS, Narkompros, 1921–32. After Lenin's death, felt strong sense of political responsibility, though earlier not politically active in her own right. Member of Opposition 1926, then broke with it. Disliked and insulted on many occasions by Stalin. In 1929 after Lunacharsky's resignation from Narkompros, appointed deputy commissar to A. Bubnov, almost certainly against her wishes. Remained in this office at Narkompros until her death.

KRZHIZHANOVSKAYA, Zinaida Pavlovna (1870–1948). Née NEVZOROVA, wife of G. M. Krzhizhanovsky, organizer of electrical industry and president of Gosplan. Both members of Lenin's Union of struggle for liberation of the working-class 1895. K. worked with Krupskaya at Smolenskaya evening Sunday school in 1890s as geography teacher. After October Revolution, Krupskaya's deputy in extramural dept of Narkompros. Later in adult-education work under GUS, Narkompros. Retired 1927 because of ill-health. Close friend and confidante of Krupskaya.

KUSEVITSKY [KOUSSEVITSKY], Sergei Aleksandrovich (1874–1951). Virtuoso double-bass player and conductor. Owner of valuable music library requisitioned 1920. Emigrated early '20s; later had very successful American career as conductor.

KUSKOVA, Ekaterina Dmitrievna (1869–1958). Wife of Prokopovich (q.v.); among oldest friends of Gorky (q.v.), having introduced him to Nizhny-Novgorod intelligentsia in 1890s. Member of Committee of Aid to Starving Population 1921; arrested on its dissolution as leader of anti-Bolshevik 'Democratic Centre'; expelled from Russia. Maintained contact with Gorky during '20s; broke with him only in 1929, when he decided to return to USSR.

LARIN, Yu. (1882–1932). Real name Mikhail Aleksandrovich LURYE. Economist. Described by Lenin in 1911 as 'the *enfant terrible* of opportunism'. Social-Democrat from 1900; Menshevik internationalist during war. Joined Bolsheviks August 1917. One of original organizers of Vesenkha. Tireless controversialist on questions of economic policy, especially in VTSIK and at Party Congresses. Member of Communist Academy. Initiator and propagandist of many social campaigns: anti-alcoholism, for the 'uninterrupted (5-day) week', for a new socialist calendar beginning at 1917, etc.

LAZURKINA, Dora Abramovna (b. 1884). Professional revolutionary, member Party from 1902. Foundation member of Narkompros, heading kindergarten dept until 1922. Later head of Herzen Pedagogical Institute and worker in Leningrad Party organization.

LEBEDEV-POLYANSKY, Pavel Ivanovich (Valerian) (1881–1948). Real name P. I. LEBEDEV. Seminary education, arrested as student, became professional revolutionary 1904. Emigrated 1908 and joined *Vpered* group. Returned to Russia with Lunacharsky in 1917; arrested and imprisoned with him during July Days; joined Bolshevik Party August 1917. Foundation member of Narkompros; president of Proletkult 1918–20. Head of Glavlit (censorship)

1921–31. Member of Communist Academy. Co-editor with Lunacharsky of *Literary Encyclopedia*. In 1940s became head of Leningrad Institute of Literature and member of the Academy of Sciences.

LENGNIK, Fridrikh Vilgelmovich (1873–1936). Party member from 1898, engineer by training. During Civil War worked in Narkompros in professional–technical education, also in Vesenkha. From 1921 member collegium of Commissariat of External Trade. Member of Central Control Commission 1927.

LENIN, Vladimir Ilyich (1870–1924). Real name ULYANOV. Founder and leader of Bolshevik Party. During Civil War years, president of Sovnarkom and STO, member Maly Sovnarkom, Central Committee and Politburo. In touch with Narkompros work through wife Krupskaya (q.v.). Spoke at every major educational conference in first years. Headed Central Committee commission on reorganization of Narkompros early 1921, and subsequently kept Litkens (q.v.) under daily supervision during reorganization. Especially interested in campaign against illiteracy, development of libraries, proper use of bourgeois specialists. Irritated when Lunacharsky appeared to give priority to the arts over education, but personally well-disposed to him (except in pre-revolutionary *Vpered* period) and shared his and Krupskaya's educational views.

LEPESHINSKAYA, Olga Borisovna (1871–1963). Wife of P. N. Lepeshinsky (q.v.). First met Lenin in Siberian exile in 1890s. Party member from 1898. Organizer of Geneva 'dining-room' which served as Bolshevik club 1903–5. Studied medicine privately in Moscow and qualified as doctor [*lekar'*] in Moscow University examination in 1915. Then worked briefly as assistant in Moscow University medical faculty. Dismissed for political reasons. After October Revolution, member of medical faculty of Tashkent University 1919, Moscow University 1920–6 (after initial boycott, as Soviet appointee, by faculty professors who claimed she was unqualified) then worked in medical institutes as biologist. Became head of department of development of living organisms of Institute of Experimental Biology under Academy of Medical Sciences of USSR, working on development of cells from non-cellular matter. Won Stalin Prize 1950. Deputy to Supreme Soviet of RSFSR. Extent of scientific achievement controversial, but highly praised in 1950s, when L. held a position of great influence in scientific world.

LEPESHINSKY, Panteleimon Nikolaevich (1868–1944). Member 'People's Will' narodnik group, then Social-Democrat from 1898. Member of collegium of Narkompros 1918–19, organizer of experimental school-commune. One of family of schoolteachers: brother Modest also organized experimental school during Civil War. Deputy Commissar of Education in Turkestan 1919–20. Later worked in Istpart (section of Party history under Central Committee), MOPR (International Society of Aid to Revolutionaries), State Historical Museum and Museum of Revolution. Active in Society of Old Bolsheviks. Late in life received doctorate of historical sciences.

LESHCHENKO, Dmitri Ilyich (1876–1937). Party member from 1900. Friend of Lunacharsky. Secretary to State Education Commission from Dec. 1917; then president of Petrograd cinema committee and head of FOTO-KINO, Narkompros. Later worked as teacher.

LILINA, Zlata Ionovna (1882–1929). Wife of Zinoviev (q.v.), née BERNSHTEIN, sister of Ilya Ionov, head of Leningrad Gosizdat after revolution. Not popular in Narkompros during Zinoviev's heyday, but kept in work after his fall from power. Head of schools sub-dept of Petrograd education dept, 1920–1; head of Leningrad education dept, 1924–5. Worked in Narkompros book commission from 1927. Signatory of opposition manifestos, expelled from Party with Zinoviev in Dec. 1927. Readmitted June 1928. Narkompros journal published article by L. in Feb. 1928, and a kind obituary by Lunacharsky.

LITKENS, Evgraf Aleksandrovich (1888–1922). Son of A. A. Litkens, chief medical officer of Artillery School in Petersburg who sheltered Trotsky in his flat 1905. Trotsky expressed warm friendship for family in autobiography. Evgraf and elder brother Aleksandr friends of Preobrazhensky (q.v.) at gymnasium in Petersburg; Aleksandr already Party member in 1905, organizer with Preobrazhensky of peasant rising in Orel district, died shortly afterwards. L. graduated Petersburg University. After October Revolution worked in extramural dept of MONO, with the 5th Army, and as Commissariat of Internal Affairs representative in Crimea. Joined Party 1919. Invited, probably on suggestion of Trotsky or Preobrazhensky, to undertake reorganization of Narkompros late in 1920. Began work as *pomnarkom* [assistant to commissar], taking over all administrative functions from Lunacharsky; but after Sovnarkom protests at unconstitutionality of such an office appointed second deputy commissar. Reorganization inevitably resented by Narkompros old guard. Results not lasting, in spite of Litkens' and Lenin's efforts. But L. appears to have been capable organizer, if over-schematic. In Feb. 1922, with failure of Narkompros reorganization apparent, L. became seriously ill and was sent to sanatorium in Crimea. Health improved. One day in April set out to walk to nearest town and disappeared. Armed detachment sent into mountains by local Special Department found bandits after 10 days' search and recovered L.'s body. Motive of killing not clear.

LOURIE [LURYE] Arthur Sergeevich (b. 1892). Avant-garde composer. Head of MUZO, Narkompros, 1918–21. In this period wrote, according to unfriendly critic (Sabaneev), quasi-proletarian marches and syncopated erotic songs. Towards end of 1920, MUZO investigated by Rabkrin, Lourie himself being under investigation by Revolutionary Tribunal. Probably acquitted; but Litkens dismissed him from MUZO in Jan. 1921. Seems to have emigrated shortly afterwards. Published book on Koussevitsky in America; worked in Princeton University.

LUNACHARSKAYA, Anna Aleksandrovna (1883–1959). Née MALINOVSKAYA, sister A. Bogdanov (q.v.), wife of Lunacharsky 1902–22. Organizer of experimental children's colonies after October Revolution. Author of satirical novel *Gorod probuzhdaetsya* (Moscow, 1927).

LUNACHARSKAYA-ROZENEL, Natalya Aleksandrovna (1902–65). Née SATS, younger sister of composer Ilya Sats, aunt of director of Moscow Children's theatre, Natalya Ilyinichna Sats. Actress of Maly theatre, later in films. Married Lunacharsky 1922. Author of memoirs of Lunacharsky.

LUNACHARSKY, Anatoly Vasilyevich (1875–1933). Born Poltava in family of State Councillor Lunacharsky (surname devised for illegitimate branch of Charnolusky family in nineteenth century); spent early years with mother Varvara Yakovlevna (née Rostovtseva) in household of State Councillor Aleksandr Ivanovich Antonov, his natural father, a man of radical views. Educated Kiev gymnasium and Zurich University. Arrested as member of Moscow Social-Democratic circle 1899; exiled to Kaluga, Vologda and Totma. Met A. Bogdanov (q.v.) in exile; met Lenin in Paris 1904 and, with Bogdanov, joined Bolsheviks. Attended Third (London) Conference of RSDRP in April–May 1905. In Nov. 1905 summoned by Lenin to Petersburg to work on journal *Novaya zhizn'*. Arrested 1906; emigrated for second time Feb. 1907. Attended congresses of Workers' International at Stuttgart (1907) and Copenhagen (1910). Lived with Gorky on Capri 1908. With Gorky and Bogdanov, one of the initiators of Capri and Bologna Party Schools. As member of

Vpered group, broke with Bolsheviks and Lenin. Lived in Italy, then (1911–15) in Paris, working as correspondent for Russian newspapers (*Kievskaya mysl'* etc.); organized proletarian culture circle. After outbreak of war, worked with Trotsky, Martov, Lozovsky and others on internationalist paper *Nashe slovo*. Moved to Switzerland in 1915 and became reconciled with Lenin. Returned to Russia May 1917. Arrested during July Days. Rejoined Bolshevik Party in August. Appointed Commissar of Education in October 1917 and held this position until 1929. From 1925–6 spent much time abroad. Litvinov's deputy at Disarmament Conference of League of Nations at Geneva 1927. Left Narkompros in 1929 after defeat of his education policy and transfer of higher technical schools from Narkompros to Vesenkha control. President of Committee for direction of scholarly and teaching institutions under TSIK USSR 1929–30. Elected member of Academy of Sciences 1930. Director of Institute of Literature, Art and Language (LIYA) under Communist Academy 1931; also headed Pushkinsky Dom in Leningrad. Subject to many political humiliations in last years. Health in sharp decline from 1930. In 1933 appointed ambassador to Spain, but died in south of France before taking up office. State funeral, but obituaries cautious and even critical. Vyshinsky (q.v.), as former head of Glavprofobr, spoke at funeral; Stalin not present. Publication of L.'s works recommenced after 1953.

MAKARENKO, Anton Semenovich (1888–1939). Educationalist. Founded colony for juvenile delinquents under Ukrainian Narkompros. In 1927 one of organizers of Dzerzhinsky labour commune under GPU in Kharkov area. From 1935 assistant to head of Ukrainian NKVD dept of labour colonies. Moved to Moscow 1937. Author of many works on education. Educational theories not congenial to Narkompros educationalists, but greatly acclaimed in USSR to present day.

MAKSIMOVSKY, Vladimir Nikolaevich (1887–1941). Party member from 1903, working in European Russia. After October Revolution, 'left Communist', later 'democratic centralist' within Party. Worked with V. N. Yakovleva (q.v.) on Moscow *oblast'* Party Committee 1917; then in Central Committee *uchraspred* [registration and appointments dept] and member collegium Commissariat of Internal Affairs. Drafted into Glavpolitprosvet, Narkompros, as deputy president 1921; member of Narkompros collegium 1921–2. Signed Platform of 46 in 1923; belonged to Opposition until Fourteenth

Congress (1925). From 1929, teacher in higher educational institutions.

MALEVICH, Kazimir Severinovich (1878–1935). Painter, theorist of 'Suprematism'. Taught in Vitebsk art school after revolution, ousting Chagal (q.v.); then in Petrograd. Belonged with Kandinsky and Gabo to 'laboratory' group of constructivists, as opposed to 'production' group of Rodchenko, Ekster, A. Vesnin. Left without a job in 1928 on closing of his institute. Painted little in last years, but continued theoretical work. Died of cancer; buried in coffin painted with suprematist designs.

MALININ, K. N. Member of Narkompros dept of state theatres and theatrical–musical section of MONO 1918–19. Deputy president of Tsentroteatr 1919–20. Opposed theatrical left.

MALINOVSKAYA, Elena Konstantinovna (1870–1942). Wife of P. P. Malinovsky (q.v.); Bolshevik from 1903. Worked in popular theatre movement before revolution. Knew Gorky and Lunacharsky. After October, worked in artistic–educational dept of Moscow Soviet and in Narkompros dept of state theatres. Director of Bolshoi theatre 1920–1; then worked in Narkompros administration of state academic theatres.

MALINOVSKY, Pavel Petrovich (1869–1943). Successful architect pre-revolution; Party member from 1904. After October, civil commissar of Kremlin, president of Moscow Soviet commission for protection of artistic and ancient monuments, acting Commissar of Property of the Republic. From 1921 worked in Gosplan and building organizations.

MASHIROV-SAMOBYTNIK, Aleksei Ivanovich (1884–1942). Old Bolshevik, member Petrograd Proletkult and Central Committee of Proletkult; member of proletarian writers' group 'Kuznitsa'. Active in union of art-workers (Rabis) during '20s. Responsible for proletarianization of Leningrad Conservatorium and its director in early '30s; also director of Institute of Theatre and Music (later LITMIK) in Leningrad.

MAYAKOVSKY, Vladimir Vladimirovich (1893–1930). Poet, futurist, revolutionary agitator. Joined Bolsheviks in 1908 as gymnasium pupil. After short period of imprisonment 1909–10 entered art school in Moscow. Joined group of 'cubo-futurists'; toured Russia reciting poetry and shocking the bourgeoisie. In 1917 active in left group of Arts union, contributor to *Novaya zhizn'*. Made contact with Bolshevik government immediately after October, but avoided

Party work and only in mid-1918 took on Soviet work in Petrograd IZO, Narkompros. Worked on agitation posters in ROSTA 1919. In 1923 founded movement and journal LEF (Left Front in Art) with Brik, Meyerhold, Eisenstein and others. Journal revived as *Novyi Lef* in 1928. Battle of LEF with RAPP (proletarian writers) ended in defeat of LEF in 1930. M. joined RAPP. Some months later committed suicide, conscious of personal as well as political failure. In 1936 Stalin declared M. to have been the best poet of Soviet epoch, after which, in Pasternak's phrase, his work was forcibly introduced to the Russian public like potatoes under Catherine the Great.

MENZHINSKAYA, Ludmila Rudolfovna (1876–1933). Sister of Vyacheslav Menzhinsky, successor to Dzerzhinsky at head of OGPU, and Vera M. (q.v.). Like Krupskaya, taught at Smolenskaya evening Sunday school in 1890s. Foundation member of Narkompros: member of Petrograd, then Moscow, collegium; head of dept of United Labour School (until Nov. 1920) and sector of social training (until Jan. 1921). Later pro-rector of Krupskaya Academy of Communist Education and member of scientific–pedagogical section of GUS, Narkompros.

MENZHINSKAYA, Vera Rudolfovna (1872–1944). Sister Vyacheslav Menzhinsky and Ludmila M. (q.v.). Teacher. After February Revolution, one of organizers of Marxist faction of teachers' union VUS. Foundation member of Narkompros. Head of TEO Feb.–Sept. 1920; then took over sister Ludmila's job as head of dept of United Labour School. Later worked in Glavpolitprosvet, and in museum and library section of GUS, Narkompros. In last years, director of Moscow external institute of foreign languages.

MESHCHERYAKOV, Nikolai Leonidovich (1865–1942). Revolutionary and journalist. Member 'People's Will' narodnik group from 1885; Social-Democrat from 1901. Member of Moscow district committee of RSDRP 1906. After October Revolution worked as editor of *Izvestiya Moskovskogo Soveta* and on editorial board of *Pravda*. President of Gosizdat 1920–4. From 1927 to 1938 chief editor of *Malaya Sovetskaya Entsiklopediya* and deputy editor of *Bol'shaya Sovetskaya Entsiklopediya*. [Note also Vladimir Nikolaevich MESHCHERYAKOV (1885–1946), member of collegium of Narkompros and deputy head of Glavpolitprosvet, 1922–8.]

MEYERHOLD, Vsevolod Emilyevich (1874–1942). Theatre producer. Before revolution worked with Moscow Arts theatre, Kommissarzhevskaya theatre and Petersburg imperial theatres. Quickly recognized Soviet government after October; head of Petrograd TEO, Narkompros, 1918–May 1919. Then went south, captured by White Army, imprisoned. After release in 1920 joined Communist Party. In summer of 1920, discovered by Lunacharsky in Rostov on Don, brought back to Moscow and appointed head of TEO. At once announced radical reorganization of traditional theatres ('Theatrical October'). But traditional theatres saved by Lunacharsky and Central Committee's letter 'On the Proletkults' attacking the artistic left. M. lost control of TEO early 1921, resigned in April. Worked as director and producer at Meyerhold theatre during '20s. Productions always controversial, influenced by avant-garde art, theory of 'bio-mechanics'. Turned to classical repertoire at end of '20s, but still controversial. M. had powerful political patrons (habitués of salon run by wife and leading actress, Zinaida Raikh), but ran into trouble in '30s when trend turned against formal experimentation in the arts. Kerzhentsev (q.v.) at Committee for Art Affairs, protected him as far as possible; nevertheless Meyerhold theatre closed 1938. M. offered job by old opponent Stanislavsky (q.v.), but made defiant speech at congress of theatre directors in June 1939 and arrested. Zinaida Raikh found murdered after his arrest. Theatre-in-the-round under construction on Mayakovsky Square for Meyerhold's use converted into Tchaikovsky concert-hall.

MITSKEVICH, Sergei Ivanovich (1869–1944). Old Bolshevik, doctor by profession. Medical student/revolutionary at Moscow University in 1890s. After October Revolution worked in MONO and extramural dept of Narkompros; opponent of Proletkult. Later member of collegium of Istpart (Party history section under Central Committee); active in section of scientific workers of teachers' union; in charge of Museum of Revolution.

NEMIROVICH-DANCHENKO, Vladimir Ivanovich (1858–1943). Co-founder with Stanislavsky (q.v.) of Moscow Arts theatre in 1897, but never in sympathy with Stanislavsky method. Legendary thirty-year antagonism between the two. N.-D. quickly established friendly relations with Lunacharsky after October Revolution. Alternate member Tsentroteatr 1919. Stayed in Moscow 1922–4, while majority of Moscow Arts company with Stanislavsky lingered in Prague. Headed Nemirovich-Danchenko musical theatre. Has been regarded as Sovietizing influence on Moscow Arts theatre, and blamed by Western critics for dead hand of realism which Moscow Arts put on Soviet theatres from '30s. This may be giving Stanislavsky less than his due.

NEVSKY, Vladimir Alekseevich. Teacher, head of Glavsotsvos, Narkompros, March–Oct. 1921. Author of textbooks pre- and post-revolution; contributor to journal of Rabpros section of scientific workers, *Nauchnyi rabotnik*.

NEVSKY, Vladimir Ivanovich (1876–1937). Real name Feodosy KRIVOBOKOV. Socialist and Party historian, Marxist philosopher. Social-Democrat from 1897. After graduating from Kharkov University, prepared master's thesis on physical chemistry. In 1920 headed VTSIK commission on Narkompros, and appointed commissar of *rabfaks* under Narkompros (June) and member of Narkompros scientific sector (Dec.). Member of Workers' Opposition 1921. From 1922 to 1924 Narkompros representative in Petrograd. Director of Lenin Library, Moscow, 1925–33. Commissioned by Lenin to write attack on Bogdanov for inclusion in 2nd edition of *Materializm i empiriokrititsizm* (1920); contributor to journals *Proletarskaya revolyutsiya* and *Pod znamenem Marksizma* in '20s. Gave paper at First Congress of Marxist historians 1928–9. Arrested 1937.

NOVIKOV, Mikhail Mikhailovich (b. 1876). Biologist, professor Moscow University. Before revolution, Cadet member of Moscow City Duma and State Duma. After revolution, dean of physical–mathematical faculty (1918) and rector of Moscow University (1919–20); member of scientific commission of NTO, Vesenkha, until his expulsion from Russia at instigation of GPU (and against wishes of NTO) in 1922. Lived in Europe until Second World War, then in USA. Reasonable and accommodating in dealings with Soviet authorities, although prepared to out-manœuvre them by good organization where possible.

OLDENBURG, Sergei Fedorovich (1863–1934). Oriental scholar of aristocratic family, member Cadet Central Committee pre-revolution. Professor Indian Language and Literature at Petersburg University from 1895; permanent secretary Academy of Sciences 1904–29. No ideological sympathy with Bolsheviks, but quickly began business dealings with Soviet government on Academy's behalf (Jan. 1918). Concerned to consolidate position of Academy of Sciences as leading scientific institution in the country, and prepared to do this by compromise. Did his best to uphold scholarly standards. Forced 1927 to cooperate in reorganization of Academy and election of official nominees. But in same year strongly attacked Lunacharsky and

Soviet government for inadequate subsidy of the Academy and science in general. Dismissed from position as permanent secretary of Academy following archives scandal and disclosure of monarchist group (to which O. did not belong) within the Academy. Expressed repentance; appointed chairman of commission for study of history of Academy of Sciences; director and organizer of Oriental Museum, later important Institute of Oriental Studies. Father of emigré monarchist S. S. Oldenburg.

PANINA, Sofia Vladimirovna (?–1957). Countess, patroness of popular education movement before revolution, founder of Petersburg *Narodnyi Dom* which offered free trade- and general-education courses, meals, books etc. Joined Cadets in 1917 to show that in spite of this she was not a socialist, but never active in party politics. Under Provisional Government, deputy minister of Social Security, then of Public Education. In Dec. 1917 brought before Revolutionary Tribunal for withholding teachers' pension fund from Narkompros. Convicted, but set free on payment of 93,000 roubles involved. Emigrated early '20s, greatly regretting loss of contact with *Narodnyi Dom* (which continued to function as *Nar. Dom im. Nekrasova*).

PETROV-VODKIN, Kuzma Sergeevich (1878–1939). Painter. Son of poor family, studied at art school in Petersburg from 1895, travelled in Europe and Africa 1905–9. Exhibition of paintings organized after return by journal *Apollon*; also exhibited with 'Mir iskusstva' and others. Sympathetic to October Revolution. Member of commission for reorganization of Academy of Arts 1918; subsequently taught there. In later '20s painting acquired greater social-political content —e.g. *Smert' komissara* [*Death of a Commissar*], commissioned for tenth anniversary of Red Army 1928. Reputation nevertheless fell during '30s, since painting too stylized for current taste. Recent revival of interest in USSR.

PLETNEV, Valerian Fedorovich (1886–1942). Joiner by profession; worked nineteen years at factory bench. Joined Mensheviks 1904; twice exiled: to Vologodskaya *guberniya* and Lena in Siberia. Social-Democratic internationalist in 1917. Began to write 1918. In 1920 joined Bolsheviks. President of Proletkult Dec. 1920–32. During Civil War also worked in Vesenkha Bureau of productive propaganda. Appointed head of Glavpolitprosvet arts dept February 1921. P.'s articles on proletarian culture in *Pravda* (1922) attacked by Krupskaya and Yakovlev (q.v.), writing on Lenin's instructions; criticized by Lunacharsky. P. also conducted polemic with Trotsky on proletarian culture. Spoke for Proletkult at 1927 meeting on theatre called by *agitprop* dept of Central Committee: described by head of *agitprop* as Bogdanovist. In 1929 attacked in journal *Proletarskaya revolyutsiya* as 'left Communist' and Bukharinist. Latterly worked Tsentrosoyuz (cooperatives), Soyuzkino, and as literary editor. Author of a number of plays performed by Proletkult theatre in '20s; work praised by Bukharin 1919. Play *Shlyapa* [*The Hat*] given unsuccessful realist production at Vakhtangov theatre 1936.

POKROVSKY, Mikhail Nikolaevich (1868–1932). Historian, pupil of Klyuchevsky; after graduation worked for some time in history dept of Moscow University. Active in revolutionary movement Moscow 1905–7, joining Bolsheviks 1905. In emigration 1908–17; member of *Vpered* group 1909–10; left in protest against proletarian culture line of group. Returned to Russia August 1917, became president of independent Moscow Sovnarkom dissolved by Lenin after move of Petrograd government to Moscow March 1918. Deputy Commissar of Education 1918–32, working mainly in GUS and Glavnauka. Organizer of Communist Academy, Institute of Red Professors. From 1929, headed Institute of History; 1929 elected to Academy of Sciences (government nominee). Held dominant position in historical world in latter years, but came under attack as historian shortly before his death; a few years later his work was posthumously condemned, as was the 'Pokrovsky school' of historians. Worked hard for the advancement of Marxism in the social sciences, sometimes, therefore, regarded by non-Marxist scholars as enemy of scholarship. Ardent polemicist.

POLETAEV, Evgeny P. Teacher. Head of dept of middle schools, Narkompros, Petrograd 1918. Author with N. Punin (q.v.) of *Protiv tsivilizatsii* (1918), an attack on decadent liberalism of Anglo-French tradition.

POTEMKIN, Vladimir Petrovich (1878–1946). Secondary school teacher, Moscow, before revolution. Worked in MONO 1918; joined Party 1919. On diplomatic work 1922–40. Then Minister of Education of RSFSR (1940–6) and president of Academy of Pedagogical Sciences. Member of Central Committee of Party from 1939; deputy to Supreme Soviet of USSR.

POZNER, Viktor Markovich (1877–1957). Teacher, also worked in philosophical field. Active in revolutionary movement from 1897; joined Bolsheviks Feb. 1917. Foundation member of Narkompros, head of dept of United Labour School 1917–19; organizer of Union of Teacher-Internationalists 1917–18. From 1939 worked in

Institute of Marxism–Leninism under Central Committee. Author of unpublished memoirs, philosophical articles.

PREOBRAZHENSKY, Evgeny Alekseevich (1886–1937). Politician, supporter of Trotsky (q.v.), and economist mainly responsible for formulating Opposition's industrialization programme. Joined Party 1903; with A. Litkens organized peasant rising in Orel district 1905. 'Left Communist' 1918; supporter of Trotsky 1920–1 in Party discussion on trade unions. Secretary to Central Committee of Party, March 1920–March 1921. In this capacity supervised first stages of Narkompros reorganization and establishment of Glavpolitprosvet. Losing political ground 1921, appointed head of Glavprofobr, Narkompros; dismissed early 1922 for mishandling of professors' strike. Critic of NEP, attacking Party policy towards peasants before and during Eleventh Party Congress (March–April 1922). Signatory of Platform of 46 (1923). Expelled from Party as oppositionist 1927; expelled from Communist Academy 1928. Readmitted to Party 1929; later again expelled and arrested.

PROKOPOVICH, Sergei Nikolaevich (1871–1955). Cadet economist, husband of Kuskova (q.v.). Dean of law faculty of Moscow University 1919, hostile to Bolsheviks. Member of Committee of Aid to the Starving Population 1921; arrested on its dissolution as leader of anti-Bolshevik 'Democratic Centre', charged with conspiracy and sentenced to death; finally deported from Russia after international protest against death sentence. Then lived in Prague and Paris. Published important pioneering study of Soviet economy (in French and German, 1944; in Russian, New York, 1952).

PUNIN, Nikolai Nikolaevich (1883–1953). Art critic. Wrote for journal *Apollon* before revolution. In 1917 member left group of Arts union. From 1918, member IZO, Narkompros, and one of editors of avant-garde journal *Iskusstvo kommuny*. Advocate of constructivist work of artist Tatlin (q.v.). Later married poetess Anna Akhmatova. Arrested and sent to labour camp late '30s.

REISNER, Larisa Mikhailovna (1895–1926). Brilliant young journalist, daughter of Professor Reisner (q.v.) and pre-revolution member of Petersburg literary circles. After October worked with Volga and Baltic fleets during Civil War; joined Communist Party 1918; then with husband Raskolnikov on first Soviet mission. Died of typhoid fever.

REISNER, Mikhail Andreevich (1868–1928). Professor of law, Petersburg University. Published statement of support for Bolsheviks in

Izvestiya, 21 Dec. 1917. Worked in Narkompros/State Education Commission on reform of higher schools 1918. Member of Communist Academy, published works on law, religion and psychology. Marxist and Freudian.

ROGALSKY, I. B. Foundation member of Narkompros, head of finance dept in first months of 1918, but had no grasp of financial affairs and lost job after criticism by deputy Azanchevskaya (q.v.). Remained in Narkompros.

ROGOZINSKY, N. V. Worked in agitation and political education field. Member of Narkompros extramural dept, head of sub-dept of schools for adults and adolescents 1918; president of central collegium of agitation-points; president of Moscow Proletarian University 1919, cooperating with Party Central Committee in taking university out of Proletkult (Bogdanovist) control.

ROSSKY, A. M. Rabkrin worker, representing Rabkrin in Narkompros collegium 1920. Learned secretary of LITO, Narkompros, in 1919–20 (disliked by Mayakovsky, but on friendly terms with Lunacharsky). Appointed by Litkens to reorganize arts sector of Narkompros into new Chief Artistic Committee (Glakhkom) 1921. Again represented Rabkrin at meetings of presidium of Narkompros 1923.

RUKAVISHNIKOV, Ivan Sergeevich (1877–1930). Of rich Nizhny-Novgorod family; poet and playwright. In 1919 organizer of Palace of Arts, Moscow, with Narkompros support. Leader of literary group 'Literaturnyi osobnyak'. Married to head of circus dept of TEO, Narkompros.

RYAZANOV, David Borisovich (1870–1938). Real name GOLDENDAKH. Marxist philosopher and historian. Social-Democrat from 1890s, Menshevik, internationalist during war. Joined Bolsheviks in August 1917. Attended meetings of State Education Commission 1918; worked in GUS and Archive Administration of Narkompros 1919–20. But main post-revolutionary work in organization and direction of Marx–Engels Institute (forerunner of present Institute of Marxism–Leninism) for collection and publication of Marxist and Social-Democratic archives. A political eccentric, often in minority of one at Party congresses, sarcastic, trouble-making, unabashed by disapproval of orthodox. 'I am not one of those old Bolsheviks who for 20 years were described by Lenin as old fools', he once told Party conference. Implicated in 'Menshevik Centre' trial of 1931, arrested and exiled to Saratov where (spirit unbroken) he continued literary work.

SCHMIDT [SHMIDT], Otto Yulyevich (1891–1956). Mathematician, organizer, explorer. Before revolution, lecturer in mathematics at Kiev University. Left Menshevik, then member of Bolshevik Party from 1918. After October Revolution, worked in Food Commissariat; 1920–Feb. 1921 deputy president of Glavprofobr, dismissed by Central Committee after polemical exchange with Krupskaya on issue of polytechnicalism in education. Head of Gosizdat 1921–4 (where, as Trotskyite, responsible for publication of Trotsky's *Lessons of October*). Deputy president of GUS; active in Communist Academy and member of its presidium from 1925. Took part in philosophical controversies of late '20s. Continued to publish mathematical work in Soviet and foreign journals. Chief editor of first edition of *Bol'shaya Sovetskaya Entsiklopediya*. Appointed deputy head of Central Statistical Administration 1928. Led Chelyushkin polar expedition in early '30s and became hero of Soviet press. Popular in Narkompros, in spite of anti-polytechnicalism; a man of great energy and talent. Nicknamed 'The beard' by Lunacharsky.

SERAFIMOVICH, Aleksandr (1863–1949). Real name Aleksandr Serafimovich POPOV. Writer. Studied science at Petersburg University, arrested as student and exiled. Had some contact with Gorky/Bunin/Andreev literary circle pre-revolution. Worked with Bolsheviks on *Izvestiya Moskovskogo Soveta* 1917, for which boycotted by literary intelligentsia. Joined Party May 1918. In 1921 appointed head of LITO, Narkompros. Unsympathetic to Narkompros leaders: savagely criticized Lunacharsky's play *Foma Kampanella* in *Pravda* (12 Feb. 1921). Established reputation as leading Soviet writer with novel *Zheleznyi potok* (1924). Prominent elderly member of proletarian writers' associations (VAPP, RAPP) in late '20s. Unhappy before revolution, uncharitable after it.

SHAPIRO, Lev Grigoryevich (1887–1957). Bundist and Menshevik from 1903; joined Communist Party 1918. Worked in Narkompros from 1918 as head of dept of scientific institutions, then member of collegium of Glavpolitprosvet. Moves to expel him from Party and dismiss him from Glavpolitprosvet frustrated by Lenin, on Krupskaya's advice, 1921. Took part in debate on economic policy in early '20s.

SHATSKY, Stanislav Teofilovich (1878–1934). Educationalist, disciple of Tolstoy, theorist of labour school. Organizer of pre-revolutionary experimental school-colony ('Settlement'). Experimental work continued after revolution with Narkompros subsidy. Krupskaya particularly interested. Member GUS from 1921. Joined Communist Party 1928. Works on education published in four-volume edition in Moscow from 1963.

SHKLOVSKY, Viktor Borisovich (b. 1893). Writer and critic, member of formalist group OPOYAZ before revolution. One of most interesting of formalist critics. In emigration 1922–3. Close to Mayakovsky, the Briks, Eisenstein, Dovzhenko, Recanted errors of formalist past in 1930. Then published little until his extremely popular memoirs *Zhyli-byli* (1964). Polished and economic prose style; ability to bow to prevailing wind without suffering internal change.

SHTERENBERG, David Petrovich (1881–1948). Avant-garde artist, in emigration in Paris before revolution. Left Bundist. First head of IZO, Narkompros, 1918–21. In 1921 head of art dept of Glavprofobr. Leading figure in MOST (Moscow Society of Artist-Workers [*khudozhnikov-stankovistov*] 1925–31, then accused of formalism. Some pictures still displayed in Tretyakov Gallery.

SHTERNBERG, Pavel Karlovich (1865–1920). Professor of astronomy, Moscow University Bolshevik from 1905; one of organizers of Moscow uprising 1917. Member of collegium of Narkompros 1918, especially concerned with reform of higher schools and scientific institutions. Failed to win re-election to chair at Moscow University 1918. Mobilized, member of War Council of 2nd Army and Eastern front. Died at front of pneumonia. Lunacharsky noted in his obituary that S.'s zeal for university reorganization seemed almost unnatural in a scholar.

SHU, Fedor Fedorovich. Engineer. Head of Petrograd *oblast'* dept of technical and professional education 1918. Ardent supporter of professionalization of education at all levels. One of the organizers of Glavprofobr, but not appointed to its collegium and replaced early 1920 as Glavprofobr representative in Petrograd.

SHULGIN, Viktor Nikolaevich (1894–1965). Educationalist. Graduated from Moscow University and became a Communist in 1917. Worked briefly in Ryazan education dept; transferred to Moscow Narkompros on Krupskaya's invitation. From 1918 to 1922 deputy head of dept of United Labour School, Narkompros. From 1922 to 1932 director of Institute of Methods of School Work, latterly known as Marx–Engels Institute of Pedagogy. Leading advocate of radical educational theories, including that of ultimate 'withering away of the school' as artificial barriers between school and outside world abolished. In 1929, when radical educational theories in vogue, appointed to collegium of Narkompros. But when tide turned against radicals (with restoration of examinations and school discipline, abolition of project method etc., 1931–2), S. lost place on collegium and his institute was dissolved. From 1938 to 1952 worked in anti-religious museum, Chernyshevsky Museum and Museum of Revolution. Career effectively ended before 40th birthday. In old age wrote short but incisive memoirs of Lunacharsky, Krupskaya, Pokrovsky. Fond of Krupskaya; rather scornful of the others.

SKVORTSOV-STEPANOV, Ivan Ivanovich (1870–1928). Real name SKVORTSOV. In revolutionary movement from 1892; Bolshevik from 1904. Worked in Moscow underground between 1905 and 1917 Revolutions. After October member of collegium of Gosizdat, apparently in effective charge 1920–1; chief editor of *Izvestiya* from 1924; member of Central Committee from 1925; head of Lenin Institute from 1926. Active propagandist against religion and for electrification. Prominent in philosophical controversies in Communist Academy. Long-standing personal connections with Vperedists, having been in exile with Lunacharsky (who used the familiar form in addressing him), Bogdanov and Bazarov (with whom he translated Marx's *Kapital*); also an old friend of Gorky. But no philosophical sympathy with empiriocriticism or Godbuilding, which he on many occasions attacked. Supported Stalin against Trotsky; the only old Bolshevik *littérateur* whom Stalin could tolerate. Stalin, Gorky and Lunacharsky all wrote obituaries for him.

SLAVINSKY, Yuvenal Mitrofanovich. Party member from 1918. Organizer and first president of Rabis (Union of art workers); remained in this post until end of '20s. Delegate to Fourteenth Party Congress (1925); Rabis spokesman at *agitprop* meeting of theatre (1927) etc. Edited series of monographs on Soviet artists mid-'30s.

SMIDOVICH, Petr Germogenovich (1874–1935). Son of aristocratic family. Educated Tula gymnasium—in same class as Bogdanov (q.v.) and Bazarov (q.v.)—and physical–mathematical faculty of Moscow University. Expelled from university 1895 for political activity. Emigrated, decided to become a worker, learned electrical trade in Paris, returned to Russia 1898 on Belgian passport as electrician, worked in Bolshevik underground and as electrician until deported to Belgium as politically undesirable foreigner. President of Moscow Soviet 1918, member of its presidium until 1920, head of MONO 1920. Later worked on various commissions on electrical industry, member of presidium of VTSIK and TSIK USSR, head of TSIK committee for the affairs of northern peoples of Russia, president subsection of literature of people of USSR of literary institute of Communist Academy. Lover of music and gardening; main interest of later life welfare of national minorities of Russian north. Good friend of Lunacharsky, who worked with him on TSIK Committee on peoples of the north. Married to Sofia Nikolaevna, widow of Lunacharsky's brother Platon and member of Central Control Commission [not to be confused with Sofia Nikolaevna Lunacharskaya, relative of Lunacharsky active in field of children's theatre].

SMIT [SMITH], Maria Natanovna (b. 1878). Marxist economist. Professor of Moscow Proletarian University 1919; protested against its closure. Then worked in Central Statistical Administration; active in Communist Academy; later professor in Institute of Economics, Academy of Sciences. Edited Ricardo's works; wrote on position of working-class in Europe, statistical method etc.

SOLOGUB, Fedor (1863–1927). Real name Fedor Kuzmich TETERNIKOV. Poet and prose writer. Leader of right-wing group in Arts union 1917; strongly opposed to Soviet government. Attempted to emigrate with wife Chebotarevskaya (distant relative of Lunacharsky, also writer) in 1920, but visas delayed and Chebotarevskaya committed suicide. S. remained in Russia, though perhaps in state of internal emigration; when he died, *Izvestiya* gave him an obituary.

SOLOVYEV, Vasily Ivanovich (b. 1890). Joined Party 1913; worked on *Pravda* 1913–14. Deputy head of PUR 1920; then member collegium Glavpolitprosvet and candidate for its deputy presidency; member *agitprop* dept of Central Committee. Worked with Litkens on project for reorganization of Narkompros. Left Narkompros May 1921. Later Soviet counsellor in Afghanistan, deputy head of press dept of Central Committee, Soviet counsellor in China, member Eastern Secretariat of Comintern, director State Publishing House of Artistic Literature early '30s, member editorial board of *Novyi mir* and collegium of Glavlit, director of All-Union Book Board [*Knizhnaya palata*] until arrest in 1937. Returned to Moscow after 1953.

SOSNOVSKY, Lev Semenovich (1886–1937). Communist journalist. Joined Party 1904. After revolution member presidium of VTSIK, editor of daily *Bednota*, contributor to *Pravda*, head of *agitprop* dept of Central Committee for short period from end of 1921. Supported Trotsky in debate on trade unions of 1920–1. Member of Trotskyite opposition, expelled from Party 1927. Not readmitted until 1935; expelled again 1936. Interested in literary and artistic questions in '20s; published several attacks on Mayakovsky's group LEF; also hostile to RAPP.

STANISLAVSKY, Konstantin Sergeevich (1863–1938). Real name ALEKSEEV. Son of rich merchant family. Co-founder with Nemirovich-Danchenko (q.v.) of Moscow Arts theatre in 1897, famous for productions of Chekhov, Gorky, Maeterlinck, originator of 'method' acting. Maintained cautious attitude to Soviet government after October. In 1922 took most of Arts Theatre company on European tour, obviously considering emigration, but returned 1924. Produced Bulgakov's *Dni Turbinykh* in 1926–7 season, providing Bulgakov with material for fine satirical portrait of S. in his *Teatral'nyi roman*. First 'revolutionary' production was Vsevolod Ivanov's *Bronepoezd 14–69* in 1927–8 season. Although artistic prestige high in '20s, it was from mid-'30s that Moscow Arts theatre established dominant position in Soviet theatrical life, and debased form of Stanislavsky method became official style of Soviet acting. Stanislavsky himself canonized, especially after his death.

SUKHANOV, Nikolai Nikolaevich (1882–?). Real name HIMMER. Menshevik internationalist. Member of executive committee of Petrograd Soviet and one of editors with Gorky (q.v.) of *Novaya zhizn'* in 1917. Recorded detached insider's view of October Revolution in *Zapiski o revolyutsii*, pub. Grzhebin, Berlin and Petrograd 1923, and criticized by Lenin. Worked in Soviet trade missions in Paris and Berlin, then in Gosplan. Took part in literary controversies of late '20s, causing great offence by telling Communist Academy in 1930 that the 'rightist danger' in literature was imaginary. Tried as leader of Menshevik conspiracy 1931. Last heard of in prison, *c.* 1934.

TAIROV, Aleksandr Yakovlevich (1885–1950). Real name KORNBLIT. Founder (1914) and director Kamerny theatre, Moscow. With Meyerhold (q.v.), the most important formal innovator in Russian theatre of his time, but did not share Meyerhold's positive revolutionary sympathies. Strongly attacked by proletarians (RAPP) in late '20s. Kamerny theatre said to have been losing popularity in '30s, but death blow was performance of Demyan Bedny's *Bogatyri* (1936), which was attacked as slanderous satire on history of great Russian people. Lunacharsky defended T. against many critics during '20s; T. spoke appreciatively of Lunacharsky at his funeral.

TATLIN, Vladimir Evgrafovich (1885–1953). Artist of constructivist school, formerly sailor. Headed Moscow IZO, Narkompros, 1918; designed well-known project for monument to Third International on commission from IZO 1919. During '20s worked in Vkhutemas (Higher Artistic–Technical Studios) and wood- and metal-work dept of Vkhutein (Higher Artistic–Technical Institute), Moscow, and in Kiev. 1931–3 worked on model of glider ('Letatlin') in laboratory in Novodevichy Monastery; exhibited work, including glider models, at one-man show in Moscow 1933. In disfavour as artist 1933–52, worked as theatrical designer. From 1950 to 1953 lectured at DOSAAF (Moscow centre for glider research).

TIMIRYAZEV, Kliment Arkadyevich (1843–1920). Distinguished biologist, professor of Moscow University. Sympathetic to Bolsheviks. Member of first collegium of GUS 1919, but age and ill-health prevented him taking more active part in Narkompros work. Son Arkady (b. 1881) trained as physicist; prominent as Communist organizer of science in '20s, defender of mechanist position in philosophical debates in Communist Academy, critic of Einstein's theories.

TROTSKAYA, Natalya Ivanovna (1882–1962). Née SEDOVA, Trotsky's second wife. Met Trotsky in Paris 1902 when studying history of art at Sorbonne. Not a politician by temperament. Worked in Narkompros from 1918 as head of museum dept. On sick leave, but still in Narkompros employment, latter part of 1927; in jubilee speech Nov. 1927 Lunacharsky paid special tribute (not reported in press) to her work in Narkompros. Exiled with Trotsky to Alma-Ata, Jan. 1928; expelled with him from USSR early 1929; with him in Mexico until his assassination in 1940; remained in Mexico after his death.

TROTSKY, Lev Davydovich (1879–1940). Real name BRONSHTEIN. Revolutionary from 1897, in emigration 1902–5, taking Menshevik side in party split. President of Petersburg Soviet 1905, publicly tried and sent to Siberia, escaped, emigrated. For next decade held independent and would-be conciliatory position among Russian Social-Democrats in Europe; on bad terms with Lenin. Internationalist, one of editors of anti-war *Nashe slovo* published in France. Expelled from France 1916; went to USA. Returned to Russia May 1917, after long detention by British naval authorities at Nova Scotia en route. Joined Bolsheviks on return; main organizer of October coup in Petrograd. Member Politburo October 1917–26.

Commissar of Foreign Affairs until after Brest peace in 1918, then Commissar of War 1918–25 (though effectively losing control of army from 1922). Initiator of labour conscription movement 1920. In bitter conflict with Stalin for leadership of Party from 1923; expelled from Party 1927; exiled to Alma-Ata Jan. 1928; expelled from USSR early 1929. Founded Fourth International in exile. Vilified in USSR, represented as leader of gigantic conspiracy responsible for all economic and organizational failure of Soviet government in '30s; assassinated Mexico 1940. Took little interest in educational affairs, although autobiography records that he was invited by representatives of Rabpros to become Commissar of Education in 1922. More interested in literature and the arts; author of *Literature and Revolution* (1923) which, *inter alia*, denied possibility of development of specifically proletarian culture; on this issue polemicized with Lunacharsky.

VOLGIN, Vyacheslav Petrovich (b. 1879). Marxist historian. Student of Moscow University, Menshevik before revolution, joined Bolsheviks 1920. Member GUS from 1919; rector of Moscow University 1921 and professor of history of socialism. Member of collegium and deputy head of Glavprofobr 1921–3. Later president of council of sector of scientific workers of Rabpros. Elected to Academy of Sciences 1930; permanent secretary 1930–5. Author of many works on history of socialist thought.

VORONSKY, Aleksandr Konstantinovich (1884–1943). Revolutionary, literary critic. Educated Tambov seminary, joined revolutionary movement as Bolshevik 1904, expelled seminary 1905. From that time, professional agitator and union organizer in various parts of Russia. After October Revolution on Soviet work in Odessa and Ivanovo-Voznesensk. With support of Lenin and other Party leaders and under auspices of Glavpolitprosvet, organized literary–political journal *Krasnaya nov'* 1921, and edited it until 1927. Signed Platform of 46 in 1923; member of Trotskyite opposition. Main target of attack by proletarian writers' group RAPP: criticized both as Trotskyite and as idealist in literary theory. Expelled from Party and exiled to Urals after Fifteenth Party Congress, but returned to Moscow in 1930 and readmitted to Party. Said to have been on good personal terms with Stalin. Arrested 1937.

VOROVSKY, Vatslav Vatslavovich (1872–1923). Polish Bolshevik intellectual. Studied at Moscow technicum in 1890s. Worked on Bolshevik emigré papers *Proletarii* and *Vpered* (1905). Head of

Gosizdat 1920. Later in diplomatic posts. Assassinated at Lausanne Conference.

VYSHINSKY, Andrei Yanuarevich (1883–1955). Born Odessa in family of intelligentsia. Menshevik. Graduated in law at Kiev University 1913, but deprived of job there for political reasons. Went to Moscow 1915. Joined Communist Party in early '20s. Taught in *rabfak* of Moscow University, then at law faculty of Kiev University, then again at Moscow. Rector of First Moscow University 1925–8; member of collegium of Narkompros and head of Glavprofobr 1928–31. Presided at Shakhty trial (1928) and trial of Prompartiya (1930). From 1931 to 1933 deputy commissar of justice; 1935–9 public prosecutor of USSR, acting in show trial of Bukharin etc. with notorious cry 'Shoot the mad dogs!'. From 1940 to 1946 first deputy commissar of foreign affairs; 1949 Minister of Foreign Affairs and Soviet delegate to United Nations. During tenancy of Glavprofobr, felt to be an alien body in Narkompros. Revealed unexpected debt to Lunacharsky at latter's funeral in 1934, when he spoke of learning from Lunacharsky's eloquence in prosecution of S-Rs, 1922.

YAKOVLEV, Yakov Arkadyevich (1896–1939). Real name EPSHTEIN. Party member from 1913. After October Revolution, member of Politburo of Ukrainian Central Committee, member collegium of Glavpolitprosvet, deputy head of *agitprop* dept of (Russian) Central Committee 1922–3. From 1923, primarily occupied with agriculture, working for Central Committee and as president of All-Union Council of Collective Farms; also deputy commissar of Rabkrin 1926. Dec. 1929 appointed Commissar of Agriculture and head of agricultural dept of Central Committee. Member of Central Committee 1931. Later president of Central Control Commission. Arrested 1937.

YAKOVLEVA, Varvara Nikolaevna (1884/5–1944). Bolshevik from 1904, daughter of rich merchant family whom she converted to revolution. Wife of P. K. Shternberg (q.v.), also converted to Bolshevik Party under her influence and her former professor at Moscow University; then wife of Trotskyist I. N. Smirnov. In 1917 member of Moscow *oblast'* Party Committee. Supported Bukharin on peace negotiations of 1918 and Trotsky on trade unions 1920–1. Head of Glavprofobr 1922; deputy commissar of education 1922–9. Broke with opposition 1927. Commissar of Finance RSFSR from 1929 until arrest 1937. Prosecution witness against Bukharin in 1938 trial.

YURYEV, Yury Mikhailovich (1872–1948). Actor of Petrograd imperial theatres, friend of Gorky (q.v.) and Andreeva (q.v.), organizer with them of Bol'shoi dramaticheskii teatr, Petrograd 1918. Co-operated with Lunacharsky from October Revolution. Author interesting memoirs.

YUZHIN, Aleksandr Ivanovich (1857–1928). Prince SUMBATOV. Playwright, under name Sumbatov, and theatre director. Radical in politics before revolution. Head of Maly theatre, Moscow. One of first major theatrical figures to come to terms with Soviet power; friend of Lunacharsky, producer of his play *Oliver Cromwell.*

ZAKS, Grigory Davydovich (1882–1937). Member S-R Central Committee from 1905. In 1917–18, left S-R. From Dec. 1917 assistant to Lunacharsky at Narkompros, also deputy president of Cheka. One of organizers of left S-R rising in June 1918. Arrested, but shortly released and joined Bolsheviks Nov. 1918. Later worked in economic field.

ZELIKSON, Ya. L. Head of Petrograd education department 1919–20. Described by M. F. Andreeva (q.v.) as nonentity under thumb of Lilina (q.v.).

ZILOTI, Aleksandr Ilyich (1863–1945). Pianist and conductor. Organizer of symphony and chamber music concerts in Moscow (from 1900) and Petersburg (from 1903), performing new music including that of young Prokofiev. Director of Mariinsky opera company from May 1917; opposed Bolsheviks; briefly arrested after October Revolution; emigrated 1919.

ZINOVIEV, Grigory Evseevich (1883–1936). Real name RADOMYLSKY. Social-Democrat from 1901; one of Lenin's closest associates in immediate pre-revolutionary years. Opposed seizure of power in October 1917; supported coalition with other socialist parties, briefly resigned from Central Committee. From 1918 to 1926 head of Party and Soviet organization in Petrograd. From 1919 to 1926 president of executive committee of Comintern. After Lenin's death formed ruling triumvirate with Stalin and Kamenev; then broke with Stalin and formed opposition alliance with Trotsky. Expelled from Party at Fifteenth Congress (1927), readmitted 1928, expelled and exiled 1932, readmitted 1933, expelled 1934 and arrested; sentenced to death in show trial of 1936 for membership of 'terrorist centre' responsible for death of Kirov. Active in educational affairs only in presiding over purge of universities in 1924. On bad terms with Lunacharsky.

ZUBOV, Valentin Platonovich. Count. Founder of Russian Institute of

History of Art in Petersburg. Worked under Provisional Government in commission for evacuation of art treasures from Palace at Gatchina; continued in this work under Bolsheviks. Quickly established contact with Lunacharsky to safeguard work of commission and Institute. Imprisoned for some months in 1922, but remained in charge of Institute until unwilling emigration 1925. Published memoirs in Munich, 1968.

NOTES

1: LUNACHARSKY

1 N. Sukhanov, *Zapiski o revolyutsii*, vol. 7 (Berlin–Petersburg–Moscow, 1923), p. 262.

2 *Ibid.*, p. 267.

3 *TSGAOR* 2306/1/152 (greeting telegrams to the People's Commissar of Education, 1918).

4 From Gorky's memoir on Lenin, in Gorky, *Sobranie sochinenii v 30-kh tomakh* (Moscow, 1949–55), vol. 17, p. 21.

5 A. V. Lunacharsky, *Velikii perevorot* (Petrograd, 1919), p. 17. This is the basic source on Lunacharsky's life before 1917. It has been republished in A. V. Lunacharsky, *Vospominaniya i vpechatleniya*, ed. N. A. Trifonov (Moscow, 1968).

6 *Ibid.*, p. 31.

7 *Ibid.*, p. 41.

8 *Ibid.*, p. 32.

9 *Ibid.*, p. 18.

10 A. V. Lunacharsky, *Religiya i sotsializm*, vol. 1 (St Petersburg, 1908), p. 39. The phrase is from Feuerbach.

11 *Velikii perevorot*, p. 31.

12 *Religiya i sotsializm*, vol. 1, p. 228.

13 *Ispoved'* was first published in the *Znanie* series, no. 23. Lunacharsky's commentary is in *Literaturnyi raspad*, vol. 2 (St Petersburg, 1909); the quotation is from pp. 92–3.

14 Lenin, preface to *Materializm i empiriokrititsizm*, in Lenin, *Pol. sob. soch.*, vol. 18, p. 11.

15 See N. Trifonov, 'A. V. Lunacharsky and M. Gorky', in K. D. Muratova (ed.) *M. Gor'kii i ego sovremenniki* (Leningrad, 1968), pp. 123 ff; and *Velikii perevorot*, p. 45.

16 Quoted N. Voitinsky, 'On the *Vpered* group (1909–1917)', *Proletarskaya revolyutsiya* (1929), no. 12, p. 73.

17 S. Lifshits, 'The Capri Party school (1909)', *Proletarskaya revolyutsiya* (1924), no. 6, p. 41.

18 *Velikii perevorot*, p. 46.

19 *Bol'shaya sovetskaya entsiklopediya* (1st ed.), vol. 31 (1937) (*Kaprii-skaya shkola*).
20 Trifonov, 'A. V. Lunacharsky and M. Gorky', p. 141.
21 *Ibid.*, p. 148.
22 *Bol'shaya sovetskaya entsiklopediya* (1st ed.), vol. 6 (1927) (*Bolon'skaya partiinaya shkola*).
23 See V. I. Lenin and A. M. Gorky, *Pis'ma, vospominaniya, doku-menty* (2nd ed., Moscow, 1961).
24 G. A. Solomon, *Lenin i ego sem'ya* (Paris, 1930), p. 62.
25 Lunacharsky 'Recollections from the revolutionary past' (1925), in *Vospominaniya i vpechatleniya*, p. 49.
26 *Velikii perevorot*, p. 55.
27 Quoted from *Vpered* (Geneva, 1915), no. 1, by Voitinsky, 'On the *Vpered* group (1909–1917)', p. 78.
28 See 'Letters on proletarian culture' (1914), in Lunacharsky, *Sob. soch.*, vol. 7 (1967), p. 169.
29 F. F. Korolev, *Ocherki po istorii sovetskoi shkoly i pedagogiki 1917–1920* (Moscow, 1958), p. 84.
30 V. V. Gorbunov, 'From the history of cultural-educational activity of the Petrograd Bolsheviks in the period of preparation for October', *Voprosy istorii KPSS* (1967), no. 2, p. 32.
31 Quoted N. Trifonov, 'Lunacharsky in the city of Lenin', *Zvezda* (1965), no. 11, p. 184.
32 *Ibid.*, p. 184.
33 Sukhanov, *Zapiski o revolyutsii*, vol. 7, pp. 266–7.
34 'On Scriabin' (1921), in Lunacharsky, *V mire muzyki*, ed. G. B. Bernandt and I. A. Sats (Moscow, 1958), p. 97.
35 V. Polyansky, *A. V. Lunacharskii* (Moscow, 1926).
36 *Ibid.*
37 V. N. Shulgin, *Pamyatnye vstrechi* (Moscow, 1958), p. 77.

2: THE ESTABLISHMENT OF NARKOMPROS

1 *Zhurnal Ministerstva Narodnago Prosveshcheniya*, new series, ed. E. Radlov, part 71 (Petrograd, September 1917), p. 38.
2 *Novaya zhizn'* (Petrograd, 1917), no. 165, 28 Oct.
3 Lunacharsky, 'From recollections of October', in *O narodnom obrazovanii* (Moscow, 1958), pp. 17–18.
4 'How we occupied the Ministry of Public Education', in *Vospo-minaniya i vpechatleniya*, pp. 180–1.

5 John Reed, *Ten Days that Shook the World* (New York, 1926), p. 262.
6 *Ibid.*
7 Yu. Flakserman, 'Pages of the past', *Novyi mir* (1968), no. 11, p. 219.
8 *Rabochaya gazeta* (1917), no. 199, 29 Oct., p. 3.
9 *Novaya zhizn'* (1917), no. 176, 9 Nov., p. 3.
10 Protocols of this meeting have been published by Trotsky in *Stalinskaya shkola fal'sifikatsii* (Berlin, 1932), pp. 116–31. Professor Schapiro, having compared the type with that of protocols published in Soviet editions, believes them to be genuine (L. B. Schapiro, *Origin of the Communist Autocracy* (London, 1955), p. 74, note).
11 Trotsky, *Stalinskaya shkola fal'sifikatsii*, p. 116 and note.
12 Speech to writers and artists, 8 May 1963, *Novyi mir* (1963), no. 3, p. 19.
13 Reed, *Ten Days*, p. 245.
14 Reported *Novaya zhizn'* (1917), no. 172, 4 Nov., p. 3.
15 The date is established by an unsigned report, possibly written by Lunacharsky, in *Novaya zhizn'* (1917), no. 185, 19 Nov., p. 3.
16 'How we occupied the Ministry of Public Education', *Vospominaniya i vpechatleniya*, p. 181.
17 *Ibid.*, p. 183.
18 Quoted Korolev, *Ocherki po istorii sovetskoi shkoly i pedagogiki 1917–1920 gg.*, p. 92.
19 See Ya. Gurevich, 'The case of Countess S. V. Panina at the Revolutionary Tribunal', *Russkoe bogatstvo* (1917), nos. 11–12. The case is mentioned by Reed, *Ten Days*, p. 233 and note; but Reed—probably following a mistaken report in *Novaya zhizn'* (1917), no. 198, 10 Dec.,—thought the money came from the Ministry of Social Security. Panina had in fact been deputy to the Minister of Social Security from May to July 1917, before moving to the Ministry of Public Education in August.
20 Quoted Gurevich, 'The case of Countess S. V. Panina'.
21 *Izvestiya TSIK* (Petrograd, 1917), no. 256, 20 Dec., p. 5.
22 V. Polyansky, 'How the People's Commissariat of Education started work', *Proletarskaya revolyutsiya* (1926), no. 49(2), p. 57.
23 *Ibid.*, pp. 56–7.
24 I. S. Smirnov, *Lenin i sovetskaya kul'tura* (Moscow, 1960), p. 340.
25 Flakserman, 'Pages of the Past', p. 224.
26 Smirnov, *Lenin i sovetskaya kul'tura*, pp. 240, 344.
27 Polyansky, 'How the People's Commissariat of Education started work', p. 51.

28 Trifonov, 'Lunacharsky in the city of Lenin', p. 187.
29 *Izvestiya VTSIK* (Moscow, 1918), no. 57, 26 March, p. 4.
30 Quoted Korolev, *Ocherki po istorii sovetskoi shkoly i pedagogiki 1917–1920 gg.*, p. 153, note 3.
31 *Ibid.*
32 From records of meetings of State Education Commission and collegium of Narkompros in *TSGAOR* 2306/1/36 and 2306/1/40.
33 Quoted Trifonov, 'Lunacharsky in the city of Lenin', p. 187.
34 Krupskaya resigned as deputy commissar on 22 May 1918, and was replaced by Pokrovsky. She remained an active member of the collegium and State Education Commission. *TSGAOR* 2306/1/36, 22 May 1918 and *passim.*
35 *Direktivy VKP(b) i postanovleniya sovetskogo pravitel'stva o narodnom obrazovanii za 1917–1947 gg.* (Moscow–Leningrad, 1947), pp. 14–16.
36 Information on attendance at meetings of the State Education Commission April–July 1918 from *TSGAOR* 2306/1/36.
37 'How we occupied the Ministry of Public Education', p. 183.
38 *TSGAOR* 2306/1/36, 31 May 1918.
39 Polyansky, 'How the People's Commissariat of Education started work', pp. 59–60.
40 'Lenin documents on education', *Sovetskaya pedagogika* (1966), no. 4, p. 120.
41 *TSGAOR* 2306/1/36, 8, 11 and 31 May (statements of Azanchevskaya and Alter).
42 *Ibid.*, 31 May 1918.
43 *Ibid.*
44 *Ibid.*, 8 May (statement of Azanchevskaya).
45 *Ibid.*, 31 May (statement of Azanchevskaya).
46 A. Aktov, 'Budget of the People's Commissariat of Education', *Nar. pros.* (weekly) (1918), no. 19, 16 Nov.
47 Minutes of State Education Commission, 5 Oct. 1918, in *Nar. pros.* (monthly) (1919), nos. 6–7, pp. 172–5.
48 *TSGAOR* 2306/1/40.
49 'Taylor's system and the organization of labour in Soviet institutions', *Krasnaya nov'* (1921), no. 1.
50 *TSGAOR* 2306/1/180, 21 Jan. 1919.
51 *TSGAOR* 2306/1/3272, instruction no. 6132, 18 Sept. 1918.
52 *Zhurnal Ministerstva Narodnago Prosveshcheniya*, new series, part 71 (October 1917), pp. 68–9.

53 *TSGAOR* 2306/1/213, 5 May 1919 (commission on current business).

54 *TSGAOR* 2306/1/320, 21 Jan. 1920 (report of Markus). Markus' plan, by an omission difficult to explain, did not include the fifth sector ('social training'). The sector was created in 1920 around the nucleus of the department of the United Labour School.

3: SCHOOL EDUCATION

1 'Address of the People's Commissar of Education', *Direktivy VKP(b) i postanovleniya sovetskogo pravitel'stva za 1917–1947 gg.*, p. 11.

2 Lunacharsky, speech to cultural-education section of 3rd Congress of Soviets, 16 Jan. 1918, quoted Korolev, *Ocherki po istorii sovetskoi shkoly i pedagogiki 1917–1920 gg.*, p. 96.

3 Korolev, *ibid.*, p. 98. The NKVD plan was published as an instruction 'On the organization of the Soviets of workers' and soldiers' deputies'.

4 Korolev, *ibid.*, p. 97.

5 *TSGAOR* 2306/1/36, 10 April 1918.

6 *Ibid.*, 9 April 1918.

7 *Ibid.*, 10 April 1918.

8 'On educational soviets' (1918), in Krupskaya, *Ped. soch.*, vol. 2, p. 76.

9 See *ibid.*, vol. 11, p. 742, and 'Educational soviets, the teaching body and *volost'* education departments', *Nar. pros.* (weekly) (1919), nos. 56–8, 25 October, p. 8.

10 *Direktivy VKP(b)*...pp. 21–6.

11 For Marx and Engels on education, see *Marks i Engel's o vospitanii i obrazovanii* (Moscow, 1957). In *Kapital* (vol. 1, ch. 13) Marx wrote that in the future 'productive labour will be united with schooling and gymnastics for all children above a certain age, not only as one of the means of increasing the society's level of production, but as the unique means of producing people of all-round development'. (Marx and Engels, *Sochineniya*, vol. 23 (Moscow, 1960), pp. 494–5.)

12 The Narkompros bibliography was published in *Vestnik narodnogo prosveshcheniya soyuza kommun severnoi oblasti* (1918), no. 1, August, p. 40. The VUS bibliography appeared in *Petrogradskii uchitel'* (1918), nos. 19–20, 7 Aug., p. 15.

13 *Vestnik narodnogo prosveshcheniya s.k.s.o.* (1918), nos. 2–3, September, p. 5.

14 *TSGA RSFSR* 2306/1/132, 10 Aug. 1918 (State Education Commission).

15 *Nar. pros.* (monthly) (1919), nos. 6–7, p. 124.

16 *TSGA RSFSR* 2306/1/132, 12 Sept. 1918.

17 *Protokoly VTSIK 5 sozyva* (Moscow, 1919), p. 231.

18 The text of the 'Declaration' is in Lunacharsky, *O narodnom obrazovanii*, pp. 522–38.

19 The text of the 'Statement' is in *Direktivy VKP(b)*..., pp. 120–7.

20 *Nar. pros.* (monthly) (1919), nos. 6–7, p. 114.

21 'Education in Soviet Russia', *Kommunisticheskii internatsional* (1919), no. 2, p. 218.

22 Resolution of 29 Oct. 1917, published *Petrogradskii uchitel'* (1918), no. 1, 6 Jan., p. 2.

23 'How we occupied the Ministry of Public Education' (1927), *Vospominaniya i vpechatleniya*, p. 181.

24 Smirnov, *Lenin i sovetskaya kul'tura*, p. 200.

25 *Ibid.*, p. 215 and Korolev, *Ocherki po istorii sovetskoi shkoly i pedagogiki*, p. 125.

26 *Petrogradskii uchitel'* (1918), no. 1, 6 Jan., p. 1.

27 'On the school strike', *Izvestiya TSIK* (Petrograd, 1917), no. 256, 20 Dec., p. 8.

28 *Petrogradskii uchitel'* (1918), no. 1, 6 Jan., pp. 2 and 4.

29 Quoted Korolev, *Ocherki*, p. 142.

30 Examples drawn from *Nar. pros.* (monthly) (1919), nos. 9–10, p. 94; nos. 11–12, p. 112 and nos. 13–14, p. 141; and from Korolev, *Ocherki*, p. 142.

31 *TSGAOR* 2306/1/36, 23 and 25 May 1918 (debates in State Education Commission).

32 *Novaya zhizn'* (1918), no. 75, 24 April, p. 4 (resolution on proposal of Ya. Gurevich).

33 *TSGAOR* 2306/1/36, 23 May 1918 (State Education Commission).

34 'Strange psychology', *Izvestiya VTSIK* (1918), education supplement no. 5, and in *Ped. soch.*, vol. 2, p. 63.

35 Lenin, *Pol. sob. soch.*, vol. 36, pp. 420–1.

36 *TSGAOR* 2306/1/36, 8 June 1918.

37 Speeches reported, apparently verbatim, in *Izvestiya VTSIK* (1918), education supplement no. 8.

38 *TSGAOR* 2306/1/40, 22 Aug. 1918.

39 *Ibid.*, 16 Dec. 1918.

40 A stenogram of the VTSIK debate is in *Nar. pros.* (monthly) (1919), nos. 6–7, pp. 181–4.
41 *Ibid.* (weekly), nos. 23–5, 28 Dec., p. 22.
42 *TSGAOR* 2306/1/180, 26 and 28 March 1919 (collegium of Narkompros).
43 *Nar. pros.* (monthly) (1919), no. 15, p. 90.
44 *Ibid.*, nos. 6–7, p. 26.
45 'Education in Soviet Russia', *Kommunisticheskii internatsional* (1919), no. 6, pp. 870–1.
46 Lunacharsky to VTSIK, 26 Sept. 1920, in *O narodnom obrazovanii*, p. 140.
47 See Krupskaya, *Ped. soch.* vol. 11, p. 742, on the dissolution of *volost'* education departments—'NKVD, not saying a word to Narkompros, had...stopped paying the salaries of their officials'.
48 Sovnarkom 'Statement on money resources and expenses of local Soviets', 3 Dec. 1918, quoted V. P. Dyachenko, *Sovetskie finansy v pervoi faze razvitiya sotsialisticheskogo gosudarstva*, part 1, 1917–25 (Moscow, 1947), p. 174.
49 *TSGAOR* 2306/1/180, 21 March 1919.
50 *TSGAOR* 2306/1/36, 13 April 1918.
51 Letter to Krzhizhanovskaya, 17 July 1919, *Ped. soch.* vol. 11, p. 190.
52 *Vestnik narodnogo prosveshcheniya s.k.s.o.* (1918), nos. 6–8, pp. 15 and 67; and *Severnaya kommuna* (1919), no. 23, 31 Jan., p. 3.
53 *TSGAOR* 2306/1/180, 28 March and 11 April 1919.
54 *TSGAOR* 2306/1/181, 23 May 1919.
55 *Ibid.*, 2 Aug. 1919.
56 *Vestnik prosveshcheniya* (Petrograd) (1919), nos. 4–6 (12–14) p. 64.
57 Letter of Feb. 1920, in *M. F. Andreeva. Perepiska. Vospominaniya. Stat'i. Dokumenty. Vospominaniya o M. F. Andreevoi* (Moscow, 1961), p. 273.
58 'Education in Soviet Russia', *Kommunisticheskii internatsional* (1919), no. 6, p. 871.
59 *TSGAOR* 2306/1/182, 30 Sept. 1919.
60 Theses published *Kommunisticheskii trud* (1920), no. 70, 16 June, p. 4.
61 *TSGAOR* 2306/1/320, 19 June 1920.
62 *Ibid.*, 6 July 1920.
63 *Nar. pros.* (monthly) (1918), nos. 4–5, p. 71.
64 RSFSR, Narodnyi Komissariat po Prosveshcheniyu, otdel edinoi trudovoi shkoly, *Pis'mo k shkol'nym rabotnikam* (Moscow, 1919).

65 A. S. Tolstov, 'At work on the organization of the labour school', *Nar. pros.* (1927), no. 10, pp. 131 and 133.
66 V. Dyushen, 'In the first years of Soviet power. Experimental-model institutions of Narkompros', *Narodnoe obrazovanie* (1966), no. 1, p. 80.
67 *TSGAOR* 2306/1/320, 17 June 1920. From a resolution on pre-school education proposed by Lazurkina, but later published over signature of Lunacharsky.
68 *Nar. pros.* (monthly) (1919), nos. 16–17, p. 16.
69 A. I. Kondakov, 'Experiment in aesthetic education in the Znamenskaya school-commune (1918–1925)', *Sovetskaya pedagogika* (1958), no. 11.
70 Tolstov, 'At work on the organization of the labour school', pp. 132–4.
71 A. N. Volkovsky, 'Formation of a Soviet pedagogue in the first years after October', *Sovetskaya pedagogika* (1957), no. 11, p. 106.
72 A. Kuchepatov, 'From a teacher's recollections', *Sovetskaya pedagogika* (1957), no. 4, p. 78.
73 V. N. Shulgin, *Pamyatnye vstrechi*, p. 48.
74 Polyansky, 'How the People's Commissariat of Education started work', p. 58.
75 'Diary of a journey on the river-steamer *Krasnaya zvezda*' (1920), in Krupskaya, *Ped. soch.*, vol. 11, pp. 729–57. Letters from Volga to Krzhizhanovskaya in *ibid.*, pp. 187–94.
76 'Letters of N. K. Krupskaya', *Sovetskaya pedagogika* (1961), no. 11, p. 138.
77 Letter of June 1920, *Ped. soch.*, vol. 10, p. 47.
78 *TSGAOR* 2306/1/320, 30 June 1920.
79 Tolstov, 'At work on the organization of the labour school', p. 135.
80 *O narodnom obrazovanii*, pp. 127–8.

4: TECHNICAL AND HIGHER EDUCATION

1 Quoted by Lunacharsky, Sept. 1920, *O narodnom obrazovanii*, pp. 128–9.
2 Narkompros statement 'On the tasks of professional-technical education in Russia', *Nar. pros.* (weekly) (1919), no. 34, 10 May, pp. 1–4.
3 *Dekrety sovetskoi vlasti*, vol. 2 (Moscow, 1959), pp. 357–9 and 487–8.

4 *Nar. pros.* (monthly) (1919), nos. 6–7, p. 131.
5 'Paths of professional education (reminiscences)', *Nar. pros.* (1927), no. 10, p. 137.
6 B. Kozelev, *Rabotnik prosveshcheniya* (1921), nos. 2–3, p. 20; N. Hans and S. Hessen, *Educational Policy in Soviet Russia* (London, 1930), p. 142).
7 *Vestnik narodnogo prosveshcheniya s.k.s.o.* (1919), nos. 1–3 (9–11), pp. 123–4, and nos. 4–6 (12–14), p. 8.
8 *TSGAOR* 2306/1/180, 17 Feb. 1919 (statement of L. G. Shapiro).
9 *Severnaya kommuna* (1919), no. 23, 31 Jan., p. 3.
10 Decree and statement on professional education published *Izvestiya VTSIK* (1919), no. 135, 24 June, p. 2.
11 *Pravda* (1920), no. 2, 3 Jan., p. 2 (announcement on commission by Trotsky); and *TSGAOR* 2306/1/320, 17 Jan. 1920 (protest by Lunacharsky on non-representation of Narkompros).
12 *TSGAOR* 2306/1/320, 17 Jan. 1920.
13 *Ibid.*, 21 Jan. 1920.
14 *Ibid.*
15 *Ibid.*, 31 Jan. 1920.
16 *TSGA RSFSR* 1565/1/22, 14 Feb., 3 March and 14 April 1920 (collegium of Glavprofobr).
17 Unsigned letter, evidently from Lunacharsky, dated 19 April 1920, in *M. F. Andreeva*, p. 280.
18 Krupskaya, *Ped. soch.*, vol. 10, pp. 44–6.
19 *Izvestiya VTSIK* (1920), no. 240, 27 Oct., p. 2.
20 On the organization of the Ukrainian Narkompros see M. Zaretsky, 'How the factory school came into being in the Ukraine', *Nar. pros.* (1927), no. 10.
21 *TSGA RSFSR* 1565/1/22, 3 Nov. 1920.
22 *O narodnom obrazovanii*, p. 159.
23 *Nar. pros.* (monthly) (1919), nos. 9–10, p. 79.
24 *Izvestiya Rossiiskoi Akademii Nauk* (6th series) vol. 12 (Petrograd, 1918), no. 14, 15 Oct., pp. 1391–2.
25 Quoted Smirnov, *Lenin i sovetskaya kul'tura*, p. 247.
26 *Izvestiya Rossiiskoi Akademii Nauk*, vol. 12, no. 14, 15 Oct., pp. 1392–3.
27 *Ibid.*, pp. 1387–91.
28 Karpinsky's letter in *Izvestiya VTSIK* (1918), no. 72, 12 April, p. 3; Oldenburg's memorandum quoted Smirnov, *Lenin i sovetskaya kul'tura*, pp. 251–2.

29 Smirnov, *ibid.*, p. 238.
30 Quoted *ibid.*, p. 273.
31 *TSGAOR* 2306/1/36, 5 April 1918.
32 Smirnov, *Lenin i sovetskaya kul'tura*, p. 274.
33 M. M. Novikov, *Ot Moskvy do N'yu Iorka* (New York, 1952), p. 307.
34 Smirnov, *Lenin i sovetskaya kul'tura*, p. 266 (Pokrovsky); Pokrovsky, *Nar. pros.* (weekly) (1920), nos. 89–90, 7 Nov., p. 18 (Shapiro); Lunacharsky, 'For the 200th anniversary of the All-Union Academy of Sciences', *Novyi mir* (1925), no. 10, p. 110 (Shternberg).
35 Lunacharsky, 'For the 200th anniversary of the All-Union Academy of Sciences', p. 110.
36 'The student body and the revolution', *Prosveshchenie i revolyutsiya* (Moscow, 1924).
37 E. N. Gorodetsky, 'Soviet reform of the higher school in 1918 and Moscow University', *Vestnik moskovskogo universiteta* (1954), no. 1 (social science series).
38 *Ot Moskvy do N'yu Iorka*, p. 120.
39 Pokrovsky, 'What Lenin was for our higher schools', *Pravda* (1924), no. 22, 27 Jan., p. 4.
40 See *Velikii perevorot*, p. 14.
41 *Izvestiya VTSIK* (1918), no. 71, 11 April, p. 4.
42 Quoted Gorodetsky, 'Soviet reform of the higher school in 1918', p. 125.
43 F. F. Korolev, 'The great October revolution and the higher school 1917–1920', *Sovetskaya pedagogika* (1957), no. 11, p. 78.
44 Domov (Pokrovsky), 'Reform of the higher school', *Nar. pros.* (monthly) (1918), nos. 4–5, p. 32.
45 Gorodetsky, 'Soviet reform of the higher school in 1918', p. 128.
46 K. A. Timiryazev, 'Democratic reform in the higher school' (1918), *Nauka i demokratiya* (Moscow, 1963), p. 420.
47 Decree of 2 Aug. 1918 'On the rules of admission to higher educational institutions'. Text in *Sovetskaya pedagogika* (1966), no. 4, p. 129.
48 Gorodetsky, 'Soviet reform of the higher school in 1918', p. 131.
49 Meeting of State Education Commission, 21 Sept. 1918, *Nar. pros.* (monthly) (1919), nos. 6–7, p. 142.
50 Gorodetsky, 'Soviet reform of the higher school in 1918', p. 133.
51 Meeting of State Education Commission, 21 Sept. 1919, *Nar. pros.* (monthly) (1919), nos. 6–7, pp. 132 ff.
52 *Nar. pros.* (monthly) (1920), nos. 18–19–20, p. 91.

53 V. I. Bessonova, 'Moscow University in the first years of Soviet power', *Voprosy istorii* (1955), no. 5, p. 57.
54 M. M. Novikov, 'Moscow University in the first period of the Bolshevist regime', in *Moskovskii universitet 1755–1930* (Paris, 1930), p. 173.
55 *Nar. pros.* (monthly) (1920), nos. 18–19–20, p. 92.
56 Narodnyi Komissariat po Prosveshcheniyu, *1917—oktyabr'—1920 (kratkii otchet)* (Moscow, 1920), pp. 62–3.
57 V. I. Bessonova, 'Creation and development of workers' faculties', in *Iz istorii velikoi oktyabr'skoi sotsialisticheskoi revolyutsii* (Moscow, 1957), p. 169.
58 Quoted Bessonova, *ibid.*, p. 163.
59 'Moscow University in the first period of the Bolshevist regime', p. 175.
60 Bessonova, 'Moscow University in the first years of Soviet power', p. 61.
61 Lunacharsky, *Prosveshchenie i revolyutsiya* (1926), p. 78.
62 Korolev, 'The great October revolution and the higher school 1917–1920', p. 87.
63 Decree of STO, 23 July 1920, *Izvestiya VTSIK* (1920), no. 186, 24 Aug., p. 2.
64 Narkompros draft in *TSGAOR* 2306/1/320, 2 Sept. 1920; Sovnarkom decree of 17 Sept. 1920 in *Sovetskaya pedagogika* (1966), no. 6, pp. 120–1.
65 S. F. Oldenburg, 'Maxim Gorky and scholars', in *Gor'kii i nauka* (Moscow, 1964), p. 245.
66 V. D. Bonch-Bruevich, 'Gorky and the organization of TSEKUBU', in *Gor'kii i nauka*, pp. 222–3.
67 *TSGAOR* 2306/1/182, 13 Dec. 1919; and Lenin, *Pol. sob. soch.*, vol. 39, p. 586 and vol. 40, p. 461.
68 *Gor'kii i nauka*, p. 110 (note) and pp. 114–15.
69 *Nar. pros.* (monthly) (1920), nos. 18–19–20, p. 7.
70 Speech to VTSIK, 26 Sept. 1920, *O narodnom obrazovanii*, p. 133.
71 *Sobr. uzak.* (Moscow, 1920), no. 82, art. 395.
72 *Ibid.*, art. 396.
73 Novikov, 'Moscow University in the first period of the Bolshevist regime', pp. 190–1.
74 N. L. Safrazyan, 'From the history of Moscow University in the first years of the reconstruction period 1921–25', in *Iz istorii Moskovskogo Universiteta* (Moscow, 1955), pp. 90–1.

75 Nar. Kom. po Pros., *1917—oktyabr'—1920* (*kratkii otchet*), p. 66.
76 Safrazyan, 'From the history of Moscow University', p. 87.
77 Quoted *Istoriya moskovskogo universiteta*, vol. 2 (Moscow, 1955), p. 59.
78 'Revolutionary education', *Izvestiya VTSIK* (1920), no. 249, 6 Nov., p. 2.
79 Nar. Kom. po Pros., *1917—oktyabr'—1920* (*kratkii otchet*), p. 66.
80 Pokrovsky, *Nar. pros.* (monthly) (1920), nos. 18–19–20, p. 7.
81 Nar. Kom. po Pros., *1917—oktyabr'—1920* (*kratkii otchet*), p. 66.

5: PROLETKULT

1 *Direktivy VKP(b) i postanovleniya sovetskogo pravitel'stva o narodnom obrazovanii za 1917–1946 gg.*, p. 11.
2 Gorbunov, 'From the history of the cultural-educational activity of the Petrograd Bolsheviks in the period of preparation for October', *Voprosy istorii KPSS* (1967), no. 2, p. 33.
3 Lunacharsky, 'Ideology on the eve of October' (1922), *Vospominaniya i vpechatleniya*, p. 166.
4 Gorbunov, 'From the history of the cultural-educational activity of the Petrograd Bolsheviks', p. 34.
5 Lunacharsky, 'Ideology on the eve of October', p. 167.
6 Gorbunov, 'From the history of the cultural-educational activity of the Petrograd Bolsheviks', p. 34.
7 *Izvestiya TSIK* (Petrograd, 1917), no. 237, 27 Nov., p. 12.
8 *Direktivy VKP(b)*..., p. 15.
9 *Nar. pros.* (fortnightly) (Petrograd, 1918), nos. 1–2, p. 22.
10 Moskovskii Proletkult, *Pervaya moskovskaya obshchegorodskaya konferentsiya proletarskikh kul'turnykh-prosvetitel'nykh organizatsii* (Moscow, 1918).
11 Lunacharsky, 'Ideology on the eve of October', p. 167.
12 *Novaya zhizn'* (1918), no. 74, 23 April, p. 3.
13 *TSGAOR* 2306/1/36, 31 March 1918.
14 *Ibid.*, 22 May 1918.
15 *Ibid.*, 8 April 1918. Minutes of this meeting have been published in I. Smirnov, 'Towards the history of Proletkult', *Voprosy literatury* (1968), no. 1, pp. 119–22; and in A. Ermakov, 'Lunacharsky and Proletkult', *Druzhba narodov* (1968), no. 1, p. 243–4.
16 *TSGAOR* 2306/1/36, 13 April 1918. Minutes published in Smirnov,

'Towards the history of Proletkult', pp. 122–4, and Ermakov, 'Lunacharsky and Proletkult', pp. 245–6.

17 Published in *Proletarskaya kul'tura* (1919), nos. 9–10, p. 63.

18 See *Izvestiya VTSIK* (1918), no. 172, 13 Aug., p. 8: 'Proletarian culture (conversation with comrade Piskunov)' and editorial comment. Budget of Moscow Proletkult for 1918 is in *TSGAOR* 2306/17/8.

19 *Protokoly pervoi vserossiiskoi konferentsii proletarskikh kul'turno-prosvetitel'nykh organizatsii 15–20 sentyabrya 1918 g.* (Moscow, 1918).

20 *Proletarskaya kul'tura* (1918), no. 3, pp. 35–6.

21 Theses published *ibid.*, no. 2 (July), p. 23.

22 *Protokoly pervoi vserossiiskoi konferentsii*..., pp. 79–80.

23 *Ibid.*, p. 55.

24 *Gorn* (organ of Moscow Proletkult) (1920), no. 5, p. 85.

25 *TSGAOR* 2306/17/8 (department of aid to independent proletarian cultural organizations).

26 'Once again on Proletkult and Soviet cultural organizations', *Izvestiya VTSIK* (1919), no. 80, 13 April, p. 2.

27 *Severnaya kommuna* (1919), no. 32, 11 Feb., p. 4.

28 *Proletarskaya kul'tura* (1919), nos. 9–10, pp. 61–2.

29 *Izvestiya VTSIK* (1918), no. 244, 9 Nov., p. 5.

30 *Proletarskaya kul'tura* (1918), no. 3, p. 19.

31 V. Khodasevich, *Literaturnye stat'i i vospominaniya* (New York, 1954), p. 326.

32 Quoted from *Gryadushchee* no. 10 in *Iskusstvo kommuny* (1919), no. 10, 9 Feb., p. 3.

33 *Proletarskaya kul'tura* (1919), nos. 9–10, p. 45.

34 'Paths of proletarian creativity (theses)', *Proletarskaya kul'tura* (1920), nos. 15–16, p. 50.

35 'Ideology on the eve of October', p. 63.

36 Quoted by N. Chuzhak, *K dialektike iskusstva* (Chita, 1921), p. 77.

37 *Pravda* (1919), no. 62, 22 March, p. 4.

38 *Izvestiya VTSIK* (1919), no. 105, 17 May, p. 3.

39 *TSGAOR* 2306/1/180, 4 April 1919.

40 See 'On the closing of the Proletarian University', *Proletarskaya kul'tura* (1919), nos. 9–10, pp. 56–9.

41 Quoted *ibid.*, p. 59.

42 Quoted *ibid.*

43 *TSGAOR* 2306/1/182, 4 Sept. and 2 Oct. 1919.

44 *Izvestiya VTSIK* (1919), no. 63, 23 March, p. 5.

45 Quoted *Proletarskaya kul'tura* (1919), nos. 7–8, p. 72.
46 'Proletkult's methods of work', *Proletarskaya kul'tura* (1919), no. 6, pp. 18–22.
47 'A few words about Proletkult', *Ped. soch.*, vol. 7, p. 60.
48 *TSGAOR* 2306/17/8—'Information relating to the activities of Proletkults and associated organizations for the 2nd half of May [1919]'.
49 'On the results of the Congress' (1919), *Ped. soch.*, vol. 7, p. 39.
50 *Proletarskaya kul'tura* (1919), nos. 7–8, p. 71.
51 Lenin, *Pol. sob. soch.*, vol. 38, p. 330.
52 *Izvestiya VTSIK* (1919), no. 99, 10 May, p. 2.
53 *Ibid.*, no. 101, 13 May, p. 4.
54 Quoted T. Knyazhevskaya, *Yuzhin-Sumbatov i sovetskii teatr* (Moscow, 1966), pp. 98–9.
55 Lenin, *Pol. sob. soch.*, vol. 38, pp. 368–9.
56 *TSGAOR* 2306/1/181, 6 June 1919.
57 *TSGAOR* 2306/17/8—'Information relating to the activities of Proletkults and associated organizations for the 2nd half of May [1919]'.
58 Quoted from *Nar. pros.* (monthly) (1919), nos. 9–10 (April–May), in *Proletarskaya kul'tura* (1919), nos. 9–10 (June–July), p. 63.

6: THE ARTS

1 Lunacharsky, *Vospominaniya i vpechatleniya*, p. 357; and *Protokoly TSK RSDRP(b) avg. 1917—fev. 1918* (Moscow, 1958), p. 36.
2 Gorky quoted in Trifonov, 'Brothers-in-arms', *Russkaya literatura* (1968), no. 1, p. 27; satirical poem in *Novaya zhizn'* (1918), no. 55, 30 March, p. 2; Desnitsky in *Novaya zhizn'* (1918), no. 22, 30 Jan., p. 1.
3 Lunacharsky, 'On Soviet rails' (1931), *Vospominaniya i vpechatleniya*, p. 277.
4 E. M. Bebutova, 'Recollections', in *Iz istorii stroitel'stva sovetskoi kul'tury. Moskva. 1917–1918 gg.* (Moscow, 1964), p. 283.
5 *Novaya zhizn'* (1918), no. 21, 28 Jan., p. 4.
6 E. V. Oranovsky, 'Kremlin-Acropolis', in *Iz istorii stroitel'stva sovetskoi kul'tury*, pp. 326–7.
7 Unsigned memorandum to Sovnarkom, probably by P. P. Malinovsky and E. V. Oranovsky, in *Iz istorii stroitel'stva sovetskoi kul'tury*, pp. 76–9.

8 *TSGAOR* 2306/1/36, 5 April 1918 (State Education Commission).
9 Interview with Kameneva in *Izvestiya TSIK* (1918), no. 67, 6 April, p. 4.
10 'On the tasks of the state theatres', *Nar. pros.* (fortnightly) (1918), nos. 1–2, pp. 23–4.
11 Quoted E. A. Dinershtein, 'Mayakovsky in February–October 1917', in *Literaturnoe nasledstvo*, vol. 65, pp. 564–6.
12 *Ibid.*, pp. 564–6; and O. Brik, 'Mayakovsky—editor and organizer', *Literaturnyi kritik* (1936), no. 4, p. 116.
13 Dinershtein, 'Mayakovsky in February–October 1917', p. 544.
14 Sovnarkom decree of 12 April 1918, *Sobr. uzak.* (1918), no. 31, art. 417.
15 N. Punin, 'In the days of Red October', *Zhizn' iskusstva* (1921), no. 816, 8 Nov., p. 1.
16 'On the tasks of the state theatres', *Nar. pros.* (fortnightly) (1918), nos. 1–2, pp. 22–5. Also published in *Izvestiya TSIK* on 13, 15 and 17 December 1917.
17 Correspondence between Lunacharsky and Batyushkov is published by V. P. Zeldovich, 'First measures of Narkompros in the administration of the theatres', *Istoricheskii arkhiv* (1959), no. 1.
18 Lunacharsky, 'To all artists and employees of the Petrograd state theatres', *Izvestiya TSIK* (1917), no. 258, 22 Dec., p. 4.
19 Zeldovich, 'First measures of Narkompros in the administration of the theatres', p. 60.
20 Flakserman, 'Pages of the past', *Novyi mir* (1968), no. 11, pp. 223–4.
21 Lunacharsky, 'On Soviet rails', p. 279.
22 Zeldovich, 'First measures of Narkompros in the administration of the theatres', p. 53.
23 Quoted Zeldovich, *ibid.*, p. 52.
24 'On Soviet rails', p. 281.
25 R. Ivnev, 'Recollections of the first days and months of Soviet power', *Prometei* (Moscow, 1967), no. 4, p. 246. Lunacharsky wrote to his wife on 18 Dec. of a meeting planned by Blok, Meyerhold, Petrov-Vodkin and Ivnev on the theme 'People's Commissars are representatives of the real masses. Intelligentsia, return to the service of the people' (quoted A. Elkin, *Lunacharskii* (Moscow, 1967), pp. 123–4).
26 Lunacharsky reported this meeting enthusiastically in *Izvestiya TSIK* (1917), no. 228, 17 Nov., p. 3. He was mocked for this,

because of Yasinsky's unprincipled reputation, by Korolenko in *Russkie vedomosti* and Gorky in *Novaya zhizn'* (Trifonov, 'Brothers-in-arms', *Russkaya literatura* (1968), no. 1, p. 27).

27 'I myself (1922.1928), in *Sovetskie pisateli. Avtobiografii v dvukh tomakh* (Moscow, 1959), vol. 2, p. 72.

28 B. F. Malkin recalled meeting Mayakovsky at Smolny shortly after October at a meeting of the Petrograd intelligentsia summoned by TSIK, and attended by only a handful of people including Mayakovsky, Blok, Meyerhold and Larisa Reisner (see *V. Mayakovskii v vospominaniyakh sovremennikov* (Moscow, 1963), p. 635). A letter written by Lunacharsky to his wife in November 1917 mentions Mayakovsky as one of his associates (quoted *Literaturnoe nasledstvo*, vol. 65, p. 572).

29 Dinershtein, 'Mayakovsky in February–October 1917', p. 566.

30 Brik, 'Mayakovsky—editor and organizer', p. 119.

31 *Ibid.*, p. 116.

32 Punin, 'In the days of Red October', p. 1.

33 'From the literary heritage of A. V. Lunacharsky' (publication of A. Ermakov), *Novyi mir* (1966), no. 9, p. 237.

34 Punin, 'In the days of Red October', p. 1.

35 'To the critics from Proletkult', *Iskusstvo kommuny* (1919), no. 10, 9 Feb., p. 3. The same issue carried an attack by Brik on the Proletkultists.

36 Punin, 'In the days of Red October', p. 1.

37 *Vestnik narodnogo prosveshcheniya soyuza kommun severnoi oblasti* (1918), nos. 4–5, p. 14.

38 Quoted *Vestnik teatra* (1920), no. 71, 22 Oct., p. 13 from speech of 26 Sept. 1920.

39 Shulgin, *Pamyatnye vstrechi*, p. 66.

40 V. Bonch-Bruevich, 'Vladimir Ilyich and the decoration of the Red capital', *Vospominaniya o Lenine* (Moscow, 1965), pp. 380–1.

41 Lunacharsky, 'Lenin and art (reminiscences)', *Ob izobrazitel'nom iskusstve* (Moscow, 1967), vol. 2, pp. 7–9, note p. 277.

42 *Ibid.*, pp. 301–2.

43 'From the literary heritage of A. V. Lunacharsky', *Novyi mir* (1966), no. 9, p. 239.

44 *Ob izobrazitel'nom iskusstve*, vol. 2, pp. 115–16.

45 Brik, 'Mayakovsky—editor and organizer', p. 116.

46 V. P. Zubov, *Stradnye gody Rossii* (*Vospominaniya o Revolyutsii 1917–1925*) (Munich, 1968), pp. 37, 93, 97–8.

47 Unpublished letter of 12 June 1918, quoted A. Elkin, *Lunacharskii*, p. 161.

48 *Iz istorii stroitel'stva sovetskoi kul'tury*, p. 126, note.

49 'Letters of A. V. Lunacharsky' (publication of I. S. Smirnov), *Novyi mir* (1965), no. 4, p. 252.

50 *TSGAOR* 2306/1/36, 22 May 1918 (statement of Lunacharsky in collegium of Narkompros).

51 'From the literary heritage of A. V. Lunacharsky', *Novyi mir* (1966), no. 9, p. 237.

52 K. Chukovsky, 'Lunacharsky', *Sovremenniki* (Moscow, 1963), pp. 424–5.

53 Quoted from an article by Lunacharsky in *Komsomol'skaya pravda* (1926), no. 222 by P. A. Bugaenko, *A. V. Lunacharskii i literaturnoe dvizhenie 20'kh godov* (Saratov, 1967), p. 151.

54 'The idea of contemporary Don Quixotism arose especially clearly when I was present at conversations between V. I. Lenin and Gorky' (Lunacharsky, *Sob. soch.*, vol. 4, p. 438). The play *Osvobozhdennyi Don-Kikhot* is published in Lunacharsky, *P'esy* (Moscow, 1963).

55 *TSGAOR* 2306/1/320, 11 March and 12 Aug. (Vyach. Ivanov); letter of 1919, published by N. Piyashev in *Russkaya literatura*, (1966), no. 1 (Balmont); *TSGAOR* 2306/1/320, 17 April 1920 (Kusevitsky and Balmont); *ibid.*, 29 April 1920 (Kusevitsky); 'Letters of A. V. Lunacharsky', *Novyi mir* (1965), no. 4, pp. 244–5 (Stanislavsky); *TSGAOR* 2306/1/320, 15 July 1920 and 20 July 1920 (Nemirovich-Danchenko—suggestion accepted on first occasion and rejected on second); *TSGAOR* 2306/1/181, 4 Aug. 1919 (Alkonost); *TSGAOR* 2306/1/180, 24 Jan. 1919 (Volfila).

56 See S. Savshinsky, 'The past does not die', *Sovetskaya muzyka* (1967), no. 1, pp. 71 ff.

57 V. Serge, *Memoirs of a Revolutionary*, tr. Sedgwick (London, 1963), p. 76.

58 B. Raikov, 'My meetings with Gorky', *Gor'kii i nauka*, p. 258; Chukovsky, 'Gorky', *Sovremenniki*, pp. 323–4; and A. I. Nazarov, *Oktyabr' i kniga* (Moscow, 1968), p. 152.

59 Nazarov, *Oktyabr' i kniga*, pp. 156–60; and *TSGAOR* 2306/1/181, 10 July 1919.

60 M. Shchelkunov, 'Legislation on printing over five years', *Pechat' i revolyutsiya* (1922), no. 6, p. 183.

61 Nazarov, *Oktyabr' i kniga*, p. 137.

62 *Ibid.*, pp. 76–83.

63 'The Commissariat of Public Education and the writers', *Izvestiya VTSIK* (1919), no. 27, 6 Feb., p. 1.
64 Nazarov, *Oktyabr' i kniga*, pp. 138–42.
65 *TSGAOR* 2306/1/182, 11 Dec. 1919.
66 *Ibid.* (undated letter appended to protocol of meeting).
67 *TSGAOR* 2306/1/320, 16 Aug. 1920 (commission on current business of Narkompros).
68 *TSGAOR* 2306/1/36, 17 June 1918.
69 Quoted Knyazhevskaya, *Yuzhin-Sumbatov i sovetskii teatr*, p. 36.
70 *Vestnik teatra* (1920), no. 48, 13–19 Jan.
71 Resolution of 20 Nov. 1917, quoted Knyazhevskaya, *Yuzhin-Sumbatov i sovetskii teatr*, p. 26.
72 'Three meetings', *Vospominaniya i vpechatleniya*, p. 304.
73 *Sovetskii teatr. Dokumenty i materialy. Russkii sovetskii teatr. 1917–1921* (Leningrad, 1968), pp. 38–9 (Statutes of autonomous state theatres) and pp. 112–13 (Maly theatre).
74 A. Yufit, 'Facts, documents, history', *Teatr* (1966), no. 6, p. 43.
75 Quoted A. Ya. Trabsky, 'Leninist decree (On the history of the drafting of the "Decree on the unification of theatrical affairs")', in *Teatr i dramaturgiya. Trudy leningradskoi gosudarstvennogo instituta teatra, muzyki i kinematografii* (Leningrad, 1967), p. 71.
76 *Ibid.*, p. 71.
77 Quoted Knyazhevskaya, *Yuzhin-Sumbatov i sovetskii teatr*, pp. 36–7.
78 E. K. Malinovskaya, 'I consult Ilyich', *Izvestiya* (1963), no. 77, 31 March, p. 5 (first posthumous publication).
79 Yufit, 'Facts, documents, history', p. 39.
80 *Ibid.*, p. 38.
81 See *Izvestiya VTSIK* (1919), no. 164, 27 July, p. 4, and no. 175, 7 Aug., p. 4.
82 *TSGAOR* 2306/1/182, 16 Aug. and 19 Nov. 1919.
83 Knyazhevskaya, *Yuzhin-Sumbatov i sovetskii teatr*, pp. 97 and 194.
84 Kerzhentsev, 'Theatrical museum', *Vestnik teatra* (1920), no. 48, 13–19 Jan., pp. 4–5.
85 Kerzhentsev, 'The bourgeois heritage', *Vestnik teatra* (1920), no. 51, 5–8 Feb., pp. 2–3.
86 Lunacharsky, 'In the name of the proletariat', *Vestnik teatra* (1920), no. 51, 5–8 Feb., pp. 3–4.
87 Lunacharsky, letter to the editor, *Pravda* (1919), no. 242, 29 Oct., p. 2 (reply to Bukharin's article of 16 Oct.).
88 Lunacharsky, 'Revolutionary theatre (answer to comrade Bukharin)',

Vestnik teatra (1919), no. 47, 23–8 Dec. Also in Lunacharsky, *Sob. soch.*, vol. 3, pp. 100–5. It is not clear whether the article was submitted to *Pravda* for publication.

89 *TSGAOR* 2306/1/320, 10 Feb. 1920.

90 E. Kuznetsov, 'Commissar of the theatres', in *M. F. Andreeva*, p. 416.

91 *TSGAOR* 2306/1/180, 24 Jan. 1919.

92 *M. F. Andreeva*, pp. 273 and 656.

93 See unsigned letter, evidently from Lunacharsky, to Andreeva, dated 19 April 1920, in *M. F. Andreeva*, pp. 279–81.

94 J. Jelagin, *Temnyi genii* (New York, 1955), p. 222.

95 *TSGAOR* 2306/1/320, 16 Sept. 1920.

96 I. Ehrenburg, *First years of Revolution 1918–1921* (London, 1962), p. 129.

97 Lunacharsky, *Sob. soch.*, vol. 7, p. 255; and *Pravda* (1920), no. 234, 20 Oct., p. 2.

98 Knyazhevskaya, *Yuzhin-Sumbatov i sovetskii teatr*, pp. 105 and 108.

99 Ya. Shapirshtein (Lers), 'On the fate of theatrical October', *Vestnik teatra* (1920), no. 75, 30 Nov., p. 2.

100 'From the People's Commissar of Education', *Vestnik teatra* (1920), no. 74, 20 Nov., p. 16.

101 Lunacharsky had written extensively on Maeterlinck's plays before the revolution—see, for example, his articles in *Obrazovanie* (St Petersburg, 1902), nos. 9, 10 and 12.

102 *Magi* (preface) (Moscow, 1919), p. 1.

103 'What kind of melodrama do we need?' *Sob. soch.*, vol. 2, p. 21.

104 *Vestnik teatra* (1920), no. 74, 20 Nov., p. 10.

105 Lunacharsky, *O teatre i dramaturgii* (Moscow, 1958), vol. 1, p. 789 (note by editor A. Deich).

106 *Vestnik teatra* (1920), no. 75, 30 Nov., p. 14.

107 *Ibid.*, pp. 2–3.

108 The debate was reported *in extenso* in *Vestnik teatra* (1920), nos. 76–7, 14 Dec., pp. 16–19.

109 Knyazhevskaya, *Yuzhin-Sumbatov i sovetskii teatr*, p. 108.

110 Lunacharsky quoted Gorky as saying that, after reading *Magi*, 'I consider it necessary to publish it, because this play was written at a time of intensive terror by a member of the Soviet government', *Vestnik teatra* (1920), nos. 76–7, 14 Dec., p. 17.

111 Lunacharsky, 'To my opponents', *ibid.*, p. 4.

112 Meyerhold, 'J'accuse!', *ibid.*, p. 5

113 Quoted Knyazhevskaya, *Yuzhin-Sumbatov i sovetskii teatr*, p. 109.
114 Reported *Vestnik teatra* (1921), nos. 78–9, 4 Jan., p. 6 and nos. 80–1, 27 Jan., pp. 10–12.

7: TOWARDS REORGANIZATION OF NARKOMPROS

1 *TSGAOR* 2306/1/180, 1 and 7 February, 5 March 1919.
2 *TSGAOR* 2306/1/182, 4 November 1919; *TSGAOR* 2306/1/320, 27 Jan. 1920; *TSGAOR* 2306/1/182, 27 Dec. 1919.
3 *TSGAOR* 2306/1/320, 26 Feb. 1920; *TSGAOR* 2306/1/182, 27 Dec. 1919; *TSGAOR* 2306/1/320, 24 Jan. 1920.
4 *Sovetskaya pedagogika* (1966), no. 10, p. 102; *TSGAOR* 2306/1/320, 18 Oct. 1920.
5 M. M. Novikov, 'Moscow University in the first period of the Bolshevist regime', in *Moskovskii universitet 1755–1930* (Paris, 1930), pp. 67–8.
6 *TSGAOR* 2306/1/320, 26 Feb. 1920 and 3 April 1920; *Nar. pros.* (weekly) (1921), nos. 89–90, 7 Nov., p. 10.
7 Resolution and document in *TSGAOR* 2306/1/320, 26 Feb. 1920.
8 Lenin, *Pol. sob. soch.*, vol. 40, p. 445.
9 *TSGAOR* 2306/1/320, 27 March 1920 (reported to collegium by Lunacharsky).
10 Speech to VTSIK, 26 Sept. 1920, in Lunacharsky, *O narodnom obrazovanii*, p. 119.
11 *TSGAOR* 2306/1/320, 2 Sept., 16 (18) Sept., 1 Nov. 1920.
12 *Ibid.*, 20 July 1920.
13 *Ibid.*, 14 Sept. 1920.
14 26 Sept. 1920. Speech published (with omissions) in Lunacharsky, *O narodnom obrazovanii.*
15 Reported by M. Zagorsky, 'On new plays', *Vestnik teatra* (1920), no. 70, 9–17 Oct., p. 6.
16 *TSGAOR* 2306/1/320, 7 Oct. 1920.
17 'In performance of the resolution of the 3rd session of VTSIK 1920', *Nar. pros.* (weekly) (1921), no. 80, 20 March, pp. 7–9.
18 *TSGAOR* 2306/1/320, 29 Jan. 1920.
19 *TSGA RSFSR* 1565/1/22, 22 July 1920.
20 *Nar. pros.* (weekly) (1921), no. 80, 20 March, p. 9.
21 *Ibid.*, pp. 7–9; and *Nar. pros.* (weekly) (1921), no. 83, 20 July, pp. 5–7.
22 Lenin, *Pol. sob. soch.*, vol. 41, p. 621.

23 *Leninskii sbornik*, vol. 35 (Moscow, 1945), p. 148.
24 Lenin, *Pol. sob. soch.*, vol. 41, p. 662.
25 *TSGAOR* 2306/1/320, 13 and 24 July, 13 Aug. 1920.
26 Lunacharsky, 'Lenin and art. Recollections' (1924), *Sob. soch.* vol. 7, p. 405.
27 Lenin, *Pol. sob. soch.*, vol. 41, p. 336.
28 *Izvestiya* did not publish Lunacharsky's letter, which was discovered in the archives and first published by P. Bugaenko, 'A. V. Lunacharsky and Proletkult', in *Problemy razvitiya sovetskoi literatury* (Saratov, 1963), p. 23.
29 Lunacharsky, 'Lenin and art. Recollections', p. 405.
30 Lenin, *Pol. sob. soch.*, vol. 41, p. 337.
31 V. V. Gorbunov, 'V. I. Lenin's struggle with the separatist aspirations of Proletkult', *Voprosy istorii KPSS* (1958), no. 1, p. 33.
32 Quoted from Central Party Archives by V. V. Gorbunov, 'Criticism by V. I. Lenin of Proletkult's theories in relation to the cultural heritage', *Voprosy istorii KPSS* (1968), no. 5, p. 91.
33 *TSGAOR* 2306/1/320, 8 Oct. 1920. This item (motion and resolution) was included in the typed minutes and later crossed out in ink.
34 Gorbunov, 'V. I. Lenin's struggle with the separatist aspirations of Proletkult', pp. 34–5.
35 *TSGAOR* 2306/1/320, 24 Oct. 1920.
36 *Izvestiya TSK* no. 22, 18 Sept. 1920, p. 16.
37 *TSGAOR* 2306/1/320, 23 March, 16 April, 6 and 8 June, 26 Aug. and 13 Sept. 1920.
38 *TSGAOR* 2306/1/182, N. K. Krupskaya, 'On working in the countryside in the field of extramural education' (memo. filed after minutes of meeting of Narkompros collegium on 15 Nov. 1919).
39 Lunacharsky, 'Communist propaganda and education' (*c.* 1921), *Prosveshchenie i revolyutsiya* (1926), p. 84.
40 Lunacharsky, 'The significance of Soviet Party schools and their place in the system of education', *ibid.*, p. 73.
41 *Desyatyi syezd RKP(b). Mart 1921 g. Stenograficheskii otchet* (Moscow, 1963), p. 154.
42 *Byulleten' vserossiiskogo soveshchaniya politprosvetov (1–8 noyabrya 1920 g.* (Moscow), pp. 2–3.
43 *Otchet o rabote politprosveta Narkomprosa* (Moscow, 1920), pp. 13–16.
44 Published *Izvestiya TSK*, no. 18, 23 May 1920, p. 2.
45 Lenin, *Pol. sob. soch.*, vol. 41, pp. 397, 542.

46 Lunacharsky, 'Questions of education', *Prosveshchenie i revolyutsiya* (1926), p. 418.
47 *TSGA RSFSR* 2313/1/1, 11 and 16 Nov. 1920.
48 Lenin, *Pol. sob. soch.*, vol. 42, p. 12.
49 The letter's attack on futurism was attributed by N. Chuzhak to Zinoviev (*K dialektike iskusstva*, pp. 98–9). According to a document from the Central Party Archives quoted in an unpublished thesis in Moscow, the Central Committee entrusted the drafting of the whole letter to Zinoviev on 10 Nov. 1920.

8: REORGANIZATION

1 I. S. Smirnov, 'V. I. Lenin and the direction of educational affairs (on the history of the reorganization of Narkompros in 1920–21)', *Sovetskaya pedagogika* (1958), no. 4, pp. 48–9.
2 Litkens, 'On the reorganization of Narkompros', in *Byulleten' VIII syezda sovetov* (Moscow, 1920), no. 7, 27 Dec., p. 1.
3 Smirnov, 'V. I. Lenin and the direction of educational affairs', p. 49.
4 Lenin, *Pol. sob. soch.*, vol. 52, pp. 21–2.
5 Smirnov, 'V. I. Lenin and the direction of educational affairs', p. 50; and Lenin, project on the reorganization of Narkompros, *Pol. sob. soch.*, vol. 42, p. 87.
6 Lenin, *Pol. sob. soch.*, vol. 42, pp. 87 and 463; and *TSGAOR* 2306/1/320, 9 Dec. 1920.
7 Smirnov, 'V. I. Lenin and the direction of educational affairs', p. 50.
8 *Byulleten' VIII syezda sovetov* (1920), no. 6, 26 Dec., p. 16; Narodnyi komissariat po prosveshcheniyu, *K. IX vserossiiskomu syezdu sovetov* (Moscow, 1921), p. 5; and *Pravda* (1921), no. 3, 5 Jan., p. 3.
9 'Reform of the school system', *Pravda* (1921), no. 40, 23 Feb., p. 1.
10 A detailed report of the meeting was published by VTSIK in *Prilozhenie k byulletenyu VIII syezdu sovetov, posvyashchaemoe partiinomu sobraniyu po voprosam narodnogo obrazovaniya* (Moscow, 10 Jan. 1921).
11 Reported in *Izvestiya TSK*, no. 27, 27 Jan. 1921, pp. 4 ff.
12 See *Prilozhenie k byulletenyu VIII syezdu sovetov*...
13 Nar. kom. po pros., *K IX vserossiiskomu syezdu sovetov*, p. 6.
14 Lenin, 'On the reorganization of Narkompros' (Dec. 8), *Pol. sob. soch.*, vol. 42, p. 87.

15 Lenin, 'On polytechnical education' (annotations to Krupskaya's theses), *ibid.*, pp. 228–30.
16 Nar. kom. po pros., *K IX vserossiiskomu syezdu sovetov*, p. 6.
17 *Prilozhenie k byulletenyu VIII syezdu sovetov...*, p. 11.
18 Lenin, *Pol. sob. soch.*, vol. 52, p. 48.
19 Smirnov, 'V. I. Lenin and the direction of educational affairs', pp. 51–2.
20 Nar. kom. po pros., *K IX vserossiiskomu syezdu sovetov*, p. 6.
21 *TSGAOR* 2308/1/21. Instruction no. 6, 16 Dec. 1920.
22 B. Plyusnin-Kronin, 'V. I. Lenin and our tasks', *Nar. pros.* (monthly) (1924), no. 2 (11), p. 1.
23 Lenin, *Pol. sob. soch.* vol. 52, p. 112.
24 Lenin to Preobrazhensky, 5 June 1921, *ibid.*, p. 256.
25 Lenin to Molotov, for members of the Politburo, 7 Sept. 1921, *ibid.*, vol. 53, pp. 79–80, 413.
26 See his letters to Preobrazhensky, 5 June 1921, and Litkens, 14 July 1921, *ibid.*, vol. 52, pp. 255–6, 274–5.
27 Letter to Litkens, 14 July 1921, *ibid.*, pp. 274–5.
28 Lenin to Litkens, 27 March 1921, *ibid.*, p. 112.
29 *TSGAOR* 2306/1/634, 18 July, 25 Aug. and 5 Sept. 1921 (closed meetings of collegium of Narkompros); and *TSGA RSFSR* 2313/1/1, report of P. Voevodin (head of FOTO-KINO), 1 June 1921.
30 *TSGA RSFSR* 2313/1/1 (collegium of Glavpolitprosvet), 11 Nov., 4 and 18 Dec. 1920, 30 Jan. 1921.
31 *Izvestiya TSK*, no. 27, 27 Jan. 1921, p. 7.
32 *TSGAOR* 2308/1/21. Instruction no. 108, 7 March 1921. Other information from *TSGA RSFSR* 2313/1/1 and 2313/1/4, *passim.*
33 *TSGAOR* 2306/1/634, 17 March 1921.
34 *Ibid.*, 25 May 1921.
35 'On the question of the review of staffs and institutions (interview with comrade Larin)', *Izvestiya VTSIK* (1921), no. 243, 29 Oct., p. 1. Members of the commission were Larin, D. I. Kursky, L. S. Sosnovsky, V. A. Avanesov, Antipov.
36 *TSGAOR* 2306/1/634, 3 Nov. 1921.
37 *TSGA RSFSR* 2313/1/1, 8 Nov. 1921 (meeting of Larin commission with representatives of Narkompros and Glavpolitprosvet).
38 See obituary in *Nar. pros.* (weekly) (1922), no. 101, 3 May, p. 3.
39 *TSGAOR* 2306/1/634, 9 Dec. 1921.
40 Yu. Larin, 'State workers and salaries', *Pravda* (1922), no. 39, 18 Feb., p. 2.
41 L. Trotsky, *My Life* (London, 1930), p. 408.

9: NARKOMPROS AFTER REORGANIZATION

1 *TSGAOR* 2308/1/21, Instruction no. 34, 6 Jan. 1921.
2 *TSGAOR* 2306/1/634, 18 Feb. 1921.
3 Smirnov, 'V. I. Lenin and the direction of educational affairs', *Sovetskaya pedagogika* (1958), no. 4, p. 55.
4 *Ibid.*
5 *Ibid.*
6 Appointed to the collegium of Narkompros by Sovnarkom on 22 March 1921 (*Izvestiya VTSIK* (1921), no. 65, 26 March, p. 3); announced as head of Glavsotsvos by Litkens on 23 March (*TSGAOR* 2308/1/21, Instruction no. 122).
7 *Ibid.*, Instruction no. 352, 25 Oct. 1921.
8 *TSGAOR* 2306/1/634, 31 March 1921.
9 *Ibid.*, 22 March 1921.
10 *Ibid.*, 11 April 1921.
11 *Ibid.*, 4 July 1921.
12 Lunacharsky, 'Economics and culture', *Nar. pros.* (weekly) (1921), no. 84, 10 Aug., p. 2.
13 Preobrazhensky, 'On professional-technical education', *Pravda* (1921), no. 201, 10 Sept., p. 2, and *Nar. pros.* (weekly) (1921), no. 85, 24 Sept., pp. 6–7.
14 Pokrovsky, 'What Lenin was for our higher school', *Pravda* (1924), no. 22, 27 Jan., p. 2.
15 N. L. Safrazyan, 'From the history of Moscow University in the first years of the reconstruction period 1921–25', in *Iz istorii moskovskogo universiteta*, pp. 90–1.
16 Lenin, *Pol. sob. soch.*, vol. 52, p. 388.
17 Lenin to Preobrazhensky, 19 April 1921, *ibid.*, p. 155.
18 *TSGAOR* 2306/1/634, 14 Feb. 1921 (Lenin's letter read to meeting by Lunacharsky; Schmidt's memo filed with minutes).
19 Letter of 5 June 1921, *Pol. sob. soch.*, vol. 52, p. 256.
20 Letter of 6 December 1921, *Pol. sob. soch.*, vol. 54, p. 66.
21 *TSGAOR* 2306/1/1199a, 2 Feb. 1922 (collegium of Narkompros); and *TSGAOR* 2306/1/2102, 22 March 1922 (presidium of Narkompros).
22 *Nar. pros.* (weekly) (1921), no. 82, 20 May [*sic*], pp. 7–9.
23 *Ibid.*, no. 83, 20 July, pp. 1–2.
24 *Ibid.*, no. 82, 20 May, pp. 7–9.

25 Lenin forwarded the protest to Litkens on 6 August, *Pol. sob. soch.*, vol. 53, p. 398.

26 *TSGAOR* 2306/1/634, 18 Aug. and 19 Sept. 1921.

27 *Ibid.*, 9 and 30 Dec. 1921; and *TSGAOR* 2306/1/1199a, 16 March 1922.

28 *Odinnadtsatyi syezd RKP(b). Mart-aprel' 1922 g. Stenograficheskii otchet* (Moscow, 1961), p. 777 (note). See also a participant's account in V. Stratonov, 'Moscow University's loss of freedom' in *Moskovskii universitet 1755–1930*.

29 See *Istoriya moskovskogo universiteta*, vol. 2, pp. 88–9.

30 Stratonov, 'Moscow University's loss of freedom', describes the work of this commission (albeit in somewhat contemptuous terms).

31 *Istoriya moskovskogo universiteta*, vol. 2, p. 88. No date is given for Preobrazhensky's dismissal. He ceased to attend meetings of the collegium of Narkompros from the end of December 1921. Yakovleva attended as Glavprofobr representative from 9 March 1922 (*TSGAOR* 2306/1/1199a).

32 *Odinnadtsatyi syezd RKP(b)*, pp. xii–xiii.

33 *Ibid.*, pp. 85–6 (Preobrazhensky) and p. 95 (Ioffe), and p. 142 (Lenin).

34 Scheffer, 'University life and the press in revolutionary Russia', *Manchester Guardian Commercial* series, *Reconstruction of Europe*, ed. J. M. Keynes, section 4 (6 July 1922), pp. 243–4.

35 Lunacharsky, 'Children's colonies near Smolensk', *Nar. pros.* (weekly) (1919), nos. 53–5, 4 Oct., p. 2.

36 See A. I. Elizarova, 'Pages of reminiscence of Vladimir Ilyich in Sovnarkom', *Proletarskaya revolyutsiya* (1929), no. 11.

37 *Bol'shaya sovetskaya entsiklopediya* (1st ed.), vol. 21 (1931), '*Detskii dom*', p. 619.

38 Narodnyi Komissariat po Prosveshcheniyu, *1917—oktyabr'—1920* (*kratkii otchet*), pp. 99 and 102.

39 *TSGAOR* 2306/1/320, 25 March, 3 Sept., 19 Nov. 1920.

40 Nar. Kom. po Pros., *1917—oktyabr'—1920* (*kratkii otchet*), p. 70.

41 Decree of 4 March 1920. Text in *Sovetskaya pedagogika* (1966), no. 6, pp. 119–20.

42 H. G. Wells, *Russia in the Shadows* (London, 1920), p. 107; and Lenin, *Pol. sob. soch.*, vol. 51, pp. 121 and 405.

43 S. S. Dzerzhinskaya, *V gody velikikh boev* (Moscow, 1965), pp. 342–3.

44 *TSGAOR* 2306/1/320, 27 and 28 Sept., 13 Dec. 1920.

45 Lunacharsky, 'F. E. Dzerzhinsky in Narkompros', *Pravda* (1926),

no. 168, 22 July, p. 2. Also in *Rytsar' revolyutsii* (*vospominaniya o Dzerzhinskom*) (Moscow, 1967), pp. 278–9.

46 Dzerzhinskaya (*V godу velikikh boev*, p. 343) gives founding date as 27 January 1921.

47 'Educational questions in the press', *Nar. pros.* (weekly) (1921), no. 80, 20 March, p. 13.

48 Quoted Dzerzhinskaya, *V gody velikikh boev*, p. 345 (in paraphrase).

49 *Ibid.*, p. 346.

50 *TSGAOR* 2306/1/634, 17 Feb. 1921 (appointment of M. I. Vasilyev); *ibid.*, 7 March (appointment of Z. G. Grinberg); *ibid.*, 23 April and 12 May (appointment of V. A. Nevsky); *ibid.*, 10 Oct. (resignation of V. A. Nevsky and appointment of M. I. Kalashnikov).

51 *Izvestiya VTSIK* (1921), no. 158, 21 July, p. 2.

52 Bertram D. Wolfe, *The Bridge and the Abyss* (London, 1967), pl. XVII (reproducing Hoover's answer of 23 July 1921 to personal appeal from Gorky) and pp. 114–5.

53 E. Drabkina, 'Winter crossing', *Novyi mir* (1968), no. 10, pp. 60 and 62 (quotation from Lenin's letter on dissolution of the committee).

54 *Izvestiya VTSIK* (1921), no. 158, 21 July, p. 2; and no. 162, 26 July, p. 1; and no. 167, 31 July, p. 1.

55 *TSGAOR* 2306/1/634, 21 July 1921.

56 *TSGA RSFSR* 2313/1/1, 9 Nov. 1921 (Glavpolitprosvet file on work of *Kompomgol*).

57 Dzerzhinskaya, *V gody velikikh boev*, p. 351.

58 *Ibid.*, p. 348.

59 *TSGAOR* 2308/1/21, Instruction no. 49, 25 Jan. 1921; and *TSGAOR* 2306/1/634, 26 May 1921.

60 *TSGA RSFSR* 2313/1/4, 26 Feb. 1921.

61 *TSGA RSFSR* 2313/1/1, 31 Jan. 1921 (Davydov); *ibid.*, 5 Feb. 1921 and *TSGAOR* 2306/1/634, 31 March 1921 (Shterenberg); *TSGA RSFSR* 2313/1/4, 26 Feb. and 6 April 1921 and *TSGAOR* 2306/1/634, 23 June 1921 (Kiselis); *TSGAOR* 2308/1/21, Instruction no. 49, 25 Jan. 1921 (Bryusov); *TSGA RSFSR* 2313/1/4, 26 Feb. 1921 (Serafimovich); *ibid.*, 26 Feb. and 5 March 1921 (Bryusova); *ibid.*, 26 Feb. and 6 April (Meyerhold).

62 *TSGA RSFSR* 2313/1/1, statement of V. V. Tikhonovich to the presidium of Glavpolitprosvet, 14 Nov. 1921.

63 *Literaturnaya entsiklopediya*, vol. 9 (1935), article by N. Belchikov on Valerian Polyansky, p. 126.

64 V. Polyansky, 'Independence, or in the paths of bourgeois culture', *Proletarskaya kul'tura* (1920), nos. 15–16, p. 48.

65 *Proletarskaya kul'tura* (1921), nos. 20–1, p. 33 (session of Central Committee of Proletkult of 16–20 Dec. 1920).

66 *Ibid., passim.*

67 *Resolyutsii Vserossiiskikh soveshchanii Proletkul'ta po voprosam teatra, literatury i izobrazitel'nykh iskusstv* (Rostov on Don, 1921), quoted P. A. Bugaenko, *A. V. Lunacharskii i literaturnoe dvizhenie 20-kh godov*, p. 45.

68 N. Bukharin, 'The proletariat and questions of artistic policy', *Krasnaya nov'* (1925), no. 4, p. 265.

69 Lunacharsky, 'Again on the question of culture', *Izvestiya VTSIK* (1922), no. 249, 3 Nov., p. 2.

70 Lunacharsky, 'Theatre and revolution', *Sob. soch.*, vol. 3, pp. 126–7.

71 See L. N. Suvorov, 'From the history of the struggle of V. I. Lenin and the Bolshevik Party against Bogdanovist "organizational science"', *Filosofskie nauki* (1966), no. 3; and Lenin, *Pol. sob. soch.*, vol. 54, pp. 23 and 561.

72 See reports of proceedings of Proletkult Congress in *Pravda* (1921), no. 263, 22 Nov., p. 4 and no. 267, 26 Nov., p. 2.

73 On Proletkult and the 'Hermitage' theatre: *Byulleten' ofitsial'nykh rasporyazhenii i soobshchenii Narodnogo Komissariata po Prosveshcheniyu* (1922, 1st series), no. 69, 15 Feb.; *TSGAOR* 2306/1/1199a, 9 Feb. 1922; Lunacharsky, 'Theatre of the RSFSR', *Pechat' i revolyutsiya* (1922), no. 7, p. 90.

74 *TSGA RSFSR*, 2313/1/4, 26 Feb. 1921.

75 *TSGA RSFSR* 2313/1/1, 18 Dec. 1920.

76 *TSGA RSFSR* 2313/1/4, 10 June 1921.

77 'Letters of A. V. Lunacharsky' (publication of I. S. Smirnov), *Novyi mir* (1965), no. 4, p. 251.

78 *Byulleten' ofitsial'nykh rasporyazhenii i soobshchenii Narodnogo Komissariata po Prosveshcheniyu* (1922, 1st series), no. 71, dated 14 Feb., signed Lunacharsky.

79 Meyerhold, Bebutov and Derzhavin, 'Theatrical pages', *Vestnik teatra* (1921), nos. 87–8, 5 April, p. 2.

80 *Izvestiya TSK*, no. 17, 30 March 1920, p. 1 (report of PUR).

81 *Izvestiya TSK*, no. 23, 23 Sept. 1920, p. 3 (report on *politprosvet* work on transport).

82 *Partiino-politicheskaya rabota v Krasnoi Armii* (*mart 1919–1920 gg.*) (Moscow, 1964), pp. 513 and 90 ff. ('Statement on the political ad-

ministration of the War Council of the Republic', 8 Sept. 1920); *Otchet o rabote Politprosveta Narkomprosa*, p. 23.

83 *TSGAOR* 2306/1/320, 8 Oct. 1920.

84 *Desyatyi syezd RKP(b)*, p. 884 (note).

85 *Ibid.*, pp. 154–5.

86 *Ibid.*, p. 165 (Krupskaya) and pp. 143–4 (Preobrazhensky).

87 *Vos'moi syezd RKP(b). Mart 1919 g. Stenograficheskii otchet* (Moscow, 1959), p. 287. The subject of debate was whether Sovnarkom should be revitalized by an injection of Central Committee members, Osinsky taking the affirmative position.

88 *Desyatyi syezd RKP(b)*, pp. 146 and 481 (Preobrazhensky) and p. 169 (I. A. Ivanov).

89 *Ibid.*, pp. 479–80, 482.

90 Krupskaya, 'Relations between Party committees and political education departments' (1921), *Ped. soch.*, vol. 7, p. 96.

91 Letter of April 1921, *ibid.*, vol. 11, p. 212.

92 Krupskaya, *ibid.*, vol. 7, p. 100.

93 Krupskaya, 'Do political education departments need to exist?' *ibid.*, pp. 100–3.

94 *Desyatyi syezd RKP(b)*, p. 178.

95 *Partiino-politicheskaya rabota v Krasnoi Armii* (*mart 1919–1920 gg.*), p. 514.

96 *TSGAOR* 2306/1/634, 18 July 1921.

97 *TSGAOR* 2306/1/1199a, 9 Feb. 1922.

98 Speech of 3 Nov. 1920, *Pol. sob. soch.*, vol. 41, p. 406.

99 Trotsky's speech was published in *Izvestiya VTSIK* of 25, 26, 27 and 28 October 1921; and in *Nar. pros.* (weekly) (1921), nos. 89–90.

100 R. Pelshe, 'Political education work in danger', *Izvestiya VTSIK* (1921), no. 259, 18 Nov., p. 1; Krupskaya, 'Perspectives of political education work' (1922), *Ped. soch.*, vol. 7, p. 106.

101 *TSGAOR* 2306/1/1199a, 2 March 1922 (statement by Krupskaya and collegium's resolution) and 9 March 1922 (statement of Rabkrin representative).

102 *Odinnadtsatyi syezd RKP(b)*, p. 454. The speaker was R. V. Pikel, a Glavpolitprosvet worker, later in charge of Zinoviev's secretariat.

103 'Letters of N. K. Krupskaya', *Sovetskaya pedagogika* (1961), no. 11, pp. 143–5.

104 'Perspectives of political education work', *Ped. soch.*, vol. 7, p. 107.

105 'On educational soviets' (1918), *ibid.*, vol. 2, p. 76.

10: NARKOMPROS AND NEP

1 Hans and Hessen, *Educational Policy in Soviet Russia*, pp. 43–4.

2 *TSGAOR* 2306/1/180, 11 Feb. 1919.

3 *Ibid.*, 21 March 1919; *Nar. pros.* (weekly) (1919), no. 33, 3 May ('Information on credits').

4 *Ekonomicheskaya zhizn'* (1919), no. 17, 25 Jan., p. 4, and *ibid.* (1919), no. 18, 26 Jan., p. 6.

5 *Ibid.* (1921), no. 58, 17 March, p. 2.

6 Litkens, 'Narkompros supply', *Nar. pros.* (weekly) (1921), nos. 87–8, p. 5.

7 Lunacharsky, 'Education in danger', *Izvestiya VTSIK* (1921), no. 214, 25 Sept., p. 1.

8 Sovnarkom resolution of 16 Feb. 1921, *Sovetskaya pedagogika* (1966), no. 11, p. 87; *TSGAOR* 2306/1/634, 23 May 1921; *ibid.*, 4 July 1921; *ibid.*, 18 Aug. and 19 Sept. 1921.

9 Lunacharsky, 'Education in danger', *Izvestiya VTSIK* (1921), no. 214, 25 Sept., p. 1.

10 *Nar. pros.* (weekly) (1922), nos. 99–100, 10 April, p. 21.

11 'On social insurance of persons working as hired labour', Sovnarkom, 15 Nov. 1921, *Sobr. uzak.* (1921), no. 76, art. 627; 'On the improvement of the state of social security of workers, peasants and families of Red Army men', Sovnarkom, 14 May 1921, *Sobr. uzak.* (1921), no. 48, art. 236; 'On the transfer of the Central Administration of the Commissariat of Social Security to self-supporting bases', Sovnarkom, 6 June 1922, *Sobr. uzak.* (1922), no. 39, art. 459.

12 'On the taking of payment for services rendered by enterprises of a communal nature', 25 Aug. 1921, *Sobr. uzak.* (1921), no. 62, art. 445; 'On the procedure for taking payment for the issue of medical supplies from chemist shops', 19 Dec. 1921, *Sobr. uzak.* (1922), no. 1, art. 16; Sovnarkom decrees on newspapers of 28 Nov. and 14 Dec. 1921, *Sobr. uzak.* (1921), no. 77, art. 648, and no. 80, art. 692; 'On the opening of private medical institutions and chemist shops', Sovnarkom, 9 Jan. 1922, *Sobr. uzak.* (1922), no. 6, art. 58.

13 *TSGAOR* 2306/1/634, 6 Oct. 1921. Pub. *Nar. pros.* (weekly) (1921), nos. 87–8, p. 26.

14 Speech to congress of heads of *guberniya* education departments, *Pechat' i revolyutsiya* (1921), no. 2, August–October, pp. 102–4.

15 *Ibid.*, no. 2, p. 236.

16 Books issued in Moscow and Petrograd 1918–21 by these publishers are reviewed in *Pechat' i revolyutsiya* (1921), no. 1.

17 *TSGAOR* 2306/1/181, 4 Aug. 1919; *TSGAOR* 2306/1/180, 15 Jan. 1919; *ibid.*, 24 Jan. 1919.

18 *Pechat' i revolyutsiya* (1921), no. 3, Nov.–Dec., p. 310.

19 *TSGAOR* 2306/1/634, 18 Aug. 1921 (Skvortsov's report to the collegium of Narkompros before congress of heads of *guberniya* education departments, and resolution); *Pechat' i revolyutsiya* (1921), no. 2, p. 235 (resolutions of Narkompros and the presidium of Moscow Soviet).

20 *Pechat' i revolyutsiya* (1921), no. 3, Nov.–Dec., p. 140. Sovnarkom subsequently issued decrees 'On payment for the works of the non-periodic press' and 'On payment for newspapers', *Sobr. uzak.* (1921), no. 77, arts. 647 and 648.

21 *Pechat' i revolyutsiya* (1922), no. 1, Jan.–March, p. 329 (Narkompros statement on Gosizdat); *Nar. pros.* (weekly) (1921), no. 94, 30 Dec., p. 3 (Gosizdat on *khozrashchet*); Lenin, *Pol. sob. soch.*, vol. 54, pp. 262–3, 647.

22 N. L. Meshcheryakov, 'On the work of the state publishing house in new conditions', *Pechat' i revolyutsiya* (1922), no. 1, p. 167; and 'On private publishers', *ibid.* (1922), no. 6, July–August, p. 130.

23 *Ibid.* (1921), no. 3, Nov.–Dec., pp. 310–11.

24 Nazarov, *Oktyabr' i kniga*, pp. 253–4.

25 Letter to I. F. Popov, Aug. 1921, pub. in 'Letters of A. V. Lunacharsky', *Novyi mir* (1965), no. 4, p. 249.

26 E. K. Malinovskaya, 'I consult Ilyich', *Izvestiya* (1963), no. 77, 31 March, p. 5.

27 Lunacharsky, letter to editor, *Izvestiya VTSIK* (1919), no. 206, 17 Sept., p. 2, answering complaint by R. Arsky, letter to editor, *ibid.* (1919), no. 205, 16 Sept., p. 2.

28 *Zhizn' iskusstva* (Petrograd, 1921) nos. 773–5, 11 July, p. 1.

29 'On taking as guidance the norms and establishments worked out for the commissariats and institutions subordinate to them by the VTSIK commission', VTSIK, 23 Aug. 1921, *Sobr. uzak.* (1921), no. 53, art. 675.

30 Letter of Lenin to Lunacharsky (rejecting Lunacharsky's complaint), 3 Aug. 1921, Lenin, *Pol. sob. soch.*, vol. 53, pp. 91–2 and 395.

31 *Ibid.*, pp. 157–8.

32 'Letters of A. V. Lunacharsky', *Novyi mir* (1965), no. 4, p. 249 (note by I. Smirnov).

33 Memo. of 4 Sept. 1921, *Pol. sob. soch.*, vol. 53, pp. 170 and 410.
34 Lunacharsky to Litkens, 20 Sept. 1921, 'Letters of A. V. Lunacharsky', *Novyi mir* (1965), no. 4, p. 251.
35 Lenin, *Pol. sob. soch.*, vol. 54, p. 110 and note p. 593.
36 'Theatre of the RSFSR', *Pechat' i revolyutsiya* (1922), no. 7, p. 90.
37 'The new economic policy and Narkompros', *Nar. pros.* (weekly) (1921), nos. 87–8, 25 Oct., p. 4.
38 *Istoriya sovetskogo dramaticheskogo teatra*, vol. 2, p. 85.
39 *Vestnik teatra* (1919), no. 43, 25–30 Nov., quoted by Knyazhevskaya, *Yuzhin-Sumbatov i sovetskii teatr*, p. 85; Zolotinsky, 'Theatre of revolutionary satire', in *Teatr i dramaturgiya* (Leningrad, 1967), p. 104.
40 V. Vladimirov, 'Art in the conditions of the new economic policy', *Kommunisticheskoe prosveshchenie* (1923), no. 2(8), March–April, pp. 20–1.
41 Narodnyi Komissariat po Prosveshcheniyu, *K IX vserossiiskomu syezdu sovetov*, p. 11.
42 Litkens, 'The new economic policy and Narkompros', *Nar. pros.* (weekly) (1921), nos. 87–8, 25 Oct., p. 4.
43 Narodnyi Komissariat po Prosveshcheniyu, *K IX vserossiiskomu syezdu sovetov*, p. 11.
44 *Ibid.*, p. 10; *TSGAOR* 2306/1/634, 4 July 1921.
45 *TSGAOR* 2306/1/634, 21 July 1921; *Sobr. uzak.* (1921), no. 64, art. 482.
46 'The new economic policy and Narkompros', speech to congress of educational administrators, September, *Nar. pros.* (weekly) (1921), nos. 87–8, 25 Oct., p. 4.
47 Litkens, *ibid.*, p. 5; Lunacharsky, *Izvestiya VTSIK* (1921), no. 214, 25 Sept., p. 1.
48 'The new economic policy and Narkompros', *Nar. pros.* (weekly) (1921), nos. 87–8, 25 Oct., p. 5.
49 See Lenin, *Pol. sob. soch.*, vol. 54, p. 287.
50 See *ibid.*, vol. 53, p. 188.
51 *TSGAOR* 2306/1/1199a, 11 April 1922 (statement of Ukrainian representative to collegium of Narkompros).
52 Lenin, letter to Zinoviev, 8 Sept. 1921, *Pol. sob. soch.*, vol. 54, p. 287.
53 *Ibid.*, vol. 53, p. 303.
54 *TSGAOR* 2306/1/1199a, 13 July 1922 (reported by Maksimovsky without further elucidation).

55 'On the prohibition of compulsory taking of payment in any Soviet educational institution', 27 Oct., *Sobr. uzak.* (1921), no. 74, art. 605.
56 *TSGAOR* 2306/1/634, 22 Oct. 1921.
57 Lunacharsky, 'Strengthening the material base of school affairs in Russia', *Nar. pros.* (weekly) (1922), no. 97, 20 Feb., p. 2.
58 Krupskaya, 'The new economic policy in the field of education', quoted from *Agitrosta* no. 23 in *Nar. pros.* (weekly) (1921), nos. 87–8, 25 Oct., p. 8.
59 'Strengthening the material base of school affairs in Russia', *Nar. pros.* (weekly) (1922), no. 97, 20 Feb., p. 2.
60 Lunacharsky, 'To the aid of the school', *ibid.* (1921), no. 91, 25 Nov., p. 1.
61 N. Osinsky, speech to IX Congress of Soviets, reported *Pravda* (1921), no. 293, 27 Dec., p. 3.
62 Narodnyi Komissariat po Prosveshcheniyu, *K IX vserossiiskomu syezdu sovetov*, pp. 17–19.
63 See 'List of locally-significant needs of Narkompros', *Nar. pros.* (weekly) (1921), no. 92, 10 Dec., p. 16; *Narodnyi Komissariat Finansov, 1917, 7.xi/25.x 1922* (Moscow, 1922), pp. 67–8.
64 Narodnyi Komissariat po Prosveshcheniyu, *K IX vserossiiskomu syezdu sovetov*, p. 26. Note that the figures differ slightly from those quoted in appendix I.
65 *Ibid.*, p. 19; and statement of Korablev in *Izvestiya VTSIK* (1922), no. 45, 25 Feb., p. 3.
66 *TSGAOR* 2306/1/1199a, 16 March 1922.
67 *TSGAOR* 2306/1/2102, 25 April 1922 (presidium of Narkompros).
68 *TSGAOR* 2306/1/1199a, 27 April 1922.
69 Report on Glavsotsvos, *Nar. pros.* (monthly) (1923), no. 1, p. 17; *TSGAOR* 2306/1/1199a, 27 April 1922; Lenin, *Pol. sob. soch.*, vol. 54, pp. 250 and 641.
70 *TSGAOR* 2306/1/2102, 21 July 1922 (presidium of Narkompros).
71 'On taking as guidance the norms and establishments worked out for the commissariats and institutions subordinate to them by the VTSIK commission', 23 Aug. 1921, *Sobr. uzak.* (1921), no. 53, art. 675.
72 *TSGAOR* 2306/1/2102, 7 Sept. 1922 (reported by Maksimovsky).
73 Figures quoted by Lunacharsky: the lower estimate for 1921 in *Na fronte prosveshcheniya*, speech to 2nd session of VTSIK, 9 Oct. 1924 (Moscow [1924]), pp. 8–9; the higher estimate in speech to

Tenth All-Russian Congress of Soviets, reported *Izvestiya VTSIK* (1922), no. 293, 26 Dec., p. 2.

74 *Kul'turnoe stroitel'stvo SSSR. Statisticheskii sbornik* (Moscow, 1956), pp. 86–7.

75 Lunacharsky, *Na fronte prosveshcheniya*, pp. 8–9.

76 Lunacharsky, 'Strengthening the material base of school affairs in Russia', *Nar. pros.* (weekly) (1922), no. 97, 20 Feb., p. 3.

77 *Kommunisticheskoe prosveshchenie* (1922), no. 2, p. 151.

78 Reports in *Izvestiya VTSIK* (1922), no. 231, 13 Oct., p. 4, and *Kommunisticheskoe prosveshchenie* (1922), nos. 4–5, p. 175.

79 Instruction signed V. N. Yakovleva, 11 Nov. 1922, *Byulleten' ofitsial'nykh rasporyazhenii i soobshchenii Narodnogo Komissariata Prosveshcheniya* (1922) (2nd series), no. 2, 9 Dec., pp. 3–4.

80 *Byulleten' ofitsial'nykh rasporyazhenii i soobshchenii Narodnogo Komissariata Prosveshcheniya* (1922) (2nd series), no. 4, 23 Dec., p. 7.

81 Speech to Tenth Congress of Soviets, 24 Dec. 1922, *Izvestiya VTSIK* (1922), no. 293, 26 Dec., p. 2.

82 *Ibid.*, pp. 2–3.

83 *Pravda* (1922), no. 295, 28 Dec., p. 3.

84 'On the procedure for taking payment for study in institutions of Narkompros', 23 March, *Sobr. uzak.* (1923), no. 24, art. 279.

85 Krupskaya, letter to Z. G. Grinberg, 9 Jan. 1923, *Ped. soch.*, vol. 11, p. 224.

86 Ya. Volk, 'Organizational problems', *Nar. pros.* (weekly) (1921), no. 92, 10 Dec., pp. 3–5.

87 Speech to congress of local education departments, *Nar. pros.* (weekly) (1922), no. 98, 12 March, p. 2.

BIBLIOGRAPHY

ARCHIVES

During 1967–8, the Narkompros archive for 1918–25 was moved from the Central State Archive of the October Revolution and Socialist Construction (*TSGAOR*) to the Central State Archive of the RSFSR (*TSGA RSFSR*) and partially reclassified. I have given the references as I found them in 1967 and 1968.

TSGAOR

2306/1/36	State Education Commission, 1918.
2306/1/40	Collegium of Narkompros, 1918.
2306/1/152	Telegrams of greeting to People's Commissar Lunacharsky, 1918.
2306/1/3272	Miscellaneous materials of Narkompros, 1918–19.
2306/17/1 /8 /10	Department of aid to independent proletarian cultural organizations of Narkompros, 1918–19.
2306/1/180 /181 /182	Collegium of Narkompros, 1919.
2306/1/213	Commission on current business of Narkompros, 1919.
2306/1/320	Collegium of Narkompros, 1920.
2308/1/21	Narkompros instructions [*rasporyazhenii po Narkomprosu*], 1921.
2306/1/634	Collegium of Narkompros, 1921.
2306/1/1199a /1199	Collegium of Narkompros, 1922.
2306/1/2102	Presidium of collegium of Narkompros, 1922.

TSGA RSFSR

2306/1/132	State Education Commission, 1918.
1565/1/22	Collegium of Glavprofobr, 1920.
2313/1/1 /4	Collegium of Glavpolitprosvet, 1921.

Bibliography

OFFICIAL DOCUMENTS AND PROTOCOLS; BULLETINS, NEWSPAPERS AND JOURNALS; BIBLIOGRAPHIES; PUBLICATIONS OF LETTERS

Mariya Fedorovna Andreeva. Perepiska. Vospominaniya. Statyi. Dokumenty. Vospominaniya o M. F. Andreevoi. Ed. A. P. Grigoryeva and S. V. Shirina. Moscow, 1961 [letters].

Byulleten' ofitsial'nykh rasporyazhenii i soobshchenii Narodnogo Komissariata Prosveshcheniya. Moscow, 1921 and 1922 (1st and 2nd series).

Byulleten' VIII syezda sovetov, pub. VTSIK. Moscow, December 1920 (nos. 1–7); and *Prilozhenie k byulletenyu VIII syezda sovetov, posvyashchaemoe partiinomu sobraniyu po voprosam narodnogo obrazovaniya.* Ed. L. Sosnovsky and B. Malkin, pub. VTSIK. Moscow, 10 Jan. 1921.

Byulleten' vserossiiskogo soveshchaniya politprosvetov. Moscow, 1–8 Nov. 1920.

Dekrety sovetskoi vlasti. Moscow, vol. 1 (25 Oct. 1917–16 March 1918), 1957; vol. 2 (17 March–10 July 1918), 1959.

Desyatyi syezd RKP(b). Mart 1921 g. Stenograficheskii otchet. Moscow, 1963.

Direktivy VKP(b) i postanovleniya sovetskogo pravitel'stva o narodnom obrazovanii za 1917–1947 gg. Moscow–Leningrad, 1947.

Ekonomicheskaya zhizn', daily organ of STO and the economic commissariats. Moscow [1921–2].

Ermakov, A. 'Lunacharsky and Proletkult' (publication of documents). *Druzhba narodov.* 1968, no. 1.

Gor'kii i nauka. Articles, speeches, letters, recollections. Moscow, 1964 [letters].

Gorn, organ of Moscow Proletkult [1919–20].

Iskusstvo kommuny, organ of IZO Narkompros. Petrograd, 1918.

Iz istorii stroitel'stva sovetskoi kul'tury. Moskva 1917–1918 gg. Ed. V. N. Kuchin. Moscow, 1964 [documents].

Izvestiya Rossiiskoi Akademii Nauk. Petrograd, 6th series, vol. 11 (1917) and vol. 12 (1918).

Izvestiya TSIK rabochikh i soldatskikh deputatov i Petrogradskogo Soveta rabochikh i soldatskikh deputatov. Petrograd, 1917 to 3 March 1918. Continued as *Izvestiya VTSIK Sovetov krest'yanskikh, rabochikh, soldatskikh i kazakskikh deputatov.* Moscow, to 21 June 1918; and *Izvestiya VTSIK krest'yanskikh, rabochikh, soldatskikh i kazakskikh deputatov i Moskovskogo Soveta rabochikh i krest'yanskikh deputatov.*

Moscow, to 13 July 1923; with education supplement to *Izvestiya VTSIK*, pub. Moscow, 1918, nos. 1–14, June–August. [The paper is referred to in text as *Izvestiya* and in notes as *Izvestiya TSIK* (Petrograd) and *Izvestiya VTSIK*.]

Izvestiya TSK VKP(b), organ of Central Committee of Communist Party [1919–22].

Kommunisticheskoe prosveshchenie, organ of Glavpolitprosvet. Moscow [1920–3].

Kommunisticheskii trud, organ of Moscow Committee of RKP(b) and Moscow Soviet [1920].

Korolenko, V. *Pis'ma k Lunacharskomu*. Paris, 1922.

'Letters of N. K. Krupskaya' (publication of V. S. Dridzo), *Sovetskaya pedagogika*, 1961, no. 11.

Krupskaya, N. K. *Pedagogicheskie sochineniya v 10-i tomakh*. Plus supplementary volume 11. Moscow, 1963 [letters].

Kul'tura teatra, journal of Moscow state theatres, 1921.

Lenin, V. I. *Polnoe sobranie sochinenii*, 5th ed., 55 vols. Moscow, 1958–65 [documents].

Lenin, V. I. and Gorky, A. M. *Pis'ma, vospominaniya, dokumenty*, 2nd ed. Moscow, 1961.

'Lenin documents on education' (Oct. 1917–Jan. 1923), *Sovetskaya pedagogika*, 1966, nos. 4, 6, 10, 11.

Leninskii sbornik, vol. 35. Moscow, 1945.

Literaturnye manifesty (from the Symbolists to October). Moscow, 1929.

Lunacharskii o kino. Ed. A. M. Gak and N. A. Glagoleva. Articles, statements, scenarios and documents. Moscow, 1965.

Moskovskii khudozhestvennyi teatr v sovetskuyu epokhu. Materials and documents. Moscow, 1962 [documents on repertoire].

Moskovskii Proletkult, *Pervaya moskovskaya obshchegorodskaya konferentsiya proletarskikh kul'turno-prosvetitel'nykh organizatsii 23–28 fev. 1918 g.* Theses, resolutions, constitution of Moscow Proletkult. Moscow, n.d. [1918].

Muratova, K. D. (ed.) *A. V. Lunacharskii o literature i iskusstve*. Bibliography. Leningrad, 1964.

Muratova, K. D. *Periodika po literature i iskusstve 1917–1932*. Leningrad, 1933.

Narodnoe prosveshchenie, fortnightly organ of State Education Commission, Petrograd, 1918, nos. 1–2, 3?; then monthly organ of Narkompros, Moscow, 1918–21, 1923–30.

Narodnoe prosveshchenie, weekly organ of Narkompros. Moscow, 1918–22.

Narodnyi Komissariat po Prosveshcheniyu, *K IX vserossiiskomu syezdu sovetov*. Annual report. Moscow, 1921.

Narodnyi Komissariat po Prosveshcheniyu, *Sbornik dekretov i postanovlenii raboche-krest'yanskogo pravitel'stva po narodnomu obrazovaniyu*, part 2, 7 Nov. 1918–7 Nov. 1919. Moscow, 1920 (1921).

Narodnyi Komissariat po Prosveshcheniyu, *1917—oktyabr'—1920 (kratkii otchet)*. Moscow, 1920.

Narodnyi Komissariat po Prosveshcheniyu RSFSR, otdel edinoi trudovoi shkoly, *Pis'mo k shkol'nym rabotnikam*. Moscow, 1919.

Novaya zhizn', Social-Democratic internationalist daily, ed. Sukhanov, Desnitsky, Gorky, Tikhonov. Petrograd, 1917–18.

Odinnadtsatyi syezd RKP(b). Mart-aprel' 1922 g. Stenograficheskii otchet. Moscow, 1961.

Otchet o rabote politprosveta Narkomprosa (for the session of VTSIK, 23 Sept. 1920). Moscow, 1920.

Partiino-politicheskaya rabota v Krasnoi Armii. Documents. Vol. 1 (April 1918–February 1919), Moscow, 1961; vol. 2 (March 1919–1920), Moscow, 1964.

Pechat' i revolyutsiya, journal of criticism and bibliography, ed. Lunacharsky, N. L. Meshcheryakov, Pokrovsky, Polonsky, Skvortsov-Stepanov. Moscow, 1921– [1921–2].

Petrogradskaya pravda, organ of Petrograd Committee of RKP(b) [1920–1].

Petrogradskii uchitel', organ of Petrograd teachers' union, 1918.

Piskunov, A. I. *Sovetskaya istoriko-pedagogicheskaya literatura (1918–1957)*. Bibliography. Moscow, 1960.

Plamya, scientific, literary and artistic illustrated daily, ed. Lunacharsky. Petrograd, 1918.

Pravda, organ of Central Committee of RSDRP and Petrograd Committee of RSDRP, Petrograd, to 18 March 1918; then organ of Central Committee and Moscow Committee of VKP(b), Moscow.

Proletarskaya kul'tura, organ of Central Committee of All-Russian Council of Proletkult. Moscow, 1918–21.

Protokoly pervoi vserossiiskoi konferentsii proletarskikh kul'turno-prosvetitel'nykh organizatsii 15–20 sentyabrya 1918 g. Ed. Lebedev-Polyansky. Moscow, 1918.

Protokoly TSK RSDRP (b) avg. 1917–fev. 1918. Moscow, 1958.

Protokoly VTSIK 2 sozyva. Moscow, 1918.

Protokoly VTSIK 5 sozyva. Moscow, 1919.

Protokoly zasedanii VTSIK 4 sozyva. Moscow, 1920.

Rabotnik prosveshcheniya, organ of Central Committee of All-Russian union of educational workers. Moscow [1920–1].

Severnaya kommuna, daily organ of the executive committee of Soviets of the Northern Commune and the Petrograd Soviet [1919].

Smirnov, I. S. 'Letters of A. V. Lunacharsky'. *Novyi mir*, 1965, no. 4.

—— 'Towards the history of Proletkult' (publication of documents). *Voprosy literatury*, 1968, no. 1.

Sobranie uzakonenii i rasporyazhenii rabochego i krest'yanskogo pravitel'stva. Moscow [1920–2].

Sovetskii teatr. Dokumenty i materialy (1917–1921). Ed. A. Z. Yufit. Leningrad, 1968.

Trotsky, L. *Stalinskaya shkola fal'sifikatsii*. Berlin, 1932. [Protocol of meeting of Petrograd Bolshevik committee, 1 Nov. 1917.]

Vestnik narodnogo prosveshcheniya soyuza kommun severnoi oblasti, organ of Petrograd Narkompros, 1918. Continued as *Vestnik prosveshcheniya*. Ed. Z. G. Grinberg, V. A. Desnitsky-Stroev, A. P. Pinkevich. Petrograd, 1919.

Vestnik rabotnikov iskusstv, organ of Central Committee of All-Russian union of art-workers. Moscow [1921].

Vestnik teatra, organ of TEO Narkompros. Moscow, 1919–21.

Vos'moi syezd RKP(b). Mart 1919 g. Stenograficheskii otchet. Moscow, 1959.

Vysshaya shkola, fortnightly. Ed. A. N. Druzhinin and D. V. Kandelaki for Shanyavsky People's University. Moscow, 1919.

Zeldovich, V. D. 'First measures of Narkompros in the administration of the theatres' (letters of Lunacharsky and Batyushkov, 1917). *Istoricheskii arkhiv*, 1959, no. 1.

Zhizn' iskusstva, daily organ of department of theatres and public performances, Petrograd, 1918–19; then organ of Petrograd TEO, 1920–1; then private weekly ed. G. Adonts. Petrograd, from July 1921.

Zhurnal Ministerstva Narodnago Prosveshcheniya, organ of Ministry of Public Education. New series ed. E. Radlov. Petrograd [1917].

MEMOIRS, LITERARY WORKS, SECONDARY SOURCES

Aleksandrov, R. 'P. N. Lepeshinsky (for the 100th anniversary of his birth)'. *Voprosy istorii KPSS*, 1968, no. 3.

Alyansky, S. M. 'Meetings with Blok'. *Novyi mir*, 1967, no. 6.

Mariya Fedorovna Andreeva. Perepiska. Vospominaniya. Statyi. Doku-

menty. Vospominaniya o M. F. Andreevoi. Moscow, 1961 [memoirs].

Anikst, Olga. 'Paths of professional education' [recollections]. *Narodnoe prosveshchenie.* 1927, no. 10.

Belykh, G. and Panteleev, A. *Respublika Shkid* (novel). Moscow, 1927.

Bendrikov, K. 'Educational questions under the Provisional Government'. *Narodnoe prosveshchenie*, 1927, nos. 3, 5, 6, 8–9; 1928, no. 4.

Bessonova, V. I. 'Moscow University in the first years of Soviet power'. *Voprosy istorii*, 1955, no. 5.

Bonch-Bruevich, V. D. *Vospominaniya o Lenine*, Moscow, 1965.

Brik, O. 'Mayakovsky—editor and organizer'. *Literaturnyi kritik*, 1936, no. 4.

Bugaenko, P. A. 'A. V. Lunacharsky and Proletkult', in *Problemy razvitiya sovetskoi literatury 20-kh godov.* Saratov, 1963.

—— *A. V. Lunacharskii i literaturnoe dvizhenie 20-kh godov.* Saratov, 1967.

Bukharin, N. 'The proletariat and questions of artistic policy'. *Krasnaya nov'*, 1925, no. 4.

Carr, E. H. *The Bolshevik Revolution 1917–1923*, 3 vols. London, 1952.

Chukovsky, K. *Sovremenniki.* Moscow, 1963 [chapters on Gorky and Lunacharsky].

Davies, R. W. *The Development of the Soviet Budgetary System.* Cambridge, 1958.

Drabkina, E. 'Winter crossing' [on last years of Lenin's life, by Gusev's daughter]. *Novyi mir*, 1968, no. 10.

Dreiden, Sim. 'In the Politburo the question has been decided in the affirmative'. *Teatr*, 1967, no. 7.

Dyachenko, V. P. *Sovetskie finansy v pervoi faze razvitiya sotsialisticheskogo gosudarstva.* Part 1, 1917–25. Moscow, 1947.

Dyushen, V. 'In the first years of Soviet power. Experimental-model institutions of Narkompros'. *Narodnoe obrazovanie*, 1966, no. 1.

Dzerzhinskaya, S. *V gody velikikh boev.* Moscow, 1965.

Ehrenburg, I. *People and life*, memoirs of 1891–1917 (1st vol. of autobiography). London, 1961.

—— *First years of Revolution 1918–1921* (2nd vol. of autobiography). London, 1962.

Elizarova, A. I. 'Pages of reminiscence of Vladimir Ilyich in Sovnarkom'. *Proletarskaya revolyutsiya*, 1929, no. 11 (94).

Elkin, A. *Lunacharskii.* Moscow, 1967.

Entsiklopedicheskii slovar' Russkogo Bibliograficheskogo Instituta Granata, 7th ed. Moscow, vol. 41:

SSSR XXI. E. Arkin, 'Pre-school training in the USSR'.
XXII. M. Rubinshtein, 'The United Labour School of the USSR'.
XXIII. M. Reisner, 'The higher school'.
XXIV. N. Tarasov, 'Professional education in USSR'.

SSSR supplement: *Deyateli SSSR i oktyabr'skoi revolyutsii* (biographies and autobiographies).

Erickson, J. *The Soviet High Command*. London, 1962.

Ermakov, A. 'From the literary heritage of A. V. Lunacharsky'. *Novyi mir*, 1966, no. 9.

Fainsod, Merle. *Smolensk under Soviet Rule*. London, 1958.

Flakserman, Yu. 'Pages of the past'. *Novyi mir*, 1968, no. 11.

Goldman, Emma. *My Disillusionment in Russia*. London, 1925.

Goode, W. T. *Bolshevism at work*. London, 1920.

Gorbunov, V. V. 'V. I. Lenin's struggle with the separatist aspirations of Proletkult'. *Voprosy istorii KPSS*, 1958, no. 1.

—— 'From the history of the cultural–educational activity of the Petrograd Bolsheviks in the period of preparation for October'. *Voprosy istorii KPSS*, 1967, no. 2.

—— 'Criticism by V. I. Lenin of Proletkult's theories in relation to the cultural heritage'. *Voprosy istorii KPSS*, 1968, no. 5.

Gorchakov, N. *The Theatre in Soviet Russia*. New York–London, 1957.

Gorky, Maxim. *Sobranie sochinenii v 30-kh tomakh*. Moscow, 1949–55. Vol. 8. *Ispoved'*; vol. 17. 'V. I. Lenin'.

Gor'kii i nauka. Articles, speeches, letters, recollections. Moscow, 1964 [recollections].

Gorodetsky, E. N. 'Soviet reform of the higher school in 1918 and Moscow University'. *Vestnik moskovskogo universiteta* (social sciences series), 1954, no. 1.

—— *Rozhdenie sovetskogo gosudarstva*. Moscow, 1965.

Gozenpud, A. *Russkii sovetskii opernyi teatr (1917–1941)*. Leningrad, 1963.

Gurevich, Ya. 'The case of Countess S. V. Panina at the Revolutionary Tribunal'. *Russkoe bogatstvo*, 1917, nos. 11–12.

Hans, Nicholas. *History of Russian Educational Policy (1701–1917)* London, 1931.

—— *The Russian Tradition in Education*. London, 1963.

Hans, N. and Hessen, S. *Educational Policy in Soviet Russia*. London, 1930.

Istoriya moskovskogo universiteta, vol. 2. Moscow, 1955.

Istoriya sovetskogo dramaticheskogo teatra v 6-i tomakh. Moscow, vol. 1 (1917–20), vol. 2 (1921–5), 1966.

Ivanov, Georgy. *Petersburgskie zimy*. New York, 1952.

Ivnev, Rurik. 'Recollections of the first days and months of Soviet power'. *Prometei* (historical–biographical almanac, published 'Molodaya gvardiya'). Moscow, 1967, no. 4.

Iz istorii moskovskogo universiteta (1917–1941). Ed. E. N. Gorodetsky, M. E. Naidenov and M. I. Stishov. Moscow, 1955.

Iz istorii stroitel'stva sovetskoi kul'tury, Moskva 1917–1918 gg. Moscow, 1964 [memoirs].

Iz istorii velikoi oktyabr'skoi sotsialisticheskoi revolyutsii. Ed. M. I. Stishov, B. G. Verkhoven and M. I. Kheifets. Moscow, 1957.

Jelagin, Juri (Elagin, Yu.). *Temnyi genii (Vsevolod Meierkhol'd)*. New York, 1955.

Kerzhentsev, P. M. *K novoi kul'ture*. Petrograd, 1921.

Kerzhentsev, V. *Kul'tura i sovetskaya vlast'*. Moscow, 1919.

Khalatov, A. B. (ed.) *Pamyati A. V. Lunacharskogo*. Moscow, 1935.

Khodasevich, V. *Literaturnye statyi i vospominaniya*. New York, 1954.

Knyazhevskaya, T. *Yuzhin-Sumbatov i sovetskii teatr*. Moscow, 1966.

Kondakov, A. I. 'Experiment in aesthetic education in the Znamenskaya school-commune (1918–1925)'. *Sovetskaya pedagogika*, 1958, no. 11.

Konovalova, K. A. 'First steps of Narkompros (from recollections)'. *Sovetskaya pedagogika*, 1958, no. 11.

Korolev, F. F. 'The great October revolution and the higher school 1917–1920'. *Sovetskaya pedagogika*, 1957, no. 11.

—— *Ocherki po istorii sovetskoi shkoly i pedagogiki 1917–1920*. Moscow, 1958.

Krupskaya, N. K. 'Taylor's system and the organization of labour in Soviet institutions'. *Krasnaya nov'*, 1921, no. 1.

—— *Pedagogicheskie sochineniya v 10-i tomakh*. Moscow, 1957–62. Plus vol. 11, 1963.

Kuchepatov, N. 'From a teacher's recollections'. *Sovetskaya pedagogika*, 1957, no. 4.

Kumanev, V. A. *Sotsializm i vsenarodnaya gramotnost'* (liquidation of mass illiteracy in USSR). Moscow, 1967.

Lebedev, A. A. *Esteticheskie vzglyady A. V. Lunacharskogo*. Moscow, 1962.

Lenin, V. I. *Polnoe sobranie sochinenii*, 5th ed., 55 vols. Moscow, 1958–65.

Lifshits, M. 'In place of an introduction to A. V. Lunacharsky's aesthetics', in A. V. Lunacharsky, *Sobranie sochinenii*, vol. 7. Moscow, 1967.
Lifshits, S. 'The Capri Party school (1909)'. *Proletarskaya revolyutsiya*, 1924, no. 6.
—— 'Bologna Party school'. *Bol'shaya sovetskaya entsiklopediya* (1st ed.), vol. 6. Moscow, 1927.
Lilina, Z. 'Ten years ago'. *Narodnoe prosveshchenie*, 1927, no. 10.
Literaturnoe nasledstvo, vol. 65 (*Novoe o Mayakovskom*). Moscow, 1958.
Lunacharskaya-Rozenel, N. *Pamyat' serdtsa*. Moscow, 1965.
Lunacharsky, A. V. *Religiya i sotsializm*, 2 vols. St Petersburg, 1908 and 1911.
—— 'On the 23rd volume of *Znanie*', in *Literaturnyi raspad*, vol. 2. St Petersburg, 1909.
—— *Velikii perevorot*. Petrograd, 1919.
—— 'Education in Soviet Russia'. *Kommunisticheskii internatsional*, 1919, nos. 2 and 6.
—— *Magi* (play). Moscow–Petrograd, 1919.
—— *Ivan v rayu* (play). Moscow, 1920.
—— 'Culture in the Soviet republic'. *Manchester Guardian Commercial* series, *Reconstruction of Europe*, ed. J. M. Keynes, section 4, 6 July 1922.
—— *Lenin i prosveshchenie*. Moscow, 1924.
—— *Na fronte prosveshcheniya* (report on education to the 2nd session of VTSIK, 9 Oct. 1924). Moscow [1924].
—— *Prosveshchenie i revolyutsiya*. Pub. 'Krasnaya nov''. Moscow, 1924.
—— 'For the 200th anniversary of the All-Union Academy of Sciences'. *Novyi mir*, 1925, no. 10.
—— *Prosveshchenie i revolyutsiya*. Pub. 'Rabotnik prosveshcheniya'. Moscow, 1926.
—— *V mire muzyki*. Ed. G. B. Bernandt and I. A. Sats. Moscow, 1958.
—— *O narodnom obrazovanii*. Ed. N. K. Goncharov, N. A. Konstantinov, F. F. Korolev. Moscow, 1958.
—— *O teatre i dramaturgii*. Ed. A. I. Deich, 2 vols. Moscow, 1958.
—— *P'esy*. Ed. A. I. Deich. Moscow, 1963 [*Oliver Kromvel'*. *Osvobozhdennyi Don Kikhot*].
—— *Sobranie sochinenii v 8-i tomakh*. Ed. I. I. Anisimov, A. I. Ovcharenko etc. Moscow, 1963–7.
—— *Siluety*. Ed. I. Lunacharskaya and I. Sats. Moscow, 1965.
—— *Ob izobrazitel'nom iskusstve*. Ed. I. A. Sats, 2 vols. Moscow, 1967.
—— *Vospominaniya i vpechatleniya*. Ed. N. A. Trifonov. Moscow, 1968.

Malinovskaya, E. K. 'I consult Ilyich'. *Izvestiya*, 1963, no. 77, 31 March, p. 5.

V. Mayakovskii v vospominaniyakh sovremennikov. Moscow, 1963.

Milyukov, P. 'Greatness and fall of M. N. Pokrovsky'. *Sovremennye zapiski*, 1937, vol. 65.

Moskovskii universitet 1755–1930. Ed. V. B. Elyashevich, A. A. Kizevetter and M. M. Novikov. Pub. 'Sovremennye zapiski', Paris, 1930.

Nazarov, A. I. *Oktyabr' i kniga. Sozdanie sovetskikh izdatel'stv i formirovanie massovogo chitatelya 1917–1923*. Moscow, 1968.

Nikulin, Lev. *Gody nashei zhizni*. Recollections and portraits. Moscow, 1966.

Novikov, M. M. *Ot Moskvy do N'yu-Iorka*. New York, 1952.

Panina, S. V. 'On the outskirts of Petersburg'. *Novyi zhurnal*, 1957, nos. 48 and 49.

Panteleev, A. I. *Zhivye pamyatniki*. Leningrad, 1966 ['American kasha'—recollections of ARA feeding].

Paquet, Alfons. 'Prolet-Kult, or Bolșevik Education'. *The New Europe* 1919, 6 Feb.

Piyashev, N. 'A. V. Lunacharsky on Balmont'. *Russkaya literatura*, 1966, no. 1.

Pokrovsky, M. N. 'What Lenin was for our higher schools'. *Pravda*, 1924, no. 22, 27 Jan., p. 2.

Poletaev, E. and Punin, N. *Protiv tsivilizatsii*. Petrograd, 1918 (preface by Lunacharsky).

Polyansky, V. 'How the People's Commissariat of Education started work'. *Proletarskaya revolyutsiya*, 1926, no. 49 (2).

—— *A. V. Lunacharskii*. Moscow, 1926.

S. S. Prokof'ev. Materialy, dokumenty, vospominaniya, 2nd ed. Moscow, 1961 [autobiography].

Reed, John. *Ten Days that Shook the World*. New York, 1926.

Rytsar' revolyutsii. Recollections of Dzerzhinsky. Moscow, 1967.

Rzhanoe slovo. Revolutionary reader of the futurists, preface by Lunacharsky. Petrograd, 1918.

Sats, I. and Dementyev, A. 'A. V. Lunacharsky and Soviet literature'. *Novyi mir*, 1966, no. 12.

Savshinsky, S. 'The past does not die'. *Sovetskaya muzyka*, 1967, no. 1.

Schapiro, L. B. *The Origin of the Communist Autocracy*. London, 1955.

Scheffer, Paul. 'University life and the press in revolutionary Russia'. *Manchester Guardian Commercial* series, *Reconstruction of Europe*, ed. J. M. Keynes, section 4, 6 July 1922.

Serge, Victor. *Memoirs of a Revolutionary, 1901–1941*, trans. P. Sedgwick. London, 1963.

Shatsky, S. T. *Pedagogicheskie sochineniya v 4-kh tomakh*. Moscow, 1963 [vol. 1].

Shulgin, V. N. *Pamyatnye vstrechi*. Moscow, 1958.

Slonim, Marc. *Russian Theatre from the Empire to the Soviets*. London, 1963.

Smirnov, I. S. 'V. I. Lenin and the direction of educational affairs' (on the history of the reorganization of Narkompros in 1920–1). *Sovetskaya pedagogika*, 1958, no. 4.

—— *Lenin i sovetskaya kul'tura*. The state activity of V. I. Lenin in the field of cultural construction (Oct. 1917–summer 1918). Moscow, 1960.

Solomon, G. A. *Lenin i ego sem'ya*. Paris, 1930.

Sovetskie pisateli. Avtobiografii v dvukh tomakh. Moscow, 1959.

Subbotina, K. *Narodnoe obrazovanie i byudzhet*. Moscow, 1965.

Sukhanov, Nik. *Zapiski o revolyutsii*, vol. 7. Berlin–Petersburg–Moscow, 1923.

Suvorov, L. N. 'From the history of the struggle of V. I. Lenin and the Bolshevik Party against the Bogdanovist "organizational science" '. *Filosofskie nauki*, 1966, no. 3.

Teatr i dramaturgiya. Trudy leningradskogo gosudarstvennogo instituta teatra, muzyki i kinematografii. Ed. A. Ya. Altshuller. Leningrad, 1967.

Timiryazev, K. A. 'Democratic reform in the higher school'. *Nauka i demokratiya*, collected articles 1904–1919. Moscow, 1963.

Tolstov, A. S. 'At work on the organization of the labour school'. *Narodnoe prosveshchenie*, 1927, no. 10.

Trifonov, N. A. 'Lunacharsky in the city of Lenin'. *Zvezda*, 1965, no. 11.

—— 'Brothers-in-arms (Lunacharsky and Gorky after October)'. *Russkaya literatura*, 1968, no. 1.

—— 'A. V. Lunacharsky and M. Gorky (towards the history of literary and personal relations before October)', in K. D. Muratova ed., *M. Gor'kii i ego sovremenniki*. Leningrad, 1968.

Trotsky, L. *My Life*. London, 1930.

—— *The History of the Russian Revolution*, 3 vols. London, 1933.

Vasilyev, A. I. 'Vladimir Ivanovich Nevsky (for the 90th anniversary of his birth)'. *Voprosy istorii KPSS*, 1966, no. 5.

Voitinsky, N. 'On the *Vpered* group (1909–1917)'. *Proletarskaya revolyutsiya*, 1929, no. 12.

Volkovsky, A. N. 'Formation of a Soviet pedagogue in the first years after October'. *Sovetskaya pedagogika*, 1957, no. 11.

Vospominaniya o N. K. Krupskoi. Ed. A. M. Arsenyev, V. S. Dridzo and A. G. Kravchenko. Moscow, 1966.

Wells, H. G. *Russia in the Shadows*. London, 1920.

Wolfe, Bertram D. *The Bridge and the Abyss*. The troubled friendship of Maxim Gorky and V. I. Lenin. London, 1967. [Committee of Aid to the Starving, 1921.]

Yufit, A. 'Facts, documents, history'. *Teatr*, 1966, no. 6.

Yuryev, Yu. M. *Zapiski*, 2 vols., ed. E. M. Kuznetsov. Leningrad–Moscow, 1963.

Zaretsky, M. 'How the factory school came into being in the Ukraine'. *Narodnoe prosveshchenie*, 1927, no. 10.

Zubov, V. P. *Stradnye gody Rossii*. Recollections of the Revolution, 1917–1925. Munich, 1968.

INDEX

Page numbers in italic type indicate a biographical note in Appendix II

Index